W. C. PRIVY

"W. C. Privy's Original Bathroom Companion—
It's not just for the bathroom anymore."

W. C. Privy's
Original
Bathroom
Companion
NUMBER 2

W. C. PRIVY

EDITED BY ERIN BARRETT & JACK MINGO

St. Martin's Griffin ❧ *New York*

www.stmartins.com

Designed, packaged, and produced by the Univark Deconstructionists

ISBN 0-312-31580-5

First Edition: December 2003

10 9 8 7 6 5 4 3 2 1

Thanks!

To the *Bathroom Companion* staff members, our family, and our friends, for helping us keep W. C. Privy's dream alive. Without you, this book wouldn't have happened. Especially...

Heather Jackson Silverman
Elizabeth Bewley
Pam Suwinsky of Thalia
Publishing Services
Kathie Meyer
Susan Shipman
Chris McLaughlin
Mary-Nell Bockman
Michele Montez
John Karle
Sarah Cocroft
Don Jollyson
Brian Marshall
Elsa Bronte
Mark Riley
Janelle Barbier

Glynne Gilmore
Cynthia Damon
Elana Mingo
Jackson Hamner
Georgia Hamner
Vera Mingo
Jerry & Lynn Barrett
Powell Hamner
Everyone at St. Martin's Press
Skip Colcord & Polaroid Corp.
Energizer
www.NJHotair.com
Gino Micheletti
The BCOMPs (members of the
W. C. Privy fan club—see p. 476)
All the Univark Truckers

· "Making Eggs" and "Money Magic" originally published in *How to Spit Nickels*, by Jack Mingo, Contemporary Books, 1993. Adapted with permission of author.

· "Our Favorite Disasters" adapted from *Just Curious About History, Jeeves*, by Erin Barrett and Jack Mingo, Pocket Books, 2002. Adapted with permission of authors.

· "Hand Shadows" series originally published in *Hand Shadows to Be Thrown Upon the Wall* (1859) and *Hand Shadows: Second Series* (1860), by Henry Bursill.

· "The Spirits Speak" adapted from *How to Spit Nickels*, by Jack Mingo, Contemporary Books, 1993. Used with permission of author.

· "Buttheads," "Elephants," and "Simian Says," originally published in *Just Curious About Animals and Nature, Jeeves*, by Erin Barrett and Jack Mingo, Pocket Books, 2002. Adapted with permission of authors.

· Some images © 2003, www.clipart.com.

· Special thanks to Aaron Trauring, Simcha Schtull, and the *Whole Pop Magazine Online* for some of the ideas and content.

W. C. PRIVY

Genius!
MORE ABOUT MR. PRIVY, THE ORIGINAL

"There will be imitators, but no matter: 'Imitation is the sincerest form of plagiarism.' They can be nothing but pale counterfeits of the genuine Privy." —W. C. Privy

Since WE RELEASED the first volume of *W. C. Privy's Original Bathroom Companion,* we have received many questions about W. C. Privy from readers, friends, lawyers, and creditors. Ironically, the more we've discovered about this reclusive and brilliant fellow, the less we seem to know. It turns out that much of what we believed to be true turned out to be false. Much of what we believed to be false turned out to be true. And much of what we believed to be neither false nor true turned out to be neither true nor false.

So, while we may not be back to square one, we are at least back to square three or even two. Here's what we currently believe that we think we know (although we could be wrong): W. C. Privy was born on a mountaintop in Tennessee. As a child, he might have worked the coal mines in Appalachia. As a teen, he may have written marital manuals under the pen name "Dr. Hiram Cheepily." He might have founded a dollhouse factory in Maine. And after he retired from writing *Bathroom Companions,* he and his wife, Lucienne ("Loo") Donniker-Privy, may have opened some sort of museum somewhere in the Pacific Northwest.

On a more definitive note, additional, rare fragments from the original, century-old *Bathroom Companions* have begun appearing. As you recall, virtually all copies disappeared shortly after publication because it was a time when good, affordable toilet paper was hard to come by. However, a few scattered sheets of *BC #6* have appeared, giving further clues about the contents of Mr. Privy's wildly popular series. In honor of the man and his commercial good sense, we've run computer analyses of the fragments and discovered some of the original pieces they've come from, in order to reproduce them in these pages. See if you can guess which three articles came directly from the editorial mind of the great latrinographist.

We hope you enjoy Volume 2. If so, you may want to track down Volume 1 in your local bookstore or on our online site {www.bathroomcompanion.com} for yourself and your friends. (Conversely, if you *don't* enjoy it, you may want to consider buying copies for your enemies.) And we hope Mr. Privy, wherever he may be, is looking down (or, just as likely, up) at our efforts with bemusement and approval.

'Til next time,

Erin Barrett   Jack Mingo

ABOUT BARRETT & MINGO
Erin Barrett and Jack Mingo are particularly suited for the task of reviving the *Bathroom Companion*. They have written dozens of entertaining books including *Just Curious, Jeeves; Doctors Killed George Washington; Cats Don't Always Land On Their Feet; The Whole Pop Catalog;* and *How the Cadillac Got Its Fins.* Their daily column, *Random Kinds of Factness,* appears in newspapers around the country.

What's Inside...

Sweet!
HOW TWINKIES GOT CRÈMED

You may be embarrassed to admit it, but you know it's true: you love Twinkies. Everyone loves Twinkies—the food of the convenience store gods.

THEY'RE GOLDEN brown, irresistibly spongy, and filled with "crème" (you don't think there's actually cream in there, do you?). And they're the Continental Baking Company's biggest seller, even beating out that other Continental food marvel, Wonder Bread. Twinkies are quite literally "the greatest thing since sliced bread," since Wonder was the first bread that came presliced and packaged.

Twinkies were invented in 1930 at the beginning of the Great Depression by the Chicago-area Continental plant manager. His name was James A. Dewar. At the time, Continental was a new company, only six years old, and Dewar wasn't completely confident in its ability to weather the new economic times. It didn't make sense to him, for example, that the plant had lots of expensive pans dedicated to a product called "Little Short Cake Fingers," which was baked for only six weeks a year. The

Fingers were designed to be made into strawberry shortcake, so they went into commission only during the strawberry season. During the rest of the year, they lay idle.

Dewar figured that the shortcake fingers could sell year-round if the company came up with something—a filling, say—to go with it. He mixed up a banana-flavored "crème" (the company switched to vanilla ten years later when, during World War II, there was a banana shortage) and figured out a way to inject it into the shortcake using three syringe-like injection tubes.

But Dewar was having trouble coming up with a name he liked until, on a business trip to St. Louis, he and a colleague drove past the Twinkle Toes Shoes factory. His friend suggested the name "Twinkle Fingers" for his new cakes; Dewar shortened it to Twinkies.

Continental started selling Dewar's new Twinkies in packs of two for 5¢. Since that time, it has made at least forty-five billion Twinkies—over two million tons. Sales records show that they sell best by far in the Midwest, and the *New York Times* has officially dubbed Chicago the "Twinkie Capital of the World" because folks in Chicago eat more Twinkies per capita than anywhere else.

Because of their success, Twinkies have had plenty of critics who call them the archetypal junk food. TV's Archie Bunker damned them with dubious praise, calling them "the white man's soul food."

In the early 1970s, they were mentioned prominently in a song called "Junk Food Junkie," and they were accused, in what was called "the Twinkie defense," of mentally unbalancing a San Francisco supervisor to the point of murder.

The company responds blandly: "We make these cakes out of the same ingredients that you'd find in a typical kitchen," says a company spokesperson. "It's a fun food. That's our position."

Dewar, before he died in 1985, was a little less soft-spoken in defending his creation, "the best darn-tootin' idea I ever had." To live 88 years like him, he advised that you should "eat Twinkies every day and smoke a pack of cigarettes." Seriously, he'd add, "Some people say that Twinkies are the quintessential junk food, but I fed them to my four kids and they feed them to my fifteen grandchildren. My boy Jimmy played football for the Cleveland Browns. My other son, Bobby, played quarterback for the University of Rochester. Twinkies never hurt them."

As to the legend that they will last forever on the grocery shelf, the company admits they do, indeed, have a long shelf life. The "crème" works to keep them moist. They're also quick to point out that unsold Twinkies are replaced in stores after only 4 to 6 days.

MORE SWEET FACTS

• There are 17 Hostess bakeries across the country.

• Five hundred million Twinkies are consumed every year across America.

• Each year it takes over a half-million chickens to lay the 160 million large eggs needed to make Hostess Twinkies.

• The bakeries at the Hostess company can put out 1,000 Twinkies every minute.

• Hostess can crème about 52,000 Twinkies in an hour.

• It takes 40,000 miles of plastic wrap a year to package Hostess Twinkies.

• When the White House put together their time capsule for the millennium, they chose the Twinkie to go in as an "object of enduring American symbolism." ☾

The T.W.I.N.K.I.E.S. Project

Tests With Inorganic Noxious Kakes In Extreme Situations, or T.W.I.N.K.I.E.S., was carried out during finals week at Houston, Texas's Rice University in 1995. The point of the tests was to determine the properties of the Twinkie snack food cake.

These tests that were conducted on Twinkies included experiments with the force of gravity, radiation, flame, electricity, water, and blender. The names of the tests were far more scientific than the actual tests themselves, including "Maximum Density Test," "Rapid Oxidation Test," "Gravitational Response Test," and "Turing Test," which was actually an extremely modified version of a real intelligence test....

Although the tests really proved very little about Twinkies in any real sense, the Web site has become a living legend. It can be found, along with haikus to Twinkies and letters to the "scientists," at *http://www.twinkieproject.com/*.

According to Mark Twain

These notations supposedly come from *Puddin'head Wilson's Calendar*, a fictitious publication that Twain "quoted" whenever he needed a maxim to head a chapter.

- "Consider well the proportions of things. It is better to be a young Junebug than an old bird of paradise."

- "Adam was but human—that explains all. He did not want the apple for the apple's sake, he wanted it only because it was forbidden. The mistake was in not forbidding the serpent; then he would've eaten the serpent."

- "Adam and Eve had many advantages, but the principal one was, that they escaped teething."

- "Why is it that we rejoice at a birth and grieve at a funeral? It is because we are not the person involved."

- "Training is everything. The peach was once a bitter almond; cauliflower is nothing but cabbage with a college education."

- "Let us to endeavor so to live that when we come to die even the undertaker will be sorry."

- "Habit is habit, and not to be flung out of the window by any man, but coaxed downstairs a step at a time."

- "One of the most striking differences between a cat and a lie is that a cat has only nine lives."

- "Whoever has lived long enough to find out what life is, knows how deep a debt of gratitude we owe to Adam, the first great benefactor of our race. He brought death into the world."

- "All say, 'How hard it is that we have to die'—a strange complaint to come from people who have had to live."

- "The holy passion of Friendship is so sweet and steady and loyal and enduring that it will last through a whole lifetime, if not asked to lend money."

- "It is easy to find fault, if one has that disposition. There was once a man who, not being able to find any other fault with his coal, complained that there were too many prehistoric toads in it."

- "When angry, count to four; when very angry, swear."

- "When I reflect upon the number of disagreeable people who I know have gone to a better world, I am moved to lead a different life."

All in the Family

FEUDS, FIGHTING, AND OTHER FAMILY FUN

By digging up family dirt, contributors Chris McLaughlin and Kathie Meyer have come up with some intriguing stories and stats about life with the people we love...and who sometimes drive us crazy.

WHY WE CALL IT A FAMILY

The word *family* comes from the Latin, *famulus,* which, mothers everywhere will be interested in learning, once meant "servant." From it, the word *familia* was derived, a collective term for all of the domestic servants in the household. That's what it meant when it first entered the English language. Sometime in the mid-17th century, the word came to include the entire household — relatives and servants. Eventually, it narrowed to mean just a group of related persons.

KEEPING UP WITH THE ITURRIBERRIGORRIGOIKOERROTAKOETXEAS

According to the Guinness Book of Records, the longest English surname that's not hyphenated is Featherstonehaugh (pronounced *Fanshaw*; go figure). Two other non-English, long, and difficult surnames are Iturriberrigorrigoikoerrotakoetxea (Basque) and MacGhilleseatheanaich (Gaelic).

JUGGLING A LARGE FAMILY

Experts advise families to become expert jugglers of work, school, and other responsibilities. The Boehmer family of Iowa took this advice perhaps a little too literally. Twenty years ago, Larry Boehmer was employed as a pipeline worker, often away from his family. Instead of pining for his wife and kids at night, he bought a juggling instruction book, and learned the basics of the craft. Once home again, Larry's children saw him practicing and wanted to try, too—even little Casey, who was born without a left forearm.

Larry and three of the children gave their first family performance at an amusement park in 1989. Today, Larry and Judy Boehmer have eleven juggling children—yes, Casey, too—and lay claim to being the world's largest juggling family.

RIDING IN NASCARS WITH BOYS

Good old brother boys: gotta love 'em. Especially if you were watching the Winston Cup race at Texas Motor Speedway, Fort Worth, in 1999. Five sets of brothers ran in the Primestar 500: Geoffrey and Brett Bodine, Kenny and Rusty Wallace, Terry and Bobby Labonte, Jeff and Ward Burton, and Darrell and Michael Waltrip. Terry Labonte won: brother Bobby was third.

MY EVIL TWIN

Twins don't usually have an evil sibling and a good sibling. However, in the case of the Han twins of Irvine, California, there might be reason to believe otherwise. Jeen decided to swipe credit cards and use them to run up debts she wouldn't have to pay off. She got busted, and believed her "good" twin Sunny was responsible for ratting her out. So what did Jeen do? She conspired to murder her sister and assume her identity. She got busted for that, too.

COMING BACK FOR MOORE

What are the odds? In the early 1990s, Richard Moore had to be rescued after he became mysteriously lodged in the ceiling of a convenience store in West Haven, Connecticut. Several years later, in 1994, his brother David had to be rescued from the same convenience store when he got stuck in the chimney while attempting to burglarize it.

A Moore brother family tradition.

DADDIES & MUMMIES
Fourteen mummies, some dating back to 1,000 BC, were discovered in an ancient tomb in one of China's old cemeteries. The Shanghai office of the *Guinness Book of Records* dubbed this the world's largest family joint burial.

Archaeologists say the custom of family joint burial was quite popular in parts of China 3,000 years ago, although the customs varied slightly from family to family. The mummies were of both genders; some were old and some were children. Their faces were covered, but underneath, the various facial openings were plugged with things like gold foil, wool, and flour paste—perhaps as part of the embalming process or for religious reasons. Buried alongside were stone, wood, bronze, and iron articles, including various bits of pottery, as well as exquisite fabrics.

HAPPY FAMILY
Perhaps you've seen "Happy Family" on a Chinese menu. It's called that because it's made with a little "family member" of all kinds of meat and seafood, and its served at family events like weddings, reunions, and so on. On a similar note, the "Mother and Child Reunion" contains chicken (the "mother") and an egg (the "child").

"Our Happy Family Life Chairman Mao Gave Us," Chinese propaganda poster,1954

TWO OR MORE

According to the Statistical Abstract of the United States, in the year 2000, 85 percent of American households fall under the "family" category. The average family household has 3.24 persons.

KISS AND MAKE UP

Fed up with family squabbling during a bankruptcy trial, Florida judge Jay Cristol came up with an interesting, although probably futile, way to resolve at least some of the differences. He ordered Judith Herskowitz to send a birthday card to her estranged sister Susan Charney. He ordered that the card must have "Happy Birthday, Sister" on it, and must include Judith's signature. Just to cover all bases, he added a proviso: "The card shall not contain any negative, inflammatory or unkind remarks."

MILITARY BRATS

Within the U.S. armed forces, 55% of military personnel are married; 630,000 members have children (only 6% of these are single parents)—a collective total of 1.2 million children of military personnel. Seventy-three percent are eleven years of age or younger; 39% are below the age of six. ☾

An ad from back in the days when birds were heavily involved in subversive politics

The Best!

THE WAYS WE SAY SOMETHING'S THE GREATEST

From "cool" to "bad" to "boss," the slang terms that
have told you, "Baby, you're tops!"

Bad: People have been using opposite words to mean "good" since the 1830s, when *nasty* meant "wonderful." The 1950s led a resurgence of the practice, leading to this exchange from "Give Him a Great Big Kiss" by the Shangri-Las (1962): "I hear he's bad!" "Well, he's *good* bad, but he's not evil."

Boss: Re-popularized in the early 1960s, *boss* first meant "the best" way back in the 1600s.

Cool: Along with *crazy, far out, real gone,* and *wild, cool* came from beatnik slang in the 1950s.

Copacetic: Popularized in the 1930s by tap dancer Bill "Bojangles" Robinson.

Cute: Came from "acute" in the 1860s.

Ducky: Now used ironically, *ducky* has meant good things since the 1830s. Before that, it was a term of endearment,

and in Shakespeare's time, it was slang for female breasts.

Fabulous: Originally having to do with fables, *fabulous* has had its current meaning since about 1600. *Fantastic,* likewise, originally meant something that existed only in fantasy; in the late 1940s it attained its present meaning.

Hot: People assume that *hot* is a recent slang term, but it came to mean sexually attractive back in 1910.

Nice: When *nice* entered English from Latin in the 1290s, it meant ignorant or foolish. It took several centuries to begin meaning something good.

Nifty: Popularized in the 1860s, *nifty* might be short for *magnificent.*

Out of sight: You think "Outta sight!" first appeared in the 1960s? Nope, try the Bowery in the 1840s.

Phenom: People began shortening *phenomenon* back in the 1890s.

Spiffy: *Spiffy* started out meaning well dressed in England, and then in America in the 1870s, it came to mean any kind of stylish excellence.

Swell: The original meaning of being swollen or enlarged began in the 9th century. By the 1720s, *swelled head* came to mean pompous and stuck-up, but the word also began taking on the additional meaning of someone very well dressed by the early 1800s and general excellence not long after.

Terrific: In the 1660s, *terrific* meant *terrifying*, but by the 1880s, it had somehow become a compliment. ☾

Stately Knowledge

12 REASONS WHY YA GOTTA LOVE IDAHO

Here are our favorite reasons to love the state of famous potatoes.

1 The state of Idaho plays host to the deepest river gorge in North America. It's Hell's Canyon, which runs along the western border of the state. It's more than 2,600 feet deeper than the Grand Canyon.

2 How can you not mention potatoes when you talk about Idaho? The state produces more than 28% of the nation's spuds. McDonald's alone uses 500,000 pounds of the state's potato crop each year.

3 In honor of all those potatoes, annual Spud Day is celebrated each year in Shelley, Idaho. Along with music and a parade are spud-specific games like Tug-O-War over a pool of mashed taters and the Potato Cook-off.

4 While we're on the topic, the World Potato Exposition is in Blackfoot. There you can see the world's largest concrete potato and the world's largest potato chip. It's a 25-inch-wide Pringle, donated by Proctor & Gamble.

5 Idaho's state capital is geothermally heated. That means hot water, naturally found about 3,000 feet underground, is pumped up and used to heat the building. We think it's pretty safe to say it's the only one of its kind in the United States.

6 Next time you're in Idaho, don't forget to visit Island Park. It's a city full of resorts, but it's laid out in a rather odd way. The resorts were all built along the same road, so when the city decided to draw boundary

lines, they stretched about 33 miles long. The results are that it's a skinny town, with a long street running through the middle of it.

7 Today it's spuds, but Idaho used to be home to a bunch of gold and silver mines. As a result, there are quite a number of ghost towns with names like Gold Dredge and Yankee Fork.

Hey, diddle-diddle: Hula, spuds, and a fiddle. It's the Idaho way!

8 If you like a good fiddle, check out Weisler, Idaho. It's home to the annual National Old Time Fiddler's Contest.

9 Several more reasons to love Idaho: Ty Cobb, Mariel Hemingway, Wyatt Earp, Lillian Disney, Philo Farnsworth (inventor of TV), Paul Revere and the Raiders, Ezra Pound, Picaboo Street, Lana Turner, Edgar Rice Burroughs, and Gutzon Borglum (designer of Mount Rushmore). They're all natives of the western state.

10 Idaho has a bit of history that's not widely known. Back in the 1830s, a large influx of Hawaiian natives came to live in the state. They all came to work in the booming fur trade. As a matter of fact, most of the staff at Fort Boise during this time was originally from the Hawaiian Islands. Remnants of this era live on in Owyhee County, which got its name from an early attempt to spell "Hawaii" in honor of its newest inhabitants.

11 Idaho is home to both the world's longest gondola (in Kellogg) and the world's longest floating bridge (in Coeur d'Alene).

12 Way back in the 1940s, a ski lodge in Sun Valley hired Larry LaPrise and his group, the Ram Trio, to entertain vacationers. To give the crowd a fun activity, Larry came up with a simple dance, and a song that told how to do it. Called the Hokey Pokey, the dance was an instant hit with the skiers, and the song was later recorded and made famous by bandleader Ray Anthony, also famous for the Bunny Hop. €

A Boy's Life in 1890
Guns & Taxidermy, Fires & Kites

In some ways, children have really lost out in the modern age. Years ago, preteen kids were expected to run wild through woods, streams, and fields. In these days of fear, over–coddling, and lawsuits, it's amazing what was considered a normal kid's life as reflected in *The American Boy's Handy Book* by Dan Beard (1890).

Gas-bubble.

"Procure a rubber tube and force it over the gas-burner. Dip your pipe into the suds and turn the gas on; the gas will be sufficient to blow the bubble. Since the gas is lighter than the air, the bubble will rapidly ascend...."

"An old-fashioned, single-barrelled pistol is securely lashed to an upright stick, and the fish-line tightly fastened to the trigger. To prevent accidents, my friend never loaded the pistol...."

Fig 309
Top View of Duck-frame

Fig 310
Side View of Duck-frame

Fig 311
Duck of Duck-frame

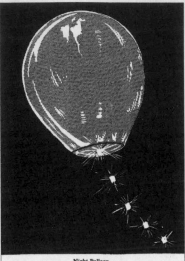

Night Balloon.

"Ducks made of wood have the usual objection—expense. You can convert dead ducks to decoys to lure their comrades to death....A **Y**-shaped stick holds the dead duck's head. Two pointed sticks keep the bird in place...."

"Cut open the Roman candle and extract the powder and balls; wrap up in a piece of tissue-paper. As the fire creeps slowly along, the balloon mounts higher and higher, sending it skyward with a ball of fire for its motive power. Showers of jagged sparks fall constantly."

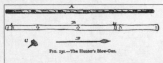

FIG. 231.—The Hunter's Blow-Gun.

"With a red-hot iron rod, enlarge the hollow in the center. The arrows must be very small, and a pin makes a simple point. You will then have a blow-gun that can be used to hunt with."

Fig 277

swims, the spoon is jerked along and fish cannot restrain themselves. Then the fun begins. The goose feels something tugging at its leg and seeks refuge on the shore where you unhook the fish."

"THE GOOSE FISHERMAN is a live goose with a line and spoon hook attached to one leg. As the bird

Position Assumed when Casting the Arrow.

Strap for Hawk's Leg.

"The hawk may be perfectly tamed if taken from the nest while young.... A tame hawk is very useful in keeping chickens out of the garden and as a decoy for catching other birds."

"Whip-lash arrowsnappers should only be used with targets or game; they are dangerous on the play-ground."

FIG. 248.—The Incision.

"He must be skinned and stuffed! Remove the eyes by breaking the bones that separate the eye orbits from the mouth....For a preservative, dissolve ten pounds soap, one pound potash, pipeclay and lime, and add ten pounds of arsenic. This preparation is, of course, very poisonous and should be so labeled."

"Fill with birdshot and bend the quill back. Allow it to fly forward — the shot from the tube can stun a small bird."

Spring Shot-gun.

FIG. 239.—Mole Trap.

"I object to dead-falls on principle, and I include this trap with some reluctance."

FIG. 30.—Cutters.

"Fasten three sharp pieces of broken glass with wax, cloth and wood. Pass twine through each apparatus. Tie to your kite's tail. To win the battle, maneuver your kite and cut your opponent's string."

"There is always a certain danger attending the use of firearms which is avoided by the crossbow....The young sportsman may shoot several times at the same bird or rabbit without frightening it away."

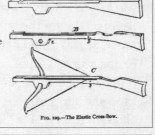

FIG. 129.—The Elastic Cross-Bow.

"To light the gas with your finger, turn it on, walk around sliding your feet on the carpet, and then touch the burner. Instantly the light will blaze up like magic."

"Taking a long pull at a cigar, he blew the smoke into the paper box and commenced to tap the sides of it with a pencil. At each tap, a tiny but perfect smoke ring shot into the air."

Smoke-Rings.

"One end cut like a quill pen, your lance seldom injures your specimens. With a quick movement push the stick and animal both into the mud."

Tom Swifties I
"TELL ME A SWIFTY," TOM SAID PUNISHINGLY

From the surreal 1960s came elephant jokes and Tom Swifties, based on bad puns and the stylistic excesses of Victor Appleton, who created the popular Tom Swift stories (see pages 53, 295 and 383).

"I can't believe I ate that whole pineapple!" Tom said dolefully.

"I dropped the toothpaste," Tom said, crestfallen.

"That's the last time I pet a lion," Tom said offhandedly.

"We don't have a homerun hitter," Tom said ruthlessly.

"I'll dig another ditch around the castle," Tom said remotely.

"I keep shocking myself," said Tom, revolted.

"I shouldn't sleep on railroad tracks," said Tom, beside himself.

"My steering wheel won't turn," Tom said straightforwardly.

"I've lost a lot of weight," Tom expounded.

"I keep banging my head on things," Tom said bashfully.

"I'll have to telegraph him again," Tom said remorsefully.

"I can't get down from the mountain!" Tom alleged.

"Let's play a C, E, and G," said Tom's band, in accord.

"You call this a musical?" asked Les miserably.

"I must make the fire hotter!" Tom bellowed.

"I have no carpet for the landing," Tom said with a blank stare.

"The girl's been kidnapped," Tom said mistakenly.

"I want a motorbike," Tom moped.

"That just doesn't add up," said Tom, nonplussed.

"Who says I have too many children?" said Mary overbearingly.

"We make a good opera duo," said Tom, callously and placidly.

Neck-rophilia

TALL TALES ABOUT GIRAFFES

Who doesn't love giraffes, the tallest land animal in the world? They may look absurd, but their design works in their environment. Let's take a short look at a mighty long animal.

WALK LIKE AN AFRICAN

Most animals alternate left and right feet as they walk. Giraffes walk by moving the two left feet, then the two right. Only cats and camels walk in the same way. Despite the awkward gait, giraffes can gallop at a speed of 35 mph.

NECK BONE'S CONNECTED TO ANOTHER NECK BONE....

The African plains giraffe, with a neck that extends 8 feet, has seven vertebrae in its neck, the same number as every other mammal, from man to mouse to whale.

SENSELESS BRUTALITY

The first giraffe ever seen in Europe was butchered at the Roman Coliseum for sport. It had been expected to put up a good fight against the gladiators, since the Romans thought it was a vicious cross between a leopard and a camel. Alas, the harmless herbivore was quickly slaughtered, to the cheers of the bloodthirsty Roman citizenry.

HOW'S THE WEATHER UP THERE?

A giraffe's heart would have to be quite a machine to reliably push blood up to its brain. Giraffe hearts can weigh more than 29 pounds and pump three times harder than human hearts. The blood pressure of a giraffe is the highest of any animal: 260/160. You'd think it would be in danger of blacking out when it bends down to drink and then suddenly stands up again. However, the giraffe comes with an amazing network of veins and valves in the neck to regulate and equalize blood flow.

This network has been compared to a sponge. If you watch a giraffe taking a drink, you will see that it doesn't stay down indefinitely, but raises its head now and again. When the giraffe tilts its head down to drink, the vessels in the head fill up, while valves partially close to keep the blood from rushing to the brain. The giraffe can perceive the pressure, and as the blood vessels approach full capacity, the giraffe knows it's time to right itself and reverse the process. Then, the valves partially close off and the blood vessels drain, so blood doesn't quickly rush out of the brain.

NEVER KISS A GIRAFFE

How long is a giraffe's tongue? On average, about 2 feet. It's not only really long, but black as well, which might serve the practical purpose of protecting it from sunburn...but it still looks really, really gross.

GIRAFFE NAP

Have you ever seen a giraffe lying down? It doesn't happen often. Adult giraffes would make a good supper for a lion on the African plain, so they've evolved some interesting sleep patterns. They sleep deeply a half–dozen times a day but for only a few minutes at a time, totalling about 30 minutes every 24 hours. At other times, they doze off lightly with their ears still perked and listening for predators. When a giraffe does lie down for resting, it usually will rest its head on its rump or a log so that its head stays elevated.

ALL IN THE FAMILY

There are only two separate species in the family *Giraffidae*. One is the steppe giraffe, the one we're familiar with, and the other is an okapi—also called a forest giraffe—that has a short neck and looks like a cross of a zebra, a mule, and a steppe giraffe. There are seven different subspecies of steppe giraffes, including the semiarid savannah giraffe, the southern giraffe, and the masai giraffe. All of these have variations in their markings; however, that's not saying much because all giraffes, even members of the same subspecies and herd, have variations in their markings. Like humans' fingerprints, no two giraffes have the same spot patterns.

An Okapi, one weird-looking animal

WELCOME TO THE REAL WORLD, SPOT BOY!

A giraffe calf is welcomed into this world in a most unpleasant way. Its mother doesn't really have the ability to squat down close to the ground when it gives birth, so the newborn giraffe baby tumbles six feet to the ground. Despite the hard landing, within an hour the new baby will be standing up and trying out its spindly legs. It will also grow quickly—about half an inch an hour.

YOU THINK YOUR CHILDHOOD WAS TOUGH?

Only about a quarter of all giraffes born in the wild make it to adulthood. This is mostly because they are a favored prey among the big cats and jackals. Although the mother giraffe puts up a battle to save her baby, and can sometimes kill a lion or tiger with her kicks, the predators usually win.

HEAD–TO–FOOT NOTES

• The average male giraffe is about 17 feet tall. The average female is about 14 feet tall. This serves a very practical purpose: Unlike in most species, the two genders don't compete for food, because each reaches different levels of tree branches.

• A giraffe's digestive system is about 280 feet long. It has to be that long to extract nutrients from the high-fiber leaf diet that giraffes eat. Like cattle, giraffes chew cud that they've already swallowed and regurgitated.

• Giraffes can't swim.

• A giraffe can close its nostrils completely to keep out sand and dust.

• Giraffes have good vision, although they can't tell green from orange.

• A giraffe seldom uses its voice, though it can utter a variety of soft sounds.

• Giraffes perpetually wag their tails.

• "Camelopard" is just another name for the giraffe.

• A few African ranches raise giraffes for meat.

• Females live in groups with their young. Occasionally, they're joined by an adult male.

• Male giraffes fight each other by butting their heads against the chest and neck of their opponent. In a serious fight, you can hear their powerful head–thwacks from a distance of 100 yards. However, they rarely injure each other.

Modern Myth

"RAILROAD TRACKS BASED ON ROMAN CHARIOTS"

The Internet's an amazing thing—a really good myth can spread around the world instantly and linger for years afterward. Hey, did you hear that railroad tracks are based on the ruts from ancient Roman chariots? Not!

YOU HAVE TO LOVE the Internet: A piece of misinformation can get posted as a joke to a small mailing list in 1994 and take on a life of its own, accepted as gospel truth by millions as it ricochets and reverberates through cyberspace a decade later. Such is the case with the myth that modern railroad track specs came from the ancient Romans.

Here's how it began. On February 9, 1994, an R & D engineer for the military named Bill Innanen typed out a joke essay about the United States' and Britain's "exceedingly odd" railroad gauge—4 feet 8.5 inches between the tracks—and claimed that the measurement was based on the ruts left by ancient Roman war chariots.

Roman chariot

Innanen sent the mock essay to a small mailing list for other military researcher/developers. It was a group he expected would appreciate his wry point: that project specifications often live long beyond their usefulness.

Hoo boy, did they appreciate it, way beyond Innanen's wildest expectations. Members of the group sent it to their friends and coworkers, who passed it further along. The story spread and mutated as it traveled through hyperspace, and it started being reproduced in books, magazines, and news stories. The fact that it had been meant as a joke quickly got lost in the tellings and retellings. Meanwhile, Innanen sat by and watched, amused and horrified, powerless to stop his creation even if he had wanted to.

"The post was never meant to be a serious historical thesis," he explained when we tracked him down. "Never did I imagine that sending this to some friends would cause it to become a bona fide urban legend. I personally sent the message out only once. From there it took on a life of its own. Every once in a while someone would unknowingly send me a copy of whatever version was being passed around. It was like a prodigal child returning home, carrying the evidence of his travels with him (the additions and modifications). It's always fun to be able to reply to the sender on these occasions saying, 'Yes I've seen this one before. In fact, I wrote it!'"

So what's the truth? Actually, there were dozens of track sizes used by railroads, but railroads eventually standardized their equipment so that all trains could run on all tracks. But why that "exceedingly odd" gauge of 4 feet 8.5 inches? It turns out to be not so strange after all. Gauge is officially measured from the inside of the track. However, if you measured from the outside of the track, you'd find that it measures 5 feet — not a particularly odd measurement at all. ☾

Daredevils on tracks after a flood washed out a North Carolina railroad bridge, 1916

Something in Common I

It's easy, really—we'll give you a list of words and you tell us what one word goes with all of them. Answers below.

1. Street, iron, rugged, purposes, double, word
2. Baby, wicked sisters, twelve, stool, training
3. Mark, shelf, work, hand, binder, mobile
4. Big, fault, note, sewing, long, best, pounds, soldier
5. Bud, flash, head, switch, meal, housework, craft
6. Buttons, Cincinnati, Rhode Island, light, pepper, cross, hot
7. Wall, back, news, toilet, tiger, tissue, term
8. Rubber, Christmas, Easter, Navy, trained, harbor, elephant
9. Navy, string, counter, Boston, kidney
10. Quarter, porch, channel, paper, stage, diamond, street, pain
11. Quarters, hunter, shrink, board, start, hammer, potato
12. List, electrical, sheet, sighted, handed, stories, order, change
13. Forest, village, bowling, sleeves, horn, party, eggs & ham
14. High, easy, person, rocking, electric, wheel
15. Brake, wooden, running, dance, tree, tennis
16. Great, flower, street, uterine, brick, Berlin
17. Knocker, front, knob, stop, dog, revolving, screen
18. Chicago, arms, necessities, grease, brown
19. Loss, net, cut, split, grey
20. House, tennis, papers, supreme, press, people's

Potty Pourri
RANDOM KINDS OF FACTNESS

• The largest ant in the world reaches lengths of about 41 millimeters, or a little over 1.5 inches. The smallest is only .8 millimeters long.

• The Beatles really didn't think their careers would last that long when they started. They didn't take themselves very seriously for quite some time. Ringo Starr, as a matter of fact, was planning on staying in the group to make the money he needed to open his own hair salon.

• The American flying squirrel has logged flights of more than 150 feet. But that's nothing compared to the giant flying squirrel of Asia. About four times bigger, it can fly about ten times farther.

• If it weren't for the help of a massive influx of French soldiers and sailors fighting on the American side, the British would've won the American Revolution. At the Battle of Yorktown, for example, George Washington's 11,000 soldiers turned the crimson tide of Redcoats with the help of 29,000 French troops.

• Most people could walk across Delaware in an afternoon. The narrowest part of the state is just 8 miles. The widest part isn't much bigger—35 miles.

• What's eating you, chum? There are approximately 2,250 flea species.

• Vincent Van Gogh was a late bloomer. He took up drawing at the age of twenty-seven, only after a failed attempt at being a missionary.

• Ross Bagdasarian, creator of the singing chipmunks—Alvin, Simon, and Theodore—was said to have gotten his inspiration from watching chipmunks in Yosemite, but he named his characters after the officers of his record company.

• What's that smell? *Musk* comes comes from *muschka*, the Sanskrit word for "testicle."

Raising a Führer

THE LIFE OF ADOLF HITLER

Adolf Hitler is undoubtedly one of the most puzzling personalities of our time. He was a vegetarian who loved animals and children, yet put millions to death without a second thought.

• Hitler's father, Alois Hitler, was the illegitimate son of Maria Anna Schickelgruber. Maria worked for the Frankenreithers, a Jewish family, as a servant. There has been speculation that Alois's father was the nineteen-year-old son of the family. Whether true or not, the Frankenreither family financially supported her until her son was fourteen. While postwar research casts some doubt on this story that portrays Adolf as one-quarter Jewish, Hitler himself feared that it might be true and he tried to cover up any evidence of the matter.

• Hitler's father had three wives (but only one divorce), seven or eight children, and at least one child out of wedlock. One wife was 13 years older than him, another 23 years younger, and one—Hitler's mother—was his foster daughter. Hitler's godfather was a Jew named Prinz.

• At the age of eight, Hitler attended a Benedictine monastery school. He longed to become an abbot, but barely escaped expulsion when he was caught smoking. The monastery's coat-of-arms, displayed in various parts of the school, prominently featured a swastika.

Little Adolf

• Hitler hated school, and his teachers hated his insolence. When he finally finished high school he celebrated by getting so drunk that he fell into unconsciousness. When he awoke he could not find his graduation certificate to show his mother. He returned to the school to get a duplicate. The headmaster was waiting for him with his original certificate. It had been torn into four pieces and used as toilet paper. The humiliated future Führer then made a vow never again to touch alcohol.

• Hitler once claimed that everything he knew about

Pa and Ma Hitler

America came from western novelist Karl May's books about cowboys and Indians, and that he got the idea for concentration camps from reading about American Indian reservations.

• Hitler's half-brother Alois, Jr., served time in jail for thievery on at least two occasions and was a bigamist. He was banished to a concentration camp in 1942 because he talked too much about Hitler as a youth.

• Hitler's first youthful love was Stephanie Jansten. He composed a number of love poems in her honor including one he called "Hymn to the Beloved," and apparently falsely believed from her last name that she was Jewish. In spite of his passion and his confession to his best friend that he would jump off a bridge into the Danube to commit suicide, taking Stephanie with him, he never once got up the nerve to talk to her. It wasn't until many years later that she discovered she had once been the object of Hitler's ardor.

• Unable to get into art school, Hitler moved to Liverpool, England, for a while to avoid the draft. Authorities caught up with him in Vienna. He became a message runner as World War I was breaking out. He was awarded the Iron Cross for bravery under fire, thanks to the recommendation of his Jewish commanding officer. By then, though, Hitler was already deeply anti-Semitic.

• During the 1920s Hitler took lessons in public speaking and in mass psychology from Erik Jan Hanussen, an astrologer and fortune teller. Hitler was a believer in astrology, telepathy, graphology, phrenology, and physiognomy, and usually sought supernatural advice when making decisions.

• Hitler was secretly financed by German industrialists and various German princes who believed the Nazis were the best group to stop the rising support of communism that threatened their fortunes. They contributed a reported 25 million gold marks in the years before the Nazis took over Germany. In return, Hitler discreetly changed the party platform, which had been, up to that point, against capitalists and royalists.

• Hitler was a very ordinary-looking man with a mincing walk. His strongest physical asset was his eyes, which were blue verging on violet with a depth and glint that made them almost hypnotic. In his earlier days he wore a pointed beard, often unkempt, and had broken, rotten teeth. He began wearing the famous little moustache during World War I. More of a British style than a German one, he may have adopted it in imitation of English officers, whom he grew to admire during his years at the front.

• Sister Angela's daughter was Geli Raubal, a pretty young woman in her twenties with whom Hitler lived for a number of years when he was rising to power. Nineteen years younger than Adolf, she was by all accounts the only woman he ever loved. Hitler made her pose for nude drawings, which were later stolen and bought back from a blackmailer, and reportedly whipped her with a bullwhip. She is quoted as telling a friend, "My uncle is a monster. You would never believe the things he makes me do."

• Hitler was insanely jealous of his niece. When his chauffeur confessed to him that he and Geli were lovers and wanted to marry, Hitler flew into a rage and fired him. One night, after a loud public fight, she apparently killed herself with a shot from Hitler's revolver.

• When Hitler learned of her death, he decided to become a vegetarian and made a vow never to eat meat again. He went into a deep depression and threatened suicide. An associate, Gregor Strasser, took heroic measures to keep him alive, a fact he regretted three years later when Hitler ordered his execution.

• Eva Braun, his final mistress, was a product of a convent school. She was only seventeen years old when Hitler began to take her out. Once, after seeing photographs of Hitler in the company of other women, Eva shot herself, severing an artery in her neck. She survived.

• In 1935, Eva Braun became despondent when Hitler's preoccupation with international affairs left little time for her. She again attempted suicide, this time by swallowing twenty sleeping pills. Her sister Ilse found her in a coma and saved her. Angela, Hitler's sister and Geli Raubal's mother, was his housekeeper at this time. She despised Eva, refused to shake hands with her, and referred to her as "the stupid cow." Because Hitler continued to bring Eva to his chalet, Angela gave up her housekeeper post and got married.

• Hitler did not like to be alone. He would often summon aides to sit with him in the middle of the night while he rambled on about anything that came to his mind. There was an unwritten rule among the aides that no one would ask a question lest Hitler go off on another tangent.

• By 1937, when the rest of the world didn't yet consider environmental degradation a significant problem, Hitler was mandating anti-pollution devices on factories in the Ruhr. All new factories, like that of the "Strength-Through-Joy" car (later renamed the Volkswagen), were required to install anti-pollution devices.

• Dr. Erwin Giesing treated Hitler after an aborted assassination attempt by German generals, and so was one of the few men Hitler trusted. However, Giesing wrote in his diary that he had once tried to kill the Führer by giving him a double dose of cocaine. The attempt went undetected, and Hitler remained alive.

• At the end of the war, when Hitler decided to commit suicide rather than fall into the hands of the Russians, his first act was to poison his favorite dog Wolf. ☾

Two Little Hitlers

During the filming of Some Like It Hot Tony Curtis commented, "Kissing Marilyn Monroe was like kissing Hitler," to which she quipped, "He only said that because I wore prettier dresses than he did."

Every Picture Tells a Story

A Friend in Need by Cassius Marcellus Coolidge (1845-1934)

• These poker-playing dogs have graced many a bar and rec room where men congregate. It shows two little dogs in the foreground passing a card while playing poker with the big dogs.

• Artist "Cash" Coolidge began his career as a druggist, sign painter, art teacher, and founder of a bank and small-town newspaper in upstate New York. After a trip to European museums, he decided to try his hand at painting.

• His sense of humor, love of dogs, and artistic limitations helped focus his artistry: "His paintings of people look like dogs," observed art historian Moira Harris. "I don't think his people are very good, but his dogs are wonderful."

• In the early 1900s, the Brown & Bigelow printing company recognized Coolidge's rare gift, and commissioned him to paint anthropomorphic dogs for calendars and posters. He generated sixteen scenes—including dogs in a courtroom and at a formal dance—with more than half featuring dogs playing cards.

• *A Friend in Need* seems timeless; most people don't guess that it's a century old. One clue: The cards are old-fashioned, without numbers in the upper-left corners. Many people also seem to believe that the painting's name is *Poker-Playing Dogs*.

Sports Match

MATCH THE TEAM TO THE LOCATION

Okay, sports fans. Included in this quiz are teams from the National Basketball Association, Major League Baseball, and the National Football League. See if you can correctly place them all.

1.	76ers	New Orleans
2.	Jaguars	Tennessee
3.	Devil Rays	Detroit
4.	Cavaliers	Oakland
5.	Wizards	Cincinnati
6.	Mariners	Texas
7.	Titans	Anaheim
8.	Angels	Washington
9.	Bengals	Tampa Bay
10.	Pistons	Baltimore
11.	Rangers	San Diego
12.	Athletics	Philadelphia
13.	Chargers	Jacksonville
14.	Ravens	Seattle
15.	Hornets	Cleveland

Answers: 1. 76ers: Philadelphia; 2. Jaguars: Jacksonville; 3. Devil Rays: Tampa Bay; 4. Cavaliers: Cleveland; 5. Wizards: Washington; 6. Mariners: Seattle; 7. Titans: Tennessee; 8. Angels: Anaheim; 9. Bengals: Cincinnati; 10. Pistons: Detroit; 11. Rangers: Texas; 12. Athletics: Oakland; 13. Chargers: San Diego; 14. Ravens: Baltimore; 15. Hornets: New Orleans

Arachnophile

A TANGLED WEB OF SPIDER FACT

If you love spiders, this one's for you. These juicy arachnid facts, written by *Bathroom Companion* staffer Kathie Meyer, are sure to trap you in their alluring web.

HOME SWEET HOME

A Portland, Oregon, homeowner and her friend were considering the subterranean cobwebs in the basement when the friend lit one to see if it would burn. It did. In the chaos of swatting out the fire, the web-burners dislodged the dryer vent, causing built-up lint to fly, creating an even bigger fire. There were no injuries, except to the spider, but a Fire Bureau spokesman said a fire lieutenant at the scene reminded the homeowner about why it's not a good idea to use fire as a cleaning agent as well as why it's a good thing to clean lint out of the dryer vent.

WHO'S FOR DINNER?

According to some estimates, the bugs that spiders eat in one year weigh as much as all the people on Earth. These estimates, of course, include the results of the spiders' well-known habit of cannibalism. For example, as many as six Australian redback spider males may compete for the ultimate prize—having sex with the female redback spider, and usually being eaten after mating. Still, not all inmates got devoured. Research indicates that the males that got eaten were apparently the ones that most satisfied the female, usually the one with the most stamina. The eaten males' sex act lasted an average of 25 minutes, while the uneaten ones went only eleven minutes.

Australian researchers have also identified some species of baby spiders that survive by dining on their mothers still-living as they grow over a period of weeks. The scientists hypothesize that the maternal sacrifice keeps the young from eating each other.

JUST SAY NO
Government scientists tested the effects of certain drugs on a spider's ability to spin webs. A spider on marijuana tried to make a web, but gave up when it was only half-done. Spiders on Benzedrine spun webs quickly, but left huge holes in them. Spiders on caffeine spun only some random threads, while those on sleeping pills never even started in the first place.

THE CLEVELAND ARACHNOIDS
The Cleveland Indians were named in honor of Louis Cockolexis, who was the first Native American to play pro-fessional baseball. However, before they became the Indians, the team was known as the Cleveland Spiders.

The Cleveland Spiders in 1895

UP, UP AND AWAY...
How do you travel far if you're a young spider? They "balloon." They climb to the top of a plant or fence post, and spin out some lines of gossamer web silk until it catches the wind and pulls the spiderlings away. This allows them to spread out and avoid competing with their brothers and sisters. It's surprising how far spiders can go this way. For example, when the volcano Krakatoa exploded in the Java Sea over a century ago, wiping out all life on nearby islands, the first re-colonizer was a spider, which presumably got there by ballooning on the wind from another island 25 miles away.

In 1981, a Japanese weather

boat discovered that such long-distance ballooning was pretty common. Stationed 240 miles from the mainland, they collected more than a hundred young spiders in nets they had mounted 60 feet in the air.

Look out below!

KISS OF THE WOMAN SPIDER

Even though the black widow bite is the most poisonous spider in Europe and America, only about 1% of bite victims die, and most of those are the very young, the very old, or the infirm. Still, being bitten isn't a pleasant experience. Everyone bitten, though, suffers from the effects. These include a stinging bite, numbing, pain, and swelling. After a half hour or so comes severe abdominal cramping, spasms in the arms and legs, temporary paralysis of some or all parts of the body, chest constriction, and difficulty in swallowing.

ARACHNID BY ANY OTHER NAME

A harvestman, or "daddy longlegs," belongs to the class *arachnid*—like mites, ticks, scorpions, spiders, and a few other invertebrates. Although similar to a spider, it isn't technically a spider.

ENTOMOLOGICAL ETYMOLOGY

Why is it called a "cobweb"? *Cob* is from the Middle English word *coppe*. It meant "spider."

A Brazilian tarantula is about the same size as a boy's hand

BUILDING A WEB SITE

If a spider begins building her traditional-looking, round web at 6 in the morning, she'll probably have it completed before 7—just in time for breakfast. But the building phase really isn't the hard part, it's the maintenance. Between meals, a spider will spend much of her time gathering up broken threads, reweaving them, and adding a new layer of stickiness, so she can keep catching insect meals.

• A spider web consists of two types of thread: *anchor* and *snare*. Anchor threads make the basic shape and

A dew-drenched web, in need of some maintenance

aren't very sticky. Snare threads catch the flies.

• Spiders never spin webs in structures made of chestnut wood. That is why so many European chateaux were built with chestnut beams—after all, spider webs on a 50-foot beamed ceiling can be difficult to clean.

• It would take an average of 27,000 spider webs to produce a pound of web.

• Tiny, woolly bats, in West Africa, live within the large webs of colonial spiders.

• The golden orb-weaver spiders of Papua New Guinea spin the biggest, strongest webs. With supporting threads reaching up to 19 feet (6 meters), their webs can reach 5 feet (1.5 meters) across.

• Among the very rich, it was a fad in the 1800s to import thousands of spiders for special occasions. They'd have servants release them into the trees to spin webs, then sprinkle gold dust into the webs. ☾

The Ten Most Venomous Spiders

1. Brazilian Huntsman (Brazil)
2. Funnelweb (Australia)
3. Redback Spider (Australia)
4. Black Widow (Europe & the Americas)
5. Tarantula (Europe & the Americas)
6. Brown Recluse Spider (Americas)
7. White Tailed Spider (Australia)
8. Spitting Spider (The Tropics)
9. Woodlouse Spider (Europe)
10. Sicarius Hahnii (South Africa)

Filboid Studge

A CAUTIONARY TALE OF ART & CAPITALISM

In this ironic short story by Saki (Hector High Munro), a struggling artist helps his girlfriend's father save the family fortune. No good deed goes unpunished.

I WANT TO MARRY your daughter," said Mark Spayley with faltering eagerness. "I am only an artist with an income of two hundred a year, and she is the daughter of an enormously wealthy man, so I suppose you will think my offer a piece of presumption."

Duncan Dullamy, the great company inflator, showed no outward sign of displeasure. As a matter of fact, he was secretly relieved at the prospect of finding even a two-hundred-a-year husband for his daughter Leonore. A crisis was rapidly rushing upon him, from which he knew he would emerge with neither money nor credit; all his recent ventures had fallen flat, and flattest of all had gone the wonderful new breakfast food, Pipenta, on the advertisement of which he had sunk such huge sums. It could scarcely be called a drug in the market; people bought drugs, but no one bought Pipenta.

"Would you marry Leonore if she were a poor man's daughter?" asked the man of phantom wealth.

"Yes," said Mark, wisely avoiding the error of over-protestation. And to his astonishment Leonore's father not only gave his consent, but suggested a fairly early date for the wedding.

"I wish I could show my gratitude in some way," said Mark with genuine emotion. "I'm afraid it's rather like the mouse proposing to help the lion."

"Get people to buy that beastly muck," said Dullamy, nodding savagely at a poster of the despised Pipenta, "and you'll have done more than any of my agents have been able to accomplish."

"It wants a better name," said Mark reflectively, "and something distinctive in the poster line. Anyway, I'll have a shot at it."

Three weeks later the world was advised of the coming of a new breakfast food, heralded under the resounding name of "Filboid Studge." Spayley put forth no pictures of massive babies springing up with fungus-like rapidity under its forcing influence, or of representatives of the leading nations of the world scrambling with fatuous eagerness for its possession. One huge

sombre poster depicted the Damned in Hell suffering a new torment from their inability to get at the Filboid Studge which elegant young fiends held in transparent bowls just beyond their reach. The scene was rendered even more gruesome by a subtle suggestion of the features of leading men and women of the day in the portrayal of the Lost Souls; prominent individuals of both political parties, society hostesses, well-known dramatic authors and novelists, and distinguished aeroplanists were dimly recognizable in that doomed throng; noted lights of the musical-comedy stage flickered wanly in the shades of the Inferno, smiling still from force of habit, but with the fearsome smiling rage of baffled effort. The poster bore no fulsome allusions to the merits of the new breakfast food, but a single grim statement ran in bold letters along its base: "They cannot buy it now."

Spayley had grasped the fact that people will do things from a sense of duty which they would never attempt as a pleasure. There are thousands of respectable middle-class men who, if you found them unexpectedly in a Turkish bath, would explain in all sincerity that a doctor had ordered them to take Turkish baths; if you told them in return that you went there because you liked it, they would stare in pained wonder at the frivolity of your motive. In the same way, whenever a massacre of Armenians is reported from Asia Minor, everyone assumes that it has been carried out "under orders" from somewhere or another; no one seems to think that there are people who might like to kill their neighbors now and then.

And so it was with the new breakfast food. No one would have eaten Filboid Studge as a pleasure, but the grim austerity of its advertisement drove housewives in shoals to the grocers' shops to clamor for an immediate supply. In small kitchens solemn pig-tailed daughters helped depressed mothers to perform the primitive ritual of its preparation. On the breakfast-tables of cheerless parlors it was partaken of in silence. Once the womenfolk discovered that it was thoroughly unpalatable, their zeal in forcing it on their households knew no bounds. "You haven't eaten your Filboid Studge!" would be screamed at the appetiteless clerk as he turned weariedly from the breakfast-table, and his evening meal would be prefaced by a warmed-up mess which would be explained as "your Filboid Studge that you didn't eat this morning." Those strange fanatics who ostentatiously mortify themselves, inwardly and outwardly, with health biscuits and health garments, battened aggressively on the new food. Earnest spectacled young men devoured it on the steps of the National Liberal Club. A bishop who did not believe in a future state preached against the poster, and a peer's daughter died from eating too much of the compound. A further advertisement was obtained when an infantry regiment mutinied and shot its officers rather than eat the nauseous mess; fortunately, Lord Birrell of Blatherstone, who was War Minister at the moment, saved the situation

by his happy epigram, that "Discipline to be effective must be optional."

Filboid Studge had become a household word, but Dullamy wisely realized that it was not necessarily the last word in breakfast dietary; its supremacy would be challenged as soon as some yet more unpalatable food should be put on the market. There might even be a reaction in favor of something tasty and appetizing, and the Puritan austerity of the moment might be banished from domestic cookery. At an opportune moment, therefore, he sold out his interests in the article which had brought him in colossal wealth at a critical juncture, and placed his financial reputation beyond the reach of cavil.

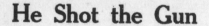

brought him in colossal wealth at a critical juncture, and placed his financial reputation beyond the reach of cavil.

As for Leonore, who was now an heiress on a far greater scale than ever before, he naturally found her something a vast deal higher in the husband market than a two-hundred-a-year poster designer. Mark Spayley, the brainmouse who had helped the financial lion with such untoward effect, was left to curse the day he produced the wonder-working poster.

"After all," said a friend, meeting him shortly afterwards at his club, "you have this doubtful consolation, that 'tis not in mortals to countermand success." ☾

Love & Romans

Et Tu Can Be a Latin Lover!

Love is hard in any language, but what if you end up in a Latin bar and everybody's wearing togas? Well, you know what they say: When in Rome, do as the Romans do. Here's a glossary to help you out.

LETTING SOMEONE KNOW YOU'RE INTERESTED

Here are a few good pick-up lines that just might be enough to impress that cute person in a toga across the bar:

• Seen any good movies lately? *Vidistine nuper imagines moventes bonas?*

• What's your sign? *Quo signo nata es?*

• Is that a scroll in your toga, or are you just happy to see me? *Estne volumen in toga, an solum tibi libet me videre?*

• How do you get your hair to do that? *Quomodo cogis comas tuas sic videri?*

• You know, the Romans invented the art of love. *Romani quidem artem amatoriam invenerunt.*

• Everyone is doing it! *Sic faciunt omnes!*

• Go with the flow! *Ventis secundis, tene cursum!*

• Let it all hang out. *Totum dependeat.*

• Bad kitty! Rrrr.... *Feles mala! Rrrr....*

"To fall in love you have to be in the state of mind for it to take, like a disease." —Nancy Mitford

KNOWING WHEN TO ICHTHUS OR CUT BAIT

It's pretty easy to tell if someone is interested in you, but the signs may be a bit more difficult to read if they're not. Here are a few phrases to let you or the other person know it's time to pack up your fishing nets and go home:

- As if! *Ut si!*

- Don't call me, I'll call you. *Noli me vocare, ego te vocabo.*

- Stupid cow. *Vacca foeda.*

- Gag me with a spoon! *Fac me cocleario vomere!*

- Eat my shorts. *Vescere bracis meis.*

- Men are slime. *Viri sunt Viri.*

- What a doofus! *Qualem blennum!*

- I'm outta here! *Absum!*

- I can't hear you. I have a banana in my ear. *Te audire no possum. Musa sapientum fixa est in aure.*

- I'm going to have to hurt you on principle. *Me oportet propter praeceptum te nocere.*

- Your mother was a hamster and your father smelt of elderberries. *Mater tua criceta fuit, et pater tuo redoluit bacarum sambucus.*

- I have a catapult. Give me all your money, or I will fling an enormous rock at your head. *Catapultam habeo. Nisi pecuniam omnem mihi dabis, ad caput tuum saxum immane mittam.*

- Get a life. *Fac ut vivas.*

- If Caesar were alive, you'd be chained to an oar. *Caesar si viveret, ad remum dareris.* ❦

Men and Women

"When a woman behaves like a man, why doesn't she behave like a nice man?" —Dame Edith Evans

"It is so many years now since Adam and Eve were first together in the garden, that it seems a great pity that we have not learned better how to please one another.... I wish that once in all the time of men and women, two ambassadors could meet in a friendly mind and come to understand each other." —Isak Dinesen

Retro-Futurism

TOM SWIFT'S WORLD OF TOMORROW

Tom Swift was a boy inventor created by Victor Appleton almost a century ago. The breathless adventure stories are great fun, but even better are the descriptions of his inventions.

TOM SWIFT & HIS SUBMARINE BOAT (1910)

The inventor did not want to depend on the usual screw propellers for his craft. Mr. Swift planned to send *The Advance* along under water by means of electricity. Certain peculiar plates were built at the forward and aft blunt noses of the submarine. Into the forward plate a negative charge of electricity was sent, and into the one at the rear a positive charge, just as one end of a horseshoe magnet is positive and will repel the north end of a compass needle, while the other pole of a magnet is negative and will attract it. In electricity like repels like, while negative and positive have a mutual attraction for each other. Mr. Swift figured out that if he could send a powerful current of negative electricity into the forward plate it would pull the boat along, for water is a good conductor of electricity, while if a positive charge was sent into the rear plate it would serve to push the submarine along.

TOM SWIFT & HIS ELECTRIC RIFLE (1911)

"How does it work?'" asked Ned, as he looked at the curious gun. The electric weapon was not unlike an ordinary heavy rifle in appearance save that the barrel was a little longer, and the stock larger in every way. There were also a number of wheels, levers, gears and gauges on the stock.

"It works by electricity," explained Tom. "That is, the force comes from a powerful current of stored electricity."

"Oh, then you have storage batteries in the stock?"

"Not exactly. There are no batteries, but the current is a sort of wireless kind. It is stored in a cylinder, just as compressed air or gases are stored, and can be released as I need it."

"And when it's all gone, what do you do?"

"Make more power by means of a small dynamo."

"How does it kill?"

"By means of a concentrated charge of electricity which is shot from the barrel with great force. You can't see it, yet it is there. It's just as if you concentrated a charge of electricity of five thousand volts into a

small globule the size of a bullet. The electric bullets will pierce anything. They'll go through a brick wall as easily as the x-rays do. You can fire through a house, and kill something on the other side."

"I should think that could very well be dangerous."

Tom took his place at the end of the range, and began to adjust some valves and levers. "Here she goes!" he suddenly exclaimed. Ned watched his chum. The young inventor pressed a small button at the side of the rifle barrel. There was no sound, no smoke, no flame and not the slightest jar. Yet, the next instant the scarecrow figure seemed to fly all to pieces. There was a shower of straw, rags and old clothes, which fell in a shapeless heap at the end of the range.

"Say. I guess you did for that fellow, all right!" exclaimed Ned.

"It looks so," admitted Tom, with a note of pride in his voice. "Now we'll try another test."

Who Was "Victor Appleton"?

The Tom Swift series was the creation of publisher Edward Stratemeyer, who also created the Hardy Boys, Nancy Drew, and the Bobbsey Twins. Stratemeyer chose the name "Victor Appleton," and hired Howard R. Garis to write the books under that name. Garis was famous under his own name as the author of the Uncle Wiggily stories.

TOM SWIFT & HIS PHOTO TELEPHONE (1914)

"It can't be done, Tom!" said Tom's dad. "To transmit pictures over a telephone wire, so that persons cannot only see to whom they are talking, as well as hear them — well, to be frank with you, Tom, I should be sorry to see you waste your time trying to invent such a thing."

"I don't agree with you. Not only do I think it can be done, but I'm going to do it. In fact, I've already started on it. As for wasting my time, well, I haven't anything in particular to do, now that my giant cannon has been perfected."

"But, Tom, this is different. You are talking of sending lightwaves — one of the most delicate forms of motion in the world — over a material wire. It can't be done!"

"Look here, Dad!" exclaimed Tom, coming to a halt in front of his parent. "What is light, anyhow? Merely another form of motion; isn't it?"

"Well, yes, Tom, I suppose it could be."

"Of course it is," said Tom. "With vibrations of a certain length and rapidity we get sound — the faster the vibration per second the higher the sound note. Now, then, light shoots along at the rate of 186,000,000 miles a second. So we have sound, one kind of wave motion, or energy; we have light, a higher degree of vibration or wave motion, and then we come to electricity — and nobody has ever yet exactly measured the intensity or speed of the electric vibrations. But what I'm getting at is this — that electricity must travel pretty nearly as fast as light — if not faster. So I believe that electricity and light have about the same kind of vibrations, or wave motion. Now, why can't I send light-waves over a wire as well as electrical waves?"

Mr. Swift was silent for a moment. Then he said, slowly: "Well, Tom, I never heard it argued just that way before. Maybe there's something in your photo telephone after all." ☾

(Interested in reading more Tom Swift theories and inventions? See pages 295 and 383.)

Tom Swifties II

"Tell Me a Swifty," Said Tom Punsively

From the surreal 1960s came elephant jokes and Tom Swifties, based on bad puns and the stylistic excesses of Victor Appleton, who created the popular Tom Swift stories.

"No need for silence," Tom allowed.

"Cobblers!" Tom said at last.

"This is where I keep my arrows," Tom said quiveringly.

"2 bdrm furn w/vu," Tom said aptly.

"This boat is leaking," Tom said balefully.

"I've swallowed a window," Tom said painfully.

"My bike wheel's badly damaged," said Tom outspokenly.

"Would you like to buy a cod?" asked Tom selfishly.

"3.14168," Tom said piously.

"Harumph!" Tom ejaculated phlegmatically.

"Are you a homosexual, too?" Tom queried gaily.

"I think I'm allergic to this fruit!" rasped Barry.

"@#$%&*!" wrote Tom in cursive.

"I'm a sloppy hot dog eater," Tom admitted with obvious relish.

"I do too know a French city and street!" Tom parried ruefully.

"So another person arrived before me?" Tom second-guessed.

"Please keep quiet about my drooling," said Tom secretively.

"I want to look at your cervix," said Dr. Tom speculatively.

"The carpet layer sneezed," explained Tom tactfully.

"I punched his stomach three times," said Tom triumphantly.

"I can't stand painting," Tom said uneasily.

Whad'ja Get?

HOW CRACKER JACK BECAME A PRIZED SNACK

Like the Ferris wheel, the ice cream cone, and Aunt Jemima pancakes, Cracker Jack premiered during Chicago's Columbia Exhibition in 1893. It never would've happened if it weren't for the Great Chicago Fire 22 years earlier.

FREDERICK RUECKHEIM was working on a farm in rural Illinois in 1871 when he heard that there were good-paying jobs in the city of Chicago cleaning up the charred ruins and debris from the Great Fire. Rueckheim, who had recently immigrated from Germany, stashed his life's savings of $200 and went.

Once Rueckheim got there, though, he discovered that the jobs weren't quite as good as promised. Instead, he opened a one-popper popcorn stand with a partner, William Brinkmeyer. Their sales were brisk enough that they expanded to more and bigger stands—and finally to popcorn wholesaling. The burgeoning company outgrew its facilities six times in the next seven years. To help out, Frederick brought his brother, Louis, over from Germany. Louis soon bought out Brinkmeyer's half of the company, but Frederick made sure Louis knew whose half was the bigger half: He named the business "F. W. Rueckheim & Brother."

In 1884, their factory burned down. The brothers quickly rebuilt, and within six months their business was popping again. They started expanding the popcorn lines, adding marshmallows and other sweet flavorings to batches. For the Columbia Exhibition, the world's first World's Fair, they decided to mix up something new and different: a molasses, peanut, and popcorn mixture. It was a huge success, garnering orders for it from retailers all over the country.

After yet another factory expansion, Frederick complained all the way to the

Bet You Didn't Know

• More than 1,200 years ago, Native Americans hybridized a special strain of dent corn that was perfect for popping. Some tribes in the New England area figured out that if they heated maple syrup and poured it over the popped corn, not only did it taste sweet, but it helped preserve the popped kernels for later consumption.

• Fast forward hundreds of years: Jack Norworth and Albert von Tilzer wrote *Take Me Out to the Ballgame* in 1908, years before either one of them had actually seen a baseball game. However, both had eaten Cracker Jack, so they included a now-famous line: "Buy me some peanuts and Cracker Jack / I don't care if I never come back...."

• During the Depression, the company came out with new products like chocolate-covered Cracker Jack and coconut-flavored corn brittle.

• Cracker Jack's largest marketing campaign, the Cracker Jack Mystery Club, lasted from 1933 to 1936. It required kids to find presidential medals hidden in a secret box compartment and return five to the company.

• Twenty dollars annually will buy you a membership into the Cracker Jack Collectors Association where you can mingle, mix, and trade with fellow Cracker Jack prize collectors.

• Since 1912, Cracker Jack gave out more than 23 billion toys, making it perhaps the biggest provider of toys in the world.

• A mint condition, full set of baseball cards from a 1915 Cracker Jack box was recently valued at $60,000.

• There are several rare Cracker Jack prizes that have been valued at $7,000 or more.

"Slide, Kelly, Slide!"

"*The More You Eat—The More You Want*"
Now comes the open season
for baseball fans and good old

Cracker Jack
America's Famous Popcorn Confection

pened in 1896. The sticky snack finally got a name. A sales rep was munching on some and he exclaimed, using Victorian slang for something very good, "That's a cracker jack!" Frederick ran down and trademarked the phrase. The rest is history. (It is sobering to realize that, had the product been born in a later decade, the caramelized corn might have been called "The Cat's Pajamas" or "Cool Stuff" or "One Groovy Thing, Man" or "Awesome, Dude.")

bank: "No matter how we try to plan for it, the orders always exceed our production."

The still-unnamed product was shipped to retailers in large wooden tubs, but there was a problem. When it arrived, due to heat and agitation, the popcorn often stuck together in one huge sticky glop. Louis went to work on the problem, and in 1896 discovered a process that kept the individual particles separate (the formula is still used by the company today and is guarded as a valuable trade secret).

But that's not all that hap-

Now that it had a name, Cracker Jack needed a package. The brothers hired one Henry Eckstein in 1899, who developed a wax-sealed, moisture-proof, individual-serving-sized box. It was this box that made the product portable enough that it could be sold anywhere snacks could be found (including baseball games, which eventually spawned the *Take Me Out to the Ballgame* musical tribute). But that wasn't enough. Hundreds of other imitators had sprung up with names like Yellow Kid, Honey Corn, Unoit, Goldenrod, Honey Boy, Kor-Nuts, Nutty Corn, Five Jacks, Maple Jack, and Sammy Jack. The brothers decided they needed a gimmick.

Their first try were coupons that kids could collect and exchange for merchandise, a system that had recently been pioneered by Sears and Roebuck. The Rueckheims issued an illustrated catalog offering more than 300 household items, sports accessories, and toys. Cracker Jack sales picked up briefly, but leveled off again shortly afterward.

It was reportedly brother Louis who first suggested putting small toys inside the packages, figuring that kids were more likely to make repeat purchases if they received immediate gratification instead of having to save coupons. The combination of Cracker Jack's built-up name recognition and the packaged premium spurred a national craze that resulted in peak sales in 1914.

Frederick decided to add the sailor boy Jack and his dog Bingo to the package in a wartime salute to our fighting boys. (One sad footnote: The boy was modeled after Frederick's beloved grandson Robert, who often wore a sailor suit. As the first of the new packages rolled off the presses, Robert came down with pneumonia and died. So, besides Cracker Jack packages, the logo can also be seen on little Robert's tombstone in Chicago.)

Cracker Jack toys at the time were of remarkable quality: little magnifying glasses, miniature books, whistles, strings of beads, baseball cards, tops, metal trains, cars, and more. The high quality continued through two World Wars and into the 1950s, when little plastic TVs and space ships were premium items. Unfortunately, the prizes today are less than impressive — high-speed packaging and a general stinginess by corporate overlords (first Borden in 1964, then bought by Frito Lay in 1997), have reduced the prizes to little more than disappointing little pieces of paper.

Despite the downgrade in prize quality, though, Cracker Jack continues to sell without new gimmicks and/or much in the way of advertising. So much of the snack has sold over the years that, laid end to end, it could circle the globe more than 70 times. ☾

True Adventures

"DOWN THE DELAWARE RIVER IN A CANOE"

Nowadays, weekend adventurers in indestructible crafts run white water for a lark, but there was a time when men were men and canoes were just wood and canvas. This is an excerpt from *Athletics and Manly Sport*, written by John Boyle O'Reilly in 1890.

Y OU CAN RUN everything on the river but the Big Foul," said the teamster at Port Jervis as he helped us launch the canoes. "It is the foulest rapid on the Delaware. You'll have to carry round."

We had before heard about this rapid with the ominous name. I had with me the notes of one of the best canoemen in the country, who had run the Delaware in the spring of last year, and found these words: "Great Foul Rift. Ran in May. Rapidity of water and danger much exaggerated."

"That's spring," said the teamster, who had heard this note read. "The river is ten feet lower now; and it's the bottom of a river that's dangerous, not the top."

Guiteras was first in his canoe. "Here goes for Philadelphia!" he cried, as he pushed off. "Are there any rapids near?"

"Listen!" and the teamster smiled. We listened and heard one, the sound coming from the bend of the river half a mile below. "It's only a little one," shouted the teamster, as we started. "Keep the left, and you'll find a channel. It's a smooth rift."

We were three, in three canoes — Mr. Edward A. Moseley in a stout boat built by Partelow of the Charles River; Dr. Ramon Guiteras, in a strong Racine; mine was a keelless, decked canoe, by the best builder in the world, Rushton, of Canton, N.Y.

It is impossible to convey the exhilarating sense of freedom one feels during the first moments in a canoe. We were silent at first, and surprised. The river was not deep—three or four feet at most; but it ran down hill like a hunted hare.

"This is superb!" said one. The others echoed the word.

TROUBLE IN THE FIRST RAPIDS

Almost before we knew, we were in the rush of the first rapid. We had not carefully followed the teamster's instructions to keep to the extreme left and had passed the narrow mouth of the channel. Before us ran an oblique bar of heavy stones, over which the river poured like a curtain. It ran clear across the river, and we found ourselves far into the closed angle. The water on the curtain to the left roared like a heavy surf, and we knew that we could not get over or through. There was no opening between the stones more than two feet wide, and below was a hundred yards of chaotic rock and roar.

We turned and paddled upstream. Inch by inch we gained, working with feverish speed, the paddle slipping back in the glancing stream as if it were in air, holding hardly any force.

But we climbed the first descent, and steered across to where

Greetings from the Delaware River

the channel hugged the right bank. Guiteras went in first; he had not gone up far enough by a boat's length, and as he shot across into the narrow channel, his canoe lurched upon one side, stood a moment and swung athwart stream. He had struck; but before a thought of danger could follow, the paddle was buried, and with a lifting push, his boat slipped over the stone and rushed down the rapid like a leaf.

The other canoes followed, avoiding the buried stone. It was a vigorous little rush—about two hundred yards in length, and not fifteen feet in width. The water was deep, but its speed made it leap over every stone on the bottom, and hurl itself in all kinds of ridges and furrows and springing whitecaps.

At the bottom of the rift we plunged into the heap of boiling breakers, still running like mad. Next moment we floated into smooth water, and turned and looked back at our first rapid with much laughing and congratulation. The teamster had called it "a little one," and "a smooth rift"; what, then, was the ominous Great Foul Rift in comparison?

The Author rests between rapids.

As we gazed back at the rapid, it receded from us swiftly. We were on the quiet surface of deep water, but going down at the rate of several miles an hour. The left bank was almost black, a clean, smooth stone with round puff-holes in it, no vegetation whatever on the steep slope.

I've given too much space to our first rapid on the Delaware, which was to be only one of scores before us, and a small one — even a "smooth one." But it will save other descriptions; and it gives our first impression of the river. The Delaware is a river of extraordinary pitch, the fall from Port Jervis to Philadelphia being nearly 1,200 feet. With deep water in May or June, the river is eight to ten feet higher than it was in this last week of August. Then, a canoeman may run two hundred miles without striking a stone. But every foot of fall in the stream makes a totally new river; and he who goes down in early summer cannot imagine what the river is like at low water in late autumn.

That afternoon we pulled the canoes ashore and plunged into the delicious water, drinking it as we swam — a sensation for epicures. We lay prone in the rapid stream, our arms outspread, and our faces under water, floating quickly and looking at the yellow and white pebbles on the bottom.

At last we came to a lovely spot, a soft white sandbank on the left, the Jersey side, formed by the junction of a bright little river with the Delaware. Every paddle was laid down. Half a mile below we heard the dull roar of a rapid. Here the river was very deep and swift, and not more than eighty yards wide. On the right, a wooded but precipitous mountain rose almost straight from the water to a height of at least 800 feet. From his eyrie we had disturbed a white-headed eagle which tipped its great wings above us as it moved slowly down river.

We camped for the night. One man erected the tent; another cooked dinner; the third went in search of a farmhouse for milk, eggs, melons and peaches — the staple of our food for the next fortnight. The sun went down on the left, above the low trees, without cloud or haze. With philosophic reflection, we spread

Delaware River

our rubber blankets on the sand of the tent, over these our woolen blankets; and then, with a big fire blazing a few feet from the tent's mouth, we lay or sat for our coffee and cigars.

Throughout our trip this quiet hour each evening with a strange scene before us was a most enjoyable part of the day.

SECOND DAY: FIDDLER'S ELBOW AND DEATH'S EDDY
We slept as if the night were an hour long, and we woke to plunge into the sweet unchilled water. The miles were long, and the river unendingly broken. It was downhill all the time, rift succeeding rift. Do what we could with careful steering, we struck again and again, and we were in constant danger of smashing boats or paddles. So common became the striking that we coined a word for it — "hung up." And we could not help laughing when one of us struck, as we swept past and saw him grimly poling his canoe over a rock, or raising his feet over the gunwale as he got out to haul her over. For this we had to be always ready; trousers tucked up, and canvas shoes on.

It came to be a jesting habit, that when one led into a rapid he would do so with a boastful shout. This was my part, at one time on this second day. I had gone into a rift with much flourish, and, a third of the way through, had been "hung up."

Down rushed the others with loud derision, avoiding the bad place. Imagine my feeling of disgust at their selfishness, as I saw their backs, leaving me there. Next moment, in the worst part of the rapid, I saw one of them strike and hold his boat with his paddle against a rock; and a second or two later the other struck just beside him. Who could help smiling? And that moment, by a fortunate lurch, my canoe floated and rushed down toward the two, who were now struggling knee-deep in the stream. They held on to let me pass, and scowled as if my laugh were in bad taste.

At ten o'clock we reached Milford, Penn. The river was a series of deep and swift reaches, and then a leaping rift, with a steep descent. In the very center of one of these rapids, my canoe struck on a covered rock and I knew in a flash that she must either get instantly over or be rolled down stream. Thought and act united. I lifted her by a vigorous push, and was whirled down, stern foremost, with my paddle broken.

Fortunately, the channel below was deep, though rough and very rapid. To meet the emergency I knelt and used the broken end of the paddle as a pole, fending off rocks, and steering occasionally with the blade end. My loss was a gain: the best way to steer down a rapid is to kneel and use a long paddle with one blade, the other end used as a pole.

The memory of that day is wholly confused with the noise of rapid water. We were no sooner through one rift than we heard another. The names of the rapids were quaint and suggestive: such as Death's Eddy, Fiddler's Elbow, Milliner's Shoe, Sambo and Mary, Vancamp's Nose, and Shoemaker's Eddy.

THIRD DAY: CALM BEFORE THE STORM

One must use colors, not words, to paint the beauty of the scene that opened before us on our third day, when we ran the upper rapid at Walpack Bend. The wooded height before us rose at least 1,200 feet. The river below was green with the immense reflection. But on the very line of union was a little flame of crimson, which held the eye and centered all the immensity. It was the small cardinal flower, a plant that grows all the way along the Delaware. The intensity of its color is indescribable, and only seen by the natives and the accidental canoe voyager.

The river affects men in a different way from the road. Never before have I seen so many quiet, contented, and gentle working people. Hundreds of farmhouses we passed, surrounded with foliage, women sitting sewing, children playing near the house, men working in the farmyard, and the bright river moving forever before their eyes.

A song sung by some country girls and boys in a boat, passing close, makes a memory as vivid as the cardinal flower. A lady in a boat, excited and joyous, holds up a splendid fish as we pass. "See! I've just caught it!" she says. A gentleman in the boat tells us that we can run all the rapids down the river — "except the Great Foul Rift!"

"Depth of mind is as safe as depth of water."

Few people are aware of the danger of rapids. To a person along a river, the rapids seem the safest spot because they are obviously the shallowest. But, as the teamster said at Port Jervis, it is "the bottom that is to be feared, not the top."

"It is just the same with humanity," says Guiteras, when this thought is spoken; "it is superficial and hasty people who make all the trouble. Depth of mind is as safe as depth of water."

We ran two or three rapids that day that tested nerves and boats, and were exasperated to hear that they were "smooth rifts," and "nothing at all to the Big Foul." Here it was again; and from this time forward, almost every one to whom we spoke warned us in about the same words. Hence grew an unexpressed desire in each of our minds to reach and run it, and have done with it.

(What happens next? Will the canoeists attempt the Big Foul Rift, or chicken out and carry their canoes around it? Does injury or death wait around the next riverbend? Turn to page 367 for the rest of the story.)

BANG!

Explosive Facts About Firecrackers

> *"Inside the palace, the firecrackers made a glorious noise...
> the rumbling of which sounded like thunder."*
> —Wu Tze-Mu, A.D. 1275

IN CHINA, firecrackers are called *pao chuk*, which means "bursting bamboo." In ancient times, they threw segments of green bamboo into a fire to make it explode with a bang. Even after the Chinese invented black-powder firecrackers, the original name stuck.

• Who invented black powder? Historians believe that as early as the 7th century A.D., a Chinese Taoist alchemist stumbled onto the recipe while experimenting with sulfur compounds. We do know that an alchemist guide book from the A.D. 800s warned against mixing sulfur, arsenic disulfide, saltpeter, and honey: "Smoke and flames result, so that hands and faces have been burnt, and even whole houses have been burned down. These things only bring Taoism into discredit, and alchemists should not do them."

• The first firecrackers to reach Europe came from the travels of Marco Polo, who sent a huge stash of them home to Italy with this (perhaps overexaggerated) description: "They burn with such a dreadful noise they can be heard for ten miles at night. Anyone who is not used to it could die, hence the ears are stuffed with cotton and clothes drawn over the head, for it is the most terrible thing in the world to hear for the first time."

• Remember the paper drives by Boy Scouts in years gone by? Until the 1970s, most of the newspapers collected were shipped to Asia and recycled into firecrackers.

• Here's how firecrackers work. The black powder inside contains saltpeter. The saltpeter releases its own oxygen so none needs to be sucked from the outside air when the powder burns, so it burns instantaneously at 3,800° C. Carbon dioxide and sulfur dioxide gases expand to fill a space 3,000 times the gunpowder's original bulk, buckling the firecracker's paper walls and exploding.

• For weddings, new year's celebrations, store openings

A Bang-Up Fourth of July

Hard to believe considering the number of casualties they've caused, but firecrackers were long encouraged as a way of making the Fourth of July a safer time. Actually, though, the standard ways of making a lot of noise were much more dangerous then. For example:

• **Guns.** Discharging pistols into the air was long considered an essential part of Independence Day. That wasn't necessarily a big problem in farmland, but in densely packed urban areas, the bullets raining down presented a grave danger to life and property.

• **Shooting the Anvil.** It was said you could hear a good anvil shoot from miles away. Celebrants put a blacksmith's anvil on the ground and placed a bag of gunpowder with a fuse on top of it. A second anvil was turned upside down on top of the bag of gunpowder. One brave (or drunk) soul lit the fuse, and everybody scattered. This was to avoid being crushed like a cartoon character.... When the gunpowder exploded, the top anvil was propelled into the air by the explosion before returning heavily, and sometimes lethally, to the ground.

and even funerals, firecrackers have been part of Chinese celebrations for more than a millennium. The firecrackers are meant to scare away unwanted bad spirits like Nian, a one-horned, mythical dragon that comes at the end of each year to savagely molest and kill people and their livestock.

• For Chinese weddings, the explosions of firecrackers are used

"Holiday in Chinatown, San Francisco" by Paul Frenzeny for *Harper's Weekly*, 1880

to clear out negative *chi* and jealous *chi* (*chi* means "energy"). It's believed that if the spirits of jealousy attack during the ceremony, the bride may begin menstruating, which is a terrible omen of bad luck indicating the marriage will shortly end in death or divorce.

• Experts of *feng shui* swear that hanging firecrackers around your home will change the *chi* of your household, resulting in harmony, balance, fame, wealth, awareness, energizing of the lazy, comfort for all and the protection of the household from harm.

• Chinese Christians celebrate Christmas with firecrackers, blowing them off while waiting for the arrival of Dun Che Lao Ren ("Christmas Old Man," or Santa Claus). What's interesting is that they're following an old European and American tradition, in which the deafening sound of firecrackers and guns marked the birthday celebration of the Prince of Peace. An Englishman visiting Baltimore in 1866 wrote that he felt as though he were in the middle of a war zone.

• Poor folks who couldn't afford Christmas firecrackers

saved the bladders from slaughtered hogs. They got good explosions by inflating them and tossing them into a fire.

• Fire experts in the early 1900s suggested scattering firecrackers in rafters, studding, flooring and walls. Not for the *feng shui* benefits (*see p. 69*), but as a fire alarm, since the firecrackers going off would likely awaken the residents in time to get out safely.

SUPER CHARGED FLASHLIGHT CRACKERS
黑貓牌頂好電光 小炮
DO NOT HOLD IN HAND AFTER LIGHTING

• An article in the March, 1955 *Farm Journal* suggested tying firecrackers to a smoldering cotton rope in order to scare birds away from crops. "The rope will smolder away at the rate of about six inches per hour, so you can time the explosions by varying the distances between firecrackers."

• Possessing cherry bombs and M-80s became a federal felony in 1967.

• Legal firecrackers are now relatively safe, resulting in only 17 percent of all fireworks injuries. (This figure includes not just explosions, but also things like toddlers swallowing them, etc.) This compares favorably to sparklers which cause 19 percent. Illegal homemade firecrackers are responsible for 40 percent.

• In England, the big firecracker holiday is November 5—Guy Fawkes Day. The holiday commemorates an aborted plot by persecuted Catholics to blow up Parliament and the royal family in A.D. 1605. For centuries, the holiday was an excuse to make anti-Catholic speeches and burn effigies of the pope with firecrackers inside.

• In India, at the end of the five-day festival of Diwali, celebrants banish Alaksmi, the goddess of bad luck, poverty and misfortune. They do this by sweeping the house, yelling in all the rooms and setting off firecrackers.

• Although some factories use hand-powered or foot-powered rolling machines, firecrackers are still mostly assembled by hand. It's dangerous and tedious work. In China, where the bulk of the world's firecrackers are made, skilled workers get paid only 80¢ to $1 an hour. ❦

"Pop" Culture

SOME KERNELS OF TRUTH ABOUT POPCORN

Have you ever thought about what a strange thing it is that corn can pop? And the fact that it tastes good—especially when watching movies—makes it all the more magical.

A CORNUCOPIA OF FACTS

• Popcorn grows in a variety of colors besides boring old white and yellow. The red, pink, and blue kinds are especially colorful. Unfortunately, no matter what the color of the kernel, the insides are still white when they pop.

• A German food scientist has identified twenty-three different natural compounds that contribute to the flavor and aroma of popcorn.

• Popcorn figures into a 1957 hoax that many people still believe is true. An unemployed market researcher named James M. Vicary claimed that by flashing "EAT POPCORN" for a split second on the movie screen, he subliminally convinced audiences to buy 57.5% more popcorn.

• Americans eat an average of more than 2

pounds—68 quarts—of popcorn a year.

• Maybe they should eat more. One cup of plain popcorn from a hot air popper has little fat and only 23 calories. Because of its high fiber content (15% total dietary fat), popcorn has earned recommendations from the American Cancer Society and the National Cancer Institute.

• Or, in the real world, maybe people should eat less popcorn. Because when we eat popcorn, it's usually slathered with artificial, buttery hydrogenated fat. A study in 1994 by the Center for Science in the Public Interest found that a medium-

An 1856 recipe for popcorn balls began with a big slather of pig fat....

sized buttered popcorn from movie theaters contains more saturated fat than an order of bacon and eggs, a Big Mac, a medium fries, and a steak dinner, *combined*—29 grams.

• In 1996, thirty-five volunteers working 10 hours straight created the world's largest popcorn ball. At 2,225 pounds, it weighed more than a Volkswagen Beetle, and was taller—nearly 6 feet high. The superball took 1,020 pounds of sugar and 425 pounds of corn syrup to stick it all together. All this excitement took place in Sac City, Iowa, to honor the town's biggest crop.

READ HISTORY & BE A-MAIZED

• Ancient fossilized corn pollen from 80,000 years ago, found in Mexico City, is nearly identical to that of modern corn.

• Archeologists believe that humanity's first use of corn

Versatile Corn

• Only 1% of all corn grown is used for direct human consumption, and only a fraction of that is popcorn. The rest is used for animal feed or made into other products like corn starch, corn oil and alcohol.

• Besides that, cornstalks can be made into soil conditioners, building materials, paper, packing materials and even explosives.

• Corncobs are used to manufacture plastics and nylon (and rustic pipes), and corn husks can be made into cigarette paper.

was for popping. The oldest known ears of popcorn, about 5,600 years old, were discovered in Bat Cave, New Mexico.

• In ancient times, they heated sand in a fire and then stirred kernels of popcorn into the hot sand.

• Some Native Americans used the same oil-and-hot pan method often used today. Others ran a sharp stick through the cob and popped the corn kernels still attached.

• 1,000-year-old popcorn found in Peruvian graves is so well-preserved that it could still pop.

• Before Columbus, popcorn had spread from Mexico through most Native American societies in North and South America. Native Americans used it for eating, of course, but also made it into popcorn soup and beer, strung it into necklaces, and woven it into headdresses.

• When Columbus and crew

Tlaloc, Aztec god of rain, fertility... and popcorn!

first landed in the Americas, the Indians offered to sell them popcorn. Early Spanish explorers told of "a kind of corn which bursts when parched and and makes itself look like a very white flower; they said these were hail-

Why Popcorn Pops

• Popcorn has a higher moisture content than other varieties of corn. To pop, a kernel must contain at least 13.5% water, encircled inside the ring of soft starch, in order for the kernel to explode.

• If the kernel heats up quickly, the water inside the starch expands and exerts great pressure against the hard outer surface. (If heated slowly, the water escapes without popping the corn.)

• Eventually the outside cannot contain this pressure, causing the skin to burst with a loud "pop!" The softened starch inside the popcorn turns the kernel inside out and instantaneously hardens into that stiff, Styrofoam consistency.

stones given to the god of water."

• While popcorn probably originated in Mexico, it was also grown in China, Sumatra and India centuries before

Columbus brought it to Europe, fueling more speculation that the Chinese discovered America years before.

• Quadequina, brother of the Wampanoag chief Massasoit,

The King of Corn

• Yes, there really was an Orville Redenbacher, even though the name and the geekish bowtie-and-suspenders persona convinced many people that he was too good to be anything but an ad agency's creation.

• After graduating from Purdue University, Redenbacher and another researcher named Charles Bowman worked for decades, crossbreeding 30,000 hybrids before coming up with a strain of popcorn in 1952 that was originally branded Redbow, a combination of Redenbacher and Bowman's names. A Chicago advertising agency, realizing Redenbacher would be good at a folksy television hucksterism, suggested changing the name.

Orville Redenbacher, from a package of microwave popcorn

• Marketing his popcorn was difficult at first. Retailers didn't see a point in a higher grade of "gourmet popcorn." It wasn't until the yuppie food faddism of the 1980s that Redenbacher's popcorn came into its own. He'd sold the business to Hunt-Wesson in 1978 for $2 million before it had really taken off, yet he continued to act as its commercial front man, eventually becoming famous. When in public, he'd pass out stickers that said, "I've met Orville Redenbacher, the Popcorn King."

• The popcorn's reputation for always popping and Redenbacher's identification with it led people to complain directly to him if they ran into problems. "Every once in a while, someone will mail me a single popcorn kernel that didn't pop. They'll tape it to a piece of paper and mail it to me," he told the LA Times in 1984. "So I'll get out a fresh kernel, tape it to a piece of paper and mail it back to them."

• Redenbacher ate a bowl of popcorn a day.

• In 1995, he drowned in a spa after having a heart attack at the ripe old age eighty-eight.

brought a deerskin bag of popcorn to the first Thanksgiving feast of the pilgrims at Plymouth, Massachusetts. After that, colonists ate popcorn with milk and sugar for breakfast.

• A man name Charles Cretors invented the very

A Cretors popcorn machine

first popcorn machine in 1885. It was pretty ingenious because of its versatility. It could be pushed on foot, pulled by horse or mounted on trucks. The Cretors family still makes machines today. ☾

Nothing to Do with Corn at All

• When the first settlers landed in America there were about 200,000 words in the English language. Now there are more than 600,000. Most Americans know only about 10,000-20,000 of them, but actually use only about half that number. In fact, 1,500-2,000 words account for about 99% of everything we ever say.

• The most common word that's spoken in the English language is *I*. The second most common is *you*. Those two words account for almost 10% of all informal conversation.

• The third and fourth most common words are *the* and *a*.

• The ten most popular words account for about 25% of what we say, and the fifty most popular words fill about 60%.

• The fifty most popular words? Alphabetically, they are *a, about, an, and, are, be, can, do, don't, have, he, her, him, I, in, is, it, for, from, just, get, go, know, me, not, now, of, on, out, over, see, she, tell, that, them, they, thing, think, this, to, want, was, we, what, will, with, would, you.*

• *"The trouble with corporate America is that too many people with too much power live in a box (their home), travel the same road every day to another box (their office)."*
• *"Send me out into another life. But get me back for supper."*

—Faith Popcorn, U.S. Management Consultant

Typhoid, yellow fever, dysentery, cholera, malaria and hookworm all were common illnesses in parts of the United States before the arrival of sanitary, non–leaking privies.

Next time, more pumice; less wine....

Say "Ah"

A Closer Look at Dental History

It's hard to believe, but most Americans didn't brush their teeth until soldiers brought the Army-enforced habit back home from World War II.

ALTHOUGH IT TOOK AMERICANS a while to catch on to good oral hygiene practices, people throughout history have worked to care for their teeth, starting as far back as the ancient Egyptians. "Chew sticks"—twigs with one end frayed into soft bristles—have been found in Egyptian tombs going back to about 3000 B.C. The first toothpaste was developed about the same time—a mixture of ground pumice and wine.

POTTY MOUTHS
The ancient Romans took teeth cleaning further, including it as part of some of their religious ceremonies. The patriarchy employed certain slaves, forerunners of modern dental hygienists, to clean their teeth. They also invented the first toothpaste and mouthwash with a secret ingredient: human urine. They especially prized

imported Portuguese urine for its strength, but that was probably more a function of evaporation on the long trip to Rome than any ethnic characteristics.

Urine continued to be an active ingredient in toothpastes and mouthwashes until well into the 18th century, because its ammonia was a great cleanser. In fact, ammonia continues to be an ingredient in many modern dentifrices, but now it's manufactured in the laboratory, not the lavatory. Other ingredients in toothpaste over the years included herbs, honey, ground shells, talc, mice, rabbit heads and lizard livers.

BRISTLING AT THE THOUGHT

The first toothbrush appeared in China around 1498. The bristles were plucked from hogs living in China's cold-weather provinces because their hair was stouter and firmer; the hairs were set into handles of bone or bamboo. The Chinese toothbrush traveled to Europe in the 1600s and became widely used.

The toothbrush stayed pretty much the same for several hundred years. Finally, the discovery of nylon in 1938 revolutionized the toothbrush, and just in time for World War II. The bristles of Dr. West's Miracle Tuft Toothbrush released that year were stiff enough to be a painful hazard to the gums; it wasn't until the early 1950s that a safe, soft nylon bristle became the standard. Since then, more than 2,000 toothbrushes have been patented across the world.

IT'S ELEMENTAL!

Dentists discovered the positive effects of fluoride on teeth in 1802 when they noticed that the citizens of fluoride-rich Naples, Italy, had brown mottled teeth but few cavities. By the 1840s, some Europeans sucked honey-flavored fluoride lozenges to prevent tooth decay, but the idea of adding the chemical to toothpaste was still a century away. Instead, manufacturers started adding soap in 1824 and chalk in the 1850s. In 1892, Dr. Washington Sheffield of Connecticut was the first to put toothpaste into tubes like those used for oil paint.

In 1945, Grand Rapids, Michigan, became the first U.S. city to deliberately add fluoride to city water to reduce cavities. Other cities followed suit to a point that nearly two-thirds of the U.S. population now has fluoridated water, despite warnings from right-wing fearmongers that fluoride was a communist plot to produce a generation of drugged and mind-controlled zombies. (Hmm, look around you—maybe they were right after all?)

Procter & Gamble was the first company to package fluoride into a toothpaste in 1956. In a brilliant ad campaign that's still quoted 40 years later, kids ran into the house brandishing notes from their dentist and screaming, "Look ma, no cavities!"

GOOD VIBRATIONS

Meanwhile, electric toothbrushes made their way from

Switzerland, where they'd been developed immediately after World War II and tested on canines for effectiveness. They first hit the U.S. market in 1960. The latest gimmick is an ultrasonic toothbrush that is reported to clean between teeth with high-pitched sound waves. Maybe true, but don't throw away the floss until all the results are in.

DRILLING FOR FACTS

• It's hard to imagine, but Colgate claims "Tooth Fairy" as a registered trademark. Hopefully, corporate sponsorship means the TF can leave a lot more money under the pillow. Your can fill out a form and get an e-mail from the Tooth Fairy® Itself.

• Colgate reportedly faced a big obstacle marketing toothpaste in Spanish speaking countries. Colgate translates into the command "Go hang yourself."

• Although Crest with fluoride came out in 1955, it just

sat on store shelves, to Procter & Gamble's bewilderment. P&G touted a high-profile study proving that fluoride prevents cavities and lobbied the American Dental Association for an endorsement. Both—touted in "Look ma, our group had 23% fewer cavities!" ads— finally brought Crest skyrocketing sales in the early 1960s.

• In 1959, dentists performed 34 extractions for every 100 people. Getting dentures was considered a natural step in the aging process. Today, it's half that rate.

• Saliva is a natural bacteria destroyer, and antidepressants, antihypertensives, antihistamines, decongestants and muscle relaxants can all inhibit saliva production.

• The old Listerine commercial notwithstanding, not even mouthwash really helps bad breath beyond a minute or two— in fact, alcohol and hydrogen peroxide can actually worsen the conditions. Baking soda makes your mouth more alkaline—exactly the wrong direction, because acidity decreases bad breath.

• We worry about bad breath to the tune of $10 billion a year of profit to mint, gum, and mouthwash manufacturers, nearly all of it wasted.

• Regular flossing and proper brushing is the best cure for halitosis, or bad breath.

• How about a tooth tattoo? Tiny gold images of hearts, butterflies and rabbits have become popular among certain trendy subgroups. The downside is that from a distance of more than about 3 feet it just looks like you have food stuck in your teeth.

• In case you've tried brushing, flossing and regular check-ups and still have problem teeth, try religion. The patron saint of dentists is St. Apollonia, who reportedly had her teeth pulled out in A.D. 249 by an anti-Christian mob. ☾

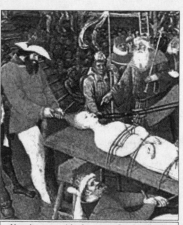
No nitrous oxide for poor St. Apollonia

Ouch!

Love Secrets of the Spiny & Hardshelled

Animal relationships can be difficult enough, but have you thought about the difficulties of animals that have prickles or shells?

PRICKLY HEAT

"How do porcupines make love?" "Very carefully!" goes the old joke, but in real life it's not quite as prickly as you'd expect. Mating is a dangerous pastime for male porcupines, but not because of the quills. They fight other males for the right to mate with a receptive female. Since the female porcupine goes into a prickly heat only once a year, the stakes are high in porcupine love. Worse, the female enjoys inciting the rivalries between males. She hangs out in a tree, urinating her sexual scents down toward them and calling saucily to the boys fighting each other below. When one man's left standing,

"Hi, boys—how's every li'l prickly thing?"

the female crawls down the tree. The male urinates on the female to excite her with his sexual scents, and the female curls her tail over her back to expose her quill-free genital region. Male porcupine genitalia is located on his underside, too, so when they mate, there are no pointed parts for the prickly pair to be watchful of. The whole messy business takes only a minute or so.

A SHELLFISH KIND OF LOVE

How do lobsters mate with all that shell in the way?

Well, it turns out there's an opportunity now and again. You see, lobsters grow by molting—they get too big for their shells and shed them like a human shedding a too–tight girdle. Without a shell they grow quickly by absorbing a lot of water, and then they grow a new, bigger shell.

It's in the time just after shedding their shells that females mate. The courtship process is sweet: When the female lobster  is ready to molt, she approaches a male's den and stands outside, releasing her scent in a stream of urine from just below her antennae. When the male emerges from his den, the

"Hey, baby, why not slip out of those wet things?"

two spar briefly, then the female signals him by placing her claws on his head that she is ready to molt and mate.

They enter his bachelor pad and she languidly strips off her shell. He tenderly turns her limp, yielding body over onto her back with his legs and his mouth. The male, still hard-shelled and passionate, passes his sperm into her body with a rigid, grooved swimmeret. Afterward, she sinks into the soft warmth of the ocean bed and stays in the safety of his den for about a week. When her new shell is hard again, she calls a cab and goes home, never to see him again.

The sperm she receives from the male goes into a special repository where it can stay viable for two years. When she decides she's ready to settle down and have a family, she fertilizes her eggs, numbering from 3,000 to 100,000, carrying them them first in her body, then—for another 9–12 months—under the swimmerets attached to her tail.

After hatching, her microscopic larva float for a month, then settle to the bottom of the ocean to turn into lobsters proper. Still, odds are not good for them—for every 100,000 eggs hatched, only five or six will typically get up to a one-pound weight.

LOVE IN THE SLOW LANE

How do snails have sex? Well, as you'd expect, it's pretty slow; it's also complicated in the many species that are hermaphroditic (in other words, each snail is both male and female).

But that's not the weirdest thing. Snail foreplay begins with each snail jabbing the other in the head, foot or brain with a calcium carbonate "love dart" that can be as long as a centimeter (one-fifth of an inch).

"Sweet Slimer, my foot has been pierced by Cupid's dart."

People have wondered for three centuries why snails do this, but it was not until a few years ago that researchers at McGill University figured it out. They discovered that mucus covering the dart contains hormones that disable the recipient's *bursa copulatrix*, an organ near the female organs that normally digests the vast majority of received sperm. With this organ temporarily disabled, more of the donor's sperm will survive.

After this mutual piercing takes place, the snails place their slimy undersides together and exchange sperm before slowly parting company. But don't expect fond, languid farewells—snails may be slow, but they're not sentimental. They copulate frequently with many different partners, and can store other snails' sperm in their bodies for up to two years. ☾

Arm in Arm in Arm in Arm...

Octopuses may not have to contend with shells and prickles, but they have their own sexual idiosyncrasies to overcome. Males have a modified third arm with a groove down the edge and a leaf-shaped grasping structure at the tip. To mate, the male moves elongated sperm packages down the groove and reaches over to place them in the female's oviducts of her mantle cavity. Beforehand, some males make a vivid display of colored skin patterns and complex body movements; however, the rock pool octopuses have sex without seeing each other—while both remain hidden behind rocks, the male snakes his long arm of love over to her.

Get a Job!

WANT A CAREER CHANGE? HERE ARE SOME SUGGESTIONS

Nob Thatcher: A peruker; wig manufacturer.
Caffler: Someone who collects bones and old scraps.
Qwylwryghte: A wagon wheel mechanic.
Jouster: A fish dealer.
Accipitrary: One who works with falcons.
Eremite: A solitary soul; a hermit.
Hankyman: A magician who moves from town to town.
Perambulator: One who surveys the land.
Chiropodist: A foot and hand disease specialist.
Garlekmonger: Someone who sells garlic.
Mold Boy: Apprentice to a glass maker; helps with molding.
Scrimer: A master fencer.
Whittawer: Someone who manufactures saddles.
Costerwife: A woman who hawks fruit.
Ankle Beater: A cattle driver.
Slubber Doffer: A mill worker who changes bobbins.
Archil Maker: One who makes violet-colored dye from lichen.
Back'us Boy: A servant who works in the kitchen.
Leech: A doctor or veterinarian ("dog leech," "horse leech").
Gerund Grinder: A Latin teacher.
Vineroon: A wine maker.
Bottom Knocker: Someone who helps a potter by knocking the bottom of clay pots.
Nedeller: Someone who makes sewing needles.
Sucksmith: A plow blade manufacturer.
Fewster: One who makes the wooden parts of a saddle.
Tappiologist: A train wheel inspector; someone who taps train wheels.
Simpler: An herbalist.
Deviller: Someone who operates a machine that shreds cloth.
Owler: Ovine thief; one who deals in stolen sheep or wool.
Blemmere: One who works with pipes; a plumber.
Fustian Weaver: A corduroy manufacturer.

T.G.I. Friggas Day

WHERE THE WEEK'S DAYS GOT THEIR NAMES

The name Sunday makes sense. It's obviously a joining of "sun" and "day." But what about the other six days? Where did the names come from, anyway? Gloria Munday brings us a day by day overview.

THE IDEA OF THE SEVEN DAY WEEK came from either the Babylonians or ancient Egyptians, depending on which source you believe. Regardless, the Greeks also adopted it, and named each of the days after the five known planets, and the sun and moon. When the Greek civilization declined, the Roman Empire took much from the Greeks, including naming rights for the days of the week, substituting their own names for the planets.

As the Romans conquered Europe, they spread their names for the week's days. Today in France and Italy, for instance, the names of the days are pretty much the same as they were in ancient Roman times. England, though, had many more influences than Latin. In about A.D. 500, for instance, the Germanic tribes—the Norse, Saxons, Anglos, collectively—conquered Britain and substituted their own names in place of the Roman days of the week, and until the next conquering army, this is where we are now.

SUNDAY
Latin: *Solis dies*
Germanic: *Sonntag*

The Greeks came up with "the day of the sun," and the Romans and Germanic tribes liked it so much, they kept it. The Romans honored the god Apollo, who flew his fiery chariot through the sky each day. The Saxons changed the Roman "solis" to *sunne*, and the day to "Sonntag."

MONDAY
Latin: *Lunae dies*
Germanic: *Monandaeg*

The Romans dedicated this day to the goddess of the

hunt, Diana, who was the twin sister of Apollo. Diana loved hunters, but only to a point. She once turned a hunter into a deer when she caught him spying on her, so she's often depicted with a stag.

The Saxons believed that the sun was a girl and the moon (or *mona*) a boy, and each drove chariots through the sky as wolves chased them. The legend had it that if the wolves caught them, day and night would disappear. It's no surprise, then, that eclipses caused a lot of anxiety for these early Germanic peoples.

TUESDAY
Latin: *Martis dies*
Germanic: *Tiwesdaeg*

The Romans named this day for the planet Mars, and the Roman god of war — Martius. In France, Spain and Italy, the name for Tuesday is directly descended from the Latin: *Mardi, Martes,*

and *Martedi,* respectively. (*Mardi Gras,* literally means "Fat Tuesday" in French.) In Roman mythology, the god Mars was the father of Romulus and Remus, the legendary founders of Rome, who were raised by a wolf.

Years later, when the Germanic tribes rode into Britain, they gave this day to their own god of war, Tiw, hence "Tuesday." Evidence suggests that Tiw was the oldest of all the Norse gods and was long their head god. However, Odin eventually replaced him as head god, and Tiw was demoted to war god only. He's depicted dressed for battle with sword and shield.

WEDNESDAY

Latin: *Mercurii dies*
Germanic: *Wodnesdaeg*

Mercury was the ancient Roman god of messages, and Wednesday (*Mercurii dies*) was named after him.

 Mercury sported a winged hat and shoes that helped him fly. He was known in mythology for being a thief. As the story goes, he stole Apollo's cows by placing shoes on their feet and having them walk backward so no one could track them. Mercury used the gut from the cows to string the first lyre, which so impressed Apollo that he forgave Mercury.

Supplanting Mercury, the Saxons decided their chief god, Odin (or Woden),

deserved his own day. Odin was believed to have invented writing. He was often depicted riding on an eight-legged horse, with two ravens who served as his messengers.

THURSDAY

Latin: *Jovis dies*
Germanic: *Thorsdaeg*

Jove, god of thunder, was the Roman honoree of the day. His better-known name, Jupiter, means "Father Jove" (the Latin *pater* means "father") — a sign of respect. Jupiter was the guardian of Rome and the head of all the gods.

The Saxon's god Thor is also the god of thunder, and he lends his name to this day. Thor is usually seen depicted with a huge hammer that produces loud thunder. He was Odin's son, and is often drawn riding around on  a wagon, led by two goats. He battled giants, and used his hammer to smash their heads. His sworn enemy was the hated World Snake — a snake so big and nasty, it wraps itself around the world and bites its own tail. (You can see a drawing of the World Snake at the top of page 85.)

FRIDAY
Latin: *Veneris dies*
Germanic: *Frigedaeg*

In ancient Rome, there was the belief in a beautiful goddess named Venus who rose from the sea on a half-shell. Her legend is about competition for male attention. A man named Paris had an apple

with "For the Fairest" written on it. The goddesses Venus, Minerva and Juno offered Paris various qualities in exchange for the apple. Minerva promised Paris wisdom; Juno, power. But Venus offered him another beautiful woman—Helen. He took Venus up on her offer, and paid dearly for it with his life, the lives of his family, and his hometown of Troy. Helen, as it turned out, was a married woman. Still, the Romans were suckers for a pretty face, and Venus's day was born.

The Saxons liked the idea of a day in honor of a pretty gal, so they named this day after Frigga. She is believed to be Odin's wife, but Frigga also had affairs with his brothers. She is the goddess of marriage and fertility.

SATURDAY
Latin: *Saturni dies*
Germanic: *Saterdaeg*

The Roman god Saturn was known as Father Time, and is depicted with a sickle. A winter festival called Saturnalia was celebrated in his honor every year in ancient Rome. Schools and businesses closed; families made and ate huge banquets, and the adults showered the children with gifts. All of these traditions— including the time of year— were adopted by the early

Christians to celebrate their own Christmas. They continue on today.

The Germanic tribes didn't really have a god that corresponded to Saturn, so they ended up adopting the ancient Roman Saturni day as is. ☾

Life of the Party!

A hundred years ago, with the help of a little candlelight, hand shadows were big fun at get-togethers. Today, we have much better lighting options and these cool pictures from Henry Bursill's book *Hand Shadows*. With just a little practice, you and your hand shadows can become the life of your next party.

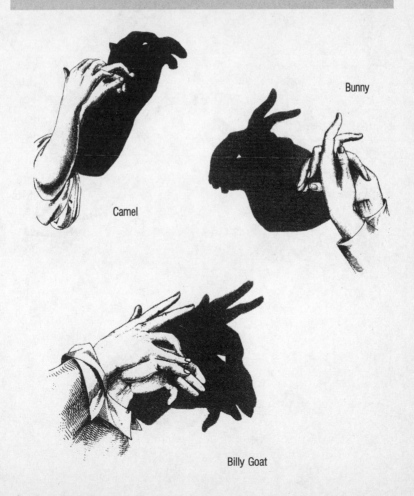

Bunny

Camel

Billy Goat

Mike

Goose

Squirrel

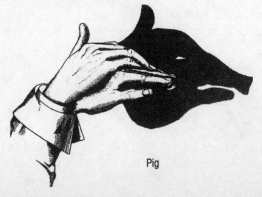

Pig

Pooh Bear

VERY LITTLE BRAIN, BUT MUCH SUCCESS

You can't discuss teddy bears without mentioning that Bear of Very Little Brain, Winnie the Pooh. He and the other cotton-brained residents of the Hundred Aker Woods have charmed kids for 75 years.

FOR THEIR IMPACT, it's hard to imagine that Alexander (A. A.) Milne wrote only two books about Winnie the Pooh and his friends plus two books of verse featuring his real-life son Christopher Robin Milne. For illustrations, he enlisted an artist he knew from writing for *Punch Magazine,* Ernest Shepard. Recognizing Shepard's contributions to the success of his books, Milne began giving him 20% of his royalties instead of just the normal flat rate for an illustrator.

Despite the books' huge success, Milne got tired of writing for children. He had been a moderately successful playwright who believed that his kid books were just a diversion from his "real" career. After his second Pooh book, he announced that it was to be his last, and stuck to that decision.

Meanwhile, his son Christopher got tired of media attention and being ribbed through school, military service and adult life with "Hey, where's Pooh?" and "Cwistopher Wobin is saying his pwayers." He became estranged from both father and his literary namesake, now seeking anonymity, now blasting both father and bear regularly in word and print.

His father began feeling similarly cursed by Winnie the bear as the public consistently rejected his more serious efforts. But in 1952, a few months before the stroke that eventually killed him, he seemed to have made peace with his fuzzy creation. He wrote in his memoirs: "There was an intermediate period when any reference to Pooh was infuriating; but now such a 'nice comfortable feeling' envelopes him that I can almost regard him impersonally as the creation of one of my favorite authors." Alexander's funeral in 1956 was the last time Christopher would see either parent, although his mother, Daphne, would live another fifteen years.

Daphne became busy during that time, further enraging Christopher by selling his father's original manuscripts.

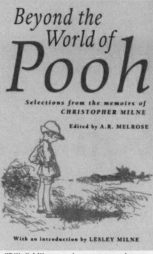

Beyond the World of **Pooh**

Selections from the memoirs of *CHRISTOPHER MILNE*

Edited by A.R. MELROSE

With an introduction by LESLEY MILNE

"Billy" Milne made a career of complaining about the difficulties of being Christopher Robin

She also infuriated much of England by giving the original stuffed animals to Milne's American publisher, which placed them in the New York Public Library, where they still reside. Many readers, too, became exasperated because Christopher's mother sold Pooh's movie rights to the Walt Disney Corporation. Its first effort was not reassuring to Pooh fans: In *Winnie-the-Pooh and the Honey Tree* Piglet got inexplicably replaced by a gopher, and all of the characters somehow developed American accents.

Christopher eventually came grudgingly to terms with his unwelcome notoriety over the years after writing two successful books complaining about it. He died in April 1996.

END PIECES OF THE TALE

• Through his real life childhood, Christopher Milne was usually called Bill or Billy Moon. ("Moon" because

92

that's the closest young Billy could get to pronouncing his own last name.)

• Most of the names of characters in the stories were the real names of Billy's stuffed animals, except Owl and Rabbit, who were real animals seen in the woods behind the Milnes' house.

• Pooh was purchased at Harrod's department store in London for Christopher Robin's first birthday, August 21, 1921. He was originally called Edward.

• Christopher Milne called

his toy bear "Winnie-ther-Pooh." Some people have speculated that "Winnie" may have come from Winston Churchill, like Teddy came from Roosevelt. But no — Winnie was the name of a very tame American black bear at the London Zoo that A. A. Milne and son Christopher visited regularly. Her name came from her first owner's hometown: Winnipeg, Canada.

• Why "-ther-Pooh"? Young Christopher believed that it was the masculine form of "the" that showed that Winnie was a male. "Pooh" seemed to be a name he used for other things, too, including a swan mentioned in one of his dad's *When We Were Very Young* verses.

• The Pooh stories have been translated into at least 40 languages, including Thai, Hebrew and Braille. A Latin version made history as the first

non-English book to hit the *New York Times* bestseller list in 1960. *Winnie ille Pu* remained there for 20 weeks.

Pooh Sticks Game

Whether they know it or not, almost everybody's played Pooh Sticks, the game that tests the speed and agility ... of twigs. The rules are very simple:

1. You and your friends drop a stick or pine cone on the upstream side of a bridge.

2. Run to the other side and see which one emerges first.

3. Repeat indefinitely.

• The very first Kanga and Roo belonged to Christopher Robin's childhood friend, Anne Darlington. Later Milne apparently got his own. Darlington later auctioned hers off to a Teddy Bear Museum in December, 1995.

• The Bear of Very Little Brain's mindlessly mindful existence awakened Benjamin Hoff to write about Pooh-philosophy in *The Tao of Pooh* (1982). His sequel, *The Te of Piglet*, came out in 1992.

• Despite outrage from England, Winnie, Eeyore, Piglet, Kanga and Tigger are on display in the children's section of the New York Public Library's Donnell Library Center. The toys are a little worse for wear, because the Milne family dog also apparently enjoyed playing with them. And, most tragically, Roo was lost somewhere in an English apple orchard in the 1930s.

• Disney Store outlets reported in 1997 that, for the first time, sales of Winnie the Pooh merchandise beat out Mickey Mouse to become Disney's top-selling character among adult toy buyers. ☾

Not Everyone Loved Pooh & Milne

"Tonstant Weader fwowed up." —Dorothy Parker as "Constant Reader" reviewing The House on Pooh Corner in the New Yorker

A. A. Milne responded: "No writer of children's books says gaily to his publisher, 'Don't bother about the children, Mrs. Parker will love it.'"

"We were supposed to be quite good friends, but, you know, in a sort of way I think he was a pretty jealous chap. I think he was probably jealous of all other writers. But I loved his stuff. That's one thing I'm very grateful for: I don't have to like an awful person to like his stuff." —P. G. Wodehouse, about A. A. Milne

"Some people are good with children. Others are not. It is a gift. You either have it our you don't. My father didn't....It seemed to me, almost, that my father had got to where he was by climbing upon my infant shoulders, that he had filched from me my good name and had left me with nothing but the empty fame of being his son." —Christopher Robin Milne

Ben's Money I
ADVICE FROM FRANKLIN'S LITTLE MONEY BOOK

In 1757, Benjamin Franklin compiled a small collection of advice on money from his *Poor Richard's Almanac*. The booklet was a huge success and made Franklin wealthy. Here is some of his wisdom. "A word to the wise is enough," said Ben.

TIME MANAGEMENT

• *Dost thou love life? Then do not squander time, for that's the stuff life is made of. Wasting time must be the greatest prodigality, since lost time is never found again.*

• *If we are industrious we shall never starve; for, at the working man's house hunger looks in, but dares not enter.*

• *Industry pays debts, while despair increaseth them.*

• *Plough deep while sluggards sleep, and you shall have corn to sell and to keep.*

• *One today is worth two tomorrows.*

• *If you have something to do tomorrow, do it today.*

• *Leisure is time for doing something useful; this leisure the diligent man will obtain, but the lazy man never; so that a life of leisure and a life of laziness are two things.*

SLOTH

• *Taxes are indeed very heavy, and if those laid on by the government were the only ones we had to pay, we might more easily discharge them; but we have many others, and much more grievous to some of us. We are taxed twice as much by our idleness, three times as much by our pride, and four times as much by our folly, and from these taxes the commissioners cannot ease.*

- *Sloth, by bringing on diseases, absolutely shortens life. Sloth, like rust, consumes faster than labor wears. The used key is always bright.*
- *How much more than is necessary do we spend in sleep? The sleeping fox catches no poultry. There will be sleeping enough in the grave.*
- *Sloth makes all things difficult, but industry all easy.*
- *He that riseth late must trot all day, and shall scarce overtake his business at night.*
- *Laziness travels so slowly, that poverty soon overtakes him.*

MINDING YOUR BUSINESS
- *Drive thy business, let not it drive thee.*
- *He that lives upon hope will die fasting.*
- *There are no gains without pains.*
- *He that hath a trade hath an estate, and he that hath a calling hath an office of profit and honor; but then the trade must be worked at, and the calling well followed, or neither the estate, nor the office, will enable us to pay our taxes.*
- *Keep thy shop, and thy shop will keep thee.*
- *If you would have your business done, go; if not, send.*
- *Handle your tools without mittens; remember that the cat in gloves catches no mice.*
- *In the affairs of this world men are saved not by faith, but by the lack of it.*
- *If you want a faithful servant, and one that you like, serve yourself.*
- *Many without labor would live by their wits only, but they break for want of stock.*
- *Three moves are as bad as a fire. I never saw an oft-moved tree nor an oft-moved family, that thrived as well as those who settled be.*

ATTENTION TO DETAIL
- *A little neglect may breed great mischief.*
- *Not to oversee workmen is to leave them your purse open.*
- *The eye of a master will do more work than both his hands.*
- *Want of care does us more damage than want of knowledge.*
- *For want of a nail the shoe was lost, for want of a shoe the horse was lost, and for want of a horse the rider was lost, being overtaken and slain by the enemy, all for want of care about a horse-shoe nail.*

(Want more of Ben's advice? See page 307.)

A Suppressed Gospel
BABY JESUS' REIGN OF TERROR

The terrible twos, the fearsome fives and the perilous preteens are bad enough, but what if your petulant kid had supernatural powers? The Infancy Gospel of Thomas, excluded from the Bible by church fathers in the 4th century, fills in the missing childhood years of Jesus.

I, THOMAS THE ISRAELITE, tell you of the childhood of our Lord Jesus Christ and his mighty deeds.

THE KILLING POOL

The little child Jesus when he was five years old was playing at a brook, and he gathered together the waters into pools, and made them clean by his word alone. Having made soft clay, he fashioned thereof twelve sparrows. It was the Sabbath when he made them and there were also many other little children playing with him.

A certain Jew, when he saw Jesus playing upon the Sabbath day, departed straightaway and told his father Joseph: "Your child has taken clay and fashioned twelve little birds, and has

polluted the Sabbath day." When Joseph came to the place and saw, he cried out to Jesus: "Why do you do these things on the Sabbath, which it is not lawful to do?" But Jesus clapped his hands together and cried out to the sparrows: "Go! Fly! And remember me now that you're alive!" The sparrows flew away, chirping loudly. When the Jews saw it they were amazed, and went to tell their leaders that which they had seen Jesus do.

The son of Annas the scribe was standing there with Joseph. He took a willow branch and dispersed the pools of water which Jesus had gathered together. When Jesus saw what he was doing, he became enraged and said unto him: "You evil, ungodly fool, what harm did the pools and the waters do to you? Behold, you are now going to wither like a tree, and you will never bear leaves, or root, or fruit." Immediately, the boy dried up completely, and Jesus went home to Joseph's house. The parents of the withered boy took him up, wailing about his young age, and brought his remains to Joseph. They accused him: "You are responsible for the child who did this."

WATCH IT, BUB

After that, Jesus went through the village, and a running child bumped against his shoulder. Jesus became angry and said to

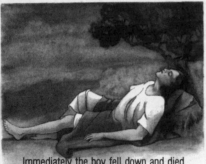

Immediately the boy fell down and died

him: "You won't get to your destination." Immediately the boy fell down and died. When people saw what was done, they asked: "Where did this young child come from, that every word of his is an accomplished work?" And the parents of the dead child came to Joseph and blamed him, saying: "With a child like that, you cannot dwell with us in the village. Not until you teach him to bless and not to curse, because he is killing our children!"

Joseph called Jesus aside and scolded him, saying: "Why are you doing such things? The neighbors are suffering and hate us. They will cause trouble for us." But Jesus said: "I know that you don't really know what you're saying. Nevertheless for your sake I will keep my silence. However, the ones who complain will bear their punishment." Immediately after he said this, the ones that accused him were stricken blind.

When the villagers saw what Jesus had done, they became frightened and confused. They said to each other: "Every word he speaks, whether good or evil, comes true." When Joseph saw what Jesus had done, he took hold of his ear and twisted it sore. The young child became angry and said: "It's bad enough that you seek and do not find, but too much for you to act so foolishly. I'm not your child, so don't bother me."

A teacher, Zacchaeus, heard when Jesus said these things to his father. After a few days he came near unto Joseph and said unto him: "You have a wise child. Give him to me that he may learn letters and not be rebellious." Joseph replied, "Nobody but God could control this child."

[*After a disastrous first lesson, in which Jesus pointed out that he already knew more than his teacher and that "nobody understands the power of my wisdom," Zacchaeus brought the five-year-old back to Joseph, saying, "I am not able to bear his stare and tongue. This child was not born of this earth. My friend, I am going out of my mind...."*]

As the villagers were counseling Zacchaeus, Jesus laughed and said: "Now let those bear fruit that were barren and let them see that were blind in heart. I am come from above that I may curse them, and call them to the things that are above, even as he commanded which hath sent me for your sakes."

Why Were Books Left Out of the Bible?

"Many have undertaken to set down accounts [about Jesus]" wrote the author of The Gospel According to Luke. And it's true—biblical scholars have identified at least thirty–four different gospels, and have translated all or parts of nineteen. Why so many? The early Christian church was a hotbed of power struggles and competing philosophies. Believing that Jesus was going to come back within their lifetimes, eyewitnesses to his life and teachings had passed their stories along orally. (None of the known gospels was written by an eyewitness or apostle, even though names of early apostles were later attached to them.)

Finally, in the A.D. 70s, it became clear that maybe Jesus' return wasn't imminent, so people began compiling anecdotes and quotations. The plethora of competing gospels was the result of authors and factions weighing in with their version of who Jesus was. A philosopher? A revolutionary leader against the Romans? A god?

One major power struggle was between the original apostles, led by Peter and James, and the Christians in Rome, led by Paul. Early church leaders, disproportionately women, also weighed in as Paul began purging women from leadership positions. Eventually the followers of Paul and Peter merged into one unholy alliance, and immediately ruled all competing gospels as "heresy." By A.D. 400, only four were officially recognized by church authorities.

Immediately all who had come under his curse were saved. After that, nobody dared make him angry, because they didn't want to be maimed or killed.

JESUS FINALLY USES HIS POWERS FOR GOOD... NOT FOR EVIL

A few days later, Jesus was playing on the roof of a house, and Zeno, one of his playmates, fell off and died. The other children fled, and Jesus remained alone. The parents accused Jesus of pushing him off. Jesus leaped down from the roof and stood by the body of the child and cried with a loud voice and said: "Zeno, arise and tell me, did I throw you down?" And Zeno arose and said: "No, Lord, you didn't throw me down, but you did raise me up." And when they saw it they glorified God for the sign which had come to pass, and worshiped Jesus.

Later, a man was chopping wood and the axe fell and cut his foot off. Losing much blood, he was about to die. There was great tumult and Jesus forced his way through the crowd. He

Jesus stretched the wood

took hold of the young man's foot and immediately it was healed. Jesus said: "Get up, chop wood, and remember me." When the multitude saw what was done they worshiped the young child.

When Jesus was six years old, his mother sent him with a pitcher to fetch water but on the way he broke it. So Jesus spread out his cloak and filled it with water. When he brought it to his mother, she kissed him, and treasured the mysteries she saw him do.

In planting season, Jesus went forth with his father to sow wheat in their land. As his father sowed, the young child Jesus planted just one kernel of wheat. From it grew an abundance; when he reaped and threshed what had grown, it had become a hundred measures. He called all the poor of the village and gave them the wheat, and Joseph took the rest. Jesus was eight years old when he wrought this sign.

Joseph was a carpenter. A rich man ordered a bed. One beam, however, was too short and Joseph knew not what to do. Jesus said to his father: "Lay down the two pieces of wood and make them even at your end." Jesus stood at the other end and took hold upon the shorter beam and stretched it to make it equal with the other. His father Joseph marvelled, saying: "Happy am I that God has given me this young child."

JESUS GOES BACK TO SCHOOL & REVERTS

Joseph saw the understanding of the child, he decided that Jesus should not be ignorant of letters; and he took him and delivered him to another teacher. Jesus said to him: "If you're real-ly a teacher, tell me the meaning of alpha and then will I tell you the meaning of beta." The frustrated teacher smacked him on the head. Jesus got angry and cursed him, and immediately the teacher fell to the ground. Jesus returned home. Joseph was distressed and commanded to Mary: "Don't let him leave the house, because when he gets angry, people die."

"Suckle your baby and remember me."

Another teacher who was a friend of Joseph: "Bring the child to me, and maybe I can flatter him into learning." Joseph said: "If you're not afraid, my broth-er, take him." The teacher took Jesus with much worry and fear, but the young child followed him gladly. Going boldly into the school, Jesus found a book lying upon the pulpit and pretended to read from it, but actually delivered a sermon. A crowd gathered and marvelled at his speaking abilities. But when Joseph heard it, he was afraid, and ran unto the school thinking this teacher also was maimed or killed, but his friend said unto Joseph: "This child is full of grace and wisdom. Now I beg you, brother, take him home." When the young child heard that, he smiled at him and said: "Since you've spoken correctly, for your sake I'll heal the other teacher." The other teacher was healed, and Joseph took the young child home.

RANDOM ACTS OF KINDNESS

Joseph sent his son James to gather firewood. While in the woods, a snake bit his hand. He was close to death when Jesus came and blew on the bite. Immediately the pain ceased, the snake burst into pieces, and James continued gathering wood.

Later, a baby fell sick and died, and his mother wept inconsolably. When Jesus heard about it, he ran there quickly. Finding the child dead, Jesus touched his breast and said: "Child, live and be with your mother." Immediately, the baby looked up and laughed. Jesus said to the mother: "Suckle your baby and remember me." Bystanders marvelled, and said: "This child is either a god or an angel, for every word of his comes true." And Jesus went out to play with other children.

A year later, a house builder fell from a great height and died. Jesus took hold of his hand and said: "Mister, rise up and get back to work." Immediately the man arose and worshiped him. When the multitude saw it, they were astonished, and said: "This child is from heaven: for he has saved many souls from death, and hath power to save them all his life long."

JESUS RUNS AWAY FROM HOME

When Jesus was twelve years old, his parents went to Jerusalem for Passover. Afterward, they began the journey home. Jesus' parents assumed he was among the crowd of relatives and neighbors, but they couldn't find him and returned to Jerusalem. After three days they found him in the temple sitting  among the rabbis, who marvelled at how the young child interpreted the law and the parables of the prophets. Mary said: "Why do you do this to us? Can't you see how worried we were?" Jesus replied: "Why are you looking for me? Don't you know that I must be in my father's house?" The scribes and Pharisees asked: "Are you the mother of this child? God has blessed the fruit of your womb. For we have never seen such glory and excellence and wisdom." Jesus arose and went home with his parents. Mary kept in mind all that came to pass, and Jesus increased in wisdom and stature and grace. ❦

Potty Pourri

RANDOM KINDS OF FACTNESS

• Galileo envisioned the body thermometer in the 17th century. Not long after, a scientist named Santorio Santorio invented one that worked. He called it the *thermoscope*.

• Neon is extracted from the air by *adsorption*. That involves superchilling the air to make it a liquid, collecting the neon with charcoal, then warming the charcoal to capture the evaporating neon gas. Unfortunately, the air just doesn't have that much neon in it, so you have to treat 88,000 pounds of air to get a pound of neon.

• Who attached the copper to the iron framework of the Statue of Liberty once it arrived in New York's harbor? Gustave Eiffel, the guy who built the Eiffel Tower.

• Marcel Proust was quite a character. He lined the walls of his writing room in cork to deaden sounds from outside, and when he went to work, he'd lie in bed, wrapped in scarves and blankets and wearing gloves.

• The guillotine got its name in "honor" of the French politician Joseph Ignace Guillotin, who promoted its use as more humane method of execution than the old block-and-axe method. Its inventor was a French surgeon, Antoine Lewis.

• Have you ever heard of the glass snake? Despite the fact that it has no legs and looks like a snake with ears, it's really a lizard. The glass snake's long tail breaks off very easily, which is how it got its name.

• In the Middle Ages, schools for knights didn't just teach jousting and sword fighting. The boys were also taught reading, writing and basic math, as well as chess, lute playing and chivalry.

• To your short list of famous newspaper editors, add Warren G. Harding. Prior to becoming president, Harding was with Ohio's Marion *Star*.

The Eyes Have It

William Hogarth painted *Frontis: Satire on False Perspective* in 1754. It is, perhaps, the original "What's wrong with this picture." The accompanying inscription (not pictured) reads, "Whoever makes a Design without the knowledge of perspective will be liable to such Absurdities as are shewn in this Frontispiece."

How many "What's wrong with this picture" things can you identify? Some people claim there are as many as thirty.

Heads Will Roll!

A Ghost Tale from Old Japan

In this story, another ancient Japanese legend collected by
Lafcadio Hearn in 1903, a samurai-priest struggles hard...
to get a head.

NEARLY 500 YEARS AGO there was a samurai named Isogai
Taketsura, in the service of the Lord Kikuji, of Kyushu.
But when the house of Kikuji came to ruin, Isogai found
himself without a master, so he cut off his hair, and became a
traveling priest, taking the Buddhist name of Kwairyo. But
always, under the robe of the priest, Kwairyo had within him
the heart of the samurai. He journeyed to preach the good Law
in places where no other priest dared to go. For that age was an
age of violence; and on the highways there was no security for a
solitary traveler, even if he happened to be a priest.

One evening, as he was traveling through the mountains of
Kai, darkness overcame him miles from any village, so he
resigned himself to pass the night under the stars. Scarcely had
he lain down when a woodcutter came along the road and said
in a tone of great surprise: "What kind of a man can you be,
good sir, that you dare to lie down alone in such a place as this?
There are haunters about here, many of them. Are you not
afraid of Hairy Things?"

"My friend," answered Kwairyo cheerfully, "I am only a wandering priest, and I am not in the least afraid of 'Hairy Things,'
if you mean goblin-foxes, or goblin-badgers, or any creatures of
that kind. Lonesome places are suitable for meditation, and I
have learned never to be anxious about my life."

"This place has a bad name and I must assure you, sir, that it is very dangerous to sleep here. Although my house is only a wretched hut, let me beg of you to come home with me at once. There is a roof at least, and you can sleep without risk."

Kwairyo, liking the man's kindly tone, accepted this modest offer. The woodcutter guided him to a small thatched cottage, cheerfully lighted from within. As Kwairyo entered, he saw four men and women warming their hands at a little fire. They bowed low in the most respectful manner. Kwairyo wondered that persons so poor, and dwelling in such a solitude, should be aware of the polite forms of greeting.

"From your speech and manners, I imagine that you have not always been a woodcutter," he said. "Perhaps you formerly belonged to one of the upper classes?"

The woodcutter smiled, "Sir, you are not mistaken. I was once a person of some distinction. My story is of a life ruined by my own fault. I used to be in the service of a master and my rank was not inconsiderable. But I loved women and wine too well; and under the influence of passion I brought about the ruin of our house, and caused the death of many persons. Retribution followed me; and I now I try to overcome the karma of my errors by repentance and helping those who are unfortunate."

Kwairyo said to the woodcutter, "My friend, it is written in the holy sutras that those strongest in wrong-doing can become the strongest in right-doing. I do not doubt that you have a good heart. Tonight I shall recite the sutras for your sake, and pray that you may overcome the karma of past errors."

Kwairyo's host showed him to a very small side-room, where a bed had been made ready. All went to sleep except the priest, who began to read the sutras by the light of a paper lantern. Into the night Kwairyo read and prayed. After a time he felt thirsty and decided to tiptoe out for a drink of water. Very gently he pushed apart the sliding-screens that separated his room from the main apartment; and he saw, by the light of the lantern, five recumbent bodies—without heads!

For one instant he stood bewildered, imagining a crime. But quickly he saw that there was no blood, and that the headless necks did not look as if they had been cut. Then he thought to himself: "I have been lured into the dwelling of a Rokuro-Kubi, a goblin that can remove its head! Now, if these be Rokuro-Kubi, they mean me no good. It is written that if one finds the body of a Rokuro-Kubi without its head and removes it to another place, the head will never be able to join itself again to the neck. When the head comes back and finds that its body has been moved, it will bounce like a ball upon the floor three times, then pant in great fear, and then die."

He seized the body of the woodcutter by the feet and dragged it out the window. While outside, he heard voices in a grove, so he stole from shadow to shadow. From behind a tree, he caught sight of the five heads flitting about, and chatting as they ate worms and insects that they'd found.

After a while the head of the woodcutter stopped eating and said: "Ah, that fat traveling priest! When we eat him, our bellies will be well filled. I was foolish to talk to him as I did — it only set him to reciting the sutras on behalf of my soul! To go near him while he is reciting or praying would be difficult, but as it is now nearly morning, perhaps he has gone to sleep. One of you go to the house and see what the fellow is doing."

Immediately, the head of a young woman flitted to the house, lightly as a bat. After a few minutes it came back, and cried out in a tone of great alarm: "That priest is gone! But that's not the worst of the matter. He has taken the body of our *aruji*, our housemaster, and I do not know where he has put it."

At this announcement the head of the aruji — distinctly visible in the moonlight — became frightful: its eyes opened monstrously; its hair stood up bristling; and its teeth gnashed. Then a cry burst from its lips; and — weeping tears of rage — it exclaimed:

"Since my body has been moved, to rejoin it is not possible! Then I must die! And all through the work of that priest! Before I die I will get at that priest! I will tear him! I will devour him! AND THERE HE IS — hiding behind that tree! The fat coward!"

In the same moment the head of the aruji, followed by the other four heads, sprang at Kwairyo. But the samurai-turned-priest had already armed himself by plucking up a young tree; and with that tree he struck the heads as they came, knocking them from him with tremendous blows. Four of them fled away. But the head of the aruji, though battered again and again, desperately continued to attack the priest, and at last caught him by the left sleeve of his robe. Kwairyo, however, quickly gripped the head by its topknot, and repeatedly struck it. It did not release its hold; but it uttered a long moan and ceased to struggle. In death its teeth still held the sleeve; for all his great strength, Kwairyo could not force open the jaws.

With the head still hanging to his sleeve he went back to the house, and there caught sight of the other four Rokuro-Kubi with bruised and bleeding heads reunited to their bodies. But when they saw him at the back-door, they screamed, "The priest! The priest!" and fled out into the woods.

The sky was brightening; day was about to dawn. Kwairyo knew that the power of the goblins was limited to the hours of darkness. He inspected the head clinging to his sleeve—its face fouled with blood, foam, and clay—and he laughed aloud as he thought to himself: "What a great souvenir, the head of a goblin!" before descending the mountain to continue his journey.

Into the main street of Suwa he solemnly strode with the head dangling at his elbow. Women fainted, and children screamed and ran away; and there was a great clamor until lawmen seized the priest and took him to jail. Kwairyo only smiled and said nothing when brought before the magistrates of the district. He was ordered to explain why he, a priest, had the head of a man fastened to his sleeve, and why he had shamelessly paraded his crime before people.

Kwairyo laughed long and loudly at these questions. "Sirs, I did not fasten the head to my sleeve: it fastened itself there, much against my will. And I have not committed any crime. For this is the head of a goblin, and I was simply taking precautions to assure my own safety." And he laughed as he proceeded to tell of his encounter with the five heads.

But the magistrates did not laugh. They judged him to be a hardened criminal and his story an insult to their intelligence. Therefore, they decided to order his immediate execution, all of them except one, a very old man. After having heard the opinion of his colleagues, he said: "Let us first examine the head carefully. If the priest has spoken truth, the head itself should bear witness for him. Bring the head here!"

So the head, still holding in its teeth the robe from Kwairyo's shoulders, was put before the judges. The old man discovered that the edges of the neck nowhere presented the appearance of having been cut by any weapon. On the contrary, the line of severance was smooth as the line at which a falling leaf detaches itself from the stem. Then said the elder: "I am quite sure that the priest told us the truth. This is the head of a Rokuro-Kubi. It is well known that such goblins have been dwelling in the mountains of Kai from very ancient time.... But you, sir," he exclaimed, turning to Kwairyo, — "what sort of sturdy priest may you be? You have the air of a soldier rather than a priest. Perhaps you once belonged to the samurai class?"

"You have guessed rightly, sir," Kwairyo responded. "Before becoming a priest, my name was Isogai Taketsura of Kyushu: there may be some among you who remember it." At the mention of that name, a murmur of admiration filled the courtroom. for there were many present who remembered it. And Kwairyo immediately found himself among friends instead of judges. When Kwairyo left Suwa, he was as happy as any priest is permitted to be in this transitory world. As for the head, he took it with him, jocularly insisting he intended it for a souvenir.

And now it only remains to tell what became of the head.

A day or two after leaving Suwa, Kwairyo met with a robber, who tried to rob him until he saw the goblin head hanging from his sleeve. "You!" he shouted, jumping backward. "What kind of a priest are you? Why, you are a worse man than I am! It is true that I have killed people; but I never walked about with anybody's head fastened to my sleeve." Deciding he could use the head to scare people, the bandit asked to buy it.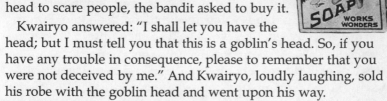

Kwairyo answered: "I shall let you have the head; but I must tell you that this is a goblin's head. So, if you have any trouble in consequence, please to remember that you were not deceived by me." And Kwairyo, loudly laughing, sold his robe with the goblin head and went upon his way.

Thus the robber got the head and the robe; and for some time he played goblin-priest upon the highways. But when his travels took him to the neighborhood of Suwa, he learned the true story of the head; and he then became afraid that the spirit of the Rokuro-Kubi might give him trouble. So he buried the head by itself in the grove behind the cottage; and he had a tombstone set up over the grave, and a funeral service performed on behalf of the Rokuro-Kubi's spirit. And that was the end of that. ☾

Kitchen Scientist
How to Make Rock Candy

Homemade rock candy is easy, fun and illustrates the scientific concept of crystallization. It also teaches patience, because you have to wait a long time before you can actually eat the stuff.

1 Tie a cotton string to a pencil and prop the pencil over the mouth of a jar so the string hangs down straight into the jar with no loops or curls.

2 Attach a nontoxic weight to the bottom of the string (say, a stainless steel paper clip) so that it hangs straight down. Heck, since you're going to the trouble, you might want to prepare several jars and double or triple the recipe below.

3 In a saucepan, bring about a cup of water to boil. Slowly stir in two cups of sugar, adding half a cup (or less) at a time and waiting for it to dissolve completely before adding the next scoop.

4 When all of the sugar has been dissolved into a thick, clear syrup, pour the mixture into your empty jar. Make sure the string is submerged into the hot liquid. Put the jars in a place where they won't be disturbed or tipped over.

5 Because the water mixture was supersaturated with sugar, the two couldn't stay mixed except when very hot. As the mixture cools, the sugar will begin to glom onto the string, creating cool crystal patterns. As the water evaporates further over the coming weeks, the crystals will grow bigger and bigger.

6 If you want to play a sadistic practical joke on someone at the same time, make a special batch of similar-looking "rock candy" by using salt instead of sugar. ☾

Word Thieves

TERMS WE'VE BORROWED FROM NATIVE AMERICANS

When Europeans landed in America, they came across things they didn't have names for. Luckily there were people living here already who could tell them what's what.

bayou: From Choctaw *bayuk*, which means "creek."

caribou: From Micmac *maccaribpoo* ("he who paws the ground").

chipmunk: From the Chippewa word for squirrel, *atchitamon* ("head first").

moose: From a Passamaquoddy observation, *moosu* ("he trims [bark] smoothly").

opossum: From Powantan *aposoum* ("white animal").

persimmon: From the Cree for "dried fruit," *pasiminan*.

powwow: The word originally had to do with gatherings for drug-enhanced religious ceremonies by the Indians. It comes from an Algonquian word *powwaw* ("he dreams").

skunk: From the Algonquian phrase, *skekakwa squnk*, which means "animal that pees" (sprays).

raccoon: The Algonquian word is *arakunen*, which means "scraper, scratcher."

squash: Shortened from Algonquian *asquatasquash* ("eaten raw").

toboggan: From Algonquian *tabakun* ("drag, small sled").

wigwam: Teepee was a western plains name for a dwelling, so until Europeans moved that far west in the 1830s, Indian dwellings were called wigwams, from the Ojibwa *wigwaum*.

woodchuck: From several similar languages, including the Algonquian word *wejack* and the Cree word *otchek*, both of which mean "fisher." Europeans turned the name into woodchuck, even though it doesn't chuck wood.

place names: Chicago ("place of bad smell"); Ohio ("beautiful water"); Shenandoah ("daughter of the skies"); Wisconsin ("beaver place"); Winnebago ("people of the filthy water").

Potty Pourri
RANDOM KINDS OF FACTNESS

• Lead was once commonly used to sweeten wine. Some historians think it might have contributed to the fall of the Roman Empire. Although the dangers of lead were understood as early as the 17th century, its use in wine wasn't banned for another 200 years.

• Remember to stop and watch the insects. Mathematician René Descartes did. A fly walking across the ceiling gave him the idea for coordinate geometry in order to trace the fly's walking path.

• Long before the Druids came along, Stonehenge existed. Ancient folks built it in three main phases from 2800 to 1500 B.C. Researchers estimate that it took about 30 million work hours and hundreds of years to complete.

• "Hedgehopper" is British slang for a pilot. A one-hit British Invasion group from the 1960s named itself Hedgehoppers Anonymous because its members met while serving in the Royal Air Force.

• The educational system in ancient Sparta seemed fairer than most: both girls and boys were educated. But the curriculum wasn't particularly well rounded: The boys were taught fighting skills, while the girls were taught what they needed to mother future soldiers.

• Lobsters are not red when alive. Because the red pigment in their shells is the most heat resistant, it remains colorful even as the natural browns, grays and greens cook away.

• The term "B.O." for body odor was coined by an advertising man in 1919 to sell Odo-Ro-No, an early deodorant. The product may be gone, but the ad campaign lingers in the air.

• "Acid rock," "country rock," and "hard rock" were all geological terms years before they became musical genres. Likewise, "heavy metal" came first from chemistry.

Stately Knowledge

12 Reasons Why Ya Gotta Love Michigan

Who needs to be reminded that Michigan's cool? Just in case, though, here are some of our favorite facts about this two-part state...

1 The very first Elvis sighting following his death occured at a Burger King in Kalamazoo. Be on the lookout; he was driving a red Ferrari.

2 Detroit is the home of motors and music, but it's also the birthplace of the Kiwanis Club. When founding members were looking for a name, someone suggested an Otchipew Indian phrase, "Nunc Kee-wanis." Members believed it meant "We trade." Actually, it translates to "We have a noisy good time." That works, too.

3 Grand Rapids was the first U.S. city to fluoridate its water supply to reduce cavities.

4 DomiNick's Pizza opened in Ypsilanti, Michigan, in 1960. Maybe you know it better by its current name, Domino's Pizza.

5 What's that extra bit of land there, above the mitten-shaped mainland of Michigan? That's called the Upper Peninsula. Literally attached to Wisconsin, it was given to Michigan as a consolation prize when they lost Toledo to Ohio in the Toledo War of 1836.

6 Three meows for Kay Draper of Cassopolis, Michigan. In 1948, she discovered that little dried bits of clay, placed in a box, made the perfect litter for a kitty.

Domino's, Post, Kellogg's, KMart, and Kiwanis
...all natives of Michigan

7 In 1907, America saw its first mile of paved road. It was a stretch of Woodward Avenue in Detroit, between Six and Seven Mile Roads.

8 About 1,500 years ago, a fungus spore somehow found its way underground in part of the forest of Michigan, and took root. Today, the fungus colony covers at least 40 acres of area underneath the ground. All in all, the fungus weighs at least 110 tons. It's the largest living organism known in the world.

9 Besides the underground fungus, famous Michiganders past and present include Charles Lindbergh, Henry Ford, Tim Allen, Eminem, Robin Williams, Francis Ford Coppola, Steven Seagal, Lily Tomlin, Ellen Burstyn, Earvin "Magic" Johnson, Diana Ross, Madonna, Ted Nugent, Bob Seger and Stevie Wonder.

10 Our favorite Michigan native, though, has got to be veterinarian and animal-lover Timothy England of Jackson, Michigan. When a stray rooster lost its legs to frostbite on a cold Michigan winter night, England fitted the cock with artificial legs.

11 Battle Creek, Michigan, is the breakfast cereal capital of the world—home to both Post cereals and Kellogg's. In the Kellogg's parking lot you can take a gander at corporate spokestoons Tony the Tiger and Tony, Jr. They both have statues erected to them, greeting visitors at the company headquarters.

12 Michigan's known as the Wolverine state; mind you, not because of a plentiful wolverine population. Truth be told, Michigan has absolutely no wolverines (little badger-like animals) whatsoever within its borders, and probably never did. So why the misnomer? During the days of Canadian fur trading, wolverine hides were shipped through the state on their way to Europe, so people indelibly associated the state with the animal. ☾

Many Happy Returns
HOW TO MAKE & THROW A BOOMERANG

Make your own boomerang? Why not? It's not hard, says *The American Boy's Handy Book* by Daniel Beard (1890). The instructions even come complete with Western cluelessness, common at the time, about the Australian aborigines.

THE BOOMERANG, or bommerang as it is sometimes called, is one of the most mysterious weapons known. Evolved by slow degrees from a simple war club

by the ignorant and savage Australians, this instrument excites the interest and astonishes the civilized man by its strange and apparently unaccountable properties. To all appearances it is a simple, roughly-hewn club, yet its movements when thrown by an expert hand are so eccentric as to make it a curious anomaly even to persons educated in natural philosophy.

HOW TO MAKE A BOOMERANG

1 With boiling water, scald a piece of well-seasoned elm, ash or hickory plank that is free from knots. Allow the wood to remain in the water until it becomes pliable enough to bend into the form indicated by the figure below.

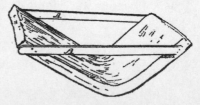

When it has assumed the proper curve, nail on the side pieces to hold the wood in position until it is thoroughly dry; after which the side pieces may be removed, with no fear that the plank will not retain the curve imparted.

2 Saw the wood into as many slices as it will allow. Each piece will be a boomerang in the rough.

3 Your rough boomerang only needs to be trimmed up with a pocket knife, and scraped smooth with a piece of broken glass to make it a finished weapon. A large wood-rasp or file is of great assistance in shaping the implement. Figure C shows a finished boomerang. Figure D

shows a cross section of the same.

The curve in two boomerangs is never exactly the same; some come round with a graceful sweep, while others bend so suddenly in the middle that they have more the appearance of angles than curves. Just what makes a good boomerang is hard to discover, although as a rule, the one that appears to have the best balance and feels as if it might be thrown easily is the best.

GOES AROUND, COMES AGROUND

To throw a boomerang, grasp the weapon near one end and hold it as you would a club; be careful to have the concave side, or inside curvature, pointed away away from you and the convex side toward you. Take aim at a stone, tuft of grass or other object on the ground about a hundred yards in front of you, and throw the weapon at the object. The weapon will in all probability not go anywhere near the mark, but, soaring aloft, perform some of the most extraordinary maneuvers then starting off again with apparently renewed velocity, either return to the spot from where it was thrown or go sailing off over the fields like a thing possessed of life.

Duck, Dingo, duck!

"FORCE ENOUGH TO CUT A DOG"

A boomerang cast by a beginner is very dangerous in a crowd, for there is no telling where it is going to alight, and when it does come down it sometimes comes with force enough to cut a small dog almost in two.* Select a large open field where the ground is soft and there is no one around to be hurt. In such a field, you may amuse yourself by the day throwing these curious weapons, and in this manner learn how to make the boomerang go through all manner of the most indescribable movements seemingly at your bidding. ☾

BABY BOOMERANG

The miniature boomerang here represented is cut out of a card. The shape represented here in the illustration is a very good one, but it may be varied to an almost unlimited degree. Card boomerangs over an inch or so in length do not work well, but they may be made much smaller.

These tiny instruments cannot be grasped by the hand. Instead, the toy should be laid flat upon a card or table, allowing one end to project, as pictured. Using your forefinger, strike it a quick, smart blow with your fingernail and the little missile will sail away, going through almost the same maneuvers that a large wooden boomerang does.

* "I have seen a dog killed on the spot, its body being nearly cut in two by the boomerang as it fell." —Rev. J. G. Wood

Pasters' Choices
WHAT TOOTHPASTE STUFF REALLY WORKS?

To drum up business, toothpastes make a lot of claims, but what's true and what's not? Here's what dentists and consumer advocates have reported so far about the most common toothpaste additives.

WHITENING TOOTHPASTES: They work only in the very loosest sense. You know, in the same way a dishrag will whiten your dishes...if you actually have white dishes. *Consumer Reports* found no whitening toothpaste that really worked. Why? Because with age natural yellowing happens below the surface. If you go that low, you destroy the enamel. Bleaching by dentists has shown to work slightly better; it cleans stains off the surface. But it still won't whiten the tooth underneath.

TARTAR CONTROL: It works, in that sorta-kinda kind of way. It doesn't take existing tartar off, but it absorbs minerals in your saliva that could collect on your teeth and become tartar.

DESENSITIZERS: They work sometimes—particularly for pain or sensitivity from receding gums. But if you have pain from cavities or tooth-grinding forget about it. Unfortunately, most dental pain is caused by cavities or tooth-grinding.

HYDROGEN PEROXIDE: It doesn't do any good. In fact, it may give you more problems with decay and bad breath by drying the mouth. The same applies to alcohol in mouthwashes.

BAKING SODA: This folk remedy doesn't do anything at all.

TRICLOSAN: Found in Colgate Total and other pastes, triclosan appears to keep killing decay germs for hours after brushing. There are some concerns about whether it has bad environmental effects, however.

FLUORIDE: Fluoride really works. It helps lay down protection where enamel is eroding. There's also evidence that it attracts calcium in the body to do the same thing. It really hardens teeth and prevents cavities. Buy it; use it. ☾

Up, Up, & Away!

How Goodyear Got Its Blimp in the Air

The Goodyear blimp seems to be ubiquitous, drifting lazily in the sky above every major outdoor event from the World Series and Superbowl to outdoor concerts. Hard to believe that Goodyear management once nearly retired it as "a waste of money."

DESPITE THE GOODYEAR NAME, the company was not founded by Charles Goodyear, the man who discovered how to vulcanize rubber in 1839. Charles Goodyear didn't get rich from his process—in fact, he died penniless in 1860. But when Frank A. Seiberling started a rubber company in Akron, Ohio, in 1898, he decided to name it after the unsung inventor. This was nice, but also likely a ploy to confuse consumers who were familiar with the long-established B. F. Goodrich Co.

Seiberling hired a recent graduate of the Massachusetts Institute of Technology, Paul W. Litchfield, and paid him $2,500 a year to be factory supervisor, tire designer, rubber compounder and head of personnel. Like his boss, Litchfield had turn-of-the-century confidence in technology and American know-how, and kept an eye open for any new application for Goodyear's rubber products. Goodyear began manufacturing airplane tires in 1909, only six years after the Wright Brothers' first flight, at a time when there were fewer than 100 airplanes in the United States.

This interest in the potential of aeronautics blossomed into a full-scale obsession. When Litchfield visited the North British Company in Scotland, which had developed a process for spreading rubber over fabric, he traded the specifications to Goodyear's straight-sided tire for the process's equipment and American rights. North British also threw in two technicians to run the machines.

Blimp Facts

• The word *blimp,* as one tale has it, came from Lt. A. D. Cunningham of Britain's Royal Navy Air Service. In 1915, he whimsically flicked the inflated wall of an airship and verbally imitated the sound—"Blimp! Blimp!"

• Another version of the word comes from a military requisition form that read "Airship B, Limp."

• The Goodyear blimps' light display consists of 7,650 blue, green, red and yellow auto tail lights connected to a computer by 80 miles of wiring. The computer is programmed on the ground, using a light-beam "pencil" to draw on a computer screen.

• Each blimp can carry nine passengers. The seats have no seat belts.

• The blimps' skin is only about as thick as a shirt collar, but it's made of Neoprene-impregnated Dacron and is quite tough. It's a good thing, too, since the company reports that their blimps are shot at about 20 times a year. In 1990, a man was arrested and accused of deliberately punching a 3-foot hole in the blimp with a radio-controlled model airplane. The blimp sagged, but made it safely home.

• The blimps are 192 feet long, 59 feet high, and hold 202,700 cubic feet of helium. The helium doesn't leak out quickly like a balloon, but it does have to be "topped off" every four months or so. The blimps have a traveling range of about 500 miles and cruise at 45 miles per hour. Each blimp has a crew of five pilots, 17 support members and one public relations representative.

• The blimps' first TV sports event was an Orange Bowl game in the mid-1960s. Since then, they have been used in about 90 televised events a year. Goodyear doesn't charge TV networks, figuring the publicity generated makes the free service worthwhile. Camera operators shoot through an open window from about 400 yards up where they can see everything, read the scoreboard and hear the roar of the crowd. On a calm day, a pilot can hold the blimp virtually still in the air by facing into the wind and idling. The hardest sport for the pilots is golf because they have to be careful not to disturb a golfer's shot with engine noise or a sudden shadow over the green.

• The company is secretive about how much the blimps cost, but acknowledged a few years ago the annual cost of operating and maintaining each blimp is about $2 million.

Within months, the Wright Brothers had signed on to use Goodyear's rubberized cloth for their airplanes. (This was back when airplanes were based on kite designs and made of mostly wood and cloth). Within a few years, most U. S. airplanes used Goodyear's cloth.

The same rubberized fabric turned out to be useful for lighter-than-air craft. Not that there weren't some glitches in the process, though. Goodyear's first dirigible, *The Akron*, was scheduled to make the first intercontinental flight from America to Europe. Its flight began from Atlantic City at daybreak, July 2, 1912, but ended 23 minutes later when the ship exploded mysteriously over the ocean. The crew of five was never seen again.

But Goodyear management was still convinced that there was a future for lighter-than-air craft, and World War I gave them a chance to prove it. Goodyear produced about 1,000 balloons and 60 dirigibles and blimps for observation and reconnaissance.

Blimps, smaller and lighter with flexible walls, were particularly useful for moving low over coastal waters and searching out enemy sub-

marines. Dirigibles, bigger and with rigid walls to keep their shape better, were better for moving large objects and groups of people.

After the war, the Navy pressed ahead with dirigible research. Having seen how well the enemy's dirigibles carried heavy loads, it commissioned the Zeppelin works in Germany to build a dirigible in 1921. They christened it the *U.S.S. Los Angeles*. The Navy was further impressed when it flew from Germany to New Jersey in 81 hours. They asked Goodyear to buy the American rights to the Zeppelin design. The result was the Goodyear-Zeppelin Corporation. In 1926, the Germans finished the Graf Zeppelin which, over the next nine years, transported 13,110 passengers and covered more than a million miles in 544 trips, including 144 ocean crossings.

Unfortunately, not all Zeppelins were so reliable. A British dirigible crashed in France, killing most of the people aboard. Goodyear's two Zeppelins, *The Akron* and *The Macon,* also went down in tragedy. *The Akron,* like its blimp namesake years earlier, crashed off the New Jersey coast. A month earlier, *The*

Macon set course for its home base near San Francisco, but hit a storm and plunged into the sea. The final blow to dirigibles occurred on May 6,

A dirigible is different from a blimp in that it has a frame with material stretched across it

1937, when the German Zeppelin *Hindenburg* burst into flames just seconds before landing in New Jersey. Actually, fewer people died than in the previous disasters, but since it took place in front of a pack of reporters and newsreel photographers, the image of the disaster was splashed all over the world.

(For half a century, people have wondered why the Germans used flammable hydrogen in the Hindenburg instead of fire-proof helium. They had no choice. Helium is actually a fairly rare natural gas, found in abundance only in America. Wary of the Nazis that ruled Germany, the U.S. government had refused to sell them helium.)

The world pretty much gave up on dirigible travel, but Goodyear continued making blimps, which they used

for research and promotion. In 1929 they had four small ones traveling around the country, each capable of carrying four passengers and a pilot. Goodyear called them the *Pilgrim, Puritan, Mayflower,* and *Vigilant.*

When World War II started, the company built dozens more for military use. One blimp was the center of a mystery that has never been solved. In the early hours of August 16, 1942, the airship *Ranger* took off from Treasure Island in San Francisco Bay with a crew of two. It carried two anti-sub depth bombs. That afternoon, residents of Daly City, down the peninsula from San Francisco, were surprised to see a blimp coming in for a perfect landing in the middle of a residential street.

The blimp was well-stocked with fuel and helium, the batteries were charged, the radio was operating, the emergency life raft and parachute were on board. Everything was fine except for a few small details: The door was open; one depth charge was gone; and both members of the crew were missing. The Navy never came up with a satis-

A blimp, like the Stars and Stripes above, has no frame. It keeps its shape by the helium inside; it's sort of like a big balloon with a motor.

factory explanation, and neither man was ever seen again.

After the war, Goodyear bought five of its blimps back from the military and began using them for promotional purposes. But the company's executives didn't seem to know the value of what it had—in 1958, its board of directors considered grounding the blimps permanently to save operating and maintenance expenses. The plan was stalled by a last-minute plea by Goodyear's publicity director, and a blimp tour generated enough favorable press that the company was convinced to keep them.

The current blimps in the United States are the *Spirit of America*, based in Carson, California, the *Spirit of Goodyear*, based near Akron, Ohio, and the *Stars and Stripes*, based in Pompano Beach, Florida. ℭ

If the Blimp is Rockin', Don't Come Knockin'

At least one child was reportedly conceived in a Goodyear blimp—Jim Maloney, whose father was a member of the blimp's ground crew in the 1940s. Apparently it had an effect, because Maloney grew up and became one of Goodyear's blimp pilots.

Potty Pourri

RANDOM KINDS OF FACTNESS

- The crack of a whip is a small sonic boom that occurs as the lash breaks the sound barrier.

- Art imitates life: A cuckoo clock reproduces nearly exactly the sound of the European cuckoo bird.

- How fast something falls depends on its weight, shape and size. A Ping-Pong ball dropped from a mile up would reach a maximum speed of about 20 mph. A baseball, 95 mph. And a bowling ball? About 350 mph.

- The average kitten weighs 3.5 ounces when it's born, about the same as a bar of soap.

- On the Colosseum's opening day in A.D. 80, 5,000 animals were killed to entertain the masses. Procuring exotic animals to slaughter in gladiator spectacles in Rome became a major undertaking. Several species were rendered extinct by the slaughter, including the North African elephant.

- There are five flamingo species, ranging in color from nearly white to deep pink.

- J. Alfred Wight wrote some of the best stories about animals and veterinarians. Perhaps you know him better by his pen name James Herriot, author of *All Things Bright and Beautiful*.

- Log cabins seem like they're the essence of Americana, but they originally came from Finland and Sweden. In the 1630s, Finns and Swedes began settling in and around Delaware, and spread the practical home design to the New Land.

- If an octopus released its ink inside an aquarium, it would kill everything inside the glass walls...including the octopus.

- If you've got *chrematophobia*, you've got a deep, unreasonable fear of money. Send us a blank check, and we'll quickly cure your problem for you.

Money Magic

TRICKS YOU CAN DO WITH A DOLLAR

Here are some easy tricks that show the magic of the Almighty Dollar.

PAPERCLIP LINK

ALTHOUGH THE PROPS are modest, the effect is pretty mind-boggling: two paperclips fly into the air and link together before your very eyes.

1 Fold a one-dollar bill into a flattened **S** shape. (Although, keep in mind that using a five for this trick gives you a wonderfully awful punch line. Read on.)

2 Take a paperclip and clip it over the two thicknesses at the end of the bill closest to you (see illustration).

3 Take the other paperclip and clip it over the two thicknesses on the other side.

4 Grab each end of the bill. Pull your hands away from each other, straightening the bill.

5 The two clips will fly into the air—and in the process, they'll have linked themselves together.

Awful punch line: If you use a $5 bill: "Why do the paperclips link together? That's because of the guy on the bill: it's Abraham Linkin'."

Variation: If you also loop a rubber band around the bill, the paperclips will again end up linked . . . and hanging from the bill by the rubber band.

STUPID MONEY TRICKS

Breaking Bread

Hold a breadstick between your hands and challenge your tablemates to break it with a dollar bill folded in half. They can hack at it repeatedly and nothing will happen.

When it's your turn, sneak your index finger into the fold. The breadstick will break cleanly.

Double Your Money

Ask a spectator for a dollar bill. Say: "I can show you how to double your money."

Fold the dollar solidly in half. Say: "I've doubled your money. Look—you can see it *in creases.*"

Turn a One into a Five

If the last trick doesn't satisfy, say that you can guarantee that you can turn a one-dollar bill into a five.

Take the dollar bill, roll it up lengthwise into a rope, and bend it into the number 5 (see picture).

Uncatchable Dollar

If you can catch it, you can keep it. That's the challenge you give when you pull out a dollar bill.

To demonstrate, you dangle a bill with your right hand. With your left hand, you hold your thumb and forefinger one inch apart at George Washington's head. When you let go with the right hand, you easily catch it with your left.

It looks simple. But it isn't. Have another person try to catch it from that position. They'll find it's virtually impossible. They don't have enough time to react before the dollar slips away...sort of a metaphor for real life.

STRONG DOLLAR

Is a dollar strong enough to hold up a water glass without the support of the International Monetary Fund?

What You'll Need

• A crisp, new dollar bill
• 3 water glasses

How You Do It

1 Place two glasses about 4 inches apart and challenge onlookers to place a dollar bill across them in a way that it will support a third glass.

2 After they pronounce it impossible, take the dollar and fold it lengthwise in tiny accordion folds.

3 Place it across the two glasses. It should now support the weight of your third glass.

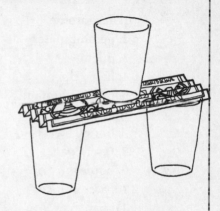

Rubber and Booze Don't Mix

A drug treatment for alcoholism is *tetraethylthiuram disulfide*, sold as the drug Antabuse. During the 1930s, workers in rubber manufacturing plants discovered that they got violently ill whenever they consumed even small quantities of alcohol. Scientists investigating the phenomenon discovered that the nausea was caused by tetraethylthiuram disulfide, a chemical used in rubber manufacturing. Apparently the drug changes the way that the body metabolizes alcohol, breaking much of it down into a chemical called acetaldehyde, which produces symptoms similar to that of a hangover: flushing, throbbing head, nausea and vomiting. Since it's nonlethal and works even when only a little bit of alcohol is consumed, doctors began using the substance in the treatment of alcoholism.

Speak English?

TRANSLATE THESE BRITISH TERMS INTO AMERICAN

Sometimes it seems like the British and Americans don't even speak the same language. How are you at translating? Translate these old and new British terms into American. (Answers below.)

1. aerodrome	a. dashboard
2. perambulator	b. car horn
3. queue	c. cotton candy
4. hair grip	d. battery
5. turf accountant	e. eggnog
6. chucker out	f. bookie
7. boiled sweets	g. bouncer
8. fascia panel	h. baby buggy
9. hooter	i. diaper
10. accumulator	j. drug store
11. pantechnicon	k. checkers
12. lorry	l. moving van
13. transport cafe	m. truck
14. draughts	n. truck stop
15. candy floss	o. line
16. nappy	p. hard candy
17. chemist's	q. bobby pin
18. egg flip	r. airfield

Answers: 1. aerodrome = r. airfield; 2. perambulator = h. baby buggy; 3. queue = o. line; 4. hair grip = q. bobby pin; 5. turf accountant = f. bookie; 6. chucker out = g. bouncer; 7. boiled sweets = p. hard candy; 8. fascia panel = a. dashboard; 9. hooter = b. car horn; 10. accumulator = d. battery; 11. pantechnicon = l. moving van; 12. lorry = m. truck; 13. transport cafe = n. truck stop; 14. draughts = k. checkers; 15. candy floss = c. cotton candy; 16. nappy = i. diaper; 17. chemist's = j. drug store; 18. egg flip = e. eggnog.

Witches' Loaves

A STORY OF GOOD INTENTIONS GONE BAD

In this ironic short story by O. Henry, a romantic bakery owner finds that there are limits to charity.

MISS MARTHA MEACHAM kept the little bakery on the corner (the one where you go up three steps, and the bell tinkles when you open the door).

Miss Martha was forty, her bank-book showed a credit of two thousand dollars, and she possessed two false teeth and a sympathetic heart. Many people have married whose chances to do so were much inferior to Miss Martha's.

Two or three times a week a customer entered in whom she began to take an interest. He was a middle-aged man, wearing spectacles and a brown beard trimmed to a careful point. He spoke English with a strong German accent. His clothes were worn and darned in places, and wrinkled and baggy in others. But he looked neat, and had very good manners.

He always bought two loaves of stale bread. Fresh bread was five cents a loaf. Stale ones were two for five. Never did he call for anything but stale bread.

Once Miss Martha saw a red and brown stain on his fingers. She was sure then that he was an artist and very poor. No doubt he lived in a garret, where he painted pictures and ate stale bread and thought of the good things to eat in Miss Martha's bakery.

Often when Miss Martha sat down to her chops and light rolls and jam and tea she would sigh, and wish that the gentle-mannered artist might share her tasty meal instead of eating his dry crust in that drafty attic. Miss Martha's heart, as you have been told, was a sympathetic one.

In order to test her theory as to his occupation, she brought from her room one day a painting that she had bought at a sale, and set it against the shelves behind the bread counter.

It was a Venetian scene. A splendid marble palazzio (so it said on the picture) stood in the foreground—or rather forewater. For the rest there were gondolas (with the lady trailing her hand in the water), clouds, sky, and *chiaro-oscuro* in plenty. No artist could fail to notice it.

Two days afterward the customer came in.

"Two loafs of stale bread, if you blease....You haf here a fine bicture, madame," he said while she was wrapping up the bread.

"Yes?" says Miss Martha, reveling in her own cunning. "I do so admire art and" (no, it would not do to say "artists" thus early) "and paintings," she substituted. "You think it is a good picture?"

"Der balance," said the customer, "is not in good drawing. Der bairspective of it is not true. Goot morning, madame."

He took his bread, bowed, and hurried out.

Yes, he must be an artist. Miss Martha took the picture back to her room.

How gentle and kindly his eyes shone behind his spectacles! What a broad brow he had! To be able to judge perspective at a glance—and to live on stale bread! But genius often has to struggle before it is recognized.

What a thing it would be for art and perspective if genius were backed by two thousand dollars in bank, a bakery, and a sympathetic heart to—But these were daydreams, Miss Martha.

Often now when he came he would chat for a while across the showcase. He seemed to crave Miss Martha's cheerful words.

He kept on buying stale bread. Never a cake, never a pie,

never one of her delicious Sally Lunns.

She thought he began to look thinner and discouraged. Her heart ached to add something good to eat to his meagre purchase, but her courage failed at the act. She did not dare affront him. She knew the pride of artists.

Miss Martha took to wearing her blue-dotted silk waist behind the counter. In the back room she cooked a mysterious compound of quince seeds and borax. Ever so many people use it for the complexion.

One day the customer came in as usual, laid his nickel on the showcase, and called for his stale loaves. While Miss Martha was reaching for them there was a great tooting and clanging, and a fire-engine came lumbering past.

The customer hurried to the door to look, as any one will. Suddenly inspired, Miss Martha seized the opportunity.

On the bottom shelf behind the counter was a pound of fresh butter that the dairyman had left ten minutes before. With a bread knife Miss Martha made a deep slash in each of the stale loaves, inserted a generous quantity of butter, and pressed the loaves tight again.

When the customer turned once more she was tying the paper around them.

When he had gone, after an unusually pleasant little chat, Miss Martha smiled to herself, but not without a slight fluttering of the heart.

Had she been too bold? Would he take offense? But surely not. There was no language of edibles. Butter was no emblem of unmaidenly forwardness.

For a long time that day her mind dwelt on the subject. She imagined the scene when he should discover her little deception.

He would lay down his brushes and palette. There would stand his easel with the picture he was painting in which the perspective was beyond criticism.

He would prepare for his luncheon of dry bread and water. He would slice into a loaf—ah!

Miss Martha blushed. Would he think of the hand that placed it there as he ate? Would he—

The front door bell jangled viciously. Somebody was coming in, making a great deal of noise.

Miss Martha hurried to the front. Two men were there. One was a young man smoking a pipe—a man she had never seen before. The other was her artist.

His face was very red, his hat was on the back of his head, his hair was wildly rumpled. He clinched his two fists and shook them ferociously at Miss Martha. *At Miss Martha.*

"Dummkopf!" he shouted with extreme loudness; and then *"Tausendonfer!"* or something like it, in German.

The young man tried to draw him away.

"I vill not go," he said angrily, "else I shall told her."

He made a bass drum of Miss Martha's counter.

"You haf shpoilt me," he cried, his blue eyes blazing behind his spectacles. "I vill tell you. You vas von *meddingsome old cat!"*

Miss Martha leaned weakly against the shelves and laid one hand on her blue-dotted silk waist. The young man took the other by the collar.

"Come on," he said, "you've said enough." He dragged the angry one out at the door to the sidewalk, and then came back.

"Guess you ought to be told, ma'am," he said, "what the row is about. That's Blumberger. He's an architectural draftsman. I work in the same office with him.

"He's been working hard for three months drawing a plan for a new city hall. It was a prize competition. He finished inking the lines yesterday. You know, a draftsman always makes his drawing in pencil first. When it's done he rubs out the pencil lines with handfuls of stale bread crumbs. That's better than India rubber.

"Blumberger's been buying the bread here. Well, today—well, you know, ma'am, that butter isn't—well, Blumberger's plan isn't good for anything now except to cut up into railroad sandwiches."

Miss Martha went into the back room. She took off the blue-dotted silk waist and put on the old brown serge she used to wear. Then she poured the quince seed and borax mixture out of the window into the ash can. ☾

Potty Pourri
RANDOM KINDS OF FACTNESS

• Both a 30-caliber bullet and a person rolled up in a tight ball fall at about the same speed: 200 mph.

• The snowy tree cricket is a white little bugger that lives in trees. Of all insects, it is the most accurate temperature gauge. If you count its chirps for 14 seconds and add 42, you'll get the temperature in Fahrenheit. This, of course, doesn't work in winter.

• For more than 4,000 years, the Great Pyramid of Egypt stood as the tallest structure in the world. No other structure has ever come close to holding the record for that long. Its reign ended in 1886, when Gustave Eiffel built a metal monstrosity in Paris.

• Edmond Rostand, the guy who wrote *Cyrano de Bergerac*, liked to write while in the bathtub.

• Some lizards come with cartilage in their tails that allow them to lose the tail without losing their life. It's simple self-preservation. Some of these lizards can regenerate new tails, but the new tail comes at great cost to the lizard's overall health.

• When Aristotle opened his school, he named it the Lyceum. People nicknamed it the Peripatetic School. *Peripatetic* means "walking around"—the teachers taught while leisurely strolling the grounds.

• Francis Cleveland, wife of Grover, was the only First Lady to deliver a baby in the White House. However, Thomas Jefferson's daughter, Martha "Patsy" Jefferson Randolph, was the first woman to give birth there.

• Wine was mighty important to the ancient Egyptians. Take King Tut as an example. The young king was entombed with 36 jars of wine to help smooth his transition into the afterlife.

• A cow that sports a black-and-white splotched face is called a *brockie*. The word can also mean a person with a dirt-smudged face.

Zen Masters
THE WISDOM OF FRANK ZAPPA

Mind-altering quotes from the late musician/philosopher Frank Zappa.

- "Art is making something out of nothing and selling it."
- "There are more love songs than anything else. If songs could make you do something, we'd all love one another."
- "The United States is a nation of laws: badly written and randomly enforced."
- "Without deviation, progress is not possible."
- "Communism doesn't work because people like to own stuff."
- "Some scientists claim that hydrogen, because it is so plentiful, is the basic building block of the universe. I dispute that. I say that there is more stupidity than hydrogen, and that is the basic building block of the universe."
- "In the fight between you and the world, back the world."
- "Fact of the matter is, there is no hip world, there is no straight world. There's a world, you see, which has people in it who believe in a variety of different things. Everybody believes in something and everybody, by virtue of the fact that they believe in something, use that something to support their own existence."
- "All the good music has already been written by people with wigs and stuff."
- "One of my favorite philosophical tenets is that people will agree with you only if they already agree with you. You do not change people's minds."
- "You can't be a real country unless you have a beer and an airline. It helps if you have some kind of a football team, or some nuclear weapons, but at the very least you need a beer."

Chews Carefully
Some Ruminations on Gum

Americans chew a lot of gum—an average of about 300 sticks per person every year. Our correspondent Elsa Bronte ruminated and masticated on the subject of gum before tucking it into our pages.

WRIGLEY FINDS HIS FIELD

William Wrigley, Jr., the father of American chewing gum, worked as a soap salesman for his father's Philadelphia business, and at age 29 moved to Chicago and started his own soap business with a total of $32 in his pocket. With an acute sensitivity to his customers' whims, Wrigley used premiums to boost his sales. When he noticed that a baking soda premium helped sell his soap, he started selling baking soda. And when a chewing gum premium proved beneficial to his sale of baking soda, he moved into the chewing gum business. His first gum flavors—Lotta Gum and Vassar—came out in 1892, followed by Juicy Fruit and Wrigley's Spearmint the following year. Wrigley was a tireless promoter—for example, in 1915, Wrigley promoted a new brand by sending a piece of it to each of the 1.5 million people listed in U.S. phone books—and it made him rich enough to branch out. In 1919, he bought the Chicago Cubs and built them Wrigley Field; next he bought Catalina Island off the coast of southern California and developed it into a lucrative pleasure resort.

THE ART & LITERATURE OF GUM

• Sculptor Les Levine immortalized gum in 18-karat gold. He cast tiny sculptures from actual pieces of chewed gum, and displayed them in his Greenwich Village Museum of Mott Art in New York City.

• Besides the immortal "Close cover before striking," this phrase may be the instruction that has been most published (and unfortunately, most ignored) in the world: "Save this wrapper for disposal after use."

IT'S THE REAL THING?

• Back in the early days of the gum industry, even Coca-Cola got in on the action. From 1911 to 1920, the company hawked "Coca-Cola Chewing Gum." Today, sticks of this gum are so rare that a piece sold for $8,000 a few years back.

GUMMING UP THE WORKS

• Liquid gum base (it hardens into chewing gum only after cooking and cooling) has been used as an organic pesticide: Insects drawn to its sweetness find their jaws stuck together and they soon starve to death.

Oh no ... Not again.

• Gum Alley: It has no official name, but it's the alley right next to 733 Higuera Street in San Luis Obispo, California. People have been depositing their chewed gum on the side of the old brick building there for more than a decade. A wonderfully tacky mural—in every sense of the word.

• New York Central Railroad once employed a full-time gum removal man to clean discarded gum from Grand Central Station. He harvested an average of seven pounds a night, with the wad growing to fourteen pounds on holiday weekends.

LOVE & GUM

• Sharing someone's ABC (already been chewed) gum is a sign of true love, as Tom Sawyer proved when he shared a piece with Becky Thatcher. The following is a selection from Mark Twain's *The Adventures of Tom Sawyer*, Chapter VII:

"'I-LOVE-YOU!'"

> ...Then they sat together, with a slate before them, and Tom gave Becky the pencil and held her hand in his, guiding it, and so created another surprising house. When the interest in art began to wane, the two fell to talking. Tom was swimming in bliss.
>
> He said:
>
> "Do you love rats?"
>
> "No! I hate them!"
>
> "Well, I do, too — LIVE ones. But I mean dead ones, to swing round your head with a string."
>
> "No, I don't care for rats much, anyway. What I like is chewing-gum."
>
> "Oh, I should say so! I wish I had some now."
>
> "Do you? I've got some. I'll let you chew it awhile, but you must give it back to me."
>
> That was agreeable, so they chewed it turn about, and dangled their legs against the bench in excess of contentment.

A section or two later, the two youngsters got engaged.

A MEMBER OF THE CHAIN GANG

Remember spending all your allowance on gum so you could have the longest wrapper chain in the entire neighborhood? It takes 50 wrappers to make a chain one foot long. On March 11, 1965, Gary Duschl of Virginia Beach,

Gum by Any Other Name

German: kaugummi
Japanese: gamu
Norwegian: tyggegummi
Russian: zhevatelnaya rezinka
Spanish: goma de mascar

Chinese: heung how chu
Portuguese: pastilka elastica
Swiss: chaetschgummi
Arabic: elki
Greek: tsikles

Gary Duschl and his record-breaking gum wrapper chain. Find out more at
http://www.gumwrapper.com/.

Virginia, began a gum wrapper chain. Thirty-eight years later, he was the world record holder for the longest gum wrapper chain, with a chain of 1,000,000 wrappers that reached 42,908 feet. The chain weighs 588 pounds and is made solely from Wrigley's gum wrappers—a total of about $50,000 worth of gum.

On his Web site, Gary draws comparisons in order to help people understand the length his obsession goes. He points out that 42,908 feet actually is about eight miles.

In case you want to challenge Gary's record (or at least have a modest-sized gum chain you can wear or display), here's how to get started: Get a pack of flat stick gum. Remove and fold the individual paper wrapper lengthwise into thirds. Fold in again, in half, crosswise. Fold each end in toward the center; this becomes the first link in the chain. Repeat with remaining wrappers to create many links. To assemble the chain, slip the ends of the second link into the **V** of the first link. Add to the chain by feeding the ends of link #3 through the ends of link #2, and so on, in a zig-zag pattern. ☾

Eyewitness

I WATCHED THE *S.S. TITANIC* GO DOWN

Margaret Graham, the 19-year-old daughter of W. T. Graham, a financial backer of the Dixie Cup Corporation, and Elizabeth Shutes, her governess, were passengers on the maiden voyage of the *Titanic*. Of the 2,227 aboard, they were two of the 375 that survived.

THE TITANIC left Southampton, England, on April 10, 1912, and headed for New York. On the night of April 15, it struck an iceberg and went down. Here's Shutes's account:

"Suddenly a queer quivering ran under me, apparently the whole length of the ship. Startled by the very strangeness of the shivering motion, I sprang to the floor. With too perfect a trust in that mighty vessel I again lay down. Someone knocked at my door, and the voice of a friend said: 'Come quickly to my cabin; an iceberg has just passed our window; I know we have just struck one.'

"No confusion, no noise of any kind, one could believe no danger imminent. Our stewardess came and said she could learn nothing. Looking out into the companionway I saw heads appearing asking questions from half-closed doors.

All sepulchrally still, no excitement. I sat down again. My friend was by this time dressed; still her daughter and I talked on, Margaret pretending to eat a sandwich. Her hand shook so that the bread kept parting company from the chicken. Then I saw she was frightened, and for the first time I was too, but why get dressed, as no one had given the slightest hint of any possible danger? An officer's cap passed the door. I asked: 'Is there an accident or danger of any kind?' 'None, so far as I know,' was his courteous answer, spoken quietly and most kindly. This same officer then entered a cabin a little distance down the companionway and, by this time distrustful of everything, I listened intently, and distinctly heard, 'We can keep the water out for a while.' Then, and not until then, did I realize the horror of an accident at sea. Now it was too late to dress; no time for a waist, but a coat and skirt were soon on;

The *S.S. Titanic* was the biggest luxury liner of its time. So large, that designers added an extra smokestack, just so it would sport an even number. The last smokestack was non-functional; it served only as ventilation.

slippers were quicker than shoes; the stewardess put on our life-preservers, and we were just ready when Mr Roebling came to tell us he would take us to our friend's mother, who was waiting above....

"No laughing throng, but on either side [of the staircases] stand quietly, bravely, the stewards, all equipped with the white, ghostly life-preservers. Always the thing one tries not to see even crossing a ferry. Now only pale faces, each form strapped about with those white bars. So gruesome a scene. We passed on. The awful good-byes. The quiet look of hope in the brave men's eyes as the wives were put into the lifeboats. Nothing escaped one at this fearful moment. We left from the sun deck, seventy-five feet above the water. Mr Case and Mr Roebling, brave American men, saw us to the lifeboat, made no effort to save themselves, but stepped back on deck. Later they went to an honoured grave.

ropes worked together, and we drew nearer and nearer the black, oily water. The first touch of our lifeboat on that black sea came to me as a last good-bye to life, and so we put off—a tiny boat on a great sea—rowed away from what had been a safe home for five days.

The *Titanic* voyage was supposed to be Capt. Edward John Smith's final working stint as head of a ship. It ended up being his last journey of any kind.

"Our lifeboat, with thirty-six in it, began lowering to the sea. This was done amid the greatest confusion. Rough seamen all giving different orders. No officer aboard. As only one side of the ropes worked, the lifeboat at one time was in such a position that it seemed we must capsize in mid-air. At last the

"The first wish on the part of all was to stay near the Titanic. We all felt so much safer near the ship. Surely such a vessel could not sink. I thought the danger must be exaggerated, and we could all be taken aboard again. But surely the outline of that great, good ship was growing less. The bow of the boat was getting black. Light after light was disappearing, and now those rough seamen put to their oars and we were told to hunt under seats, any place, anywhere, for a lantern, a light of any kind. Every place was empty. There was no water— no stimulant of any kind. Not a biscuit— nothing to keep us alive had we drifted long....

"From: Mr. Franline, The White Star Line, To: Captain Smith, The Titanic, Date: April 15, 1912. 'Anxiously awaiting information and probably disposition passengers.'" There was no reply.

"Sitting by me in the lifeboat were a mother and daughter. The mother had left a husband on the Titanic, and the daughter a father and husband, and while we were near the other boats those two stricken women would call out a name and ask, 'Are you there?' 'No,' would come back the awful answer, but these brave women never lost courage, forgot their own sorrow, telling me to sit close to them to keep warm.... The life-preservers helped to keep us warm, but the night was bitter cold, and it grew colder and colder, and just before dawn, the coldest, darkest hour of all, no help seemed possible....

"The stars slowly disappeared, and in their place came the faint pink glow of another day. Then I heard, 'A light, a ship.' I could not, would not, look while there was a bit of doubt, but kept my eyes away. All night long I had heard, 'A light!' Each time it proved to be one of our other lifeboats, someone lighting a piece of paper, anything they could find to burn, and now I could not believe. Someone found a newspaper; it was lighted and held up. Then I looked and saw a ship. A ship bright with lights; strong and steady she waited, and we were to be saved. A straw hat was offered as it would burn longer. That same ship that had come to save us might run us down. But no; she is still. The two, the ship and the dawn, came together, a living painting." ☾

142

Grandville
Kids' Illustrator, Father of Surrealism

Jean Ignace Isidore Gerard (1803–1847), who went by the name "Grandville," was a French illustrator who drew the most peculiar things. A century later, surrealist artists adopted him as a forerunner of their movement. For the rest of the story, see page 247.

The Spirits Speak
HOW TO PERFORM A PHONY SEANCE

When Houdini tried to find a genuine psychic to talk to his beloved dead mother, he discovered only frauds. You can be a fraud, too— here's a method used by professional paranormals of the past.

THE BEST THING about seances is that everything takes place in the dark. There's a reason, as you'll see when you set up your own visitation by the spirits.

WHAT YOU'LL NEED
- Table big enough for you and your unsuspecting friends
- Cigarette lighter
- Candle
- 2 pieces of cardboard
- Pen
- 2 rubber bands
- Ambient music (optional)

HOW YOU DO IT

1 Get everything ready. Black out windows and door cracks —your room must be made completely dark.

2 Have your friends sit around the table, lit candle in center. Say: "We are here tonight in a circle to see if the spirits are among us and whether they will communicate to us from the Other Side."

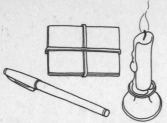

3 Show that the sides of both sheets of cardboard are blank. Wrap rubber bands around each end and put the package on the table with the pen on top of it. Say: "This is in case anybody from the Other Side wants to send us a message."

4 Have everyone place their hands palms down on the table. As you talk for a few moments about the spirits and the Other World, casually slide your hands to within a few inches of each other.

5 Tell everyone to reach over with their right hand and grasp the left wrist of the person to their right. Say: "This ensures that everybody can be trusted not to interfere with the process."

6 You announce that you are now going to extinguish the candle. Take your right hand from your neighbor's wrist and reach toward the candle. In the movement of leaning forward, you'll casually pull your left hand toward the center. Snuff the flame with your fingers, and lean back in the darkness.

7 Here comes the trick: Pull your left hand over and use *it*—*not* your right hand—to grip your neighbor's wrist. Now, unbeknownst to either of your neighbors, you have your right hand free.

8 Encourage everyone to concentrate on the spirits. As you talk about how to feel the presence of spirits (this is to mask any sounds you make), feel around gently for the pen. Write "I AM WITH YOU" in ghostly letters on the cardboard. Turn the package over so the writing is on the bottom.

9 After a short, meditative silence, say: "We have been in the dark long enough; let us see if there has been a message. I shall light the candle." This gives you a reason to take your "right" hand from your neighbor's wrist.

10 Actually, you slip your *left* hand off your neighbor's wrist. Use your right hand to find your lighter and light the candle, using the movement of leaning forward to slide your left hand back toward your left neighbor.

11 Take the rubber bands from the cardboard without showing the writing on the bottom. Lift the top piece and show it. Say, with a sigh of resignation and subtle reproach: "Apparently we didn't all have our energies fully focused on reaching the spirits. Let's try again."

12 When you put the rubber band back, lift the piece of cardboard with writing on the bottom and slide the blank piece *underneath,* so the writing is now inside. Put the rubber bands back around.

13 Say: "I think we need more direct psychic energy. Let us all lay our hands directly on the piece of cardboard."

14 Snuff the candle again. Tell everyone to focus all of their energies on receiving a message from the Other World. After a short while, say: "I sense that perhaps we have waited long enough." Light the candle once more.

15 Ask: "Will somebody please open the package again to see if we received a message?"

16 Keep a blank, unsurprised face when people gasp at the sight of "I AM WITH YOU." Explain nothing.

GETTING IN THE SPIRIT

Use your imagination. You can do a lot more with that free right hand. For example, you can create a noisy spirit manifestation by tossing something to the far side of the room. You can also move things around the table, wave a white silk over the table for a ghostly visual manifestation or just about anything to create an eerie mood. ☾

Sports Match 2
MATCH THE TEAM TO THE LOCATION

One more time: See if you can match these NBA, MLB, and NFL teams to their correct home location.

1.	Diamondbacks	Utah
2.	Timberwolves	Florida
3.	Marlins	Toronto
4.	Rams	Arizona
5.	Grizzlies	Montreal
6.	Padres	Arizona
7.	Jazz	Milwaukee
8.	Raptors	Carolina
9.	Buccaneers	San Diego
10.	Saints	New Orleans
11.	Expos	Minnesota
12.	Cardinals	Colorado
13.	Rockies	St. Louis
14.	Panthers	Memphis
15.	Bucks	Tampa Bay

Answers: 1. Diamondbacks: Arizona; 2. Timberwolves: Minnesota; 3. Marlins: Florida; 4. Rams: St. Louis; 5. Grizzlies: Memphis; 6. Padres: San Diego; 7. Jazz: Utah; 8. Raptors: Toronto; 9. Buccaneers: Tampa Bay; 10. Saints: New Orleans; 11. Expos: Montreal; 12. Cardinals: Arizona; 13. Rockies: Colorado; 14. Panthers: Carolina; 15. Bucks: Milwaukee

Tom Swifties III

"Some You Lose," Said Tom Winsomely

From the surreal 1960s came elephant jokes and Tom Swifties, based on bad puns and the stylistic excesses of Victor Appleton, who created the popular Tom Swift stories. Here are some more.

"I've found Moby Dick!" Tom wailed.

"Does Heisenberg have principles?" asked Tom uncertainly.

"How long before my table's ready?" Tom asked reservedly.

"I don't want to die intestate," said Tom unwillingly.

"Ever hear a lion catapulted?" asked Tom over the uproar.

"How do you stop a horse?" Tom said woefully.

"I've had some ventricles removed," Tom said halfheartedly.

"My specialty is milking cows," Tom uttered.

"Anyone know a rebel army leader?" Tom asked generally.

"Got any Velveeta?" asked Tom craftily.

"This is leftover calf meat," Tom revealed.

"I can hear a member of that hive in pain!" Tom bemoaned.

"I cut too much off my toenails," Tom said quickly.

"I've forgotten the guitar part," Tom fretted.

"You brought cheese I can't shred," Tom said ungratefully.

"Unclog the drain with a vacuum cleaner," said Tom succinctly.

"I forgot to buy perma-pressed clothes," Tom said ironically.

"I come from the Dog Star," Tom said seriously.

"I think I pulled a tendon," Tom insinuated.

"I hate metal on my teeth," said Tom abrasively.

"I'd give that honey-gatherer an 80 out of 100," Tom berated.

Speak English? 2
TRANSLATE THESE BRITISH TERMS INTO AMERICAN

Sometimes it seems like the British and Americans don't even speak the same language. How are you at translating? Translate these old and new British terms into American. (Answers below.)

1. power point	a. french fries
2. lift	b. mailbox
3. dust bin	c. installment plan
4. rubbers	d. electrical outlet
5. chargehand	e. molasses
6. chips	f. grab bag
7. crisps	g. merry–go–round
8. lucky dip	h. hassock
9. pouffe	i. foreman
10. ironmonger	j. long–distance call
11. solicitor	k. elevator
12. never–never	l. parka
13. trunk call	m. lawyer
14. pillar box	n. hardware store
15. loud hailer	o. megaphone
16. roundabout	p. garbage can
17. treacle	q. potato chips
18. anorak	r. erasers

Answers: 1. power point = d. electrical outlet; 2. lift = k. elevator; 3. dust bin = p. garbage can; 4. rubbers = r. erasers; 5. chargehand = i. foreman; 6. chips = a. french fries; 7. crisps = q. potato chips; 8. lucky dip = f. grab bag; 9. pouffe = h. hassock; 10. ironmonger = n. hardware store; 11. solicitor = m. lawyer; 12. never–never = c. installment plan; 13. trunk call = j. long–distance call; 14. pillar box = b. mailbox; 15. loud hailer = o. megaphone; 16. roundabout = g. merry–go–round; 17. treacle = e. molasses; 18. anorak = l. parka

Ripe Ol' Corn

"The Punkin Centre & Paw Paw Valley Railroad"

"Uncle Josh," Cal Stewart's country bumpkin, tells a story about the coming of one of those newfangled railroads.

WONDERS will never cease—we've got a railroad in Punkin Centre now; oh, we're gettin' to be right smart cityfied. I guess that's about the crookedest railroad that ever was built. I think that railroad runs across itself in one or two places; it runs past one station three times. It's so durned crooked they hav to burn crooked wood in the ingine.

Cal Stewart

Well, the first engine they had on the Punkin Centre was a wonderful piece of machinery. It had a five-foot boiler and a seven-foot whistle, and every time they blowed the whistle the durned old engine would stop.

Well, we've got the railroad, and we're mighty proud of it; but we had an awful time a-gettin' it through. You see, most everybody give the right of way 'cept Ezra Hoskins, and he didn't like to see it go through his meadow field, and it seemed as though they'd have to go 'round for quite a ways, and maybe they wouldn't come to Punkin Centre at all.

Well, one mornin' Ezra saw a lot of fellers down in the meadow most uncommonly busy like; so he went down to them and he said, "What be you a-doin' down here?" And they said, "Well, Mr. Hoskins, we're surveyin' for the railroad." And Ezra

said, "So we're goin' to have a railroad, be we? Is it goin' right through here?" And they said, "Yes, Mr. Hoskins, that's where it's a-goin', right through here." Ezra said, "Well, I s'pose you'll have a right smart of plowin' and diggin', and you'll just about plow up my meadow field, won't you?" They said, "Yes, Mr. Hoskins, we'll hav to do some gradin'."

Ezra said, "Well, now, let me see, is it a-goin' just the way you've got that instrument pointed?" They said, "Yes, sir, just there." And Ezra said, "Well, near as I can calculate from that, I should judge it was a-goin' right through my barn." They said, "Yes, Mr. Hoskins, we're sorry, but the railroad is a-goin' right through your barn."

Well, Ezra didn't say much for quite a spell, and we all expected there would be trouble; but finally he said, "Well, I s'pose the community of Punkin Centre needs a railroad and I hadn't oughter offer any objections to its goin' through, but I'm goin' to tell you one thing right now, afore you go any further. When you get it built and a-runnin', you've got to get a man to come down here and take care of it, because it's a-comin' along hayin' and harvestin' time, and I'll be too durned busy to run down here and open and shut them barn doors every time one of your pesky old trains wants to go through." ☾

Simian Says

A BARREL OF APES & MONKEYS

Climbing up the human family tree, you'd be surprised at what you'll find swinging from its branches. Here are feats and tales of some of our closest living relatives.

MONKEYS MOCK US FOR THIS
What does *Homo sapiens* mean? The name we human apes have modestly given ourselves means "wise person."

THE PRIMATE COLORS
Apes and monkeys pretty much see the same colors we do. However, many of the New World monkeys don't see reds quite as well.

Orangutan

PRIMATE COLORS II
Many people assume that the orangutan got that name because of its color, but they're wrong. *Orangutan* means "person of the forest" in the Malay language.

GORILLA WARFARE?
Chimps have been known to murder, steal and rape. They are also very human in their capacity for war. In clashes with other chimpanzee groups, they will brutalize and kill their enemies. And, although the practice is uncommon, chimpanzees have been known to eat other chimps.

MUTILATED MONKEY MEAT
How many primates are major meat eaters? Besides humans,

only chimpanzees eat any quantity of meat. About 75% of the chimps' meat consists of red colobus monkey babies ripped from the arms of their mothers. Researchers found that a chimp's major motivation for hunting monkeys is sex—if members of a hunting party offer fresh meat to a female in heat, most or all of them are likely to get lucky.

Don't be fooled by the chimp's innocent face

MONKEY LOVE

If chimps share humans' most violent attributes, bonobos are the flip side.

Even though bonobos and chimps are humans' closest relatives, sharing 98.4% of our genes, the bonobos are not as well known. They weren't even discovered by Westerners until 1929. Coincidentally, local natives along the Zaire River, where the bonobos live, have many myths about how humankind and bonobos were once brothers.

Bonobos are most interested in making love, not war—they've developed a female–led, cooperative, and egalitarian society in which promiscuous sex is a powerful substitute for aggression.

Compare bonobos with chimpanzees: If a group of chimps come upon food, the dominant male claims it as his own, using a display of aggression to eat his fill before allowing others to eat. In contrast, a group of bonobos coming upon food will immediately get aroused and begin sexually stimulating each other—male and female, male and male, and (most commonly) female and female, rubbing their genitals against each other while grinning and making cooing sounds. After about five minutes, the bonobos go ahead and feed as a community without regard to rank. A similar orgiastic thing happens when something threatens to disturb the peace. For example, when researchers in a zoo dropped a cardboard box into the chimp compound, the dominant chimp threatened violence in order to be the first to explore it. The bonobos, in contrast, engaged in a brief orgy and then approached the box together.

Unlike most simians, bonobos

often copulate face to face, looking deeply into each others' eyes. Humans once thought that they were unique in this especially intimate activity. They were wrong.

WHAT'S THE WESTERN LOWLAND GORILLA'S LATIN NAME?

Gorilla gorilla gorilla.

RELATIVE HUMILITY

Humans and gorillas are closer relatives than are gorillas and monkeys.

IN THE BLOOD OF RHESUS

The *rh* in "rh factor" stands for "rhesus," the monkey that was once widely used in medical research. When Dr. Karl Landsteiner discovered properties of blood in 1940, he decided to honor the rhesus monkeys that were deprived of their freedom, blood and lives to make his discovery.

WON'T YOU BE MY NEIGHBOR?

Koko the signing gorilla went positively ape over *Mr. Rogers' Neighborhood.* When Mr. Rogers came to visit Koko, her first response was to wrap her powerful arms gently around him. Then, as she had seen him do hundreds of times on TV, she reached down and took off his shoes.

Monkeys, Apes & Gorillas—What's the Difference?

WHAT'S A MONKEY and what's an ape? To clear up confusion, let's do a quick list. Primates have two main groups: **anthropoids** and **prosimians**.

1. **Anthropoids** include:

Monkeys. New World monkeys include marmosets, tamarins, capuchins, howlers, squirrel monkeys, woolly monkeys, spider monkeys and even woolly spider monkeys. Old World monkeys include baboons, colobus monkeys and macaques.

Apes. Chimpanzees, gibbons, gorillas, orangutans and humans. Apes have no tails and are smarter than monkeys. Apes walk in an upright position instead of on four feet like monkeys. If there's a tree to be scaled, apes climb it; monkeys take a leap into it. Excluding humans, these are known as **simians**.

2. **Prosimians** include a number of lesser-known animals like aye-ayes, galagos, lemurs, lorises, pottos and tarsiers. *Prosimian* means "pre-monkey" because they are more primitive than monkeys and actually resemble monkey ancestors. Prosimians are not as strong or smart as the anthropoids, and survive competition with them by hunting at night as their smarter cousins sleep.

Ring-tailed lemur, a prosimian

HAND GESTURES OF BIG APES

Gorillas aren't the only simians to learn sign language—so have chimps and orangutans. Washoe, the most accomplished chimpanzee, has a vocabulary of at least 240 words—nowhere near the claims for Koko that she can understand 2,000 spoken words and respond with a vocabulary of up to 1,000 signs.

ARMS OF DESTRUCTION

Gorilla arms are longer than their legs. The record gorilla arm span is 9 feet, 2 inches; a more typical adult male arm span is about 8 feet.

NOT A HEAVY DRINKER

Gorillas don't drink water. They get all the moisture they need from the leaves, tubers, flowers, fruit, fungus and insects they eat—roughly 50 pounds of food a day.

GORILLA WARFARE

What should you do if charged by a gorilla? First of all, complain to your credit card company. Okay, so it's an old joke.... The good news is that gorillas are normally very shy and amiable; the bad news is that if you wander into their territory, the male leader will charge at you beating his chest and growling. So what do you do?

You must not do the apparently rational thing of running for your life. Intruders who run are often chased and killed. Instead, screw up your courage, stand up straight, and hold your ground. Expert say that those who stand their ground are almost never harmed.

CAPPUCCINO MONKEYS

Do capuchin monkeys have anything to do with cappuccino? More than any reasonable person could expect. Both were named after the robes worn by Capuchin monks. The coffee drink is the same distinctive brown color. The monkey has a

distinctive marking that looks like a monk's hood on top of its head.

EURO-MONKEY INSOUCIANCE
Few people know about the wild monkeys of Europe. Barbary apes live in Gibraltar, the British colony south of Spain. Despite its name, this "ape" is really a monkey related to rhesus monkeys of India. There are only 5,000 worldwide, with most in remote areas of Morocco and Algeria.

SEA MONKEYS?
Gorillas don't swim. A pursuing gorilla won't follow you into the water. But some monkeys do swim. For example, the proboscis monkeys of Borneo are as graceful gliding through the water as they are swinging from the trees.

SMALL AND LOUD
Smallest monkey is the pygmy marmoset. It's the size of a small squirrel, and it weighs as much as a Quarter Pounder, bun and all.

Pygmy marmoset there'd be days like this

Loudest monkey is the howler. A small band can make as much noise as a stadium full of people. They can be heard 3 miles away.

RHESUS PIECES
Not many things hunt tree monkeys, but eagles do, swooping down with powerful talons to grasp and crush. Still, tree-dwellers are better off than monkeys that spend a lot of time on the ground. All of the meat eaters from lions to hyenas seem to want rhesus pieces. ☾

WE WOULDN'T TRUST ANY OF THEM WITH NO. 2 PENCILS
IF YOU gave animals an IQ test, primates would rule in the smartness scale. Of the top ten, seven are primates. Here's how they stack up:
1. Humans
2. Chimpanzees / Bonobos
3. Gorillas
4. Orangutans
5. Baboons
6. Gibbons
7. Monkeys
8. Small-toothed whales
9. Dolphins
10. Elephants

Potty Pourri
RANDOM KINDS OF FACTNESS

• President Millard Fillmore never had any formal education. Oxford University once offered him an honorary doctorate of Civil Law. He turned it down, saying, "No man should accept a degree he cannot read."

• Some archeologists claim that the soup ladle was the first single-use kitchen utensil invented.

• *Raash* is another name for the electric catfish—an African catfish that grows up to 3 feet in length. The name means "thunder," although its effects are far more like lightning.

• J. R. R. Tolkien was a procrastinator, it's safe to say. It took him fourteen years to write *The Lord of the Rings*. Granted, the epic ran about a thousand pages, and included complex histories and cultures that he made up out of thin air. But still, he averaged fewer than 100 words per day. (To compare, this paragraph uses 60 words.)

• Teachers' salaries have always been bad, but Confucius didn't complain. Once he said that he would never turn away a prospective student, "even if he came to me on foot, with nothing more to offer as tuition than a package of dried meat."

• Mark Twain was one of the first people to own the newly invented Remington typewriter. Its success convinced him to sink a lot of his hard-earned money into an early typesetting machine. That investment didn't pan out, and years later he traded his Remington for a $12 saddle.

• President Calvin Coolidge was sworn in as president by his own dad, who happened to be a justice of the peace.

• Until they got smart in 200 B.C., the French didn't make their own wine. They bought it from the Italians. The going price was one slave for a large jug of wine.

Ol' Smokey

WHERE THERE'S FIRE, THERE'S SMOKEY

Forest fire prevention goes back decades before the introduction of Smokey the Bear, but no publicity campaign has ever been anywhere near as successful as the Smokey campaign. Here's how it happened.

EARLY FOREST FIRE PREVENTION ads used Uncle Sam. In a campaign in 1937, initiated by President Franklin D. Roosevelt, the bearded old guy reminded us: "Your Forests; Your Fault; Your Loss." It was a powerful message that people took seriously at first, but after several years of use, the United States Forestry Service decided it was in need of a new approach.

In 1943, the Foote, Cone & Belding advertising agency took over the Forest Service account and decided it was a time for an aggressive, hard-sell campaign. Tying the effort to Japanese bombing of Pearl Harbor and an oil field near the Los Padros National Forest in California, the firm pumped out slogans like "Careless Matches Aid the Axis," to play up Americans' fears that the nation's forests were in danger from alien forces. The pictures accompanying the message showed stereotypical Japanese and Nazis leering menacingly at us, their faces illuminated as if gleefully watching a forest burn.

ALAS, ALL TASTELESS THINGS MUST COME TO AN END

As the war ended, however, it became clear that the old approach wouldn't work any more. Foote, Cone & Belding managed to get permission to use Bambi, the Disney deer, in one ad—but after that, Disney didn't want to grant further permissions. Next they tried using squirrels as a spokes-animal but after one poster, they decided that the cute little creatures didn't have sufficient seriousness and authority.

Finally, the ad agency convinced the Forest Service that a bear would best represent the authoritative yet gruffly lovable image the U.S. Forest Service wanted to project.

Early Forest fire prevention posters. Top: Uncle Sam, 1937. Left: Anti-Japanese, anti-Nazi, and pro-Bambi campaign. Right: "Careless matches aid the Axis" campaign

The first Smokey the Bear poster came out in 1945 from an illustration by New York artist Albert Staehle. In 1947 a copywriter penned the slogan "Remember, only YOU can prevent forest fires." Not long after, announcer Jack Weaver put his head into a barrel for resonance and gave a voice to Smokey in his first radio spots.

MYTHMAKING

Smokey the Bear actually became flesh, fur and blood in 1950, when a state game protector rescued a scorched bear cub from a New Mexico forest fire. The Forest Service quickly named the cub Smokey, created an after-the-fact story which claimed that the little charred cub was the inspiration for the Smokey ad campaign, instead of vice versa, and transferred the cub to the National Zoological Park in Washington, D.C.

The first living Smokey, rescued in 1950

Ben Michtom, chairman of the Ideal Toy Company and son of the original creators of the teddy bear, won permission to market a toy Smokey in 1952. Ideal produced millions of the ranger-hatted bears and included a certificate with each, which children could fill out and send to the Service to become Junior Forest Rangers. More than 5 million kids enlisted.

The original living Smokey the Bear mascot died in 1967. Another bear, Smokey II, died in 1990.

MORE SMOKEY FACTS

• The Koochiching County Keep Minnesota Green Committee in International Falls, Minnesota erected a 26-foot wooden Smokey the Bear in 1954.

Snoopy stepped in to help in 1972, and the Forest Service brought back Bambi again in 1982

• Smokey was given his own zip code number in 1964, in recognition of the large volume of mail he receives. Smokey's zip: Washington, D.C., 20252.

• In 1969, Smokey the Bear appeared in his own weekly half-hour animated comedy adventure. The show ran for two years on the ABC-TV network. ℭ

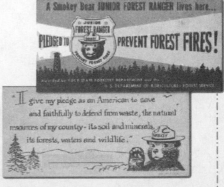

According to Mark Twain

More from *Puddin'head Wilson's Calendar*, a fictitious publication that Twain "quoted" from whenever he needed a maxim.

• "Each person is born with one possession which outvalues all his others — his last breath."

• "It takes your enemy and your friend, working together, to hurt you to the heart: the one to slander you, and the other to get the news to you."

• "If the desire to kill and the opportunity to kill always came together, who would escape hanging?"

• "Grief can take care of itself; but to get the full value of a joy, you must have somebody to divide it with."

• "Wrinkles should merely indicate where smiles have been."

• "Don't part with your illusions. When they are gone, you may still exist, but you have ceased to live."

• "Often the surest way to convey misinformation is to tell the strict truth."

• "In the first place God made idiots. This was for practice. Then he made school boards."

• "Everyone is a moon, and has a dark side which he never shows to anybody."

• "The ink with which all history is written is merely fluid prejudice."

• "When people do not respect us we are sharply offended; yet deep down in his private heart, no man much respects himself."

• "Let us be thankful for the fools. But for them, the rest of us could not succeed."

• "We begin to swear before we can talk."

• "The autocrat of Russia possesses more power than any other man in the earth, but he cannot stop a sneeze."

• "Let me make the superstititions of a nation and I do not care who makes its laws or its songs, either."

• "There are two times in a man's life when he should not speculate: when he can't afford it, and when he can."

• "Be careless in your dress if you must, but keep a tidy soul."

• "There is no such thing as 'the Queen's English.' The property has gone into a joint stock company and we own the bulk of the shares."

Quakes, Floods, and Fire

SOME OF OUR FAVORITE DISASTERS

Based on the question-savvy virtual butler's book *Just Curious About History, Jeeves*, here's a little Q & A about famous disasters.

ASH FROM A HOLE IN THE GROUND

How many people did Vesuvius kill?

Which time? Mount Vesuvius, the active volcano on the coast of Italy, has erupted more than 50 times since burying Pompeii and Herculaneum in A.D. 79. That first reported eruption killed about 3,400 people, it's estimated, mostly by burying them in thick pumice deposits. From that date, and probably before that date, Mount Vesuvius erupted every 100 years until about 1037, when it went quiet. Almost 600 years later, however, in 1631, it surprised nearby inhabitants by erupting and causing more than 4,000 deaths in the area. It was during this eruption's cleanup that the ruins of Pompeii were uncovered.

Was Vesuvius the worst volcano in history?

No. The deadliest-volcano-in-history award goes to Mount Tambora, Indonesia, in 1815. Judith Coan in Discovery.com described it like this:

> The largest eruption during the last two centuries, as well as the deadliest volcano in recorded history, Mount Tambora exploded April 10–11, 1815. It killed an estimated 92,000 people. Almost 80,000 of the victims died of starvation brought on by the agricultural devastation in the volcano's wake. The eruption and the resulting massive clouds of dust and ash affected most of the Northern Hemisphere, causing unusually cool temperatures and failed crops in 1816—sometimes referred to as "the year without a summer."

Mt. Pelee blows its top

How many people survived the 1902 Mount Pelee volcanic eruption in Martinique?

Two, one of whom was saved because he was in a windowless jail cell. The other 29,000 inhabitants living nearby were wiped out.

Had Mount St. Helens ever had a larger eruption than the one in 1980?

According to those who study these things, the Washington volcano erupted more violently about 2000 B.C. Mount St. Helens has been an active volcano for over 40,000 years, and scientists have predicted that another eruption could happen in the next 20 or 30 years.

ANOTHER BIG GAS BAG GOES DOWN IN FLAMES

What's listed on the official report as the cause of the fire that destroyed the Hindenburg in 1937?

St. Elmo's Fire—or, to a lay person, static electricity.

WIPE OUT!

What was the name of the dam at Johnstown, Pennsylvania that broke loose and flooded the town?

It shares a name with J. R. Ewing's homestead: South Fork.

Has a tidal wave ever hit the U.S.?

"Tidal waves"—or, more accurately, tsunamis—have hit the U.S. several times, most often in Hawaii and Alaska. California has been hit a couple of times this century as well. The most deadly tsunami to strike the contiguous U.S. happened in 1964. A record-shattering earthquake in Alaska was the catalyst for a series of huge waves that crashed into America's west coast. One in Shoup Bay, Valdez Inlet, measured 67 meters high. All in all, 120 people lost their lives throughout Canada, Alaska, Oregon, Washington and California. The deaths included 106 Alaskan residents, four campers on a beach campground in Newport, Oregon, and eleven people in the city of Crescent City, California, which was engulfed.

In 1946, Hawaii was also caught unaware by a devastating tsunami and 173 people were killed, prompting the foundation of the Pacific Tsunami Warning System (PTWS), for all U.S. regions in the Pacific, which watches for tsunamis in the hope of giving timely warnings of their approach.

SHAKE, RATTLE AND ROLL

Which San Francisco earthquake was more costly: the 1906 or 1989 one?

In dollars and cents, the 1989 Loma Prieta quake was the costliest at $5.9 billion, whereas the 1906 San Francisco quake totaled $400 million. In 1989 money, that would equal just over $5 billion—close but no cigar.

How many people were killed in the 1906 San Francisco earthquake?

From both the quake and the burning aftermath, about 3,000 people. The San Francisco city government at the time deliberately underreported the numbers and blamed most of the deaths on the fire, because they figured that tourists and newcomers would be less frightened of death by a familiar danger like fire than a terrifyingly unfamiliar one like an earthquake.

Was the 1906 San Francisco earthquake the deadliest U.S. natural disaster?

No. Hurricane Frederick, which pounded Galveston, Texas, in 1900 holds that honor. It left over 6,000 dead.

What's the worst earthquake in recorded history?

On January 23, 1556, in Shansi, China, a quake killed over 830,000 people. Other "big ones" in history:

- **Tangshan, China**, 1976: officially 255,000 dead; unofficial estimates put it at around 600,000
- **Aleppo, Syria,** 1138: 230,000 dead
- **Xining, China**, 1927: 200,000 dead
- **Messina, Italy**, 1908: 70,000 - 100,000 dead
- **Peru**, 1970: 66,000 dead

The Mississippi quake of 1811 ranks up there with "biggest," as well. The quake was so strong that it changed the course of the Mississippi River. However, there's no record of any human life lost. Next time, though....

A STICKY SWEET ENDING
What was the great Boston Molasses Flood?

That's exactly what it was: a flood of molasses. Don't laugh--people and horses died in it.

Just after noon on January 15, 1919, a fifty-eight-foot-tall, 90-feet wide steel structure burst open. It held 2.5 million gallons of hot molasses on the grounds of the United States Alcohol Company. Metal flew everywhere and a wave of sticky, boiling goo spewed up and out. The wave washed through a loading pit in the factory, boiling and smothering those standing nearby, and continued down on, washing freight cars off the tracks and pulling the front off a neighboring house. killing its inhabitants. Molasses poured through the nearby Public Works Department, boiling and smothering workers who were casually eating lunch around a table. Meanwhile, the town fire station was washed off its foundation and down toward the ocean.

When all was said and done, 21 people and numerous horses had come to a sticky end. The lawsuits that followed cost the molasses factory about a million dollars in damages.

A lengthy investigation decided that the tank hadn't been strong enough to hold that much molasses. In addition, a heat wave for several days in Boston had significantly increased the pressure inside the tanks. ☾

Hunt and Peck

THE SECRET LIVES OF TYPEWRITERS

From the keyboard of regular contributor Kathie Meyer comes little-known facts about typewriters.

THE TYPEWRITER — an invention initially thought up to help blind people communicate — eventually became an enormous aid for sighted people as well. Although Christopher Latham Sholes is often credited as the inventor of the first typewriter, the honor should actually go to Englishman Henry Mill who patented a kind of type-writing machine in 1714. Actually, dozens of typewriters are known to have been designed prior to the Sholes model. Some were built with piano keyboards and had names like "writing harpsichord" and "piano printer." Others had names such as "machine kryptographique" (1833), "cembalo scrivano" (1837), "machine tachygraphique" (1839), "universal compositor" (1840), "chirographer" (1843), "rapigraphe" (1843), "clavier imprimeur" (1850), "stéréographe" (1814), "phonetic writer & calico printer" (1850), "mechanical typographer" (1852), "printing machine" (1857), and "the pterotype" (1866).

TYPEWRITER MIGHTIER THAN THE GUN

In 1874, gunmaker E. Remington & Sons Arms Company came out with "The Sholes & Glidden Type Writer." Remington entered the typewriter market because the demand for guns decreased after the Civil War ended and the Wild West was tamed. Remington had also branched into the farm equipment and sewing machine markets, which explains why the Sholes & Glidden ended up looking uncannily like a sewing machine. In fact, two of Remington's mechanics, William Jenne and Jefferson Clough, had been assigned the job of making the Sholes & Glidden device suitable for producing on the sewing machine assembly line.

The type-writer diversification didn't pan out that well for Remington—the retail price was a whopping $125 ($1,800 in today's money), but they managed to sell 5,000 of them. Still, the Sholes & Glidden goes down as the first production line-manufactured typewriter, and it did sell better than any other machine on the market at the time.

The Sholes & Glidden typewriter (right) was the same boxy shape of the Sholes & Glidden sewing machine (left).

UNDONE BY A TYPEWRITER

In the famous 1924 Chicago murder trial of teenagers Nathan F. Leopold, Jr., and Richard Loeb, a typewriter was the clinching piece of evidence eliciting confessions from both Leopold and Loeb. A fourteen-year-old boy, Bobby Franks, had been brutally murdered, but the killers attempted to extract $10,000 in ransom money from the boy's wealthy father anyway. Neither of the killers needed the money, for Leopold was the son of a wealthy manufacturer and Loeb, the offspring of the vice president of Sears Roebuck & Co.

Experts determined the ransom note, supposedly composed by "George Johnson," was typed on a specific brand of portable typewriter. Leopold's classmates recalled that he had once owned a portable typewriter, and provided specimens of typewriting done on the machine. They were a match to the Johnson ransom letter. In his confession, Leopold led police to the spot where he'd dumped the machine off of a bridge. Although other damning pieces of material evidence also materialized, the typewriter (which, incidentally, had been stolen from a University of Michigan classmate) was regarded as the most important.

The young ages and wealthy background of both the perpetrators and the victim made for a sensational investigation and trial. The two killers were defended by Scopes' Monkey Trial defender Clarence Darrow, who successfully argued for long-term incarceration instead of the death penalty.

Sometimes endings are a mix of tragedy and happily-ever-after. During their time in prison, Loeb and Leopold met distinctly separate fates. After expressing intense remorse, Leopold was released from prison in 1958. During his years in prison, he had mastered 28 languages and fulfilled a vow to become a full time volunteer for various social causes. Loeb, however, was never released—he had been killed by his cellmate.

EARLY ADOPTER

Mark Twain quickly realized that the typewriter could be a writer's tool. It has been claimed (even by Twain himself) and widely accepted that *Tom Sawyer* was the first novel written on a typewriter. This fact is in dispute by historians, but regardless, the manuscript of *Life on the Mississippi,* written in 1883, proves that Twain was the first author to submit a typewritten manuscript to a publisher.

TINS OF THE TIMES

After George K. Anderson of Memphis, Tennessee, patented the typewriter ribbon on September 14, 1886, they came in colorful tin containers. Some from the Art Deco

period were quite pretty. Considered "poor relations" among antique collectors compared to tobacco, coffee and talc tins, ribbon tin collectors  are a relatively small group, but they make up for that with their enthusiasm.

IT TAKES A CERTAIN TYPE

The Underwood typewriter was the creation of German-American inventor Franz X. Wagner, but the name comes from John T. Underwood, an entrepreneur who bought the company early in its history. The Underwood family was already a successful manufacturer of ribbons and carbon paper under contract with Remington. When Remington decided to produce its own line of ribbons, Underwood retaliated by building typewriters designed by Wagner. Underwood quickly grabbed a large share of the market.

QUICK FACTS & TRIVIA

• Pellegrine Tarri invented carbon paper in 1808.

• The echoing sounds of typewriter keys striking paper in the opening scenes of the movie *All the President's Men* were created by layering gunshots and whiplashes over typewriter sounds. It was meant to illustrate the film's theme that words could be powerful weapons against official skullduggery.

• The Blickensderfer Co. made the first electric typewriter in 1902.

• In 1944, IBM designed the first typewriter with proportional spacing.

GO AHEAD, TRY THIS AT HOME

• *Typewriter* is one of the longest words that can be made using the letters on only one row of the standard typewriter keyboard.

• *Europe* is the only name for a continent that can be typed using a single row of letters.

• There are no vowels in the bottom row. The only word that can be typed using it is *Zzz* (to indicate sleeping).

• *Aftercataracts* (a condition that sometimes follows cataract surgery), *tesseradecades* and *tetrastearates* are the longest words that can be typed using only the left hand in touch-typing.

• *Deeded* is the longest word that can be typed using just one finger.

• *Johnny-jump-up* (the name of a flower) is the longest word that can be typed using only the fingers of the right hand.

ONE MAN'S JUNK

Most old gadgets, especially typewriters, have little antique value, but sometimes you can get lucky. Irene Martin sure did. While at a tag sale, Irene spied a typewriter with an ornate copper nameplate with "FORD" cast in the center.

Martin paid $50 for the machine, and assorted parts and attachments. As she carried it back to the car, her husband, Marty, joked, "What pile of junk did you buy now?"

It turned out the "pile of junk" was designed in 1895 by a New Yorker named E. A. Ford (no known relation to Henry Ford). Only 12 or so are known to exist. When the Martins put the typewriter up for auction on eBay, the winning bidder paid $15,500 for the prize. ☾

"I'm all in favor of keeping dangerous weapons out of the hands of fools. Let's start with typewriters." — Frank Lloyd Wright

172

Pot Shots

Privy's favorite privy shots. Send us yours! (See page 476.)

(Left) Sent in by BCOMP member Alan Levy, this was the outhouse that serviced his camping area in the snowy mountains of Australia's Broken Dam Hut. For perspective, Alan says there was about a meter of snow on top from a recent snowfall.

An open privy (right) in New Haven, Connecticut, in 1917. This photo was part of a Yale study on public health in the New Haven area. Nearly 400 privies were inspected by a Mr. O'Brian, Special Inspector. Two-thirds of them were exposed to rats, flies and other vermin.

This iron-shaped outhouse (above) is an engineered toilet serving dune shacks in Provincetown, Cape Cod, Massachusetts. Photo donated by Linda Coneen of Cape Cod & Islands Appraisal Group.

This permanent toilet (below, left), cemented on this desert island, serves a several-hundred-mile area in the South Pacific, including Suvarov Atoll, Anchorage Island and the Cook Islands group.

The privy opens into the sea below, where, at low tide, hermit crabs await what's dropped....

Photo courtesy of Matt Sponer. Thanks Matt!

Every Picture Tells a Story

George Washington: Unfinished Portrait by Gilbert Stuart (1755–1828)

• This is the most famous painting of George Washington, the one reproduced in schools, governmental offices and on the dollar bill. So why didn't Gilbert Stuart ever finish it?

• Artist Stuart was a deep-in-debt alcoholic. He'd painted Washington twice before. Each time, he secretly dashed off a dozen quick copies to sell before delivering the originals.

• Martha Washington, who commissioned this painting, was wise to Stuart's way. She got the artist to agree that he would surrender the painting the moment he finished it.

• George hated posing, but Stuart was able to get the general to stop scowling by discussing horses with him. Also, a new set of false teeth rounded out his face. Stuart quickly knew he had the best portrait ever painted of Washington. He started working on a plan to keep the painting long enough to make copies.

• This was his solution: he deliberately left it unfinished. Over time, he dashed off more than 200 replicas, calling them his "hundred dollar bills." Martha never got the original.

J. P. Morgan

STRAIGHT SHOOTER OR MAN OF LOW CALIBER?

Sometimes a company undergoes a dramatic change during its years of operation. That was true for the J. P. Morgan Company, as correspondents Eddie Fein and Billy Rubin found out.

J. P. MORGAN and Company and its subsidiary, the Morgan Guaranty Trust Company of New York, are respected institutions. They were founded by the man is still immortalized in their names, John Pierpont ("I owe the public nothing") Morgan, who amassed a mammoth fortune before he died in 1913. Not bad, considering that Morgan's first big financial deal—a wartime swindle against the U.S. government that involved a cache of dangerously defective guns—probably should have landed him in jail.

When America's Civil War broke out, 24-year-old Morgan successfully evaded serving in it. This was not too unusual; many sons of the affluent discovered that they could buy themselves out of the draft. It's also not surprising that the young financier would try to make a profit out of the war. But how he did it—well, judge for yourself.

Before the war started, the commander of the Army arsenal in New York City decided he wanted to unload some outdated and dangerous guns that were prone to backfire in such a way that they occasionally blew a soldier's thumb off. He arranged to sell them for scrap, cautioning potential buyers that they were "thoroughly unserviceable, obsolete, and dangerous."

Knowing that weapons of any kind would be a hot commodity in the upcoming

Young J. P. Morgan

war, Morgan teamed up with a speculator named Simon Stevens to bid $3.50 each on the guns.

After a Union loss at the Battle of Bull Run, the commander of the U.S. Army in St. Louis put out a desperate call for rifles. When Stevens and Morgan telegraphed him an offer of "5,000 new carbines in perfect condition" for $22 each, the commander accepted the offer, sight unseen. Morgan and Stevens didn't have the money to buy the guns from the New York arsenal, but with the Army's purchase order in hand as collateral, Morgan had no trouble arranging a loan.

So the U.S. Army bought its own unusable rifles from itself at a mark-up of about 500%. To save shipping costs, the partners even arranged to have the defective rifles shipped directly from the arsenal in New York to the one in St. Louis.

That took chutzpah—not to mention stupidity. The Army suddenly figured out what was happening and refused to pay for the rifles. Morgan sued. The government tried to settle out of court, offering $13.31 per rifle, but Morgan demanded full payment. When the case went to court,

the judge—incredibly—ruled in Morgan's favor, setting an unfortunate precedent for thousands of so-called "dead horse claims" in which shady suppliers were paid in full for dying animals, putrid meat, moldy bread, leaky ships, flimsy tents, dangerous weapons and breakaway shoes.

A year later, a congressional committee investigation recommended that the Army's purchasing procedures needed tightening up. It reported: "The government not only sold one day for $17,486 arms which it had agreed the day before to repurchase for $109,912—making it a loss to the United States of $92,426— but virtually furnished the money to pay itself the $17,486 which it received." The committee also ruled that Morgan and Stevens had knowingly conspired to defraud the U.S. government. Despite that, the partners were not prosecuted for the actions.

Did Morgan learn his lesson? You bet. He stopped dealing in weapons. Instead, he spent the rest of the war speculating in gold and currency. At one point in 1863 he and a partner, Edward Ketchum, quietly bought up a large amount of gold and then conspicuously shipped half of it overseas so that the price of their remaining stash went way up. They quickly made a profit of $160,000, but the effect was to suddenly and precipitously devalue the dollar in a time of national crisis. Ketchum later went to jail for other price-fixing schemes, but Morgan continued flying high.

After the war, decrying the "waste" inherent in free enterprise competition, he made it his life's work to stamp out "wasteful' competition wherever he could profitably do so, allowing him to set monopolistic rates he wanted.

Morgan was not the only robber baron of the time. Many of them through the haze of time are now thought of as philanthropists, like John D. Rockefeller and William Vanderbilt, thanks in no small part to the efforts of their P.R. folks at the time.

At the same time, these business lords came up with some business ideology that continues to live on today.

One of Rockefeller's philosophical contributions was "Silence is golden" (meaning "no explanation or is apology to the public is necessary"). William Vanderbilt weighed in with an infamously crass flip-off line, "The public be damned!"

A political cartoon depicting the Vanderbilt railroad monopoly

In context, Morgan, believe it or not, was considered a softy to some, despite his famous, "I owe the public nothing" line.

Until his death in 1913, Morgan created powerful monopolies and trusts in the fields of manufacturing, steel and railroads. His spirit, for better or worse, lives on. ☾

Cheers!

WHAT'S IN THIS DRINK, ANYWAY?

This one's easy: In Column A, we give you the names of some beverages. In Column B, we give you a list of main ingredients. Match them, and then (if you want) mix them.

1. Gin	a. Licorice & anise
2. Vermouth	b. Juniper berries
3. Rum	c. Honey
4. Whiskey	d. Wormwood
5. Sake	e. Flavored beer
6. Mead	f. Grapes
7. Champagne	g. Coffee
8. Vodka	h. Potatoes
9. Ouzo	i. Cactus
10. Absinthe	j. Barley, rye & corn
11. Kahlua	k. Molasses
12. Tequila	l. Rice
13. Zima	m. Wine with herbs

ANSWERS: 1b, 2m, 3k, 4j, 5l, 6c, 7f, 8h, 9a, 10d, 11g, 12i, 13e

The Corpse Eater

A Ghost Tale from Old Japan

In this story, another ancient Japanese legend collected by Lafcadio Hearn in 1903, a wandering priest discovers the horrifying secret of a small village.

MUSO KOKUSHI was a priest of the Zen sect. One day, when he was journeying alone, Muso lost his way in a remote mountain-district. For a long time he wandered helplessly; and he was beginning to despair of finding shelter for the night, when he saw, on the top of a hill lit by the last rays of the sun, one of those little hermitages called anjitsu, which are built for solitary priests. It seemed to be in ruinous condition; but he hastened to it eagerly, and found that it was inhabited by an aged priest, from whom he begged the favor of a night's lodging. This the old man harshly refused; but he directed Muso to a hamlet in a nearby valley where lodging and food could be obtained.

Muso found his way to the hamlet and he was kindly received at the village leader's dwelling. Forty or fifty persons were assembled in the principal apartment, but Muso was shown into a separate room and supplied with food and bedding. Being very tired, he lay down to rest, but a little before midnight he was awakened by loud weeping in the next apartment. Soon, the sliding-screens were gently opened and a young man carrying a lantern respectfully saluted him.

"Reverent sir," he began, "it is my painful duty to tell you that I am now the head of this house. Yesterday I was only the eldest son. But when you came here, tired as you were, we did

not wish that you should feel embarrassed in any way: therefore we did not tell you that father had died only a few hours
before. The people assembled here are going to another village,
about three miles off—for by our custom, we make the proper
offerings and prayers, then we leave the corpse alone. No one
may remain in this village during the night after a death has
taken place, because strange things always happen, so we think
that it will be better for you to come away with us. But perhaps,
as you are a priest, you have no fear of demons or evil spirits. If
so, you will be very welcome to use our poor house. However, I
must tell you that nobody, except a priest, would dare to remain here tonight."

Muso responded: "For your kind intention and your generous hospitality I am deeply grateful. But I am sorry that you
did not tell me of your father's death when I arrived, so I could
have done my duty as a priest before your departure. As it is, I
shall perform the service after you have gone away; and I shall
stay by the body until morning. I am not afraid of ghosts or
demons, so please feel no anxiety on my account."

The young man expressed his gratitude in fitting words. Then
the assembled villagers came to thank him, after which the
master of the house spoke. "Now, reverent sir, much as we
regret to leave you alone, we must bid you farewell. We beg,
kind sir, that you will take every care. And if you happen to
hear or see anything strange, please tell us when we return in
the morning."

All then left the priest, who went to the room where the dead
body was lying. The usual offerings had been set before the
corpse; and a small lamp was burning. The priest performed
the funeral ceremonies, after which he entered into meditation.
So meditating he remained through several silent hours. But,
when the hush of the night was at its deepest, there noiselessly
entered a Shape, vague and vast; and in the same moment
Muso found himself without power to move or speak. He
watched the Shape lift the corpse, as with hands, and devour it
more quickly than a cat devours a rat: beginning at the head,
and eating everything—the hair and the bones and even the
shroud. And the monstrous Thing, having thus consumed the
body, turned to the offerings, and ate them also. Then it went
away, as mysteriously as it had come.

When the villagers returned next morning, they found the priest awaiting them at the door of the dwelling. All in turn saluted him; and when they looked about the room, no one expressed any surprise at the disappearance of the corpse and the offerings. "Reverent sir," said the master of the house, "you have probably seen unpleasant things during the night. All of us were anxious about you. But now we are very happy to find you alive and unharmed. Gladly we would have stayed with you, but whenever the village law has been broken, some great misfortune has followed. Whenever it was obeyed, the corpse and the offerings disappear during our absence. Perhaps you have seen the cause."

Then Muso told of the dim and awful Shape that had entered the death-chamber to devour the body. No person seemed to be surprised by his narration; and the master of the house said: "What you have told us, reverent sir, agrees with what has been said about this matter from ancient time."

"Does not the priest on the hill sometimes perform the funeral service for your dead?" asked Muso.

"What priest?" the young man asked.

"The priest who yesterday evening directed me to this village," answered Muso. "I called at his anjitsu on the hill yonder. He refused me lodging, but told me the way here."

The listeners looked at each other in astonishment; and the master of the house said: "Reverent sir, there is no priest and there is no anjitsu on the hill. For the time of many generations there has not been any resident-priest in this neighborhood."

Muso said nothing more on the subject; for it was evident that his kind hosts supposed him to have been deluded by some goblin. But after bidding them farewell, he decided to look again for the hermitage on the hill. He found the anjitsu without any difficulty; and, this time, its aged occupant invited him to enter. When he had done so, the hermit humbly bowed down before him, exclaiming: "Ah! I am very much ashamed! I am exceedingly ashamed!"

"You need not be ashamed for having refused me shelter," said Muso. "You directed me to a village where I was very kindly treated, and I thank you for that favor."

"I can give no man shelter," the recluse said, "and it is not for the refusal that I am ashamed. I am ashamed only that you should have seen me in my real shape—for it was I who devoured the corpse and the offerings last night before your eyes. Know, reverent sir, that I am a jikininki, an eater of human flesh. Have pity upon me, and suffer me to confess the secret fault by which I became reduced to this condition.

"A long, long time ago, I was a priest in this desolate region. There was no other priest for many miles around, so the bodies of the mountain-folk who died were brought here, sometimes from great distances, in order that I might repeat over them the holy service. But I repeated the service and performed the rites only as a matter of business—I thought only of the food and the clothes that my sacred profession enabled me to gain. And because of this selfish impiety I was reborn, immediately after my death, into the state of a jikininki. Since then I have been obliged to feed upon the corpses of the people who die in this district: every one of them I must devour in the way that you saw last night. Now, reverent sir, let me beseech you to perform a cleansing ritual for me: help me by your prayers, I beg you, so that I may escape from this horrible state of existence."

When the hermit uttered this prayer he disappeared; and the hermitage also at the same instant. And Muso Kokushi found himself kneeling alone in the high grass, beside an ancient and moss-grown tomb, which seemed to be that of a priest. ☾

MARK TWAIN WRITES TO THE GAS COMPANY

Hartfield, February 12, 1891

Dear Sirs;

Some day you will move me almost to the verge of irritation by your chuckle-headed God-damned fashion of shutting your Goddamned gas off without givng any notice to your Goddamned parishioners. Several times you have come within an ace of smothering half of this household in their beds and blowing up the other half by this idiotic, not to say criminal, custom of yours. And it has happened again to-day. Haven't you a telephone?

Yours,
S. L. Clemens

Stately Knowledge

12 Reasons Why Ya Gotta Love Washington

Who needs more reasons to love the state of Washington? Well, in case you do, here are a dozen of our favorites.

1 Our favorite Washingtonian? Roxann Rose of Pullman, Washington, who used a hula hoop for 90 hours in a marathon display of stamina on April 2–6, 1987.

2 Or, if you prefer, businessman and pilot Kenneth Arnold, who said he was flying a small plane over Washington's Cascade Mountains and saw nine circular objects flying in formation at hyper-fast speed. He told reporters that the mysterious objects "flew like a saucer would if you skipped it across water." The reporters reported that Arnold had seen "flying saucers" and the name stuck.

3 Here's a place you might not want to stay. Kitsap County, Washington, was originally called Slaughter County, and the first hotel there was called the Slaughter House. Another place to avoid? Quillayute, Washington. It's the wettest city in the United States.

4 Washington is the only state to be named after a president. When the state was being considered for statehood, the people wanted to name it "Columbia." However, the United States Congress was afraid there'd be confusion with the new District of Columbia,

so they made them change it to Washington. Only one problem, the District of Columbia became more popularly known as Washington D.C., so the state was *still* confused with the District. They would've done better sticking with Columbia.

5 You thought it was just apples and cherries? Heck no! Washington also leads the nation in producing red raspberries, spearmint oil, dry peas, lentils, pears and hops—the stuff that beer's made from.

Ice-cream, hoops, and hops. It's a Washington thing.

6 King County, Washington, was originally named after William R. King, who was Franklin Pierce's vice president. In 1986, it was named King County *again*. The only difference was that this time, the name honored Martin Luther King, Jr.

7 The longest floating bridge in the world is the Evergreen Point Bridge, connecting Seattle and Medina across Lake Washington.

8 Firsts and oldest: Not only does Seattle hold the title of the first city to open a revolving restaurant (the Space Needle), but Olympia boasts the Dairy Queen that was the site of the first soft-serve ice cream machine ever. And Zillah, Washington, has the oldest still-operating gas station.

9 Father's Day was originated by Sonora Louise Smart Dodd, a woman with too many names who hailed from Spokane, Washington. It was first celebrated on June 19, 1910.

10 Under the Aurora Bridge in Seattle lives a troll. Well, not a real one, but huge one created out of concrete by four Seattle artists.

11 Next stop, the corner of Bing and Maraschino! There's a city named George, Washington. That's funny enough, but another odd thing is that it has streets named after all the different kinds of cherries.

12 Washington is the smallest state west of the Mississippi River, but it's larger than any state east of the Mississippi River. ☾

Tricky Dick

THE LOWDOWN ON RICHARD NIXON

Richard Milhous Nixon, the 37th President of the United States, was the second president to seriously risk impeachment and the first to actually resign from office.

• Richard Nixon was a mass of contradictions: He was raised a pacifist Quaker, yet became the U.S. president who ordered more bombs dropped than any man in history. He made a career out of the fear of communism, yet was the first to try rapprochement with China. He hated how he appeared on TV, yet, apparently, won because of it. He managed to get re-elected in 1972 by a landslide, yet before his death he was rated among the least popular politicians in recent history.

• His earliest memory was falling out of a horse-driven buggy that his mother was driving, splitting his scalp in a long cut. From that point until his death he combed his hair straight back to hide the scar, even "when the vogue of parting hair on the left side came along," he said regretfully in a later interview.

• In first grade, his mother made a point of telling his teacher, "Never call him Dick—I named him Richard." Every day he wore a freshly starched white shirt with a black bow tie and knee pants, and his teacher was quoted as saying later that she could not remember him ever getting dirty. He took great pains in brushing his teeth, and before he left for school asked his mother to smell his breath to make sure he would not offend anyone on the bus. He didn't like to ride the school bus, saying the other children smelled bad.

• He was a very solemn child who rarely ever smiled, and nobody can recall him ever really laughing. When the older boys made fun of him, Nixon cried bitterly. "I was the biggest crybaby in Yorba Linda," he admitted decades later. "My dad could hear me even with the tractor running."

• He was uncoordinated, and too small for football, but his father wanted him to play so that nobody would think Richard effeminate.

• For three summers Richard was a barker at the local fair. He was quite good at it.

• His father lent him the money for his years at law school, but Richard had to pay back every penny. At school, Nixon lead a monastic life in an abandoned tool shed in a heavily wooded area near the campus. It was an eight-by-twelve-foot shed, lined with corrugated cardboard for warmth. He did not date any girls for the entire three years. His nickname was "Gloomy Gus."

• In a foreshadowing of his future, he once broke into the dean's office to get an advance look at the grades.

• After he graduated and passed the bar exam, he bungled his first court case in a way that looked as if he were unethically trying to gain a financial advantage. The case wound up costing the firm $4,800 in an out-of-court settlement. In the course of the proceedings, he was threatened with disbarment by a judge, who said, "Mr. Nixon, I have serious doubts whether you have the ethical qualifications to practice law in the state of California. I am seriously thinking of turning this matter over to the Bar Association." Nixon thought of abandoning the United States and setting up a law practice in Havana, Cuba. He traveled there to check out the possibilities before World War II interrupted his law career.

• After the war, Nixon attempted to pass himself off as a veteran who had seen actual combat while stationed on Green Island in the Pacific. There's more data available on Nixon's poker playing—he made a great deal of money—than on any other single aspect of his war experience. Nixon also opened "Nixon's Snack Shack" near the airstrip, where SCAT pilots and their crews were able to get basic food, munchies and liquor.

• After the war, he considered going back to practicing law. Instead, he decided to become a politician. Through a series of outrageous, mean-spirited, but brilliantly opportunistic campaigns, he made a successful career of accusing opponents of being communists. He rose quickly in California politics and ended up in the House of Representatives, where he served on the House UnAmerican Activities Committee—a red-hunting group of dangerous buffoons, including proudly anti-Semitic John Rankin of Mississippi and John Wood, an active member of the Ku Klux Klan. "It was," said George Reedy, covering the committee for United Press, "the worst collection of people that have ever been assembled in the entire history of American politics." With publicity from this job, during an era of anti-communist hysteria, Nixon was soon elected to the Senate in time to make a name for himself on Joseph McCarthy's witch-hunts, and then became the premiere candidate for vice president, placating the extreme right wing which was unhappy with comparatively moderate Dwight Eisenhower.

• Long before Watergate, Nixon counseled a friend,

"You don't know how to lie. If you can't lie, you'll never go anywhere."

• Truman called Nixon "a shifty-eyed goddamn liar." Nixon was for the war in Korea, until it became unpopular. Then he blamed Truman for incurring American casualties.

• In 1958, Nixon traveled to Hong Kong and met Marianna Liu, a tour guide. They became inseparable and there were rumors of an affair—rumors that eventually ended up in J. Edgar Hoover's personal files. It became one of the bits of information that Hoover later used to keep his job when Nixon was threatening to replace him.

• Nixon had a terrible temper and a salty vocabulary, which he almost always succeeded in keeping under control in public. Once though, during the 1960 campaign, he was sitting in the back seat behind his aide, Air Force Maj. Don Hughes, during a long car ride between cities. Frustrated and impatient, Nixon suddenly went into a tantrum, swearing and repeatedly kicking the back of Hughes's seat with both feet, refusing to stop. Hughes had the car stopped and got out to walk until aides got Nixon quieted down again.

• After a meeting with a group of young college editors at Cornell University who had thrown some tough questions at him, he screamed at his aide, Ted Rogers, "You son of a bitch, you tried to destroy me in front of thirty million people!"

• After losing the 1962 race for California governor and telling the press that they "won't have Nixon to kick around any more," he joined the firm of Mudge, Stern, Baldwin and Todd and signed on Pepsi, long a backer of GOP causes.

• A "new Nixon" came back in 1968 and got elected to the presidency.

• Nixon was a bit strange, even before the pressures of the Watergate investigations reportedly drove him near to the brink of paranoia and insanity. He instructed the members of the White House staff not to talk to him or to his wife, even when greeted by them. He would not let the *Washington Post* be delivered to his home, so his teenage daughters wouldn't see the political cartoons about him.

• Nixon's brother, Donald, was suspected to have had shady business dealings. Because journalist Tom Braden questioned Donald's practices, Nixon had Braden audited by the IRS every year he was in the White House. To avoid further embarrassments, though, Nixon put Donald under surveillance. There was evidence that the Watergate break-in was an attempt to find out what the Democrats knew about his brother's questionable business dealings.

• Nixon authorized secret investigations into the habits of his political rivals and others on his "enemies list." He ordered surveillance on Edward Kennedy, telling his chief of staff Bob Haldeman, "Catch him in the sack with one of his babes." However, when his own conduct was questioned, he answered indignantly, "A candidate's personal life and that of his family are not fair subjects for discussion unless they somehow bear directly on his qualifications for office." ❦

How They Work
Hidden Stories Behind Gadgets We Love

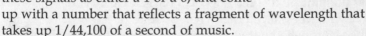

From DVDs to inkjet printers, there's an explanation behind
everything, as Brian Marshall tells us in this piece.

HOW DOES A CD PLAY MUSIC?

The "groove" on a compact disc isn't really a groove, but a path
of microscopic bumps stretched over a 3 mile path. The bumps
reflect light from a laser beam differently
than the flat parts do, shining back into a
sensor that interprets the flashing reflec-
tions as shining either "on" or "off." The
electronics of your CD player interpret
these signals as either a 1 or a 0, and come
up with a number that reflects a fragment of wavelength that
takes up 1/44,100 of a second of music.

A CD player varies its speed as it plays, so that the speed of
the bumps below stays constant. Beginning at the disc's inside
groove, the CD spins at 500 revolutions per minute (RPM) and
gradually slows to 200 RPM as the laser beam approaches the
outside edge.

HOW DO THEY GET MORE ON A DVD THAN ON A CD?

Part of the solution was making the data bumps smaller and

jamming them closer together, making the
"groove" of a DVD 7.5 miles long, more than
twice what you get on a CD. But wait, there's
more. The designers managed to double that
capacity to 15 miles per side, because the DVD
uses a sandwich of two different levels of

bumps. Like a CD, the DVD has a reflective aluminum base behind the inner layer. However, on top of that is a semi-reflective gold layer, also containing data bumps. The result is that the laser can read the top layer of bumps, then shine through it and read the inner layer, too. The cumulative effect is that a typical DVD stores 7.5 gigabytes of information.

HOW DOES A GPS FIGURE OUT WHERE YOU ARE?
A Global Positioning System (GPS) receiver is a pretty cool little 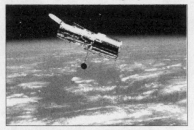 gadget. There are 24 GPS satellites orbiting the Earth, so that wherever you are in the world, your GPS receiver can pick up at least four of them. A cluster of three satellites is the bare minimum for locating your latitude and longitude, but if you also want to know your altitude, you need a fourth one as well.

Each satellite broadcasts an identifying signal and a timing code that allows your GPS to measure the time it took the signal to get there, and thereby figure out how far away the satellite is. By comparing the distance from several satellites, your GPS can tell exactly where you are (give or take a few feet).

HOW DO INKJET PRINTERS SPRAY LETTERS SO PRECISELY?
Have you ever noticed that when bubbles pop, a little of the liquid gets propelled outward? Sure you have—think of the misty feeling you get when you put your nose up to ginger ale.

Popping bubbles inspired the inkjet printer. Its designers wanted to be able to propel microscopic dots of ink quickly and accurately onto a piece of paper without actually touching it. A tiny amount of ink waits inside each nozzle, and as the print head jerks quickly along the page (so quickly that it seems like a continuous motion), jolts of electricity heat up a resistor in the nozzle. This heat instantaneously boils the ink, vaporizing it into a bubble and launching ink from the print head to dot neatly onto the surface of the paper. How small are these neat little splatters? A bubble jet print head typically has 300 to 600 microscopic nozzles that fire ink simultaneously onto the page. It can take dozens of them, precisely fired, to make up a single letter on the page.

HOW ABOUT A LASER PRINTER?

Inside the printer is a large metal roller (called the "photoreceptive drum"). As it rotates past an electrified wire ("the corona"), the surface of the drum gets a positive electrical charge.

Next, the computer guides a laser beam that scans text and images onto the photoreceptive drum. Metal hit by the laser gets a negative electrical charge. The toner powder, a mix of positively charged plastic and pigment dust, sticks to the parts of the drum zapped by the laser, but is repelled from the parts of the drum that carry the negatively charged image, so that the drum looks like a mirror image of the page being printed.

But not for long, because the drum immediately makes contact with the paper. An electric wire under the paper (the "transfer release corona") zaps the paper with negative electricity, which pulls the powdery pattern off the roller and onto the page.

The ink, held by gravity, gets melted onto the paper with the "fuser," a pair of hot metal rollers. Which is why laser-printed paper comes out toasty warm.

WHY DOES A MICROWAVE OVEN HEAT FOOD, BUT NOT PLASTIC?

Microwaves are radio waves that have a very high frequency, which makes them very short (that's why the *micro* is in microwave). On your radio dial, you'd hear your microwave oven broadcasting at 2500 megahertz, if your radio dial actually went that high. (It doesn't—108 megahertz is the highest a standard radio picks up.) Microwaves have a powerful effect on water molecules, twisting them back and forth rapidly. As they rub against each other, the molecules heat up rapidly from the friction. Luckily, nearly all foods have at least a little moisture in them—otherwise they wouldn't heat up. Which explains why the plastic doesn't heat up, while the frozen lasagna does. €

Judged by Its Cover

A BOOKSHELF FULL OF STRANGE BOOKS

Can you tell a book by its title? If so, these have got to be some of the most fascinating books on the shelves, indeed. Gleaned from *Bizarre Books* by Russell Ash and Brian Lake (St. Martin's, 1985).

Queer Shipmates—Archibald Bruce Campbell (1962)

The Gay Boys of Old Yale!—John Denison Vose (1869)

The History of the Self-Winding Watch (1770–1931)—Alfred Chapuis & Eugene Jaquet (1952)

The Ups & Downs of Lady Di—Annette Lyster (1907)

Scouts in Bondage—Geoffrey Prout (1930)

The Onion Maggot—Arthur L. Lovett (1923)

Harnessing the Earthworm—Thomas J. Barrett (1949)

100 Proofs That the Earth Is Not a Globe!—W. Carpenter (1871)

How to Abandon Ship—Phil Richards & John Banigan (1942)

Manhole Covers of Los Angeles—Robert & Mimi Melnick (1974)

A Toddler's Guide to the Rubber Industry—D. Lowe (1947)

Who's Who in Cocker Spaniels—Marion Mangrum (1944)

Cool It or Lose It: Dale Evans Rogers Raps with Youth—Dale Evans Rogers (1971)

Constipation & Our Civilization—James C. Thomson (1943)

Animals as Criminals—J. Brand (1896)

Swine Judging for Beginners—Joel Simmons Coffey (1915)

The Romance of Proctology—Charles Elton Blanchard (1938)

How to Be Plump—Thomas Cation Duncan (1878)

!!!—George H. Hepworth (1881)

Whitewash

HOW COLGATE'S BLACKFACE TURNED RED

Here's an embarrassing bit of Colgate history the company would rather just forget.

DARLIE TOOTHPASTE is a popular brand in much of Asia. Its dark secret is that it used to be called Darkie, complete with a stereotyped logo of a minstrel man. Apparently the company's founder had come to the United States in the 1920s and seen Al Jolson in his blackface show, and had been impressed with how white Jolson's teeth looked.

Stereotypes of this sort were not unusual before World War II. What was unusual about Darkie was that its racist name and logo were still intact in 1985, when Colgate bought the brand from Hong Kong's Hawley & Hazel Chemical Company.

Here's where the story gets a little twisted. According to Alecia Swasy in her book *Soap Opera,* Colgate's arch-rival Procter & Gamble learned about the sale and immediately went to work to use it to their advantage. Both companies were releasing a tartar-control formula that year, and P&G was happy to have the opportunity to portray its rival as racist. It hired a public relations firm to surreptitiously slip information to activists and newspapers about Colgate's disreputable Asian brand.

The strategy worked. There was a storm of uproar: stories and editorials in major newspapers, threats of boycotts and even Eddie Murphy expressing his outrage on David Letterman. Colgate was unfairly attacked for a brand it had just purchased; however, the attacks became more and more justified as the toothpaste giant dragged its feet on changing the brand, fearing a loss of business. Finally, nearly four years later,

Before and After shots

it announced that it was changing the name to Darlie and making the man on the package an abstraction of indeterminate race.

The name change placated Western critics, who pointed out that the toothpaste actually sold better after the name change. What they didn't know, and apparently still don't, is that only the English was changed. The Cantonese name ("Haak Yahn Nga Gou") stayed the same, and the Chinese-language ads reassured users that, despite a cosmetic change to placate those inscrutable Westerners, "Black Man Toothpaste is still Black Man Toothpaste."

WHAT'S IN A NAME?

One of the nice things about the toothpaste industry is that there are still some local brands out there, despite the best efforts of Colgate, Lever and Procter & Gamble to make every country dance to the tune of Crest and Pepsodent.

The healthiest indigenous industry seems to be in Asia. Shanghai Toothpaste Company is one such manufacturer. Besides a brand called Evafresh, they've got White Jade ("Your teeth will be health and no usual oral disease can occur....It does no harm to animal, it for smok-

ers quite well") and Bulb Poll brand for children ("With fresh melon flavour...brushing teeth would be of interest for children and they can easily get into good habits"). The significance of the names? Nobody seems to know. Supirivicky brand, an herbal toothpaste developed in Ceylon, promises to relieve "obnoxious odours, spongy gums, cough, vomiting, gripe,

colic, and paralysis of tounge." (Original spelling left intact.)

Heibao toothpaste from Hong Kong goes several steps beyond that. For a mere $96 per tube, Heibao promises an even more profound rejuvenation: "You will find your hair loss to be reduced by up to 90%. You will look younger, move younger and feel younger TEN to FIFTEEN years back because your hair becomes darker (as your good old days) and thicker and most important of all, your organic systems will function at their best!...Suitable for all ages, sex and race without any bad side effect."

Pasta Medicinal Couto is "a completely natural toothpaste" from Portugal. However, given the historical record of completely natural toothpastes from Portugal (see page 77), we're a little cautious, despite the company's assurance that this one is made from plant extracts.

Other brands of note include Pooneh and Nassim from Iran, Babool and Karma from India, and Vademecuum

from Sweden. None of these are particularly weird, but we like the names.

Finally, coming full circle back to the purely tasteless, Taiwan has a brand that's a real winner called White Men Toothpaste.

OTHER FISH IN THE SEA

"Bill's Best Places," a personal Web site, that critiques "Bill's" favorite places to visit, reports as follows:

There you are, in the South Pacific, diving in sandy-bottomed, coral-ringed waters, just off the island nation of Fiji. The water is teeming with life—some of it benign, some of it deadly, all of it beautiful. You head for a tiny crevice where a pair of cleaner shrimp live and you dive down for a closer look. You remove your mouthpiece and open your mouth wide. A shrimp spies your pearly teeth and comes over for a closer look. You hold still. It pokes and prods between them, expertly removing bits of food and plaque. This is no joke—you really can find shrimp that will clean your teeth, on the ship, Nai'a in Fiji....

D.D.S. ON 35MM

They're only there to help you keep your gums and teeth healthy, but dentists don't get much respect in movies—they're portrayed, often as not, as sadists and sometimes worse (nitrous oxide abusers, unrepentant Nazis, that sort of thing). We'll show you what we mean:

- *Little Shop of Horrors* (1960, musical; 1986, movie): Dentist as drug-abusing, woman-abusing, laughing gas sniffer who deserves to be fed to a large mutant carnivorous plant. In the movie, the dentist was played by a maniacal Steve Martin.

- *The Dentist* (1932): The first movie of this name was a short one, and featured comedian W. C. fields as a  bumbling, sadistic tooth extractor. (Available in a collection of five short features called *A Fifth of Fields*.)

- *The Dentist* (1996): A campy horror film in which a deranged dentist goes on a drilling spree.

- *The Marathon Man* (1976): Sadistic Nazi dentist drills excruciatingly through Dustin Hoffman's front tooth.

- *Eversmile, New Jersey* (1989): This one is unusual—about a wacky traveling dentist who preaches the benefits of dental health. ☾

Oral Advice

Dentists are now recommending this brushing method, to be used after flossing: Place the toothbrush at the gums at a 45-degree angle. Brush down and away to remove plaque from gum and tooth. Brush each tooth individually, inside and out, then brush chewing surfaces horizontally.

But be aware. Two out of three people brush too hard, says Dr. Trucia Drommond of Chicago, causing damage to gums and teeth. His prescription? Soft bristles, a loose grip between thumb and forefinger, just a smidgen of toothpaste and 2–5 minutes of oh-so-gentle caressing instead of 1 minute of scrubbing.

Modern Myth

"Spontaneous Human Combustion"

For centuries, people have marveled at mysterious stories of victims apparently going up in flame with nothing else burning in the room. We hate to ruin a good story, but...

SPONTANEOUS COMBUSTION stories of people mysteriously going up in flames have appeared in legend, fiction and even Temperance tracts. Novelist Frederick Marryat in *Jacob Faithful* (1834) wrote about a character's disreputable mother who "perished in that very peculiar and dreadful manner, which does sometimes occur to those who indulge in an immoderate use of spirituous liquors.... She perished from what is termed spontaneous combustion, an inflammation of the gases generated from the spirits absorbed into the system."

Herman Melville recounted an incident in *Redburn* (1849) in which a drunken sailor spontaneously combusts in front of his shipmates. And in *Bleak House* (1853) Charles Dickens wrote a gruesome description of drunkard Mr. Krook's fiery demise:

"There is a smouldering, suffocating, vapour in the room and a dark, greasy coating on the walls and ceiling....Here is a small burnt patch of flooring; here is the tinder from a little bundle of burnt paper, but not so light as usual, seeming to be steeped in something; and here is—is it a charred log of wood

Mr. Krook's fiery demise in *Bleak House*

197

> sprinkled with white ashes, or is it coal? Oh, horror, he is here! Call
> the death by any name, it is inborn, inbred, engendered in the corrupt-
> ed humours of the vicious body itself—Spontaneous Combustion."

Most 19th-century stories blamed alcohol in the body for a victim going up in flames. (Not surprisingly, the Temperance movement also often played up this angle in its literature.) Strangely enough, that's a recurring theme in more modern stories as well. Purported victims of spontaneous combustion are typically heavy drinkers (or sedative users), smokers, overweight, and elderly. They're found thoroughly burned, sometimes with a part of their body—for example, a foot or hand—strangely unscathed. Oftentimes nearby furnishings remain unburnt, and a peculiar greasy soot covers walls and ceiling.

Scientists have looked into the phenomenon, and have found that abusers of alcohol, tobacco and other drugs are disproportionately victims of the phenomenon. But not for the reasons that 19th-century chroniclers put forth.

One scientist dressed dead pigs in night clothes and placed them in chairs, beds and couches. He managed to replicate the effect, common to most "spontaneous combustion" stories, of burning with a hot, greasy fire that consumed flesh and bones without burning nearby combustibles.

Another scientist went through 200 mysterious cases and did not find one that couldn't be explained by more likely causes. Here's what he found in common for a large number of the cases: A smoker alone at home becomes unconscious from alcohol, sleeping pills, or a heart attack, and drops a cigarette. It begins smoldering in the smoker's clothes and eventually starts them on fire. The fat of the person, deeply unconscious, begins melting and gets wicked into the clothes like wax from a candle. This wicking keeps the clothes from burning away, yet burns with a continuous, smoky flame. Like a candle, the flame is contained and controlled. The heat flows upward toward the ceiling, covering it with a greasy soot, but keeping the flame from spreading.

So, the good news is that research shows no evidence that "spontaneous human combustion" has ever really happened. If you're afraid of ending your life in that way, you can stop worrying... and instead strive to lose weight, drink in moderation and avoid smoking. ☾

Mascot Miracles
HOW THE BUNNY SAVED ENERGIZER'S BATTERY

He's a shades-wearing, drum-beating, hot pink cultural icon that almost never was. Here's his story.

DID YOU KNOW that the Eveready battery line is the oldest in existence? In 1896, the National Carbon Company produced the first commercially marketed dry-cell battery. Two years later, the American Electric Novelty and Manufacturing Corporation produced a novelty flashlight and called it the "Eveready." When the two companies merged and became the Union Carbide Corporation, it decided to expand the Eveready name to the battery line as well.

Years later, Union Carbide decided to market a line of alkaline batteries. They decided that the alkalines needed to be differentiated from their line of normal batteries, so they downplayed the Eveready name and came up with a new one, the "Energizer." But Union Carbide's advertising was uninspired, bordering on awful: In one ad, tough-guy actor Robert Conrad dared us to commit assault on a battery by knocking it off his shoulder; in another, Olympic star Mary Lou Retton compared her high-energy routines to high-energy Energizers.

FROM BAD TO WORSE

In 1986, cereal and pet food company Ralston-Purina bought the Eveready line from Union Carbide. Ralston had a good reputation for marketing its products well. On the other hand, it never tried to sell a battery before. It made a huge mistake.

Its name was Jacko. Mark "Jacko" Jackson, to be exact— a wildly popular Australian Rules Football player. If the ads with Conrad and Retton were mediocre, though, Jacko's were horrible. Even though his commercials were a big hit Down Under, Americans found him loud and uncouth; he grated on everybody's nerves. The company received a dozen hate letters a day. Sales started dropping. Eveready stuck with Jacko for a year, even ludicrously trying to soften his obnoxious image with a sweater and easy chair, but it was a disaster.

Meanwhile, Duracell started a line of commercials that implied that its alkaline batteries lasted longer than those of its main competitor, Eveready. A viewer had to pay close attention to understand that the ads were comparing Duracell with Eveready's "ordinary" (carbon-zinc) batteries, not its alkalines. The commercials featured a group of battery-operated toys, each of them grinding to a stop until only the Duracell toy was still running.

WHEN OPPORTUNITY KNOCKS

Energizer decided to hit back. Their ad agency, D. D. B. Needham, set up a battalion of stupid-looking mechanical bunnies playing cymbals, looking similar to those in the Duracell ads. But the demonstration was interrupted by the ultra-cool pink Energizer Bunny wearing shades and playing a marching-band bass drum. The voice-over complained that Duracell had "never even invited us to your party."

It was an attention-getting spot, but what to do next resulted in "creative differences" between the agency and client. "We said, 'We think there's a campaign idea here. Let's do more of these,'" Eveready CEO J. Patrick Mulcahy told *Advertising*

The Energizer Bunny

Age. "But Needham said, 'We don't think so. We don't think we can campaign this out. We think it's a one-shot deal, a limited tactical vehicle. We should put it on the air for a while and then go back to something else.'"

The client, of course, is always right. Eveready went shopping for a new agency. In February 1989, they found Chiat/Day/Mojo, which came up with the electrifying jolt Eveready was looking for. "We kind of started the way we always do, by saying 'Let's assume people don't like advertising, and they have the means to zap us with their remote control,'" said C/D/M vice president Dick Sittig in an interview in *AdWeek.* "Given that, what are you going to do to grab people's attention for 30 seconds? We decided that since the battery business is kind of a low interest category, we'd have to do something pretty out there to get people's attention. The main idea is 'How do you demonstrate long-lasting batteries?' Our notion was that you couldn't do it in just one thirty-second

Keeps going...

spot, so that's where we came up with our idea."

SERIAL BUNNY STRIKES AGAIN, AND AGAIN, AND AGAIN....

C/D/M decided to begin with the spot that Needham had done, but with a different ending. In the new commercial, the bunny runs amok and escapes from the studio. "It was just a simple idea based around the fact that the Energizer keeps going and going," said C/D/M CEO Bob Kuperman. "So it became the unstoppable bunny. And we thought not only will it escape from the commercial that we had done for it, but it would continue going through other commercials for other products. From there we decided to actually use the other commercial forms that we've all grown up with. The key was to make them believable and have people immediately see them as part of the real world of commercials. It had to be instantly recognizable as a coffee or nasal spray commercial."

The agency did extensive research on different types of

...and going...

commercials in order to stay true to the genre of each. Staff members found the components of each type of commercial that made them unique and distinctive: a certain editing rhythm, type of actor, copy and delivery style, lighting, film vs. video and so on. The hard part for the directors, they discovered, was trying to exactly emulate the style they were making fun of and not add any of their own individual stylistic flourishes.

A SMASHING SUCCESS

The cleverness of the approach got a lot of positive attention from the press and the people sitting on their couches. And there was another element as well: "People would rather not see those commercials anyway," said Sittig. "That's what makes the bunny a hero. If he interrupts your favorite commercial, you don't like him. But if he interrupts something you don't like, he's a hero."

HOP, HOP, AND AWAY!

The Energizer Bunny has another claim to fame. He's the tallest hot air balloon in the world, the company claims. The Energizer "Hot Hare Balloon" is 15 feet taller than the Statue of Liberty.

So what, exactly, are his other measurements?

• **Ears.** The Hot Hare's ears are about the size of the average hot air balloon, which equals the height of one of the presidents' faces on Mt. Rushmore.

• **Glasses.** A bunny this cool demands a monstrously cool set of glasses. This pair measures 32 feet across.

• **Drum.** His drum's about 45 feet in diameter, and 20 feet wide.

• **Nose.** His shnoz is 16 feet wide.

• **Tail.** His tail measures 20 feet across.

• **Shoe Size.** This Hot Hare wears a 98 EEEEE shoe size.

The company says he's so big, 550,000,000 double-A batteries could fit inside. On the outside, he took 5,000 yards of 60-foot-wide material, and 84 miles of thread. €

...and going...

Triumph of the Egg
A Tale Both Hardboiled & Scrambled

Eggs embodied the dreams of a family...and end up being its downfall in this funny yet touching story by Sherwood Anderson, author of *Winesburg, Ohio.*

MY FATHER WAS, I am sure, intended by nature to be a cheerful, kindly man. Until he was 34 years old he worked as a farmhand near Bidwell, Ohio. He on Saturday evenings drove into town to spend a few hours in social intercourse with other farmhands. Songs were sung and glasses thumped on the bar. At ten o'clock father drove home and went to bed, quite happy in his position in life. He had at that time no notion of trying to rise in the world.

It was in the spring of his thirty-fifth year that father married my mother, then a country schoolteacher, and in the following spring I came wriggling and crying into the world. Something happened to the two people. The American passion for getting up in the world took possession of them.

It may have been that mother was responsible. Being a school-teacher she had no doubt read of how Garfield, Lincoln, and other Americans rose from poverty to greatness, and dreamed that I would someday rule men and cities. She induced father to give up his place as a farmhand and embark on an independent enterprise of his own. For herself she wanted nothing. For father and myself she was incurably ambitious.

The first venture turned out badly. They rented ten acres of poor stony land and launched into chicken raising. I grew into boyhood on the place and got my first impressions of life there. If I am a gloomy man inclined to see the darker side of life, I attribute it to the fact that what should have been for me the happy joyous days of childhood were spent on a chicken farm.

One unversed in such matters can have no notion of the many and tragic things that can happen to a chicken. It is born out of an egg, lives for a few weeks as a tiny fluffy thing such as you see on Easter cards, then becomes hideously naked, eats quantities of corn and meal bought by the sweat of your father's brow, gets diseases called pip, cholera, and other names, stands looking with stupid eyes at the sun, becomes sick, and dies. It is all unbelievably complex. Most philosophers must have been raised on chicken farms. One hopes for so much from a chicken and is so dreadfully disillusioned. Vermin infest their youth, and fortunes must be spent for curative powders.

In later life I have seen literature on the subject of fortunes to be made out of the raising of chickens. Do not be led astray by it. Go hunt for gold on the frozen hills of Alaska, put your faith in the honesty of a politician, believe if you will that the world is daily growing better and that good will triumph over evil, but do not believe the literature concerning the hen.

For ten years my father and mother struggled to make our chicken farm pay and then they gave up that struggle and began another. They embarked in the restaurant business. Packing our belongings on a wagon, we drove a tiny caravan of hope looking for a new place to start on our upward journey through life.

Father rode on top of the wagon. He was then a bald-headed man of 45, a little fat and from long association with mother and the chickens he had become habitually silent and discouraged. Mother and I walked the entire eight miles—she to be sure that nothing fell from the wagon and I to see the wonders of the world. On the seat of the wagon beside father was his greatest treasure. I will tell you of that.

Where thousands of chickens come out of eggs, surprising things sometimes happen. The accident does not often occur—perhaps once in a thousand births. A chicken is born that has four legs, two pairs of wings, two heads or what not. They go quickly back to the hand of their Maker. The fact that the poor little things could not live was one of the tragedies of life to father. He had some notion that if he could but bring into henhood or roosterhood a five-legged hen or a two-headed rooster his fortune would be made. He dreamed of taking the wonder to county fairs and of growing rich by exhibiting it.

At any rate he saved all the little monstrous things, preserved in alcohol in its own glass bottle. These he carried on the wagon seat beside him. All during our days as keepers of a restaurant, the grotesques in their little glass bottles would sit on a shelf back of the counter. Mother sometimes protested but father was a rock on the subject of his treasure. The grotesques were, he declared, valuable. People, he said, liked to look at strange and wonderful things.

Pickleville once had a cider mill and pickle factory near its railroad station, but both had gone out of business. The restaurant business was mother's idea. Buses came down to the station from the hotel on the main street of Bidwell. Traveling men, she said, would be waiting around to take trains out of town and town people would come to await incoming trains. They would come to the restaurant to buy pie and coffee.

I went to school in the town and was glad to be away from the presence of discouraged, sad-looking chickens. Still I was not very joyous.

Mother decided that our restaurant should remain open at night. At ten in the evening a passenger train went north past our door followed by a local freight. The freight crew came to our restaurant for hot coffee and food. In the morning at four they returned. A little trade began to grow up. Mother slept at night and during the day tended the restaurant while father slept. While mother and I slept, father cooked meats that were to go into sandwiches for the lunch baskets of our boarders.

Then an idea in regard to getting up in the world came into his head. The American spirit took hold of him. He became ambitious.

In the long nights when there was little to do father had time to think. That was his undoing. He decided that he had in the past been an unsuccessful man because he had not been cheerful enough and that in the future he would adopt a cheerful outlook on life. In the early morning he came upstairs and got into bed with mother. She woke and the two talked. From my bed in the corner I listened.

It was father's idea that both he and mother should try to entertain the people who came to eat at our restaurant. When young people from the town of Bidwell came into our place, as on very rare occasions they did, bright entertaining conversation was to be made. It was father's notion that a passion for the company of himself and mother would spring up in the breasts of the younger people of Bidwell. In the evening bright happy groups would come singing with joy and laughter into our place.

For weeks this notion of father's invaded our house. We in our daily lives tried earnestly to make smiles take the place of glum  looks. Mother smiled at the boarders and I, catching the infection, smiled at our cat. Father became feverish in his anxiety to please. He did not waste his ammunition on the railroad men but seemed to be waiting for a young man or woman from Bidwell to come in to show what he could do.

On the counter was a basket filled with eggs, and there was something pre-natal about the way eggs kept themselves connected with the development of his idea. At any rate an egg ruined his new impulse in life.

Late one night I was awakened by a roar of anger. Both mother and I sat upright in our beds. Downstairs the door of our restaurant shut with a bang and in a few minutes father tramped up the stairs. He held an egg and there was a half-insane light in his eyes. As he stood glaring I was sure he intended throwing the egg at either mother or me. Then he laid it gently on the table and dropped on his knees beside mother's bed. He began to cry like a boy and I, carried away by his grief, cried with him. It is ridiculous, but I can remember only that mother's hand continually stroked the bald path that ran across the top of his head.

As to what happened downstairs, I know the story as well as if I had been a witness to my father's discomfiture. On that evening young Joe Kane, son of a merchant of Bidwell, came to Pickleville to meet his father, who was expected on the ten o'clock evening train from the south. The train was three hours late and Joe came into our place to loaf about and to wait for its arrival, alone in the restaurant with father.

From the moment he came into our place the young man must have been puzzled by my father's actions. It was his notion that father was angry at him for hanging around. He thought of going out. However, it began to rain and he did not fancy the long walk to town and back. He bought a five-cent cigar and ordered a cup of coffee. He had a newspaper in his pocket and took it out and began to read. "I'm waiting for the evening train. It's late," he said apologetically.

For a long time father remained silently gazing at his visitor. He was no doubt suffering from an attack of stage fright. As so often happens in life he had thought so often of the situation that now confronted him that he was somewhat nervous in its presence. For one thing, he did not know what to do with his hands. He thrust one of them nervously over the counter and shook hands with Joe Kane. "How-de-do," he said. Joe Kane put his newspaper down and stared at him. Father's eye

Columbus cheats and stands an egg

lighted on the basket of eggs that sat on the counter and he began to talk. "Well," he began hesitatingly, "you have heard of Christopher Columbus, eh?" He seemed to be angry. "That Columbus was a cheat," he declared emphatically. "He talked of making an egg stand on its end, then he went and broke the end of the egg."

My father seemed to his visitor to be beside himself at the duplicity of Christopher Columbus. He muttered and swore. He declared it was wrong to teach children that Columbus was a great man when, after all, he cheated: when his bluff had been called he had done a trick. Still grumbling at Columbus, father took an egg from the basket and rolled the egg between the palms of his hands. He smiled genially. He declared that without breaking its shell he could stand the egg on its end. He explained that the warmth of his hands and the gentle rolling movement gave the egg a new center of gravity, and Joe Kane was mildly interested. "I have handled thousands of eggs," father said. "No one knows more about eggs than I do."

He stood the egg on the counter and it fell on its side. He tried the trick again and again, each time rolling the egg between his hands. When after a half hour's effort he did succeed in making the egg stand, he looked up to find that his visitor was no longer watching. By the time he had succeeded in calling Joe Kane's attention to the success of his effort, the egg had again rolled over on its side.

Afire with the showman's passion and disconcerted by the failure of his first effort, father now took the poultry monstrosities down from the shelf. "How would you like to have seven legs and two heads like this fellow?" he asked, exhibiting the most remarkable of his treasures. A cheerful smile played over his face. He tried to slap Joe Kane on the shoulder as he had seen men do when he was a young farmhand in town on Saturday evenings. His visitor was made a little ill by the sight of the terribly deformed bird floating in the alcohol and got up to go. Father took hold of the young man's arm and led him back to his seat. He grew a little angry and had to force himself to smile. In an outburst of generosity he compelled Joe Kane to have a fresh cup of coffee and another cigar at his expense. Then he declared himself about to do a new trick. "I will heat this egg in this pan of vinegar," he said. "Then I will put it through the neck of a bottle without breaking the shell. The egg will resume its normal shape and the shell will become hard again. Then I will give the bottle to you. People will want to know how you got the egg in the bottle. Don't tell them. Keep them guessing. That is the way to have fun with this trick."

Father grinned and winked at his visitor. Joe Kane decided that the man was mildly insane but harmless. He drank the cup of coffee and began to read his paper again. When the egg had been heated in vinegar, father got an empty bottle. He was angry because his visitor did not watch him, but nevertheless went cheerfully to work. For a long time he struggled, trying to get the egg to go through the neck of the bottle. He put the pan of vinegar back on the stove to reheat the egg and burned his fingers. The shell had been softened a little but not enough. A spirit of desperate determination took possession of him. When he thought that at last the trick was about to be consummated, the delayed train came in at the station and Joe Kane started to go nonchalantly  out at the door. Father made a last desperate effort to conquer the egg and establish his reputation as one who knew how to entertain guests. The egg broke under his hand. When the contents spurted over his clothes, Joe Kane turned and laughed.

A roar of anger rose from my father's throat. He danced and shouted inarticulate words. Grabbing another egg from the basket on the counter, he threw it, just missing the head of the young man as he dodged through the door and escaped.

Father came upstairs to mother and me with an egg in his hand. I imagine he had some idea of destroying it, of destroying all eggs, and that he intended to let mother and me see him begin. When, however, he got into the presence of mother something happened to him. He laid the egg gently on the table and dropped on his knees by the bed as I have already explained. He blew out the light and after much muttered conversation both he and mother went to sleep. I awoke at dawn and for a long time looked at the egg that lay on the table. I wondered why eggs had to be and why from the egg came the hen who again laid the egg.

The question got into my blood. It has stayed there, I imagine, because I am the son of my father, and the problem remains unsolved in my mind. And that, I conclude, is but another evidence of the complete and final triumph of the egg—at least as far as my family is concerned. ❦

The Eyes Have It

Hold the page horizontal at eye-level.

A good optical illusion is an eye-catching way to sell your products. Notice how the wheel looks like it's turning.

Rappers' Delite

WHERE DID RAP MUSIC COME FROM?

Yo, it's not just clueless adults who don't know the story of rap—neither do most of its biggest fans.

RAP IN THE 1960s meant to talk seriously about something. At the time, "rap lines" sprung up for troubled teens to dial into; black militant H. "Rap" Brown got his nickname from his abilities at public speaking and persuasion. The term all but disappeared for more than a decade, until a hybrid of talk and music revived it. A subculture called "hip-hop" (a term used in the very first successful rap record) emerged around the music, featuring stylized graffiti, break dancing, gang-inspired clothing styles and a bad-guy attitude.

• Ad-lib rhyming over a beat had a history in the black culture long before rap. For example, competitions in good-natured rhyming insults and brags were a feature of the "dozens" in the 1940s and '50s. African American radio DJs from the 1940s into the 1970s made a practice of it, as did black poets in the 1960s like the Last Poets and the Watts Prophets. And Jamaican "toasters" or "dub artists" made an art of the same wordplay traditions.

• Jamaican influence most directly spurred rap in the 1970s. Its earliest practitioners were of Caribbean descent. One of them, Kool Herc, who left Jamaica for the South Bronx in 1967, is credited as the first

DJ to buy two copies of the same record because he liked a 15–second instrumental segment in the middle. With two turntables, Herc could repeatedly switch between them to create an endless rhythm track to rap over.

• It's hard to imagine that in the earliest days of rap, the

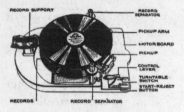

instrumentation was provided by playing short music segments from vinyl records repeatedly using two DJ turntables, manually cuing and starting the records right on beat. (Digital sampling recorders have made this process easier, so that tracks can be easily programmed before the fact instead of performed "live.") According to rap pioneer Kurtis Blow, it was largely a matter of economics: "Gifted teenagers with plenty of imagination but little cash began to forge a new style from spare parts. Hip-hop was a product of pure streetwise ingenuity; extracting rhythms and melodies from existing records and mixing them up

with searing poetry."

• As with punk rock in the white teen culture, rap was largely a homemade reaction against the slickness of disco, which had taken over much of black culture.

• While "cutting" with his two turntables, Herc also joked and boasted into the microphone in Jamaican "toasting" style. It was a time when carrying a blaring boombox everywhere was *de rigueur*; fans recorded Herc's live performances on them, then used the boomboxes to spread the music through the Bronx, Brooklyn and uptown Manhattan.

• Herc's sound inspired imitators, including Afrika Bam-

baataa, a Black Muslim who got good enough to engage Herc in direct competitions at clubs, parties and in city parks (where they powered their sound systems with hotwired street lamps). While Herc primarily used sounds from funk and disco, Bambaataa added rock music and even TV themes into the mix, inspiring other rap DJs to

plunder samples from Third World folk recordings, spoken-word tapes, bebop music and anything else that suited their fancy. (Bambaataa reportedly owned more than 25 crates of records that he could choose from.) "It became a little like 'Name That Tune,' trying to figure out what snippet came from which record," remarked one observer of the scene.

• In 1976, Grandmaster Flash (Joseph Saddler) introduced "quick mixing," using dozens of short sound bites combined for a sound–collage effect, and "backspinning," in which the record was spun quickly backward to repeat a snippet of sound. Shortly after, his

partner and "MC" (master of ceremony), Grandmaster Melle Mel, added the next important component to rap—real words. Before that, rappers improvised simple rhymes on the spot, often referring to what was going on at the club or party (for example, this early Herc couplet: "Davey D is in the house / An' he'll turn it out without a doubt"). Mel composed the first pre-planned, full-length rap song.

• In 1978, either Grandmaster Flash or thirteen-year-old

Grandmaster Flash and his turntables

Grand Wizard Theodore (there's some controversy about this) introduced the technique called "scratching"—manually turning a record back and forth so the needle would make a rhythmic *fwheet-fwheet* sound.

• In 1979, the first two rap records appeared: "King Tim III (Personality Jock)," by the

Fatback Band, and "Rapper's Delight" by the Sugarhill Gang, a band manufactured by the owners of Sugarhill Records, who had heard the

new sound and decided it had commercial possibilities. The producers bypassed the DJs that had been the backbone of rap: They hired studio musicians to replicate the basic groove of the disco hit "Good Times" by Chic, and then hired three employees of a New Jersey pizza parlor and coached them in performing a rap song that stole heavily from the style and lyrics of more genuine rappers. Still, the song became the first rap record to hit the top 40. Another successful record that year was Kurtis Blow's "Christmas Rappin'."

• Ironically, the next rap record to hit the charts was "Rapture" in 1980, by the New Wave band Blondie.

• In 1982, Afrika Bambaataa's "Planet Rock" became the first rap record using synthesizers and a drum machine, starting a trend away from depending on others' pre-recorded backing tracks.

• In 1986, rap became assimilated into mainstream pop culture with "Fight for Your Right (to Party)" by the Beastie Boys and "Walk This Way" by Run-DMC and Aerosmith. It began rivaling rock as the dominant musical form among young people.

Rap goes commercial: Run-DMC action figures "walk this way."

• Still, sampled sounds from pre-existing tracks continued to be the rule, to the consternation of much-sampled artists like George Clinton and James Brown, who found their work appearing on other people's hit records without compensation. Finally, by the early 1990s, threats of legal action established a standard practice of compensating for samples. The effect was that Clinton and others released CDs containing dozens of sound bites for the express purpose of facilitating sampling by others.

• Through the 1990s, rap moved from being just party and bragging songs into politics, and then mutated into subcategories, including the most controversial: "gangsta rap," with lyrics glorifying guns, drugs and misogyny. Feuds and vendettas among the self-proclaimed gangsters resulted in several prominent rappers being shot, maimed and killed.

• Other spinoffs, inspired by the "black science fiction" of Bambaataa's "Planet Rock" and using many of the same techniques, include electronic–heavy house and techno music. ☾

London Bridge Isn't *Really* Falling Down

Did London Bridge really ever fall down? Yes, once. Back in 1014, when the Danes controlled London. Their enemies, the Saxons and Norwegians, rowed their warships up the Thames to the then-wooden bridge, hitched cables around the bridge's pilings, and rowed away at full speed, pulling the bridge down.

What do the people in London do, now that Arizona has London Bridge? The bridge over Lake Havasu in Arizona is the third of four London Bridges in history, and it was quickly replaced by another. After the first was torn down by the Danes, city leaders wanted the next London Bridge to be more durable, so in 1176, the city built the first stone London Bridge, a drawbridge that lasted 600 years. This was the most famous London Bridge, the one where heads of executed criminals, from common thieves to Oliver Cromwell, were displayed on poles in groups of up to 30 at a time.

But all good things must come to an end. In 1823, the city tore down the aged structure. There was no rich American waiting to buy it, so they recycled it into building projects and replaced it with the "New London Bridge" made of granite. It didn't last as long as its predecessor—not even 150 years—before it began sinking into the mud and had to be replaced.

In 1962, the city sold the "New London Bridge" to an American developer for $2,460,000. He rebuilt it over an artificial lake in Arizona. (Rumors at the time had it that he thought he'd bought the picturesque London Tower Bridge instead of the ordinary-looking bridge he got.) The fourth London Bridge continues to stand.

(To Be Tacked Inside of the Privy and NOT Torn Down.)

Sanitary Privies Are Cheaper Than Coffins

For Health's Sake let's keep this Privy CLEAN. Bad privies (and no privies at all) are our greatest cause of Disease. Clean people or families will help us keep this place clean. It should be kept as clean as the house because it spreads more diseases.

The User Must Keep It Clean Inside. Wash the Seat Occasionally

How to Keep a Safe Privy:

1. *Have the back perfectly screened against flies and animals.*
2. *Have a hinged door over the seat and keep it CLOSED when not in use.*
3. *Have a bucket beneath to catch the Excreta.*
4. *VENTILATE THE VAULT.*
5. *See that the privy is kept clean inside and out, or take the blame on yourself if some member of your family dies of Typhoid Fever.*

Some of the Diseases Spread by Filthy Privies:

Typhoid Fever, Bowel Troubles of Children, Dysenteries, Hookworm, Cholera, some Tuberculosis. The Flies that You See in the Privy Will Soon Be in the Dining Room.

Walker County Board of Health

A line at the top cautions *NOT* to remove this poster from the side of the privy. The National Library of Medicine Web site states that incidences of both typhoid fever and hookworm were lowered as a result of sanitary education campaigns like this one in the 1920s.

I See London, I See France

HERE'S ONE ALL ABOUT UNDERPANTS

Rifling through the drawers from the Indies to the Andies,
Bathroom Companion regular Kitty Martindale's found some pretty
risqué facts and stories on undies.

EQUAL RIGHTS TO UNDIES

In 1991, the Texas chapter of the American Civil Liberties Union
threatened to sue the Dallas County Sheriff's Department
because, while male inmates were routinely issued underwear,
female inmates had to supply their own. Only indigent women
could apply for free underwear. The female prisoners were further limited to plain white, not colorful or frilly.

AND THE CHEST, THEY SAY, IS HISTORY....

The brassiere is a twentieth-century invention, but ancient
Greek women strapped cloth or leather around their breasts to
minimize them under their clothes. Even earlier, women of
Crete used a device to push their breasts up and out of their
tops. Archeologists think a solid gold breastplate resembling a
bra from around 1000 B.C. was used by a Greek woman
to cover her breasts.

But who invented the modern bra? It's hard to say.
A "bust improver" made of wire and silk, looking
something like two tea strainers hooked together, first
appeared in 1886. Hermione Cadolle, a French seam-
stress is credited for designing a version in 1889, and
Paul Poiret, a couturier from Paris, began to build similar underpinnings into his clothes a bit later. The garment
gained enough notoriety for *Vogue* magazine to coin the term
"brassier" in 1907. Prior to this, the bra was called a *soutien-
gorge,* translating to "throat support" or "breast support."

In 1914, an American socialite, Mary Phelps Jacobs, patented a bra-like garment made from two silk hankies and some pink ribbons. She eventually sold the patent for $1,500 to the Warner Corset Company which, in turn, became very well-endowed from sales of the item.

William Rosenthal, an immigrant from Russia, patented the first "uplift" bra in 1927. Rosenthal's wife, Ida, and her business partner, Enid Bassett, owned a dress store called Enid Frocks in Manhattan. They were of the mind that dresses looked better when worn over a natural bosom instead of the flattened chest that was the popular look at the time. This innovative idea led Enid and Ida to create cup sizes for women of all shapes, and ultimately led to the Maidenform Bra. Its advertising campaign, "I dreamed I [did just about anything] in my Maidenform Bra," had a memorable run from 1949–69.

NAMES FOR UNMENTIONABLES

Bra. An abbreviation of the French word *brassiere*, "bra" first appeared in English in the 1930s. In 17th century France, *brassiere* simply meant "bodice" and was an alteration of an earlier, Old French word *braciere*, meaning a "piece of armor for the arm or wrist."

Garter. The word "garter" probably came from a Gaulish word meaning "leg," related to the Welsh *gar*. Adopted into Old French it was used as the basis for the noun *garet* meaning "place where the leg bends; knee." *Garter* then means "band just above or below the knee." Legend even has it that while the Countess of Salisbury danced with King Edward III, her garter slipped off. The king bent down, retrieved it, and saucily put it on his leg. It was this incident, some say, that inspired name given to the order of knighthood Edward founded, the British Order of the Garter. Incidentally, the garter snake is named for its resemblance to the undergarment.

Girdle. The modern use of the word "girdle" was first seen in 1925. Although today we think of girdles as a ladies' underthing, that was not the case for much of history. The name comes from the Old English *gyrdel*, which meant a belt, worn around the waist. *Gyrdel* came from Old Germanic prefixes *gurd-*, *gard-*, or *gerd-* meaning "surrounding."

Through history, a belt-like girdle has been more than just a fashion statement for men, but also a means of carrying small articles such as a money purse or weapon. The "military girdle" was worn as a piece of armor.

Made of metal, leather, fabric or cord, a girdle was usually worn with one or two hanging ends—particularly the ones worn by women. The dangling strings were used to tote essentials like a mirror or book.

In the tenth century, a colored girdle was quite common. Priests took to wearing golden ones. Not long after, the girdle became a symbol of status and wealth. To keep the extravagance in check, a law was decreed: Squires were forbidden from wearing any girdle with gold or silver, and knights who made under a certain amount of money couldn't wear bejeweled girdles. Still, the girdles of this time period were very beautiful and expensive, often bequeathed upon death to favored family members. Others, though, took their girdles to the grave. They were so valued that stealing a girdle could mean a sentence of death.

STICKY SITUATION

A lawyer, after wearing his new J. C. Penney skivvies for the first time, found the tag "Inspected by No. 12" firmly stuck to his delicate parts. After a failed attempt at removing it himself, he sought medical help. A doctor managed to remove the tag, but the treatment left the lawyer with a nasty rash. Eventually, it cleared, but a scar in the shape of the sticker remained. The lawyer sued (surprise!) and was awarded $3,000 for the time in which he lost work and marital comfort.

UNDERNEATH, WE'RE PRETTY MUCH THE SAME

King Tut of Egypt was buried with 145 loincloths. Thousands of years later, World War II Japanese soldiers wore something similar to loincloths under their uniforms. Most clothing historians agree that modern men's briefs evolved pretty directly from early loincloths.

Even though the garment is universal, not all cultures wear them. Traditionally, Arabs are pretty modest, and cover themselves from head to toe. But underneath their robes, they don't wear any undergarments (it's hot enough with the robes!). The Scottish, too, traditionally wear nothing under their kilts. Samoans are pretty immodest, and enjoy loose clothing to go with the intense island heat, but their historical dress included underthings, and they believed that something should cover the navel — but not necessarily the female breasts — at all times.

Keep those legs down, boys!

FOR YOUR EYES ONLY
In 2002, Germany's spy agency, the Federal Intelligence Agency (or BND), announced that it would begin offering BND Brand underwear in its public shop in Berlin. The underwear will be imprinted with phrases like "Not for Public Use" and "Top Secret."

"It's not just fun and games," insisted a spokesperson for the agency. "It's all part of our plans to inform the public more about who we are and what we do."

"PATHETIC!"
What do you call one who steals women's underwear? Technically, he's a *melcryptovestimentaphiliac.*  Personally, we can think of a dozen other names to call him....

GOLF BUFFS
Harpo Marx and George Burns once nearly got kicked out of Hillcrest Country Club in Beverly Hills when they played a round of golf in their underwear.

AIRING DIRTY LAUNDRY
During an MTV interview with Bill Clinton during the 1992 presidential campaign, the democrat was asked what type of underwear he wore. After a long silence, he answered, "Boxers." ☾

Curses!

PREGNANT SCHOLAR: "One who was drunk by the middle of the morning." — *University Slang*, Morris Marple, 1950

MAMMOTHREPT: "A spoilt child." — *Dictionary of Obsolete and Provincial English*, Thomas Wright, 1857

SPATHERDAB: "A chatterer, gossip, scandal-monger who goes from house to house dispensing news." — *Leicestershire Words, Phrases and Proverbs*, A. Benoni Evan, 1881

WINDY-WALLETS: "A noisy fellow; one who romances in conversation." — *Dictionary of Archaic and Provincial Words*, James Halliwell, 1855

COUNTER-CASTER: "Contemptuous name for an arithmetician." — *Oxford Shakespeare Glossary*, C. T. Onion, 1911

PILGARLICK: "A poor, ill-dressed person; an object of pity or contempt." — *Sheffield Glossary of Words*, Sidney Addy, 1888

BEARD-SPLITTER: "An enjoyer of women." — *Dictionary of the Canting Crew*, B. E., 1699

KEYHOLE-WHISTLERS: "Persons who sleep in barns or outhouses from necessity, or in preference to sleeping in lodging houses." — *Slang Dictionary*, J. C. Hotten, 1887

SNOKER: "One who smells at objects like a dog." — *Etymological Dictionary of the Scottish Language*, John Jamieson, 1808

Bearing It All
THE INNER WORKINGS OF THE TEDDY BEAR

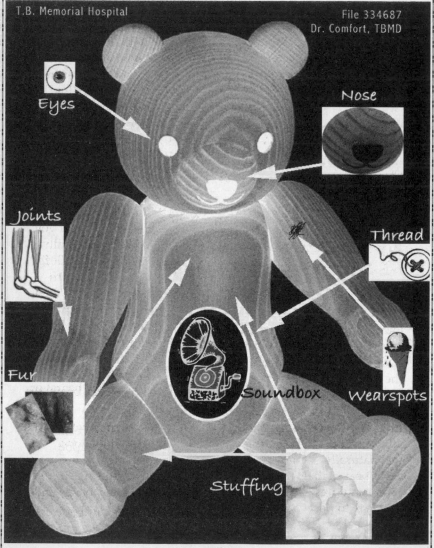

T.B. Memorial Hospital

File 334687
Dr. Comfort, TBMD

Eyes

Nose

Joints

Thread

Fur

Soundbox

Wearspots

Stuffing

Eyes: The best eyes are glass, made specifically for this purpose. In the bad old days, they were attached to a long, sharp hatpin and just thumbtacked into the head; concerned parents would routinely remove these and sew on buttons. Nowadays, eyes are safely sewn in with extra-strong nylon "eye-floss," and the really good ones come in several lifelike colors from Germany.

Paws & Nose: On some bears, just more plush of a different color. Classically, though, it's virgin wool felt. Some modern bear artists use ultrasuede.

Joints: Some inexpensive teddies don't have joints; they are merely sewn permanently sitting or reclining. Bears with "fully articulated" joints use a two-disks-on-one-axle assembly on arms, legs and head so they can turn; the really sophisticated ones have "Loc-Line" armatures that look like little Dixie Cups nestled into each other that allow the bear to bend and flex naturally. Some very early bear makers used metal rods and wires to get arms and legs to pose, but sharp

ends sometimes wore through the fabric.

Thread: Colored pearle cotton.

Fabric: Mohair is the fabric of choice for quality bears, but not for a bear that you might actually give a real kid to love and play with. Kid-gunk and dirt easily sponge off synthetic fake furs; some are even machine washable. Other popular bear fabrics include silk and rayon plush...and, in the bad old days, real fur from real bears.

Soundboxes: Electronic voice boxes exist for bears, but most use mechanical voices. Bears were traditionally either "squeakers" (squeeze them) or "growlers" (turn them upside down and then right side up). Wind-up bears with music-box parts playing lullabies came later. The sound mechanism is shielded from the stuffing material with muslin (earlier bears) or plastic (later).

Stuffing: Excelsior (very fine wood shavings) was long the preferred stuffing for its solid-packing and heft. While some stubborn hand-sewers still use wood shavings, fire safety laws be damned, most modern bears contain fire-safe polyester fill, sometimes augmented with tiny plastic beads (made from recycled milk cartons) to add a heft that collectors love.

 Wear Spots: Most collectors like antique bears in mint condition, but some actually like to see evidence that they've been well-loved by a real kid. Typical signs? Bare spots near the center belly seam from the fingers of children falling asleep. Missing or weak ears once used as handles. Mashed and threadbare hands and feet from being grasped and chewed. Dirt marks from backyard bear dens, food stains from tea parties...well, you get the idea. ❄

The Right to Bear Arms, Legs and Torsos

A N ARCTOPHILE is a person who loves bears. It comes from *arko,* which in Greek means "bear," and *philo,* which means "friend." While kids have known for decades that teddy bears offer therapeutic comfort, the professionals are finally catching on:

• Six out of ten adults surveyed for *Emotional Health* magazine said that they own or wish they owned a teddy bear.

• Some police, fire and paramedic departments routinely issue teddy bears to their officers because they're a useful tool in reaching scared, lost and traumatized children.

A firefighter lays out his comforting bears

• Following the lead of a famous old Norman Rockwell painting, several years ago the Children's Museum in Boston helped calm kids' fears of hospitals by having them bring in their teddy bears for a free checkup by trained medical professionals.

• To provide therapeutic comfort to someone suffering from illness or trauma, let the patient hold a Teddy WarmHeart that emits four hours of "human-like warmth," after being popped for a few minutes into a microwave oven (the teddy bear, that is, not the traumatized person).

Pick 'n' Chews
TAKE THE CHEWING GUM CHALLENGE

We have a pop quiz for you. If you read about gum on page 135, it'll help. Not much, but some.

1 **Gum made from the resin of the mastic tree was popular**

A. in Greece about A.D. 50

B. in Macedonia in the second century

C. in ancient Egypt

D. from the Middle Ages in Europe

2 **British settlers in the New World were introduced to chewing spruce resins by**

A. fellow settlers from Holland

B. William Wrigley, Jr.'s grandfather

C. Native Americans

D. the inventor, Thomas Adams, Sr.

3 **Chewing gum as we know it today is made from chicle,**

A. a plant with blue, pink or white flowers

B. the dried sap of the sapodilla tree

C. a stiff, prickly shrub that grows in alkaline regions

D. a common weed with small white flowers

4 **Chicle was introduced to the Americans**

A. by Mexican laborers working in California in the early 20th century

B. by a Prussian general in the late 19th century

C. by Native Americans in the early 19th century

D. by a Mexican general after the Civil War

5 **The "Nostalgia Gum program" was an advertising campaign in the 1980s**

A. to reintroduce 100-year-old chewing gum brands

B. to introduce sugarless gum to conservative gum chewers

C. launched by the Gum Wrappers Collectors Association

D. launched by an aggressive

new gum company in an attempt to grab some of Wrigley's market.

6 **The initial problem with bubble gum when invented in the early part of the century was its**

A. over-stickiness

B. high manufacturing cost

C. unreliable bubble-blowability (the bubbles burst too early)

D. horrible color (no one wanted to chew or blow mucky green gum)

7 **Liquid gum base has been used**

A. as an organic pesticide

B. to seal tiny parts in airplane engines

C. in the manufacture of super-adhesive glue

D. in the manufacture of rubber shoe soles

Grudge Match

WHY COKE HATES PEPSI (PART 1)

Few competitors have gone after each other with the battle-scarred, no-holds-barred, take-no-prisoners fervor of Coke and Pepsi. How and when did it start? It depends on who you ask. But to understand it, you have to go back to the beginning.

IN SPRING OF 1886, Atlanta was still smarting and depressed by its defeat in the Civil War. The South turned en masse for solace to religion and patent medicines. The cure-all "snake oils" of the North tended to be heavy on alcohol—an unacceptable ingredient for most Bible-thumpin', anti-demon rum Southerners. Under pressure from Temperance groups, patent medicine makers in the South began replacing alcohol with another active ingredient that was believed to be safe, healthy and morally pure...cocaine.

Atlanta druggist John Styth Pemberton had been reformulating his "French Wine Coca—Ideal Brain Tonic" to remove the alcohol, yet replace it with something that would give a nice kick. He had found it in the African kola nut—a stimulant

Coca leaves—the source for cocaine

with the reputation of being a wonder hangover cure. He blended it with coca extract, bringing together the two strongest stimulants known at the time. The concoction was indeed a potent "brain tonic." Unfortunately, it tasted terrible. So the gray-bearded druggist spent spent six months hunched over a 30-gallon brass kettle in his backyard mixing up dozens of concoctions, before finally settling on what he decided was the ideal mixture to mask the flavor of the potently psychoactive mix.

Cocaine was a common ingredient in many 19th and early 20th century remedies, including this toothache medicine for children

The result was Coca-Cola, a thick, sweet, brown syrup, packaged in reused beer bottles. Pemberton sold it to other Atlanta drugstores for 25¢ a bottle. The druggists would sell the entire bottle, or administer individual doses of the "Intellectual Beverage and Temperance Drink," often mixed into a glass of tap water to make it a little easier to get down. It became moderately successful as a pick-me-up and hangover remedy.

That summer an earthshaking event occurred in one of Coke's outlets in Atlanta, Jacob's Drug Store. A customer came in complaining of a severe hangover. Handed a bottle of Coca-Cola syrup, he asked Willis E. Venable, the soda fountain man, to open it and mix it with water right there so he could get immediate relief. Rather than walk to the tap in the back, Venable asked if the man minded soda water. The distressed customer wasn't particular. He gulped the fizzing mixture and said, "Say, this is really fine. Much better than using plain water like the label says." Word got around, and people started requesting the bubbly version all over town.

Pemberton had been marketing Coca-Cola as a medicine "for all nervous afflictions—Sick Headache, Neuralgia, Hysteria, Melancholia, Etc." He hadn't even considered that it might be drunk for refreshment recreation. But he saw the opportunity and jumped. His ads changed to "Coca-Cola makes a delicious, exhilarating, refreshing, and invigorating beverage" in addition to touting its medicinal qualities.

That same summer, Atlanta passed its first "dry laws," making alcohol illegal. Coke syrup sales jumped from 25 gallons that year to 1,049 gallons the next, largely through the marketing efforts of Pemberton's associate and financial backer Frank M. Robinson, who coined the name and drew the script "Coca Cola" logo that is still used today. Robinson was Coke's real "secret ingredient" in its early years. He was a shrewd salesman and promoter.

Meanwhile, despite consuming large quantities of his "health tonic," Pemberton's health began to fail in 1887. Coke sales were still not brisk enough to make him financially solvent, so for a very modest amount of money, he sold two-thirds of his interest in the business to Willis Venable, the man who first brought the fizz to Coke. Pemberton's inventory, which he drew up at the time of the transfer, gives a clue to Coca-Cola's closely guarded "secret ingredients": oil of spice, oil

of lemon, oil of lime, oil of nutmeg, fluid extract of nutmeg, fluid extract of coca leaves, vanilla, citric acid, orange elixir, oil of neroli, and caffeine.

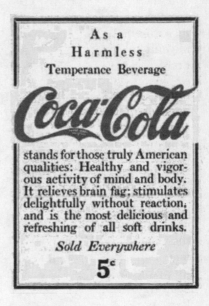

As a Harmless Temperance Beverage

Coca-Cola

stands for those truly American qualities: Healthy and vigorous activity of mind and body. It relieves brain fag; stimulates delightfully without reaction, and is the most delicious and refreshing of all soft drinks.

Sold Everywhere

5¢

Pemberton died destitute on August 16, 1888, and was buried in an unmarked pauper's grave. Before he died, he sold the last of his stock to Asa Candler, a more prosperous fellow druggist. With the help of two partners, Candler quietly bought up all the rest of the stock in Coca-Cola from Venable and other investors. Full ownership of the company—lock, stock and secret formula—cost Candler a grand total of $2,300.

Candler was a devout Christian and teetotaler, and he wholeheartedly believed that Coke was the ideal Temperance drink and all-purpose medicine. He and Frank Robinson immediately set to work reformulating Pemberton's original recipe to improve the taste and shelf life while keeping the same heart-pounding jolt of coca leaves, kola nuts and caffeine.

the arm"; soda fountains became "hop joints" and "dope stores." In 1903, Coca-Cola quietly switched to a new recipe that used coca leaves that had already been stripped of cocaine. (Coca-Cola continues to use spent coca leaves. It obtains them from the Stepan Chemical Company in New Jersey, the only legal processor of medical cocaine in the United States.)

Memorable (or Not!) Coca-Cola Ad Campaigns

"Coca-Cola Revives and Sustains" (1905)
"The Great National Temperance" (1906)
"Three Million a Day" (1917)
"Thirst Knows No Season" (1922)
"Six Million a Day" (1925)
"Around the Corner from Everywhere" (1927)
"The Pause that Refreshes" (1929)
"When you think of Refreshment, think of ice-cold Coca-Cola" (1942)
"The only thing like Coca-Cola is Coca-Cola itself. It's the Real Thing" (1942)
"The Cold, Crisp taste of Coke" (1958)
"Things go Better with Coke" (1963)
"I'd Like to Buy the World a Coke" (1971)
"Coke Adds Life" (1976)
"Coke is It!" (1982)
"Always Coca-Cola" (1993)
"Real" (2003)

Candler reformulated Coke again a few years later when anti-cocaine hysteria hit a peak. Newspapers carried shameless stories about crazed blacks rampaging with insatiable lust, superhuman strength, and even enhanced marksmanship as a result of cocaine. Slang terms for an order of Coca-Cola quickly expanded from "a Coke" to "a cold dope" and "a shot in

Right about this time, a soldier named Benjamin Franklin Thomas, stationed in Cuba during the Spanish-American War, saw the Cubans drinking something called Piña Fria from bottles. Suffering from Coke withdrawal, he wondered: Why not bottle it pre-mixed in fizzy water and make it available everywhere? When Thomas got back to the U.S., he and a partner named Joseph Whitehead called on Candler who, seeing little profit in the venture, signed over bottling rights to them. Thomas and Whitehead immediately began selling regional bottling franchises.

Candler, in a mixture of Southern Methodist piety and good business sense, began lobbying aggressively for anti-alcohol laws all over the South. By 1907, 825 of the 994 counties in the former Confederacy had gone "dry." Sales of Coca-Cola soared.

Its success spawned dozens of imitators. In 1916 alone, busy Coke attorneys went after 153 wannabes with names like Cafe Cola, Afri-Cola, Charcola, Co-Co-Colian, Dope, Kola Kola, Pau-Pau Cola, King Kola, Fig Cola, Sola Cola, Candy Cola, Toca-Cola, Cold Cola, Kos Kola, Cay-Ola, Coke Ola, Koca-Nola, Kel Kola, Kaw-Kola, Co Kola, Kola-Nola, Caro-Cola and Coca-Kola. By 1926, Coke attorney Harold Hirsch had run more than 7,000 competitors out of business.

The company began searching for a unique bottle design —one, as Thomas put it, "a person will recognize as a Coca-Cola bottle even when he feels it in the dark. The bottle should be so shaped that, even when broken, a person could tell at a glance what it was."

After a succession of rejected designs, the bottlers adopted the now-classic bottle designed by the C. J. Root Company of Terre Haute, Indiana. The alternately tapered and bulging shape was brilliant artistry, but astoundingly lousy botany: The bottle designers, thinking they were copying the shape of the *coca* bean, mistakenly copied the *cacao* bean, from which chocolate is made.

Coke's famous "hobbleskirt bottle" was named after a short-lived 1914 fashion

The bottle was a huge success. The bottlers liked it because its extra-thick glass gave a heft that disguised how little Coca-Cola was actually in it (6.5 ounces). The company liked it because it gave them a potent weapon that would kill all infringers. Or so they thought.

(For the rest of the story, see page 335)

Zen Masters
THE WISDOM OF MICHAEL JACKSON

Mind-bending quotes from the self-described "King of Pop."

- "I never smile when I dance."
- "It hurts to be mobbed. Not mentally, but physically. Your body feels like a noodle...."
- "People think they know me, but they don't. Not really. Actually, I am one of the loneliest people on this earth. I cry sometimes, because it hurts. It does. To be honest, I guess you could say that it hurts to be me."
- "Ours developed into a real close relationship. I fell in love with her (Tatum O'Neal), and she with me, and we were very close for a long time. Eventually the relationship transcended into a good friendship."
- "Me and Janet really are two different people."
- "When I'm not onstage, I'm not the same. I'm different. I think I'm some kinda stage addict. When I can't get onto a stage for a long time, I have fits and get real crazy. I start crying, and I act weird and all freaked out. No kiddin', I do. I start to dancin' round the house."
- "There are fans who actually have pieces of my hair. I could go to England right now, and they'd show me and say, 'This is your hair from three years ago.' I'd say, 'Oh my gosh.' And it's sitting in their wallet. They collect hair."
- "Most people don't know me, that is why they write such things in which most is not true. I cry very very often because it hurts and I worry about the children. All my children all over the world, I live for them.... Animals strike not from malice, but because they want to live, it is the same with those who criticize, they desire our blood, not our pain. But still I must achieve. I must seek truth in all things. I must endure for the power I was sent forth, for the world, for the children. But have mercy for I've been bleeding a long time now."

Potty Pourri

RANDOM KINDS OF FACTNESS

• Unless you're an exceptional monkey, you are likely *ecaudate*. It means "tailless."

• Anthropologist James Schaefer studied how music affected the drinking in bars. He found that people listening to country music drank more than those listening to pop or rock.

• In the wine-making process, it can take up to 2 years to remove all the solids (grape skins, dead yeast cells, and other debris). This step, called "racking," consists of letting the wine sit and draining out the gunk at the bottom now and again.

• Throwing a penny off the Empire State Building in New York won't really slice open a car or make a crater in the sidewalk. The fastest a penny can flutter from a height is only about 80 mph. In theory, a person below could catch it with baseball mitt. But don't try it.

• The dog days of summer come between July 3 and August 11. The Egyptians coined the term, believing that Sirius, the Dog Star, helped the sun warm the Earth during that time.

• The Greek Parthenon was wrecked by much more than time or weather. In 1687, the Turks battled the Venetians for control of the city, and stored their gunpowder in the ancient temple. It exploded, knocking over pillars and blowing the roof clean off. Renovations are currently underway.

• The original Rin Tin Tin— dog star of the silent screen—was picked up in Germany by U.S. Army corporal Lee Duncan during World War I.

• Wall-climbing lizards don't have suction cups on their feet. They have grooves with microscopic bumps that can get a toe-hold on the tiny imperfections on all surfaces, even glass.

"I'm Two with Nature"
QUOTES FROM WOODY ALLEN

An acting, directing, writing comedian: Woody Allen's done it all.
Here are a few things he's had to say along the way.

• "If only God would give me some clear sign! Like making a large deposit in my name at a Swiss Bank."

• "To *you* I'm an atheist; to God, I'm the Loyal Opposition."

• "I'm not afraid of dying, I just don't want to be there when it happens."

• "I was thrown out of N.Y.U. my freshman year...for cheating on my metaphysics final. I looked into the soul of the boy sitting next to me."

• "I am two with nature."

• "I don't want to live on in my work, I want to live on in my apartment."

• "My success has allowed me to strike out with a higher class of women."

• "I sold my memoirs of my love life to Parker Brothers — they're going to make a game out of it."

• "I took a course in speed reading and was able to read *War and Peace* in twenty minutes."

• "I was the best I ever had."

• "And how can I believe in God when just last week I got my tongue caught in the roller of an electric typewriter."

• "If you want to make God laugh, tell him about your plans."

• "Showing up is 80% of life."

• "What if everything is an illusion and nothing exists? In that case, I definitely overpaid for my carpet."

- "What if nothing exists and we're all in somebody's dream? Or what's worse, what if only that fat guy in the third row exists?"

- "Some men are heterosexual, and some are bisexual, and some men don't think about sex at all.... They become lawyers."

- "I think a relationship is like a shark. It has to constantly move forward or it dies. Well, what we have on our hands here is a dead shark."

- "Basically my wife was immature. I'd be at home in the bath and she'd come in and sink my boats."

- "The prettiest women are almost always the most boring, and that is why some people feel there is no God."

- "It seemed the world was divided into good and bad people. The good ones slept better... while the bad ones seemed to enjoy the waking hours much more."

- "My brain is my second favorite organ."

- "The lion and the calf shall lie down together but the calf won't get much sleep."

- "It is impossible to travel faster than light, and certainly not desirable, as one's hat keeps blowing off."

- "More than any time in history, mankind now faces a cross-roads. One path leads to despair and utter hopelessness, the other to total extinction. Let us pray that we have the wisdom to choose correctly."

- "I don't want to achieve immortality through my work. I want to achieve immortality through not dying."

- "There are worse things in life than death. Have you ever spent an evening with an insurance salesman?"

- "I don't think my parents liked me. They put a live teddy bear in my crib."

- "Human Beings are divided into mind and body. The mind embraces all the nobler aspirations, like poetry and philosophy, but the body has all the fun."

- "Love is the answer, but while you're waiting for the answer, sex raises some pretty interesting questions." ℰ

Potty Pourri

RANDOM KINDS OF FACTNESS

• If you're looking for a career change to an area with a cool name, try becoming a colporter. It has nothing to do with the famous songwriter. Instead, it's another name for a Bible salesman.

• The surface of the moon has more than 30 trillion craters that measure at least a foot wide. Of those a mile or more wide, there are at least half a million, many overlapping.

• We remember that Benedict Arnold was a traitor, but history also records that he was a great general. He nearly captured Canada and won a major battle at Saratoga for the revolutionaries, then won battles for the British in Richmond, Va., and New London, Conn. After the war, he moved to London, England.

• Pluto, Venus and Uranus all spin in the opposite direction as Earth.

• Besides being a renowned American writer, John Dos Passos invented the Soap Bubble Gun.

• Despite what you've heard, it's not true that a cow has four stomachs; it has one stomach with four compartments for the different stages of digestion. The compartments are called the rumen, the reticulum, the omasum and the abomasum.

• Rudolph Valentino was the stage name that the silent-screen actor whittled down from his real name. The original was a little too difficult to work into movie credits: Rodolfo Alfonzo Raffaelo Pierre Filibert Guglielmi di Valentina d'Antonguolla.

• One out of seven Continental soldiers in the Revolutionary War was black.

• The longest running newspaper still published in the United States is the *Hartford Courant*. It was established in 1764.

Big Mac
How It Became the Hottest Thing
Between Buns

The Big Mac was an idea "borrowed" from another restaurant chain.
When it ended up on the McDonald's menu in 1968, it wasn't because
of the company's top management, but despite it.

IN THE EARLY 1950s, the McDonald brothers of San
Bernardino, California, created the first genuine fast food
restaurant. They came up with an assembly-line formula
that they called the Speedy Service System, dishing out low-cost
burgers, fries and shakes in a fraction of the time of most drive-
ins.

KROC'S EMPIRE
When entrepreneur Ray Kroc began franchising McDonald's
outlets a few years later, he refined the Speedy System further,
making it even more regimented. Each worker was assigned
only one function, which worked out fine because the menu
featured only a few items. Kroc hired only team-oriented, col-
lege-aged men, and dressed them in white military-style uniforms. (Kroc wouldn't hire women workers for more than a
decade because he was afraid their presence would disrupt the
military-like efficiency and attract loitering male admirers.
When McDonald's finally stopped this blatant gender discrimi-
nation in 1968, the unwritten directive at the time was to hire
only "flat-chested, unattractive women.")

Unfortunately, the military-like efficiency was a curse as well
as a blessing. It forced Kroc to resist adding any new menu
items, fearing they would slow down the system. Instead, he
concentrated on perfecting the products he had, spending, for

example, more than $3 million to research the secret of consistently perfect french fries. After a while, customers naturally started getting tired of the same old thing every time, and McDonald's profits began leveling off. McDonald's franchisees began griping—loudly—about the lack of variety.

KROC'S FLOPS

Kroc tried his best. He test-marketed a series of new products that he thought could be fit into the Speedy Service System. Unfortunately, he didn't have the same genius for developing new products that he did for selling franchises. All of his new products were disasters. For example, he decided in the late 1950s that the menu needed a dessert. He tried selling brownies and strawberry shortcake. When they failed to sell, he tried miniature pound cakes at 15¢ a loaf. Nobody bought them. In desperation, he tried offering *kolacky*, a Bohemian pastry his mom used to bake for him. No luck.

Frustrated, Kroc gave up on desserts. He decided that what McDonald's really needed was a non-meat burger for Catholics on Fridays. He went into the kitchen and concocted a product that he called a "Hulaburger": two slices of cheese and a grilled pineapple ring on a toasted bun. Not surprisingly, it bombed, and was ultimately replaced with a fish sandwich.

For the next decade, Kroc would fly into a rage whenever franchisees suggested new menu items. Finally, a desperate franchisee willing to risk Kroc's wrath introduced McDonald's most popular product.

Jim Delligatti was one of Kroc's earliest franchise holders. He operated a dozen stores in and around Pittsburgh. When he noticed his customer base was dwindling, he began lobbying McDonald's managers to allow him to broaden the menu.

STOLEN GOODS MAKE GOOD

His idea? He wanted to sell a double-decker hamburger with "special sauce" and all the trimmings—an idea that he unabashedly stole from the Big Boy hamburger chain. He badgered Kroc until he received reluctant permission in 1967 to test-market what was to become the Big Mac. Kroc forced some conditions. Delligatti had to agree that the product would be offered in only one marginal suburban store. He also had to promise to use the standard McDonald's patty and bun—a promise he quickly reneged on when it became clear that the standard bun was too small, making the sandwich impossible to eat without it falling to pieces. He quietly ordered oversized sesame seed buns from an independent baker and had them sliced into thirds.

The Big Mac—a fat & calorie behemoth—is featured prominently on this McDonald's nutrition flier

Within a few months, the new Big Mac had increased Deligatti's store's sales volume by a healthy 12%. He started serving it in his other stores. Other franchisees saw what was happening and began clamoring for their own Big Macs. McDonald's quickly tried the Big Mac in other test markets. The Big Mac increased sales by at least 10% in each market. At the end of 1968, it was put into nationwide distribution.

TONGUE-TIED TWISTER

The commercials that McDonald's created featured a recital of the Big Mac's ingredients. Max Cooper, a retired McDonald's publicist who owned several franchises in Birmingham, Alabama, thought the ads were boring and ineffectual. So he took matters into his own hands and held a contest in his stores: Anyone who could correctly recite the ingredients of the Big Mac in 4 seconds got one free. An ad agency recorded his customers' attempts at "Two all-beef patties special sauce lettuce cheese pickles onions on a sesame seed bun" and eventually produced radio spots using botched recitals by real customers.

The ads were an instant hit in Birmingham. Within weeks, radio stations were co-sponsoring "Recite the Big Mac" contests. Schoolkids all over town practiced the slogan at home and recess. Sales of Big Macs soared 25%. Other franchises in the South followed. Finally, McDonald's national marketing department took notice and spread the same strategy nationwide.

ONE THING LEADS TO ANOTHER

The Big Mac's success opened a floodgate of innovation among franchise holders. In 1969, Litton Cochran in Knoxville got permission to try a variation on the deep-fried apple pie his mother used to make for him. His idea was a success and spread to the national menu.

Another franchise holder discovered that customers wouldn't normally buy two orders of fries, but many would buy a double order if it were disguised as a single order. Thus was born the now-popular Large Fries, offering 60% more product for 75% more money. Another franchisee invented the McDLT; another, the Egg McMuffin, ensuring McDonald's domination of breakfast sales among fast food restaurants for many years to come. ☾

The Big Mac Super Sized Extra Value Meal: What You're Getting Besides the Deal

The Big Mac: One sandwich contains 590 calories—over a quarter of what you need in a day if you eat a 2,000-calorie diet. It also has 34 grams of total fat, or 53% of your Daily Value, 11 grams of saturated fat (57% D.V.), 85 milligrams of cholesterol (29% D.V.), 1,090 milligrams of sodium (45% D.V.), 8 grams of sugar and only 3 grams of dietary fiber (12% D.V.).

The French Fries: One order of Super Sized Fries has a whopping 610 calories. These same fries have 29 grams of total fat, 5 grams of saturated fat, 390 milligrams of sodium and 7 grams of dietary fiber.

The Soft Drink: One Super Sized Coke contains 410 calories, 40 milligrams of sodium and 113 grams of sugar.

Thinking of topping off your meal with a Vanilla Shake? Add 570 calories, 16 grams of fat (11 of which are saturated fat), 65 milligrams of cholesterol, 400 milligrams of sodium, 76 grams of sugar and 0 grams of dietary fiber.

To stay healthy, you'll need to not eat anything else for the rest of the day: this Super Sized™ meal gives you more calories, fat and saturated fat than you need in a 24-hour period.

Elephants

A TRUNKFUL OF UNFORGETTABLE FACTS

They're smart, they're big, and on the beach they walk around with their trunks down. Who could not love elephants?

ELEPHANT HITS & MYTHS

No, elephants aren't really deathly afraid of mice. Nor is there an "elephants' graveyard" where all pachyderms go to die. And despite their intelligence, elephants *do* sometimes forget. Still, Westerners aren't the only ones who have spun elephant tales. The people of India—who live with elephants and should know better—have come up with some whoppers. For example, elephants show up in the Indian creation story (the earth sits on an elephant's head and when the head moves, an earthquake happens). Elephants were said to have appeared in the sky at the birth of Buddha. The Indians even explain why elephants no longer fly today. Here's the story:

Elephants used to have wings. One day an elephant was flying and grew tired. Spotting an old banyan tree below, he thought it looked like a good resting place. As he settled on a branch, it snapped and he plummeted toward the ground. Unfortunately for him, he landed on a meditating hermit named Dirghatapas, who was as grouchy as he was magical. Dirghatapas cursed the oafish winged beast to walk on his legs from that day on. The wings disappeared, and the elephant was henceforth forever earthbound.

BUT CALLING THEM "DUMBO" JUST TEES THEM OFF

An elephant's big, floppy ears can be 6.5 feet long and are nearly as wide. The ears have several functions, but helping the elephant hear better is not one of them. One thing the ears are good for is to make the elephant look bigger than it is when it defends or attacks (as if they aren't already big enough). Another is to wave away flies. But the primary use for the elephant's big ears is unexpected: they keep the animal cool. No,

not by waving them like a fan, but because the ears are thin, yet rich in blood vessels. Heat escapes easily into the air when you have ears like that—when elephants wave them around, the blood inside cools by as much as 9° F.

African elephants live in a hotter, sunnier climate, so it makes sense that their ears are bigger than those of Asian elephants.

TUSK A LOOSA

Elephants love sweets. Alas, they are susceptible to tooth decay, so it's a good thing that most elephants don't have many sugar-saturated foods available in the wild. Even without excessive sugar in their diets, elephants suffer from natural tooth loss in old age, which can result in starvation. Most zoos try to prevent the problem by forbidding visitors from feeding elephants. However, at least if a captive elephant loses its teeth, keepers can feed it soft foods.

SING LOW, SWEET PACHYDERM

Elephants communicate in low-frequency nasal tones that humans can't hear. Herds of elephants actually sing to each other over distances of up to 5 miles.

Elephants' natural musical ability is what inspired the Elephant Conservation Center in Thailand to create the Thai Elephant Orchestra, featuring larger, sturdier versions of Thai instruments—gongs, xylophones and percussion instruments.

GRAND OLD PACHYDERM

The elephant became the symbol for the Republican Party in 1874, thanks to political cartoonist Thomas Nast. Nast was in need of a way to depict the Republicans' policies that he considered nothing but random destructiveness. When a hoaxster reported that animals were breaking free at the New York Zoo, the image of rampaging elephants was too good for Nast to pass up.

Despite Nash's intention, the Republicans became so associated with the elephant that they eventually embraced the insulting icon while laying claim to the animal's positive traits.

The Blind Men & the Elephant
Interpretation by John Godfrey Saxe (1816–1887) of an old tale from India

It was six men of Indostan
To learning much inclined,
Who went to see the Elephant
(Though all of them were blind),
That each by observation
Might satisfy his mind.

The First approached the Elephant,
And happening to fall
Against his broad and sturdy side,
At once began to bawl:
"God bless me! but the Elephant
Is very like a wall!"

The Second, feeling of the tusk
Cried, "Ho! what have we here,
So very round and smooth and sharp?
To me 'tis mighty clear
This wonder of an Elephant
Is very like a spear!"

The Third approached the animal,
And happening to take
The squirming trunk within his hands,
Thus boldly up he spake:
"I see," quoth he, "the Elephant
Is very like a snake!"

The Fourth reached out an eager hand,
And felt about the knee:
"What most this wondrous beast is like

Is mighty plain," quoth he;
"'Tis clear enough the Elephant
Is very like a tree!"

The Fifth, who chanced to touch the ear,
Said: "E'en the blindest man
Can tell what this resembles most;
Deny the fact who can,
This marvel of an Elephant
Is very like a fan!"

The Sixth no sooner had begun
About the beast to grope,
Than, seizing on the swinging tail
That fell within his scope.
"I see," quoth he, "the Elephant
Is very like a rope!"

And so these men of Indostan
Disputed loud and long,
Each in his own opinion
Exceeding stiff and strong,
Though each was partly in the right,
And all were in the wrong!

Moral:
So oft in theologic wars,
The disputants, I ween,
Rail on in utter ignorance
Of what each other mean,
And prate about an Elephant
Not one of them has seen!

GOOD THING ELEPHANTS DON'T FLY ANYMORE

African forest elephants spend about 16 hours a day eating. Each consumes up to 500 pounds of leaves and grasses every day, and 50 gallons of water. Of that, about 165 pounds of solids return to the soil as poop. It's good for the forest, and it contains lots of seeds that sprout in the nutrient-rich excrement.

PACK A TRUNK

The elephant's trunk is an extremely versatile organ, good for trumpeting, pulling down branches, caressing elephant babies, drinking and smelling. Using fingerlike lobes on its end and the sucking action of its nostrils, elephants can pick up small objects, including such hard-to-get items as a coin on the ground. The trunk's capacity? 1.5 gallons of water.

When elephants greet each other, they place the tips of their trunks in each other's mouths. Young males play-wrestle with their trunks. (In a true fight, elephants protect their trunks by curling them under their chins.)

HOW DO YOU MAKE AN ELEPHANT FLOAT?

An elephant can't gallop, jump or leap, but it can swim for miles at a time. If you weighed as much as an elephant, you'd probably rather float and kick than walk, too: An Indian elephant weighs in at 11,000 pounds; an African elephant, at more than 15,400. Yes, despite the elephant's weight, its body displaces enough water to float quite nicely. Even in rough water, it can hold its trunk out of the water to use as a snorkel.

SOME ELEPHANT FACTS TO NEVER FORGET

• During the Ice Age, elephants roamed every continent but Australia and Antarctica.

• Besides humans, the Asian elephant is the only animal that is able to stand on its head.

• Elephants are the heaviest living land animal. They are second only to the giraffes in the tallest animal competition.

• An elephant's gestation period is a whopping 22 months. Imagine the relief for the mom when birth finally takes place, since an elephant calf can weigh 250 pounds at birth.

• Elephants live about as long as humans. One difference: Their last permanent tooth comes in when they're about forty.

• Elephant herds number from 15 to 40 members, and they're a matriarchy, led by an aged female.

• Elephants were used as work animals in Asia as early as 2000 B.C. Working elephants have learned to recognize as many as forty voice commands.

• Thick foot pads and a rolling gait allow elephants to walk almost soundlessly. They normally walk at a speed of about 4 mph, but can get up to 25 mph when charging.

• The earliest known elephant ancestor was the *moeritherium*, a pig-sized animal with a snout like a tapir's, which lived about 60 million years ago in Africa.

• The earliest use of elephants in war was recorded in 331 B.C., when Persian soldiers riding elephants lost to the Macedonian army led by Alexander the Great. In 218 B.C., Hannibal of Carthage used war elephants more successfully when he crossed the Alps and invaded Italy.

• *Pachyderm* means "thick skin" in Latin. An elephant's skin is 1.5 inches thick in places, but is tender enough that mosquitoes and flies can penetrate it.

• Elephants have no sweat glands. They keep cool by submerging themselves in water and by covering themselves with mud.

• Besides rumbling, elephants use at least twenty-five different calls to communicate specific messages to each other.

• Elephants can knock down trees of up to 2 feet in diameter.

• Elephants have few natural enemies because of their size. A big cat could kill a baby, but that rarely happens because an elephant herd surrounds the babies in a circle when attacked, and anything that threatens them will get gored with tusks or fatally stepped on. ☾

Word Thieves

TERMS WE'VE BORROWED FROM THE GERMANS

After a potato blight hit Germany in 1845, followed by a revolution in 1848, a tide of German emigrants hit America's shores, and their language added scores of words to the national vernacular.

bum: From German *bummler* ("loafer") and *bummelm* ("waste time").

check: The restaurant term came from the German *zeiche,* which means a bill for drinks. (However, all of the other kinds of checks come from the British word *cheque.*)

cookbook: From *kochbuch.*

dachshund: Germans thought the wienery dog looked like a badger, so called it *dachshund,* which means "badger dog."

delicatessen: The German word comes from *delicatesse* ("good things to eat").

dumb: Although the English used the word to mean "unable to speak," Americans got the "stupid" meaning from the German *dum.* The word *dumkopf* means "stupid head."

ecology: From the German *okologie* ("home" or "habitat").

frankfurter and **hamburger:** Both of these delicacies get their names from German cities (Frankfurt and Hamburg, of course).

gesundheit: "To your health."

hoodlum: Originally *hodalum.*

kindergarten: Literally, "children's garden."

klutz: From *klotz* ("block of wood").

nix: From the German *nichts* ("nothing").

ouch!: From *autcsch*!

pumpernickel: From *pumpen nickel* ("fart of the devil") because the coarse bread was hard to digest.

shyster: Probably from the German word *scheisse* ("shit").

spiel: From *spielen* ("play a musical instrument").

yesman: A literal translation of *jaherr.*

zwieback: This favorite of teething infants has a name that literally means "twice-baked."

More Grandville
Kids' Illustrator, Father of Surrealism

Jean Ignace Isidore Gerard (1803–1847), who went by the name "Grandville," became quite successful, illustrating *Gulliver's Travels* and other books. Unfortunately, that surrealistic genius apparently came with a price: He died insane in a mental institution.

Man of Steel

ALL ABOUT JOSEPH STALIN

In 1880, Yekaterian and Vissarion Dzhugashvili became parents to a son who would become one of the world's most feared personalities; his name was Iosif, nicknamed "Soso." To the world, he would be known as Joseph Stalin—the post-Lenin leader of the USSR.

• Joseph Stalin had a rather humble and uneventful childhood in the Georgian village of Gori. His two brothers, Mikhail and Georgii, died before reaching the age of one. Joseph's father Vissarion, a shoemaker, was an alcoholic who abused his wife and child. His mother was supportive, ensuring that he was educated first in a theological school and later in seminary in Tiflis. As he progressed in the Russian Communist Party, however, Joseph evidently did not feel a strong bond with her; when she died in 1937, he had not visited her for two years.

• Stalin was expelled from seminary in 1899 and became politically active shortly before Lenin and Martov began their revolutionary newspaper *Iskra* (*The Spark*). In 1901, Stalin became an elected member of the Tiflis Social Democratic Committee. This began his "career" as a political activist.

• Tsarist officials kept an eye on him between the times when he was either imprisoned or exiled. This physical description was circulated among the police at that time:

— 5'4" male

— sunken hazel eyes

— soft voice

— birthmark on left ear

— pock-marked face

— thick black hair and mustache (but no beard)

— withered left arm

— second and third toes of left foot grown together.

• Stalin escaped the Tsarist prisons a record five times. The prisons weren't as bad as you would imagine — they were thought of as universities of sorts because the prisoners had access to vast libraries. Stalin vowed that "his" prison system would neither allow escapes nor be an educational system. It would, he said, become a grim exercise in survival.

Stalin when he took over as head of the Bolshevik party—sometime around 1912

• In June 1904, Stalin married Yekaterina "Kato" Svanidze. He had no real career, and they were forced to live "on the run." He became known as a Robin Hood of sorts, taking part in robberies to assist the Party. (He was eventually expelled for these "expropriations.") His son, Yakov, was born in 1905. In 1907, his wife died of typhoid.

• In 1912, he officially changed his name to Stalin, meaning "man of steel," and made an aggressive entrance into Bolshevik politics. After escaping deportation in Western Siberia, Stalin visited with Lenin in Cracow and proceeded to Vienna, where he met Trotsky and began writing political tracts. Stalin was selected for the Bolshevik Central Committee at a Party Conference in Prague.

• Stalin avoided being drafted into the World War I service of Russia because of his withered arm and deformed foot. During the war, he was exiled for four years to Turukhansk.

• When the Bolsheviks seized power from the temporary revolutionary government after the assassination of the Tsar, Stalin became Commissar of Nationalities. Following this revolution, there continued to be unrest in Russia and neighboring states, which would later be defeated by the Red Army to form the Union of Soviet Socialist Republics. In 1922, Stalin was elected General Secretary of the Party, positioning himself to take over as

Lenin's health failed.

• In 1924, Lenin died and Stalin seized power. The only real opposition to Stalin's power grab came from Leon Trotsky, whom Lenin had trusted and valued. However, Trotsky was more of a revolutionary thinker and philosopher, and he did not pay close attention to politics, allowing Stalin to easily gain the support and power needed to lead the Party from the General Secretary's position. Trotsky was expelled from the Party, later permanently exiled from the USSR, and eventually assassinated in Mexico.

• Stalin pretty much lived to rule. Although he remarried and was the father of more children, his personal life hardly existed as he rose in power. Stalin's second wife and mother of two of his children, Nadezhda, committed suicide on November 8, 1932. Stalin did not appear to blame himself for her death (as most others around him secretly did); instead he viewed her action as treachery on her part. He did not attend the funeral.

• His relationship with his children was so distant as to be virtually nonexistent, and his children did not lead happy lives. Stalin's eldest son, Yakov, attempted to shoot himself, but the bullet missed vital organs and he survived after a long recuperation. Shortly after this suicide attempt, Stalin reportedly greeted his son with, "Ha! You missed!" Yakov later joined the Army and became a commander; he was killed while attempting to escape from a prison camp during World War II. Stalin's other son, Vasili, was also in the Army, but he finished life an invalid from alcoholism.

• Stalin did appear to have a closer relationship with his daughter, Svetlana, but that faded quickly as she grew older and he grew more paranoid. The relationship became seriously strained when he had her first boyfriend, Alexander Yakovlevich

Stalin loved vodka, and Russians still remember that. A bottle of Stalin's Tears vodka (left), and an inset of Stalin's face featured on another Russian brand.

Kapler, sentenced, on a trumped-up charge, to ten years in a prison camp.

- Meanwhile, Stalin focused on ferreting out or "unmasking enemies of the people." He made accusations against friends and even family members who were previously regarded as allies, and he did nothing to assist those who might have been unjustly accused. Instead, he grew more intensely suspicious.

- By the time Stalin began his infamous Five-Year Plans, he was far removed from the people, and he had little regard for the human difficulties associated with collectivization. The *kulak* (farming peasant class) became desperate as their properties were confiscated. The agricultural life of the USSR was in turmoil: half to two-thirds of all livestock was slaughtered by 1933 to feed hungry people; the amount of cultivated land fell sharply; and families torn from their land became homeless. Hunger and desperation led to petty thievery of food and basic supplies, which was punishable by an unconditional ten-year imprisonment. By 1933, more than 50,000 people had been sentenced to the concentration camps.

- During this time, Stalin was trusting aides and colleagues less and less, preferring to direct Soviet life personally. He purged anyone who seemed to threaten his power. The relationship between Stalin and the rest of the Party became so strained in the early 1930s that almost a quarter of the Party delegates voted against Stalin in a leadership vote. After that, Stalin no longer took the chance of putting himself up for re-election. He directed that Party and state documents stop listing him as General Secretary, an elected position, and he continued ruling without an official title.

- Toward the latter 1930s, Stalin became more hardlined and paranoid. Anyone could be accused of "Trotskyism" and sentenced to death. In a two-year period, 30,514 people were sentenced to be shot for disloyalty to the State. The NKVD, Stalin's police force, rounded up thousands of people suspected of capital crimes; Stalin and the chief of NKVD signed orders for their executions without considering circumstance or proof.

- By the end of the 1930s, the purges began tapering off. Party membership had understandably declined, so that

Stalin seemed less inclined to purge and more inclined to work on filling the ranks with properly dogmatized young Stalinists.

• The USSR entered the war, joining the allies against Germany, but after, the wary allies quickly split again. Stalin continued his hard-line tactics, and continual unrest was in the Party. Military standards thrived while living standards suffered.

• When Stalin died in 1953, an inventory of his possessions revealed only a government-issue piano; there were no valuable furnishings of any kind. Stalin's clothes were largely inexpensive and included a marshal's uniform. His linens consisted of Army-issued blankets. The only original art he owned was a photo of himself and Lenin together in a friendly pose at Gorky Park. This was later determined to be a carefully constructed photo montage — a fake rendition of a scene that never happened. ☾

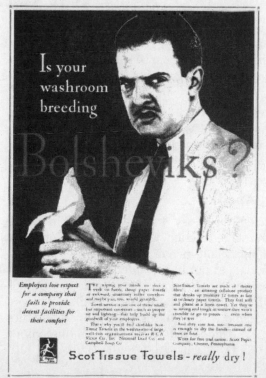

Thanks to Stalin's reign of terror, hating Bolsheviks became America's favorite pastime, as evidenced by this old ScotTissue ad

Kitchen Scientist
BAKING SODA BOMBS AWAY!

Mixing baking soda and vinegar is probably the best-known kitchen science combo around. Try this one and you'll see why.

1 Start with a leak-proof Ziploc bag, vinegar, warm water, a tissue and a carton of baking soda.

2 Place about a half-cup of vinegar and a quarter cup of warm water into your Ziploc sandwich bag. Carefully zip the bag halfway closed.

3 Pour the baking soda into the tissue and twist the top. This will prevent the baking soda from spilling into the mixture immediately when it's added.

4 Insert the baking soda tissue baggie into the bag, but don't let it fall into the liquid yet. Squeeze it from the outside while you completely seal the baggie. Let the tissue fall into the liquid and run.

5 When the baking soda, which is a base, hits the vinegar — an acid — the mixture reacts, creating carbon dioxide. The carbon dioxide fills the Ziploc baggie pretty quickly, causing it to burst open with a bang. Oh wait, did we forget to mention that this experiment is best done in a bathtub or outside? Sorry!

VARIATION ON THE THEME
Here's another, quieter, less messy, and therefore less interesting way of exploiting the same reaction. Get a soda bottle and pour a half-inch of water and a half-inch of distilled vinegar into it. Take some baking soda and put it into a deflated balloon. Fit the end of the balloon over the mouth of the bottle without letting the baking soda spill into the liquid yet. Hold the balloon securely on the bottle and let the baking soda drop down into the liquid mixture. The balloon will likely inflate to the point of exploding, or flying off the bottle. ☾

Stately Knowledge

12 REASONS WHY YA GOTTA LOVE NEW YORK

There are so many reasons to love New York, but we've somehow managed to pick out our 12 favorites.

1 Want to stand at the most crowded street corner in the United States? Get yourself to the corner of 59th and Lexington in New York City. New York also hosts the busiest highway in the nation: the George Washington Bridge.

2 The Statue of Liberty's index finger is 8 feet long. If you plan to buy her a ring, keep in mind that her finger joint is almost 3.5 feet around.

3 Grace Bedell, an eleven-year-old from Chautauqua, New York, convinced Abraham Lincoln to grow his beard while campaigning for president in 1860 by writing him in a letter: "You would look a great deal better for your face is so thin. All the ladies like whiskers and they would tease their husbands to vote for you." It seems to have worked, because he won.

4 We love LeRoy! LeRoy, New York, that is—the birthplace of Jell-O.

5 Want to know where ice cream maker Ben met Jerry? In 1963, Bennett Cohen and Jerry Greenfield were "smart, nerdy, fat kids" at Merrick Avenue Junior High School in Long Island, New York, undergoing humiliations that come with being overweight in junior high P.E. class. They ended up on the same running track, trailing behind the other guys. Recalled Jerry: "We were the two slowest, chubbiest guys in the class. Coach yelled, 'Gentlemen, if you don't run the mile in under 7 minutes, you're going to have to do it again.' And Ben yelled back, 'Gee, coach, if I don't do it in under 7 minutes the first time, I'm certainly not going to do it in under 7 minutes the second time.' To me this was brilliance. This was a

guy I wanted to know." Years later, when they decided to go into business together, they decided it should be food-related because they were into eating.

6 Created by Arthur Wynn, the first crossword puzzle appeared in the pages of the *New York World* newspaper on December 21, 1913. A national crossword puzzle craze ensued.

7 In the 1860s, some guys from the drinking society, "The Jolly Corks," visited Barnum's Museum in New York City and spied a stuffed elk. Thereafter, they decided to call themselves the Benevolent and Protective Order of Elks, aka the Elks Club.

8 In 1908, a sign reading "Baseball Today—Polo Grounds" in a New York City subway station inspired Jack Norworth and Albert von Tilzer to write a song. They'd never seen a baseball game, but they'd heard enough about it to know it was popular, so they penned "Take Me Out to the Ballgame."

9 The teddy bear was first created in Brooklyn, New York, in 1902.

10 In 1853 at the Moon Lake Lodge in Saratoga Springs, New York, a snack industry was born. A picky patron—Commodore Cornelius Vanderbilt—kept complaining that his fried potatoes were too thick. The restaurant's chef, George Crum, finally sliced them paper-thin as a joke. Vanderbilt's loved them, and Crum eventually opened a specialty shop dealing only in potato chips.

11 Peekskill, New York, is the place where Edwin Binney and C. Harold Smith invented "dustless" blackboard chalk and Crayola crayons in 1903.

12 Skyscrapers in New York were going up so fast in the 1930s that the director of *King Kong* had to change his script three times before filming ended. Kong was to climb the world's highest building, so the script first read, "the N.Y. Life," then, "the Chrysler," and finally, "the Empire State." ☾

The Jolly Corks!

Crayola

CHIPS

Spooky Tales

3 SHORT GHOST STORIES FROM OLD JAPAN

More ancient Japanese legends collected by Lafcadio Hearn in 1903, about ducks, decapitation and faces like eggs....

THE MANDARIN DUCK

There was a falconer and hunter named Sonjo. One day at Akanuma he saw a pair of mandarin ducks swimming together in a river that he was about to cross. To kill a mandarin duck is not considered good luck at all, but Sonjo happened to be very hungry, and he shot at the pair. His arrow pierced the male: the female escaped into the rushes of the further shore, and disappeared. Sonjo took the dead bird home, and cooked it.

That night he dreamed that a beautiful woman came into his room, stood by his pillow, and began to weep. So bitterly did she weep that Sonjo felt as if his heart were being torn out. The woman cried to him: "Oh! why did you kill him? What harm did he ever do you? Of what wrong was he guilty? We were so happy together, and you killed him! Me too you have killed, for I will not live without my husband!"

Then again she wept so bitterly that her crying pierced into the marrow of the listener's bones, and she sobbed out a poem: "At the coming of twilight I invited him to return with me. Now to sleep alone in the shadow of the rushes—Oh, what misery unspeakable!"

After reciting these verses, she exclaimed: "You do not know, you cannot know what you have done! But tomorrow, when you go to Akanuma, you will see, you will see...." And weeping very piteously, she went away.

When Sonjo awoke in the morning, this dream remained so vivid in his mind that he was greatly troubled. And he resolved to go to Akanuma at once, that he might learn whether his dream was anything more than a dream.

So he went to Akanuma; and there at the riverbank he saw the female mandarin duck swimming alone. The bird looked up and saw Sonjo; but, instead of trying to escape, she swam straight towards him, looking at him all the while in a strange fixed way. Then, with her beak, she suddenly tore open her own body, and died before the hunter's eyes.

Sonjo shaved his head and became a priest.

ON THE AKASAKA ROAD

On the Akasaka Road, in Tokyo, there is a slope called Kii-no-kuni-zaka. On one side of this slope you see an ancient moat with high green banks rising up to gardens; on the other, long walls of an imperial palace. Before the era of street-lamps, this neighborhood was very lonesome after dark; and many pedestrians would go miles out of their way rather than climb the Kii-no-kuni-zaka, alone, after sunset.

One night long ago, an old merchant was hurrying up the Kii-no-kuni-zaka, when he saw a woman crouching by the moat, all alone and weeping bitterly. Fearing that she intended to drown herself, he stopped to offer her assistance or consolation. She appeared slight and graceful, handsomely dressed; and her hair was like that of a young girl of good family. "Young lady," he exclaimed, approaching her. "Do not cry like that. Tell me what the trouble is. I would be glad to help you." (He really meant what he said, for he was a very kind man.) But she continued to weep, hiding her face from him with one of her long sleeves. "Young lady," he said again, as gently as he could, "please, please listen to me! This is no place for a young lady at night! Do not cry, I implore you! Only tell me how I may be of some help to you!" Slowly she rose up, but turned her back to him, and continued to moan and sob behind her sleeve. He laid his hand lightly upon her shoulder, and pleaded: "Young lady, listen to me, just for one little moment!"

The young woman slowly turned around, and dropped her sleeve. She stroked her face with her hand...and the man saw that she had no eyes or nose or mouth. He screamed and ran away. Up Kii-no-kuni-zaka he ran, and all was black and empty before him. On and on he ran, never daring to look back; and at last he saw a lantern, so far away that it looked like the gleam of a firefly; and he made for it.

It proved to be only the lantern of an itinerant noodle-seller, who had set down his stand by the roadside; but any light and any human companionship was good after that experience; and he flung himself down at the feet of the noodle-seller, crying out, "Ah!—aa!!—aa!!!"

"Hey now!" exclaimed the soba-man roughly. "What is the matter with you? Anybody hurt you?"

"Nobody hurt me," panted the merchant, "only...Ah!—aa!"

"Only scared you?" queried the peddler, unsympathetically. "Robbers?"

"Not robbers—not robbers," gasped the terrified man. "I saw—I saw a woman—by the moat—and she showed me.... Ah! I cannot tell you what she showed me!"

"Well! Was it anything like THIS that she showed you?" cried the noodle-man, stroking his own face—which was also smooth and featureless, like an egg. And, simultaneously, the light went out.

DEATH, WHERE IS THY BITE?

An execution was about to take place in the garden of an important samurai. The condemned man was made to kneel down in a wide sanded space with arms bound behind him. Retainers and servants packed rice-bags around the kneeling man, wedging him in that he could not move. The master came, and observed the arrangements. He found them satisfactory, and made no remarks.

Suddenly the condemned man cried out to him. "Honored sir, the fault for which I have been doomed I did not wittingly commit. It was only my very great stupidity that caused the fault. Having been born stupid, by reason of my Karma, I could not always help making mistakes. But to kill a man for being stupid is wrong—and that wrong will be repaid. So surely as you kill me, so surely shall I be avenged. Out of the resentment that you provoke will come the vengeance, and evil will be rendered for evil."

It's believed that if any person is killed while feeling strong resentment, his ghost will be able to take vengeance upon the killer. The samurai knew this, and he replied very gently, almost caressingly: "We shall allow you to frighten us as much as you please—after you are dead. But it is difficult to believe that you mean what you say. Will you try to give us some sign of your great resentment—after your head has been cut off?"

"Assuredly I will," answered the man.

"Very well," said the samurai, drawing his long sword. "I am now going to cut off your head. Directly in front of you there is a stepping-stone. After your head has been cut off, try to bite the stepping-stone. If your angry ghost can help you to do that, some of us may be frightened. Will you try to bite the stone?"

"I will bite it!" cried the man angrily. "I will bite it! I will—"

There was a flash, a swish, a crunching thud: the bound body bowed over the rice sacks—two long blood-jets pumping from the shorn neck—and the head rolled upon the sand. Heavily toward the stepping-stone it rolled: then, suddenly bounding, it caught the upper edge of the stone between its teeth and clung desperately for a moment. Then it dropped off and stood still.

None spoke; but the retainers stared in horror at their master. He seemed to be quite unconcerned. He merely held out his sword to the nearest attendant, who, with a wooden dipper, poured water over the blade from haft to point, and then carefully wiped the steel with soft paper. And thus ended the ceremonial part of the incident.

For months thereafter, the retainers and the domestics lived in ceaseless fear of ghostly visitation. None of them doubted that the promised vengeance would come; and their constant terror caused them to hear and to see much that did not exist. They became afraid of the sound of the wind in the bamboos, afraid even of the shadows in the garden. At last, after taking counsel together, they decided to petition their master to have an exorcism service performed on behalf of the vengeful spirit.

"Quite unnecessary," the samurai said, when his chief retainer uttered the general wish. "I understand that the desire of a dying man for revenge may be a cause for fear. But in this case there is nothing to fear."

The retainer looked at his master beseechingly, but hesitated to ask the reason of the alarming confidence.

"Oh, the reason is simple enough," declared the samurai,

divining the unspoken doubt. "Only the very last intention of the fellow could have been dangerous; and when I challenged him to give me the sign, I diverted his mind from the desire of revenge. He died with the set purpose of biting the stepping-stone; and that purpose he was able to accomplish, but nothing else. All the rest he must have forgotten. So you need not feel any further anxiety about the matter."

And indeed the dead man gave no more trouble. Nothing at all happened. ☾

Chatty Letter from a Salem "Witch" Persecutor

To John Cotton, Jr.
August 5, 1692

Reverend Sir,

Our good God is working of miracles. Five witches were lately executed, impudently demanding of God a miraculous vindication of their innocency. Immediately upon this, our God miraculously sent in five Andover witches, who made a most ample, surprising, amazing confession of all their villainies, and declared the five newly executed to have been of their company, discovering many more, but all agreeing in Burroughs being their ringleader, who, I suppose this day receives his trial at Salem. Since those, there have come in other confessors; yea, they come in daily. About this prodigious matter my soul has been refreshed with some little short of miraculous answers of prayer, which are not to be written: but they comfort me with a prospect of a hopeful issue.

The whole town yesterday turned the lecture into a fast, kept in our meeting-house; God give a good return. But in the morning we were entertained with the horrible tidings of the late earthquake at Jamaica, on the 7th of June last. When, on a fair day, the sea suddenly swelled, and the earth shook and broke in many places, and in a minute's time, the rich town of Port-Royal, a very Sodom for wickedness, was immediately swallowed up, and the sea came rolling over the town. No less than seventeen-hundred souls of that one town are missing, besides other incredible devastations all over the island, where houses are demolished, mountains overturned, rocks rent, and all manner of destruction inflicted. Behold, an accident speaking to all our English America.

I live in pains, and want your prayers. Bestow them, dear Sir, on your,

Cotton Mather

Something in Common 2

It's easy, really—we'll give you a list of words and you tell us the one word that goes with all of them. Answers below (don't cheat!).

1. Job, holy, judgment, camp, opening, earth, arbor
2. Main, chicken, water, fever, silent, hot, cleaning
3. Eye, looking, fiber, wine, drinking, stained
4. Cloth, chalk, gold, moon, bin, cosmic, bowl, fairy
5. Tray, wood, tree, Wednesday, volcanic, soda
6. Hair, combination, door, Soo, pad, picking, bike
7. Mill, ill, instrument, solar, westerly, shield
8. Fish, strawberry, naval, bean, roll
9. Gun, monkey, bear, hair, palm, elbow
10. West, board, minor, skeleton, stone, ignition
11. Pearl, traffic, session, raspberry, toe
12. Drive, backer, air, railroad, assembly, phone, sales, dotted
13. Right, out, bag, cuff, wash, made, stamp, delivery, puppet
14. Lunch, ears, car, cardboard, soap, match
15. Club, mail, site, ceiling, dancer, exhaust, tail, window, belt
16. Frost, tire, car, hi, lumber, hammer, Monterey
17. Seven, cheer, beat, chuck, speed, end, town, wind
18. Fighter, wild, forest, place, starter, pit, alarm, Chicago
19. Two, up, smiley, clock, rock, off, facts, powder
20. Finger, penny, hob, file, finishing, rusty, polish, salon, gun

Life Lessons
HOW TO MAKE A 12-FOOT "TEEPEE"

Long before log cabins, the housing of choice in North America was the tipi. Building one isn't that difficult. Here's how.

Blackfoot tipis from the 1800s

BUILDING A "TEEPEE" (tipi) can be easy or hard, depending on how authentic you want it to be. For example, if you want one in the style of some tribes, our instructions would begin: "Skin 30 bison...."

WHAT YOU'LL NEED
- 30 bison skins, or 32 yards of canvas duck fabric
- 12 lodge poles, straight and slender, 14 feet long
- 2 poles for the smoke flaps, 16 feet long
- Rope
- Strong needle and thread
- Stakes or rocks

HOW YOU DO IT
1 Cut your 32 yards of canvas into three strips 8 yards long. Sew them side by side into a rectangle 4 yards by 8 yards. As below, draw the designs on the fabric using chalk and cut them out. (Using

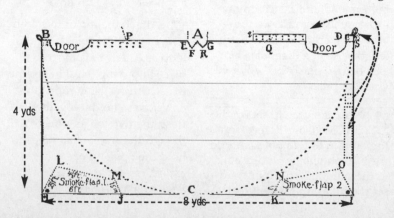

a 4-yard length of string anchored at **A** will help you draw the giant semicircle.)

2 Sew the smoke flaps and connecting strips as below. If you're a traditionalist, make reinforced holes at **B, P, Q** and **D** to lace rope through; otherwise, try using industrial-strength Velcro. Attach loops of rope or fabric strips every

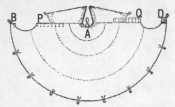

4 feet around the circle as well as one at the center point of the circle at **A** and one at the bottom of each smoke flap. Make a 2-inch hole at the top of each smoke flap.

3 About the supporting poles: using store-bought lumber is not a bad idea. For stability, you want the poles to be about 2.5 inches thick on the bottom end and 1 inch on the top. Buy 2x4s and ask a lumberyard worker to halve them lengthwise at a diagonal slant (see below). Each 2x4 will give you two poles.

4 Now it's time to set up the tipi. Measure 12 feet from the bottom of two poles and tie them together. Tie a third pole to them to make a tripod, and set the poles up on their feet.

On the ground, draw a circle 12 feet in diameter and place the bottoms of the poles equal distances around it.

5 Take all the rest of the support poles but one and lean them up against the three, spacing them as regularly as you can around the circle. Lash them all together at the top by walking around the circle with a rope two or three times. Decide where the door will be — preferably facing away from the wind — and anchor the rope with a stake driven inside the

circle opposite the door. Leave a space for the 12th pole.

5 Attach the top of the cloth to the 12th pole using the loop at **A**. Lift the pole into place and wrap the skin around the structure, using rope, pins or Velcro to hold it together. Push the two longer poles though the smoke flap holes to hold the opening open. If necessary, reinforce with ropes and a wooden crosspiece.

Stormcap.

Door

Chipewyan Teebee
with Tent Bedroom.

Teepee with Stormcap

E.T.Seton

6 You can stake the tent down with the ropes at the bottom, but you won't need to unless the wind picks up substantially.

7 Using leftover fabric, make a door flap (see above).

8 In cold weather, a small fire can be set in a fire circle in the middle of the tent. In hot weather, the open top adds cooling ventilation. During rain, you can make a fabric cap to rest on top of the poles. ☾

Wigwam or Tipi?

Despite this page from an old children's book (*right*), a wigwam is not the same as a tipi. Wigwams were small, single-family domes (*below*) used as shelter in rain and bad weather.

The above is a wigwam. The picture to the right—despite the charming rhyme—is not.

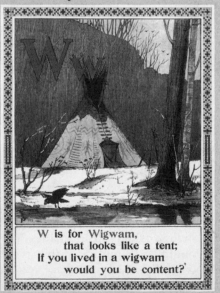

W is for Wigwam,
    that looks like a tent;
If you lived in a wigwam
    would you be content?

Every Picture Tells a Story

Nude Descending a Staircase No. 2 by Marcel Duchamp, 1912

• Marcel Duchamp was born to a family of artists. He became a founder of Dada, an absurdist, avant garde movement. (The name doesn't come from child-speak for father, as some suppose, but from the French word for a hobbyhorse.)

• In *Nude Descending a Staircase No. 2*, Duchamp tried to show each incremental step of a moving person.

• There is also *Nude Descending a Staircase No. 1*. The main difference is that *No. 2* has the little comic-booky curved lines and dots that indicate movement.

• After about twenty paintings, Duchamp decided he didn't want to repeat himself, so he gave it up. For a while he exhibited what he called "Readymades," which were common objects he bought and signed as if they were art.

• Eventually, Duchamp decided he was bored with art. He retired and became a champion chess player.

VW

BUGGING DETROIT'S AUTOCRACY

Today, they're the ultimate sign of yuppiedom, and the cost is comparable to any other car. Originally, though, the VW Beetle was a way for Americans to vote with their dollars and good sense against the excesses of Detroit.

THE BUG was designed by Ferdinand Porsche, the brilliant auto designer. He fathered a succession of high-powered yet elegant autos, including the Mercedes, for a succession of German manufacturers.

Porsche decided that his *volksauto* ("people's auto") would have to be a completely new design. He gave the car a reverse-teardrop shape to increase fuel efficiency. Brilliantly, he redesigned parts that were too heavy or expensive. Heavy wheel springs gave way to a new kind of suspension system that used torsion bars. Porsche replaced the heavy chassis with a sheet-metal floor pan, creased and corrugated for strength. He mounted a small air-cooled engine in back of the car, which improved traction, cut the expense of the drive train, and did away with the space-wasting hump in the passenger compartment.

Porsche went looking for a backer and found one in Adolf Hitler. Hitler was an auto enthusiast, even though he had never learned to drive.

He was an admirer of the Mercedes and Porsche racing cars, which were winning prestige for Germany in international races. In quick order, Porsche produced 33 cars and ran them around test tracks. They satisfactorily performed.

In 1938, the Reich built an ultramodern factory, and Hitler announced that the car would henceforth be known as the *Kraft-durch-Freude Wagen* ("Strength-Through-Joy Car").

But only 210 Strength-Through-Joy Cars were built before the factory had to be diverted to the war effort.

Staffed by slaves from the concentration camps, the factory produced some 70,000 Jeep-like *Kübelwagens* and amphibious *Schwimmkübels,* and various supplies for soldiers on the Eastern Front.

As a result, the Volksvagenwerk factory was a target of American planes and was in shambles when captured in April of 1945. The factory was scheduled for dismantling, but a few of the former car workers—hungry, having nothing much to do, and remembering the dream of Volkswagen prosperity—started coming in to see what was left of the production line. They located tools and dies, scrounged materials, and managed to hand-build a few Strength-Through-Joy Cars. These they bartered to the occupying British officers for food.

At first the plant did well, going from 1,785 cars the first year to 10,020 cars the next. Then things started sagging. In 1947, the factory produced only 8,987 cars, including the first VWs ever earmarked for export. But the plant couldn't continue building cars in an unmanaged plant that used scrounged parts.

No British car makers wanted to save the plant. They described the car as ugly, noisy, outlandish and unsalable. Henry Ford II, as well, turned down the opportunity to take over the company (Ford once described the car as a "little %#*!-box"). The Soviet Government was willing to take control if they could renegotiate the German/Soviet border to include the land the factory was on. The Allies refused the offer.

Finding no takers, the British appointed pre-war car executive Heinrich Nordhoff director of the plant. Nordhoff didn't like the VW, but he needed a job, and his family was hungry. On New Year's

Day 1948, he moved into the factory, sleeping on a cot.

Because Nordhoff had no executives looking over his shoulder, he was able to do as he saw fit. He met regularly with his workers, listening to them, and inspiring them to higher productivity and quality. All profits he plowed back into the facilities and equipment, but it became clear that the struggling company would need a larger market than postwar Germany to survive and grow. Because much of Europe was still in ruins, Nordhoff decided to go where the money was: the United States. He shipped two Beetles to his only international distributor, Ben Pon in the Netherlands.

Pon was a great car dealer. He had to be, selling German cars in the Netherlands, where residual bitterness toward Germany was still powerful. Pon took one of the Beetles to the United States. The Bug got only a little publicity, much of it negative (newspapers referred to it as "Hitler's car"). U.S. auto dealers refused to take it seriously. Finally, Pon sold his model for $800 to pay his travel costs. He returned to Holland, defeated.

It was just a temporary defeat.

American vets stationed in Europe had discovered how good the cheap little cars were and began bringing them back to this country.

Their word-of-mouth praise and a write-up in *Consumer Reports* stimulated a modest demand. In 1950, 330 VWs sold in America; in 1955, 30,000; in 1957, 79,000.

Nordhoff felt vindicated in deciding not to restyle the ugly little car. "The only decision I am really proud of," he said years later, "is that I refused to change Porsche's design. It's hard to remain the same. You can always sell cars by being new. But we chose a different course."

All this stood in stark contrast to the road traveled by American manufacturers. This was, after all, the era of planned obsolescence, of fins, chrome and outlandish doodads of almost every sort, of bigger and bigger "jukeboxes on wheels." Detroit didn't know what to make of VW's success. It was the opposite of what they believed consumers wanted.

The Beetle was cheap, and American car executives were shaken to find that the people buying them weren't poor. VW customers were generally people who could afford more expensive cars but who liked the VW's no-frills design and good engineering. "The Volkswagen sells because it is, more than anything else, an honest car," noted Arthur Railton in *Popular Mechanics* in 1956.

"It doesn't pretend to be anything it is not. Being an honest piece of machinery, it is one the owner can be proud of. Wherever he looks, he sees honest design and workmanship. There are no places where parts don't fit, where paint is thin, where the trim is shoddy. There are no body rattles, no water leaks. Neither, of course, is there overstuffed, false luxury either. There is nothing about the car that is not sincere. One cannot imagine, for instance, a Volkswagen with a fake air scoop or tail fins to make it look like an airplane in flight."

Feeling pressure, GM responded with what it thought was a comparable car in 1959—the Corvair. The problem was that they thought the success of the VW had to do solely with its price, which was, at best, half-right. They cut costs on the Corvair by scrimping on key parts. Possibly the worst American car ever, the Corvair caused much unnecessary injury and death. It inspired Ralph Nader to write his best-seller, *Unsafe at Any Speed,* and spawned hundreds of product liability lawsuits.

The VW Bug and van, virtually unchanged year after year and bolstered by brilliant, honest, low-key advertising, thrived for more than a decade. Detroit's refusal (or inability) to respond in a meaningful way to the VW challenge opened the door to other low-cost, quality imports. ☾

Modern Myth

DOWNWARD MOBILITY OF THE UPPER GLASS

It's a great story, often spread unknowingly by tour guides at historic sites: Pointing out that the glass is thicker at the bottom of an ancient window, they say it's because the glass is liquid and slowly flowing. But it panes us to say that it's a transparent fiction....

IS IT TRUE that windows get thicker at the bottom over years because glass is really a slow-moving liquid? Before we knock this story down, let's look at reasons why even some scientists have considered the idea plausible enough. Their reasoning goes something like this: Solids and liquids have different molecular structures. The molecules of solids occur in regular patterns, while the molecules in liquids are bonded in patterns that are irregular and haphazard. The structure of glass is irregular, so maybe it's really just a very, very thick liquid. Casting around for evidence that would fit this intriguing theory, researchers found that antique windows often had glass that was thicker on the bottom than it was on the top. Aha! they

Getting Down to Glass Facts

• How come you can see through glass if it's a solid? It's not a very dense solid. There's enough space between molecules to let light shine through.

• Glass is made of silica sand, with a little soda ash and limestone added to lower the sand's melting temperature. Humans figured out how to make glass after finding chunks of obsidian formed by lightning strikes on the beach. Early humans originally cast it like metal and then ground and polished it. In about 50 B.C., the Romans figured out how to blow glass using hollow metal tubes, which suddenly made glass inexpensive and practical for a variety of cups, bottles and other vessels.

said, here's evidence that glass slowly seeps downward with time, just like a really thick syrup would.

Well, not so fast. After a lot of shouting and bickering, it looks like the "You idiots, glass is a solid" side wins this one. Yes, glass has a different molecular structure than most solids, but it doesn't necessarily follow that it's a liquid. In fact, although scientists once called glass a "supercooled liquid," most now believe it is really an "amorphous solid," which means that it solidifies haphazardly without forming crystals.

Panes-Taking Work

MAKING GOOD glass windows long eluded human ingenuity. The ancient Romans molded glass and then ground and buffed it, but the results were cloudy and very expensive. On the other hand, their climate was such that they really didn't need windows, anyway.

In much cooler Germany, glassmakers made a giant leap in A.D. 600. They figured out how to blow a large sphere and wave it vigorously until it became a large, hollow cylinder, which the glassblower quickly sliced and flattened onto a metal table. However, this glass was thick and still hard to see clearly through.

Normandy glassmakers finally came up with a clever method of making much thinner windows that remained the state of the art until the late 19th century. Thin and transparent, these glass sheets were invariably thicker on one end, leading to the urban myth about glass oozing (see above). Using about 9 pounds of molten glass, a glassmaker blew a shape with a round body and straight neck on top. He'd attach a metal cap to the center of the round end, flatten the flask into a decanter shape, attach a metal rod called a "punty" to the metal cap and remove the blow pipe, leaving a hole. Now the real fun began as the glassmaker spun the punty rod inside a hot furnace. To quote an 1860 account by college professor Sheridan Muspratt:

> The action of heat and centrifugal force combined is soon visible. The hole, caused by the removal of the blowing pipe, enlarges. The opening grows larger and larger; for the moment is caught in a glimpse of a circle with a double rim; the next moment, before the eyes of the astonished spectator, is whirling a thin, transparent, circular plate of glass.... The sound of the final opening of the piece has been compared to that produced by quickly expanding a wet umbrella. In this way a flat circular disc, sixty inches (five feet) in diameter is produced, of almost uniform thickness, except at the point of attachment to the punty, and the glass at the edge of the disc is also in some cases a little thickened.... The cutting of a circle into rectangle sheets, must necessarily be attended with waste and confined to fairly small sizes.

Nowadays, glass manufacturers pour molten glass onto a pool of molten tin. Since tin stays melted at a lower temperature than glass, the glass can harden into a uniform thickness without coming in contact with anything solid. As a result, the process creates panes that are flawless on both sides.

Looking at other ancient glass gives better evidence than old windows do. For example, glass bottles from ancient Rome show no sign of seeping. Telescope lenses that were precision-ground centuries ago show no distortions. And arrowheads from prehistoric times made of obsidian (a glass made when lightning struck sand on

FLINT AND SAND

the beach) are still symmetrical and razor-sharp — something that wouldn't be the case if glass droops, seeps and weeps over time.

Okay, you ask, then how do they explain away the bottom-heavy windows on ancient buildings? Simple. In the old days, glassmakers didn't use the modern technique of floating liquid glass on molten tin, which provides a pane of uniform thickness. They hand-blew and spun window glass, a technique that all but guaranteed that each pane of glass would have varying thickness.

If you were putting a fragile, heavy pane of glass into a window frame, would you place the thicker edge or the thinner edge at the bottom where all the weight of the pane would be resting? Right, the thicker side. So rather than provide evidence of glass seepage, the bottom-heavy windows merely prove that glaziers in the past weren't fools. ☾

Words from the Wise

THINGS TO NEVER, NEVER DO

"Never put anything on paper...and never trust a man with a small black mustache." —P. G. Wodehouse

"Never get a mime talking. He won't stop." —Marcel Marceau

"Never underestimate the power of human stupidity." —Robert Heinlein

"Never send a man to do a horse's job." —Mr. Ed

"Never lend books, for no one ever returns them; the only books I have in my library are books that other folks have lent to me." —Anatole France

"Never trust a man with short legs—brain's too near their bottoms." —Noel Coward

"Never say anything on the phone that you wouldn't want your mother to hear at your trial." —Sydney Biddle Barrows

"Never drop your gun to hug a bear." —H. E. Palmer

"Never steal anything so small that you'll have to go to an unpleasant city jail for it instead of a minimum-security federal tennis prison." —P. J. O'Rourke

"Never put off until tomorrow what you can do the day after tomorrow." —Mark Twain

"Never date a girl named 'Ruby.'" —Tom Waits

"Never offend people with style when you can offend them with substance." —Tony Brown

"Never put a razor inside your nose—even as a joke." —Jake Johansen

Tom Swifties IV

"The PH Is Low," Said Tom Acidly

From the surreal 1960s came elephant jokes and Tom Swifties, based on bad puns and the stylistic excesses of Victor Appleton, who created the popular Tom Swift stories. Here are more.

"What a grand dam," said Tom cooly.

"May I introduce the Family Stone?" Tom asked slyly.

"I'd like to teach the world to sing..." Tom began coaxingly.

"*Niña, Pinta, Santa Maria* and *Titanic*," Tom said forebodingly.

"Add three cans water," said Tom with great concentration.

"I still haven't struck oil," said Tom boringly.

"I'm dying," Tom croaked.

"Your embroidery is terrible," Tom needled cruelly.

"The woodland goat-boy is no more," Tom deadpanned.

"Mink-lined coats are cruel," Tom deferred.

"I can't hear," Tom said deftly.

"Speak, or I'll emasculate you!" Tom demanded.

"All we brought was gold and frankincense," the magi demurred.

"They canceled my doctor's visit," said Tom, disappointed.

"Hey Egyptians, I'm drowning!" Tom said, deep in denial.

"You look like Venus de Milo," Tom said disarmingly.

"Out, damned spot," said Lady Macbeth disdainfully.

"It's June," said Tom, dismayed.

"I lost someone who can't speak," said Tom dumbfoundedly.

"Emily's put on weight," said Tom emphatically.

"I have an alternate personality," said Tom, being frank.

Zen Masters
MODELING ZEN

Here's something to meditate on: words from some of the world's top fashion models—Tyra Banks, Niki Taylor and more.

"I don't know what to do with my arms. It just makes me feel weird and I feel like people are looking at me and that makes me nervous."
—Tyra Banks

"I haven't seen the Eiffel Tower, Notre Dame, the Louvre. I haven't seen anything. I don't really care." —T.B.

"I liked college guys but they could tell I was just a skinny girl."
—T.B.

"I love the confidence that makeup gives me." —T.B.

"It was God who made me so beautiful. If I weren't, then I'd be a teacher." —Linda Evangelista

"All my doctors said I should become a model." —Niki Taylor

"I wish my butt did not go sideways, but I guess I have to face that."
— Christie Brinkley

"In the studio, I do try to have a thought in my head, so that it's not like a blank stare." —Cindy Crawford

"It's a huge change for your body. You don't even want to look in the mirror after you've had a baby, because your stomach is just hanging there like a Shar-Pei." —C.C.

"You start out happy that you have no hips or boobs. All of a sudden you get them, and it feels sloppy. Then just when you start liking them, they start drooping." —C.C.

"Flying is awful, there's nothing to do when you're up in the air. I bloat up, my skin gets dry, and when we hit turbulence, I'm terrified. I was coming back from Tel Aviv recently, and we had forty minutes of bumps. I got so scared I grabbed a paper and pen and put them in my pocket, just in case we crashed and I needed to write a letter from wherever we landed." —Daniela Pestova

Mascot Miracles

How Chiquita Gave Bananas Appeal

"I'm Chiquita Banana and I've come to say: Bananas have to ripen in a certain way...." Before Chiquita—a direct rip-off of a popular south-of-the-border singer—United Fruit advertised fruitlessly.

C HIQUITA BANANA, the wacky singing Latin American banana, was the response that the United Fruit Company came up with to counteract their negative image.

In the court of world public opinion, the United Fruit Company was guilty as charged. The company had a well-deserved reputation of ruthlessness among our Good Neighbors down in South America. It bought up millions of acres of land (sometimes merely to keep it out of the hands of competitors) and as many government officials as it could. The governments it couldn't buy, it undermined and overthrew. Often, as in places like Guatemala in 1954, it received the support of the U.S. government. In fact, the term "banana republic" was originally coined as a backhanded tribute to United Fruit's ability to keep in power whatever corrupt government it wanted, by ballot or bullet.

The company had so much cheap land that it wouldn't bother with maintaining the soil—when a plantation was exhausted, the company would abandon it. They'd load everything of value onto rail cars, tearing up the railroad tracks after them, and bulldoze another plantation out of the rain forest. It was costly to the land and the company, but absolutely disastrous for its local workers, who were usually abandoned at the same time.

All of these practices engendered hard feelings and unfavorable publicity for the company. In Cuba, United Fruit lost all its holdings when two sons of a lifelong United Fruit employee, Angel Castro, led a successful revolution against the banana-corrupted government. (Years later, company executives who knew Angel couldn't help but shake their heads and wonder aloud how a couple of quiet and polite kids like Fidel and Raul Castro could have gone so wrong.) It was a revolution that even United Fruit could not undo. Not that it didn't try—the company secretly provided two freighters from its "Great White Fleet" to transport fighters and weapons into Cuba during the ill-fated Bay of Pigs invasion.

But that was later. Lovable Miss Chiquita Banana was born two decades before Castro's revolution, as World War II began winding down. The Great White Fleet had been repainted battleship gray and pressed into emergency service by the Navy. The numbers of bananas coming into the United States turned into a trickle. United Fruit's corporate leaders had kept their plantations going even though they didn't have a way to get the bananas to market. Now they began

GREAT WHITE FLEET
Caribbean Cruises

SHIPS and men of the Great White Fleet know their tropics... a matter of prime importance to the traveler in the Caribbean. It means cruises planned by experience, and ships specifically designed for the traveling guest's every comfort.

Wide decks for games, promenading, and luxurious lounging...outside staterooms open to the sea breeze...excellent food prepared by chefs experienced in the art of tempting palates.

Great White Fleet Ships sail from New York twice weekly, New Orleans three times weekly. Cuba...Panama...Colombia... Jamaica...Costa Rica...Guatemala...Honduras. Cruises 16 to 24 days, all expenses included. All first class cabins. Full details from

CRUISES **UNITED FRUIT COMPANY**
$225 STEAMSHIP SERVICE
PASSENGER TRAFFIC DEPARTMENT
Room 1608, 17 BATTERY PLACE, NEW YORK CITY

A 1931 ad for United Fruit's Great White
Fleet cruise and banana line

planning a postwar blitz. As soon as they could, they once again began shipping a hundred million bunches of bananas a year.

Most Americans hadn't seen a banana since shortly after the attack on Pearl Harbor, three years earlier. United Fruit's directors decided this was a splendid opportunity to carve out a brand-new, cute and cuddly image for the company.

Carmen Miranda on the DVD cover of the 1995 documentary Carmen Miranda: Bananas is my Business, by Helena Solberg and David Meyer

They turned the problem over to their radio ad agency, Batten, Barton, Durstine & Osborn, which came up with the idea of a wacky but sexy female Latin American singer modeled after Carmen Miranda, even choosing a name that mimicked hers and stealing her trademark, a fruit-covered hat. BBD&O assigned two staff jingle writers, lyricist Garth Montgomery and songsmith Len MacKenzie, to write a suitable song. And indeed they did.

United Fruit pushed the "Chiquita Banana" song into the public's consciousness by insisting that it be performed on all the radio shows the company sponsored. Radio listeners heard the song rendered by such varied performers as Fred Allen, Alec Templeton, Arthur Fieldler, Bert Lahr, the King Sisters, Xavier Cugat, Charlie McCarthy, Carmen Miranda herself and even fictional detective Ellery Queen ("I'm Chiquita Banana and I'm here to say/You have to catch a criminal in a certain way/Now here's the strategy I've tried to use/I have paid strict attention to all the clues…"). At its peak, the song was played around the country on radio 276 times in one day. Recorded on disk by Ray Bloch and the King Sisters, it became a juke box hit as well.

"Chiquita Banana" was a genuine hit, and the public began clamoring to see what she looked like. The company commissioned comic artist Dik Browne, who had just finished redesigning the Campbell Kids but had yet to create the comic strip Hägar the Horrible. He drew Chiquita as a banana with a ruffled skirt, puffy sleeves and a fruit-covered hat. She began appearing in magazine ads and in 80-second cartoon shorts where she sang her song to movie audiences in 850 movie theaters across the country.

There have been many stickers over the years. Above: A 1947 commemorative and a "Chiquita Precious" from Japan.

At first, United Fruit was happy, even delirious, about the success of Chiquita and her song. But over time they began getting uneasy. True, Chiquita sold the idea of banana consumption, which helped them—but she also helped their competitors, because consumers couldn't differentiate United Fruit bananas from the others in the store.

Jack Fox, an executive who had been hired away from Coca-Cola, called a meeting one day to complain that Chiquita was a brand name of United Fruit and all the other banana companies were getting a free ride. He announced that, somehow, they were going to start branding their bananas within 6 to 8 weeks.

The old-timers scoffed—the company had been trying to figure out how to brand bananas for years, and now this new Soft Drink Guy was going to do it in 6 weeks. Fox continued that he didn't know exactly what form the branding would take—maybe a rubber stamp or electrostatic printing (like a Xerox machine), or maybe a gummed sticker attached to every third banana.

"Stickers?" snorted one old-timer who felt secure enough in his job to challenge the vice president. "Shee-it! Do you realize how many that would be in a year? One billion stickers. You've got to be out of your mind!"

Fox, clearly taken aback by the number, asked him to repeat the number of labels he had calculated.

"One billion!"

The room erupted in nervous laughter. Fox looked at him steadily and the laughter stopped. Fox nodded his head. "That's just what I make it. One billion."

Stickers did seem like the best way to go, even though

further calculations made it clear that the company would actually need 2.5 billion stickers that year. When the company contacted its printing vendor with the order, his eyes rolled back, and he quietly fell backward in a faint.

Designing labels with the Chiquita name and drawing prominently displayed against a field of light blue was easy. The hard part was finding a way to apply the labels inexpensively. Machinery experts from around the country worked on the problem, but none of their solutions was simple and cheap enough. (Estimates for the cost of the machinery, operator and the labels came out to anywhere from 10¢ to $10 per label applied, all of which were way too expensive.)

The solution came from an unexpected source: a young worker on a Honduran plantation who came up with a simple device that had no moving parts and was powered by a squeeze of the operator's hand.

United Fruit quickly became the largest single user of pressure-sensitive labels in the world, buying more than 3 billion a year. The commercials and stickers had such an impact that the Chiquita name became much more famous than that of United Fruit. The company called itself United Brands in the 1960s, but finally got smart and changed its name to Chiquita Brands International in 1990, using the smiling banana lady as its corporate symbol. ☾

Updated for Your Listening Pleasure

The original 1944 Chiquita Banana jingle: "I'm Chiquita banana and I've come to say/Bananas have to ripen in a certain way/When they are fleck'd with brown and have a golden hue/Bananas taste the best and are best for you/You can put them in a salad/You can put them in a pie-aye/Any way you want to eat them/It's impossible to beat them/But, bananas like the climate of the very, very tropical equator/So you should never put bananas/in the refrigerator."

1999 Update: "I'm Chiquita Banana and I've come to say/I offer good nutrition in a simple way/When you eat a Chiquita you've done your part/To give every single day a healthy start/Underneath the crescent yellow/You'll find vitamins and great taste/With no fat, you just can't beat 'em/You'll feel better when you eat 'em/They're a gift from Mother Nature and a natural addition to your table/For wholesome, healthy, pure bananas/look for Chiquita's label!"

Speak English? 3
TRANSLATE THESE BRITISH TERMS INTO AMERICAN

Sometimes it seems like the British and Americans don't even speak the same language. How are you at translating? Translate these old and new British terms into American. (Answers below.)

1. full stop
2. inquiry agent
3. mackintosh
4. wireless
5. off the peg
6. elastic
7. fitter
8. ladder
9. scribbling block
10. footway
11. sledge
12. kipper
13. plimsolls
14. minerals
15. patience
16. reel of cotton
17. tube
18. braces

a. solitaire
b. raincoat
c. sneakers
d. mechanic
e. ready-to-wear
f. scratch pad
g. period
h. spool of thread
i. smoked herring
j. rubber band
k. sled
l. soft drinks
m. run in your stocking
n. suspenders
o. private detective
p. subway
q. sidewalk
r. radio

Answers: 1. full stop = g. period; 2. inquiry agent = o. private detective; 3. mackintosh = b. raincoat; 4. wireless = r. radio; 5. off the peg = e. ready-to-wear; 6. elastic = j. rubber band; 7. fitter = d. mechanic; 8. ladder = m. run in your stocking; 9. scribbling block = f. scratch pad; 10. footway = q. sidewalk; 11. sledge = k. sled; 12. kipper = i. smoked herring; 13. plimsolls = c. sneakers; 14. minerals = l. soft drinks; 15. patience = a. solitaire; 16. reel of cotton = h. spool of thread; 17. tube = p. subway; 18. braces = n. suspenders

Tissue, No Lies
THE ACCIDENTAL HISTORY OF KLEENEX & KOTEX

Most new products are the results of trying to solve a problem. But sometimes innovations come as a result of having too much of something and trying to find a purpose for it.

WAR AND PAPER

Kimberly-Clark had been making paper in Wisconsin since 1872. In 1914, they hired a paper technician named Ernst Mahler to develop new products. A recent graduate from the Technical University of Darmstadt, Germany, Mahler had studied cellulose chemistry. He set up a laboratory across the street from Kimberly-Clark headquarters and convinced company president J. C. Kimberly to accompany him to Germany to check out some new products that had been developed over there, including a fluffy paper wadding product that absorbed liquids better than cotton.

While Mahler and Kimberly were in Germany, World War I broke out. They cut their trip short and hurried back to the United States with enough samples and formulae to begin developing their own version of the wadding material. Mahler tested a variety of native wood pulps before deciding that spruce trees yielded the longest and most absorbent fibers.

As the war got going full swing, a cotton shortage developed, giving Kimberly-Clark a ready market for their new product. "Cellucotton," so called because it was like cotton but made from wood cellulose, was used as pads in bandages, filters in gas masks, and stuffing for emergency jackets. When America entered the war, Kimberly-Clark patriotically decided they'd sell Cellucotton to the War Department and Red Cross at no profit.

Chinese Red Cross women sew gauze together, standard practice before Cellucotton became a medical supply

When the war ended abruptly, Kimberly-Clark had partially-filled orders for 750,000 pounds of Cellucotton for the war effort. Kimberly-Clark allowed the orders to be cancelled without penalty, leaving the company with a huge surplus. Worse, the Army also had a large surplus of Cellucotton—and began selling it to civilian hospitals for a ridiculously low price, killing the market. The company floundered around for new uses for the product until two good ones dropped into its lap.

KOTEX PADS COMPANY PROFITS

One of Kimberly-Clark's grateful nonprofit wartime customers had been the American Fund for the French Wounded. An official of the organization knew that Kimberly Clark's business had been hurt by canceled war orders and passed on some helpful information:

During the war, French nurses had tried using Cellucotton during their periods and found that they made excellent sanitary pads in that they didn't have to be washed but could be disposed of. Might American women be ready for a new product of this sort?

Up to that time, menstrual pads were made of felt and had to be washed after every use. They were never spoken of in public. Still, doing some extensive but very discreet market research, the company determined that women hated the felt pads and would very much welcome an alternative. So, early in 1920, Kimberly-Clark began marketing the first disposable sanitary napkin under the less-than-catchy name "Cellunaps."

MARKETING WAS A PROBLEM

Menstrual products had never been commercially displayed or advertised. Cellunaps were too sensitive to be placed in public display, and so stayed behind the druggists' counter. Company marketers found that customers were embarrassed to ask their pharmacists for Cellunaps because of the "naps" part of the name (short for "napkins"). The company decided to change the name to one that was meaningless—that would not reveal anything in a crowded drugstore. They coined the word Kotex.

The first Kotex ads appeared in women's magazines in 1921

Even with the name change and an unrevealing package, many retailers insisted that the company take the extra step of wrapping the box in unprinted brown paper so that even the Kotex name would be hidden.

While Kimberly-Clark could see the need for discreet marketing, officials at the company refused to wrap the product. They were spending millions of dollars for advertising in women's magazines and felt that the product should be treated like any other consumer product. They encouraged retailers to take Kotex out from behind the counters and put it on display. It took a few years, but eventually most retailers got with the program.

Meanwhile, letters to the company poured in, mostly favorable. Some women, however, asked questions that showed a deep ignorance of their bodies and the menstrual process. Kimberly-Clark beefed up its Education Division and began mailing out information packs, including a pamphlet called "Marjorie May's 12th Birthday," which met with a torrent of criticism from religious leaders, self-styled moralists and others who believed that too much knowledge was a dangerous thing. Several states specifically banned "Marjorie May" and other similar mailings as being too sexually explicit. But women, unable to get the information elsewhere, continued ordering them, and

eventually, the bans were lifted. Kimberly-Clark also worked with the Disney Co. to create a color movie, *The Story of Menstruation* for schools, which has been seen by over 70 million kids.

By 1939, use of the reusable felt pads was down to 20%. During World War II, large numbers of women entered the labor pool. Kimberly-Clark, in the spirit of patriotism and good marketing, made it a highest priority—despite war shortages—that war plants were well-equipped with Kotex feminine napkins. By 1947, use of old washable felt pads was down to less than 1%.

SOMETHING TO SNEEZE AT

Meanwhile, Kimberly-Clark decided to try manufacturing Cellucotton in thin sheets. Kleenex was the result. But they misjudged the market and almost had a flop.

Printed on the first boxes, each containing a hundred

N EW but tried and proved, Kotex enters universal service from a romantic background. For, although a woman's article, it started as Cellucotton — a wonderful sanitary absorbent which science perfected for use of our men and allied soldiers wounded in France.

With peace came an idea suggested in letters from nurses in France, regarding a new use for this wonderful absorbent, and early in 1919 our laboratory made the first sanitary pads of Cellucotton enclosed in gauze and placed them on sale in various cities. Requests for more followed every sale, and we devoted two years to perfecting the new article—named KOTEX from "cotton-like texture"—and to the building of machinery which makes and seals it hygienically without contact of human hands. Kotex are now ready for every woman's use.

The gauze envelope is 22 inches long, thus leaving generous tabs for pinning. The filler, thirty-six layers of finest Cellucotton, is 3½ inches wide by 9 inches long. Kotex are cool, more absorbent, and of lasting softness. Kotex are cheap in price and easy to throw away.

CELLUCOTTON PRODUCTS CO.
208 South LaSalle Street, Chicago, Illinois

The text that ran with the first Kotex ad in 1921

Cellucotton sheets, was "Kleenex Sanitary Cold Cream Remover." Kimberly-Clark thought that it had found a niche market as a disposable cloth for removing makeup and cold cream. It hadn't even occurred to them that the soft little sheets might have more universal uses as well.

One problem was the price: 65¢ per box—high at the time. Marketers then aimed for an upscale crowd, associating the Kleenex with wealth, glamour and the theatrical crowd. The company sent promotional samples to makeup artists in Hollywood and then tried to capitalize on the fact that the best Hollywood stylists used the new "scientific way to remove cold cream." Company advertisements showed movie stars using the tissues after a long day of shooting movies. Despite the hype, the tissues achieved only lukewarm sales.

FIND A NICHE AND SCRATCH IT

The Kimberly-Clark marketing people kept trying. They invented a way to make tissues pop up automatically by shuffling two piles of overlapping tissues together like a deck of cards. They introduced colors. But whatever they did, the marketplace yawned, and sales stayed flat.

A Discovery
That offers you a marvelous NEW WAY to remove cold cream
Cheaper than Spoiling and Laundering Towels

KLEENEX
ABSORBENT
KERCHIEFS

In 1930, a desperate marketing department decided to go and see why Kleenex was not playing in Peoria. In fact, they literally went to Peoria, Illinois, with clipboards and a series of questions, asking people if they had any suggestions, comments, ideas, hints—anything. They were surprised to discover that nearly two-thirds of the people in Peoria who bought Kleenex used them as disposable handkerchiefs, not as make-up removers.

The marketers headed back to the main office and immediately changed their advertising to reflect this newly discovered use. "Don't put a cold in your pocket!" said one ad. "During colds, smother sneezes with Kleenex Tissues! Use once, then destroy, germs and all." The same ad also suggested using Kleenex tissues as a filter in the coffee maker. "Now my coffee's clearer—my husband's happier!" Within two years, sales increased four-fold. Kleenex—appropriately considering all the tears and sniffling in the genre—became the sponsor of the first radio soap opera, *The Story of Mary Marlin*.

HISTORICAL ADDENDUM

Although Kleenex was the first commercial tissue, they weren't the first use of paper for noses. The 17th century Japanese used *hanagami* ("sneezing paper"), which was just regular paper that they crumpled repeatedly until soft. In 1637, an English visitor wrote, "They blow their noses with a certain soft and tough kind of paper which they carry about them in small pieces, which having been used, they fling away as a filthy thing." ☾

Judged by Its Cover

MORE STRANGE BOOK TITLES

Can you tell a book by its title? If so, these have got to be some of the most fascinating books on the shelves, gleaned from *Bizarre Books* by Russell Ash and Brian Lake (St. Martin's, 1985).

The Muck Manual: A Practical Treatise on the Nature and Value of Manures—F. Falkner (1843)

Frog Raising for Pleasure and Profit—Dr. Albert Broel (1950)

Full Revelations of a Professional Rat-catcher After 25 Years' Experience—Ike Matthews (1898)

Onania; or The Heinous Sin of Self-Pollution, and All Its Frightful Consquences, in Both Sexes, Considered—Anonymous (1725)

Colon Cleanse the Easy Way!—Verna Burnett and Jennifer Weiss (1979)

Let's Make Some Undies—Marion Hall (1954)

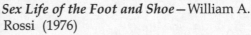

Eleven Years a Drunkard; or, The Life of Thomas Doner, Having Lost Both Arms through Intemperance, He Wrote This Book With His Teeth As a Warning to Others—Thomas Doner (1878)

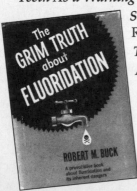

Sex Life of the Foot and Shoe—William A. Rossi (1976)

Teach Yourself Alcoholism—Meir Glatt (1843)

Amputation Stumps: Their Care and After-Treatment—Sir Godfrey Martin Huggins (1918)

The Grim Truth About Fluoridation—Robert M. Buck (1964)

Living Without Eating—Herbert Thurston (1931)

Inventing Champagne
A SHORT & BUBBLY PRIMER

That glass of bubbly you toast the new year with...making it is both an art and a science. Here's the story.

DOM PÈRIGNON was a Benedictine monk in Hautvillers, near Reims in France. To his annoyance, he accidentally invented champagne in the 1660s, while trying to improve the abbey's white wine.

Pèrignon had been making a batch late in the season and thought that the fermentation had stopped, so he bottled it. However, some yeast remained alive and became active again when the weather warmed up, causing a second fermentation inside the bottle. When he opened a bottle, he was disgusted to find that it had gone "bad" but drank some anyway. His reaction? According to legend, he blurted out, "I'm drinking stars!" Still, he considered the bubbles were an unwelcome "impurity"—that is, until people tried the wine and asked him to try to repeat the accident. With experimentation, Pèrignon came up with the process still used today.

Although sparkling wine in America is often called "champagne," it is not technically that. By definition, true champagne comes from the Champagne district of France. The varietal can be Chardonnay, which is white, Pinot Noir or Pinot Meunier (red), or some combination thereof.

RIDDLE ME THIS, YOU BRUT

Most wines only go through one fermentation, but sparkling wine goes through two. The first takes place in big

"Riddling" the bottles

vats for two to three weeks. After that, the winemaker puts the wine in its bottle for the second fermentation and adds a sugar-yeast syrup to it before "corking" it with a temporary crown cap, like those used on soda pop bottles. Inside the sealed bottle, carbon dioxide can't escape and gets trapped in the wine, waiting for a release in the pressure to make its escape.

It then waits a long time—

six months to two years. Only one problem: Over time, the yeast dies and sinks to the bottom of the bottle, making an ugly sediment.

How do you get it out without losing the carbonation? By "riddling." For six to eight weeks, winemakers rack the bottles upside-down and occasionally turn them so the yeast settles against the caps. When it's time to disgorge the sediment, the upside-down bottles go into a super-cold brine. The sediment freezes in the neck, forming an icy plug. When the winemaker pries off the bottle caps, pressure inside ejects the frozen plug.

Since there's now some wine missing from the bottle, the winemaker determines how sweet to make the champagne by topping the bottle off with a blend of sugar syrup, white wine and sometimes brandy. A little sugar makes a *brut*; increasing amounts of sugar make a *sec*, a *demi-sec*, or a *doux*.

EXPLODING BOTTLES

For centuries, champagne was a nightmare for glassblowers. With all that pressure building up inside, a good proportion of bottles exploded in wine cellars. Winemakers began the practice of closely inspecting every bottle upon arrival. The ones that were clearly irregular were set aside for uncarbonated red wine. The others were tested by smartly banging them together. Any that broke were charged to the glassblower; the ones that survived were deemed strong enough. Still, this was a less than foolproof method.

The exploding bottle crisis hit its peak with the vintage of 1828. Weather conditions

Put a Cork in It

• The Romans had first used corks in wine bottles before A.D. 200, but the practice fell out of favor for some reason and was forgotten for about fourteen centuries. During the medieval era, bottlers used a twisted cloth, leather or sealing wax.

• Finally, wine corks were reinvented in the early 16th century, soon enough for Shakespeare to write in *As You Like It,* "Take thy cork out of thy mouth, that I may drink thy tidings." Still, many winemakers preferred glass stoppers because they found, as one complained, that "much liquor is being absolutely spoiled by the defect of the cork." Cork-induced spoilage is still a big headache, with about 8 percent of all corked wine being damaged to some degree.

• Bottlers pushed corks only halfway in to make it possible to get them out again. Uncorkers wouldn't be invented for many more decades. The first mention of "bottlescrews" was recorded in 1681; they weren't called "corkscrews" until 1720.

• Corks are very elastic because they're filled with more than 300 million tiny air-filled cells. A cork can be compressed enough to get it into a bottle, yet it will immediately spring back to fill any gaps around the edge. They keep their structural integrity for up to fifty years before going brittle and crumbly.

• About 75 percent of the wine corks in the United States come from Portugal—over 360 million a year. They're made from the four-inch-thick, fire-resistant bark of the cork oak, a slow-growing evergreen. Every ten years, the trees are almost completely stripped of bark, leaving only enough to ensure that the tree will survive. A tree can be stripped twelve to fifteen times during its natural life span.

• The sheets of cork are stacked to dry for three months. They're then boiled in fungicides, dried again and cut into bottle-sized tapered cylinders that cost wine bottlers about 20 to 40 cents each. That's sometimes more than the wine itself cost to make.

• Screw tops are better and cost only a nickel each. Synthetic corks are also better at sealing bottles than corks. However, many consumers have resisted both, wrongly believing that a cork somehow indicates a good bottle of wine.

that year resulted in extra sugar in the grapes, super-charging the fermentation process. It was a booming, bang-up year for champagne makers as 80 percent of the vintage burst its bottles.

How explosive can a champagne bottle be, you ask? Ever have a blowout on a ten-speed bicycle? The pressure inside a champagne bottle is *normally* 90 pounds per square inch, about the same as a high-pressure bike tire — however, in 1828, the pressure was even higher than that. With shards of jagged, wine-soaked glass flying in all directions, spending time in a wine cellar became more dangerous than going to war.

As a result of the 1828 fiasco, a French chemist invented the *sucre-oenometre,* an instrument that measures sugar content in grapes. With its use, the champagne bottle breakage rate went way down. But "way down" is a relative thing: 15–20 percent of all champagne bottles continued to explode in storage. Wine stewards adapted their own strategies. They began storing champagne in isolated nooks and routinely wearing wire masks when in the cellar. Nowadays, that's not usually a problem.

DRINKING IT

Does champagne get you higher faster than unbubbly wine? Yes, and there are two reasons for it. The first is chemical: The carbon dioxide in the bubbles of the wine speeds the alcohol into your bloodstream quicker. The second reason is contextual: People don't usually drink champagne unless they're celebrating something, and the giddiness of the moment can have them half-drunk even without the direct effects of the alcohol.

One last thing: Although it's fun to pop the cork, it's not a great idea. Every year, popping corks blind eyes, knock out teeth and do damage to valuable furnishings. Furthermore, you lose a lot of wine and carbonation. The best way to open champagne is to hold the cork firmly and release the gas not with a bang, but with a whisper. €

Retro-Futurism
MORE OF TOM SWIFT'S WORLD OF TOMORROW

Tom Swift was a boy inventor created by Victor Appleton almost a century ago. The breathless adventure stories are great fun, but even better are the descriptions of his inventions.

TOM SWIFT & HIS BIG TUNNEL (1916)

As soon as Tom had received the samples of the rock he had begun to experiment. First he tried some of the explosive that was so successful in the giant cannon. As he had feared, it was not what was needed. It cracked the rock, but did not disintegrate it, and that was what was needed. The hard rock must be broken up into fragments that could be easily handled. Merely to crack it necessitated further explosions, which would only serve to split it more and perhaps wedge it fast in the tunnel.

So Tom tried different mixtures, using various chemicals, but none seemed to be just right. The trials were not without danger, either. Once, in mixing some ingredients, there was an explosion that injured one man, and blew Tom some distance away. Fortunately for him, there was an open window in the direction in which he was propelled, and he went through that, escaping with only some cuts and bruises. Another time there was a hang-fire, and the explosive burned instead of detonating, so that one of the shops caught, and there was no little work in subduing the flames.

But Tom would not give up, and finally, after many trials, he hit on what he felt to be the right mixture. A day after receiving Tom's message Mr. Titus came in and a demonstration was given of the powerful explosive. "Tom, that's great!" cried the tunnel contractor. "Our troubles are at an end now."

TOM SWIFT & HIS WAR TANK (1918)

The visitors entered the great craft through the door by which Tom had emerged. At first all they saw was a small compartment, with walls of heavy steel, some shelves of the same and a seat which folded up against the wall made of like powerful material.

"I don't see how you ever thought of it!" exclaimed the girl.

"Well, I didn't all at once," Tom answered, with a laugh. "I first got the idea when I heard of the British tanks. I concluded that with a bigger tank—one capable of more speed and crossing bigger excavations—more effective work could be done against the Germans."

"And will yours do that?" asked Ned. "I mean will it do ten miles an hour, and straddle over a wider ditch than twelve feet?"

"It'll do both," promptly answered Tom. "I think we straddled one about fourteen feet across back there, and we can do better when I get my grippers to working."

"Grippers!" exclaimed Mary.

"And what does your tank do except travel along, not minding a hail of bullets?" asked Mr. Nestor.

"Well," answered Tom, "it can demolish a good-sized house or heavy wall, break down big trees, and chew up barbed-wire fences as if they were toothpicks. I'll show you all that in due time. Just now, if the repairs are finished, we can get back on the road—"

TOM SWIFT & HIS WIZARD CAMERA (1912)

Work went on rapidly on the Wizard Camera. Briefly described it was a small square box, with a lens projecting from it. Inside, however, was complicated machinery, much too complicated for me to describe. Tom Swift had put in his best work on this wonderful machine. It could be worked by a storage battery, by ordinary electric current from a dynamo, or by hand. On top was a new kind of electric light. This was small and compact, but it threw out powerful beams. With the automatic arrangement set, and the light turned on, the camera could be left at a certain place after dark, and whatever went on in front of it would be reproduced on the moving roll of film inside.

In the morning the film could be taken out, developed, and the pictures thrown on a screen in the usual way, familiar to all who have been in a moving picture theatre.

A number of rolls of films could be packed into the camera, and they could be taken out, or inserted, in daylight. Of course after one film had been made, showing any particular scene, any number of films could be made from this "master" one. Just as is done with the ordinary moving picture camera. Tom had an attachment to show when one roll was used, and when another needed inserting.

"I'll tell you what I'll do !" Mr. Period went on eagerly. "After you make the camera, and take a lot of films, showing strange and wonderful scenes, I'll put at the end of each film, next to my picture, your name, and a statement showing that you took the originals. How's that? Talk about being advertised! Why you can't beat it! Millions of people will read your name at the picture shows every night."

"I am not looking for advertisements," said Tom, with a laugh. ☾

(Interested in reading more Tom Swift theories and inventions? See page 383.)

In the Future Year A.D. 2000

"In 2000, commuters will go to the city, a hundred miles away, in huge aerial buses that will hold 200 passengers. Hundreds of thousands more will make such journeys twice a day in their own helicopters." —*Popular Mechanics*, 1950

"Computers are multiplying at a rapid rate. By the turn of the century, there will be 220,000 in the U.S." —*Wall Street Journal*, 1966

"By the end of this century, we're going to put a man on Mars." —Spiro Agnew, 1969

"Housewives in 50 years may wash dirty dishes right down the drain. Cheap plastic will melt in hot water." —*Popular Mechanics*, 1950

"Dishwashing will be a thing of the past. Disposable dishes will be made from powdered plastic for each meal by a machine in the kitchen...for a few pennies a meal." —The Philco Corporation, 1967

"Using wonderful new materials much lighter than aluminum, houses will be able to fly....Whole communities may migrate south in the winter, or move to new lands whenever they feel the need for a change of scenery." —Arthur C. Clarke, 1966

"Keeping house will be a breeze by the year 2000. Sonic cleaning devices and air-filtering devices will just about eliminate dusting, scrubbing, and vacuuming.... Electrostatic filters will be installed in entrances to remove dust from clothes with ultrasonic waves." —*Wall Street Journal*, 1966

"By 2000, housewives will probably have a robot 'maid.'" —*New York Times*, 1966

The Eyes Have It

These illusions don't come free. Both have to be fiddled with a bit

This is one frame from Gustave Verbeek's New York Herald cartoon series. Which way's the right way: Upside down or right side up?

This goose looks hungry! Slowly bring the girl and the goose closer and closer to your face.

What's in a Name?

We wondered where some of our favorite products got their names, so we did a little digging. Here's what we found.

• When Cheerios came out in 1941, they were called Cheery Oats. But in 1946, Quaker Oats threatened to sue, claiming that it had exclusive trademark rights to the name "Oats." Rather than fight it, General Mills changed the name to Cheerios.

• Fritos Corn Chips were named by ice cream salesman Elmer Doolin. He stopped in a Mexican restaurant and started eating tortilla chips for the first time. He liked them so much that he bought the factory from the owner. He named the chips "Fritos"—Spanish for "fried."

• Borden's Häagen-Dazs and Kraft's Frusen Glädjé were artifacts of the 1980s, when people were led to believe that imported beer, cars and ice cream were better than domestic ones. Both made-in-America ice creams were given names that sounded Scandinavian. Although Frusen Glädjé roughly translates to "Frozen Joy," Häagen-Dazs can be found in no known language. Possibly the first known case of "artificially Swedened" ice cream?

• In a similar impulse, the name Atari was chosen so that people would think the company was Japanese.

• Would it surprise you to know that Chun King isn't really Chinese? Probably not. The company was founded by an Italian American named Jeno Paulucci in mostly Scandinavian-American Duluth, Minnesota.

• Kool-Aid was originally named Kool-Ade until bureaucrats in the Food & Drug Administration banned the use of "ade" in the name because it means "a drink made from..." (take note, Gatorade!). In response, inventor E. E. Perkins simply changed the spelling to "aid," in the sense of "help."

• Fig Newtons were invented by Kennedy Biscuits (now part of Nabisco) in Cambridgeport, Massachusetts. The plant manager, to make it easier to keep track of as-yet-unnamed products, gave each of them a temporary name chosen from nearby towns. One neighboring town is Newton, and his makeshift name for the new fig cookie eventually stuck. Similiarly-named products like the Beacon Hill, the Quincy and the Brighten didn't survive.

• The Gap stores were named in the hopes that their clothes would be able to bridge (ready for a 1960s flashback?) "the Generation Gap."

• Sony, Kodak and Exxon were all coined for the same reason: They were easy to say and remember, and are not closely related to any words in any known language. ☾

The Book I Was Born to Write, by Ima Writer

Some say fate dictates most of our actions. After receiving this list of reportedly genuine book titles and their authors, we're beginning to believe....

• *A Treatise on Madness,* by William Battie, M.D. (1768)
• *Riches and Poverty,* by L. G. Chiozza Money (1905)
• *The Boy's Own Aquarium,* by Frank Fin (1922)
• *How to Live a Hundred Years or More,* by George Fasting (1927)
• *Diseases of the Nervous System,* by Walter Russell Brain (1933)
• *Causes of Crime,* by A. Fink (1938)
• *Your Teeth,* by John Chipping (1967)
• *The Cypress Garden,* by Jane Arbor (1969)
• *Running Duck,* by Paula Gosling (1979)
• *Motorcycling for Beginners,* by Geoff Carless (1980)
• *Writing with Power,* by Peter Elbow (1981)
• *Crocheting Novelty Potholders,* by L. Macho (1982)
• *Illustrated History of Gymnastics,* by John Goodbody (1983)

The poet e.e. cummings did have a real name with capital letters and everything. He was born Edward Estlin Cummings.

Antiquated Etiquette

LEARNING CIVILITY THROUGH HISTORY

In today's fast-paced world, politeness seems scarce. But being rude has been a problem since time began, as you can see from these rules of etiquette from days gone by.

DUTCH PHILOSOPHER Erasmus of Rotterdam authored "On civility in children" in 1530. He originally wrote it for a young prince. When that prince grew up he became King Henry II, at which time the whole Western world had become familiar with Erasmus's guide.

• "Turn away when spitting lest your saliva fall on someone. If anything purulent falls on the ground, it should be trodden upon, lest it nauseate someone."

• "You should not offer your handkerchief to anyone unless it has been freshly washed. Nor is it seemly, after wiping your nose, to spread out your handkerchief and peer into it as if pearl and rubies might have fallen out of your head."

• "To lick greasy fingers or to wipe them on your coat is impolite. It is better to use the table cloth or the serviette."

• "Some people put their hands in the dishes the moment they have sat down. Wolves do that."

• "Keep your two 'pinkies' out of the serving pot. Three fingers are enough to get what you want."

• "Take the first thing you touch; do not fish around in the pot for a bigger piece."

• "If you cannot swallow a piece of food, turn around discreetly and throw it somewhere."

- "Do not be afraid of vomiting if you must; for it is not vomiting but holding the vomit in your throat that is foul."

- "Do not move back and forth on your chair. Whoever does that gives the impression of constantly breaking or trying to break wind."

- "Retain the wind by compressing the belly."

- "If your friend uses bad manners, point it out kindly and when you are alone." ☾

Universal Truths

The Dutch weren't the only ones to get in on laying down the rules of etiquette.

- *"Use silver-tipped chopsticks; if your food has been poisoned, the silver will turn black and serve as a warning to you."* —400 B.C., China

- *"If you are not using your knife to eat, keep it in its sheath."* —A.D. 1200, France

- *"Wash your hands before you dip them into the serving pot."* —A.D. 1200, France

- *"Use a thick piece of bread for a plate; when you're finished eating, give your gravy-soaked "trencher" to the poor for their dinner."* —A.D. 1200, France

- *"Do not dip your meat into the salt bowl; instead, use your little finger to sprinkle salt on your food."* —A.D.1400, England

- *"Take your own knife, fork, and spoon when you travel because inns do not provide tableware."* —A.D.1400, England

- *"Wait until you are finished eating to scratch yourself."* —American Pilgrims

- *"Never laugh at your own jokes."* —19th-century America

- *"Never use nicknames in public."* —19th-century America

- *"Children must wait to eat until all the adults are served."* —19th-century America

- *"Children must not eat greedily, cram their mouths full, smack their lips, tilt their chairs back, or drop their knives on the tablecloth."* —19th-century America

- *"At the table, do not cough or breathe into your neighbor's face, fidget in your seat, whisper secrets, or drum the table with your fingers."* —19th-century America

The Mouse

CAUGHT NAKED WITH A STRANGER ON A TRAIN

In this short story by Saki (Hector High Munro), a nervous young man finds himself in a compromising position with a stranger.

T HEODORIC VOLER HAD been brought up, from infancy to the confines of middle age, by a fond mother whose chief solicitude had been to keep him screened from what she called the coarser realities of life. When she died she left Theodoric alone in a world that was as real as ever, and a good deal coarser than he considered it had any need to be. To a man of his temperament and upbringing even a simple railway journey was crammed with petty annoyances and minor discords, and as he settled himself down in a second-class compartment one September morning he was conscious of ruffled feelings and general mental discomposure.

He had been staying at a country inn, the inmates of which had been certainly neither brutal nor bacchanalian, but their supervision of the domestic establishment had been of that lax order which invites disaster. The pony carriage that was to take him to the station had never been properly ordered, and when the moment for his departure drew near, the handyman who should have produced the required article was nowhere to be found.

In this emergency Theodoric, to his mute but very intense disgust, found himself obliged to collaborate with the innkeeper's daughter in the task of harnessing the pony, which necessitated groping about in an ill-lighted outbuilding called a stable, and smelling very like one—except in patches where it smelled of mice. Without being actually afraid of mice, Theodoric classed them among the coarser incidents of life, and considered that Providence, with a little exercise of moral courage, might long ago have recognized that they were not indispensable, and have withdrawn them from circulation.

As the train glided out of the station Theodoric's nervous imagination accused himself of exhaling a weak odor of stable yard, and possibly of displaying moldy straw on his unusually well-brushed garments. Fortunately the only other occupation of the compartment, a lady of about the same age as himself, seemed inclined for slumber rather than scrutiny; the train was not due to stop till the end of the line was reached, in about an hour's time, and the carriage was of the old-fashioned sort that held no communication with a corridor, therefore no further traveling companions were likely to intrude on Theodoric's semiprivacy.

And yet the train had scarcely attained its normal speed before he became reluctantly but vividly aware that he was not alone with the slumbering lady; he was not even alone in his own clothes. A warm, creeping movement over his flesh betrayed the unwelcome and highly resented presence, unseen but poignant, of a strayed mouse, that had evidently dashed into its present retreat during the episode of the pony harnessing.

Furtive stamps and shakes and wildly directed pinches failed to dislodge the intruder, and the lawful occupant of the clothes lay back against the cushions and endeavored rapidly to evolve some means for putting an end to the dual ownership. It was unthinkable that he should continue for the space of a whole hour in the horrible position of a house for vagrant mice (already his imagination had at least doubled the numbers of the alien invasion). On the other hand, nothing less drastic than partial disrobing would ease him of his tormentor, and to undress in the presence of a lady, even for so laudable a purpose, was an idea that made his ear tips tingle in a blush of abject shame.

He had never heen able to bring himself even to the mild exposure of openwork socks in the presence of the fair sex. And yet— the lady in this case was to all appearances soundly asleep; the mouse, on the other hand, seemed to be trying to crowd a year's sabbatical into a few strenuous minutes. If there is any truth in the theory of reincarnation, this particular mouse must certainly have been in a former state a member of the Alpine Club. Sometimes in its eagerness it lost its footing and slipped for half an inch or so; and then, in fright, or more probably temper, it bit.

Theodoric was goaded into the most audacious undertaking of his life. Crimsoning to the hue of a beet and keeping an agonized watch on his slumbering fellow traveler, he swiftly and noiselessly secured the ends of his railway rug to the racks on either side of the carriage, so that a substantial curtain hung athwart the compartment. In the narrow dressing room that he had thus improvised he proceeded with violent haste to extricate himself and the mouse from the surrounding casings of tweed and wool.

As the unraveled mouse gave a wild leap to the floor, the rug, slipping its fastening at either end, also came down with a heart-curdling flop, and almost simultaneously the awakened sleeper opened her eyes. With a movement almost quicker than the mouse's, Theodoric pounced on the rug and hauled its ample folds chin-high over his dismantled person as he collapsed into the farther corner of the carriage. The blood raced and beat in the veins of his neck and forehead, while he waited dumbly for the communication cord to be pulled. The lady, however, contented herself with a silent stare at her strangely muffled companion. How much had she seen, Theodoric queried to himself; and in any case what on earth must she think of his present posture?

"I think I have caught a chill," he ventured desperately.

"Really, I'm sorry," she replied. "I was just going to ask you if you would open this window."

"I fancy it's malaria," he added, his teeth chattering slightly, as much from fright as from a desire to support his theory.

"I've got some brandy in my hold-all, if you'll kindly reach it down for me," said his companion.

"Not for worlds—I mean, I never take anything for it," he assured her earnestly.

"I suppose you caught it in the tropics?"

Theodoric, whose acquaintance with the tropics was limited to an annual present of a chest of tea from an uncle in Ceylon, felt that even the malaria was slipping from him. Would it be possible, he wondered to disclose the real state of affairs to her in small installments?

"Are you afraid of mice?" he ventured, growing, if possible, more scarlet in the face.

"Not unless they came in quantities. Why do you ask?"

"I had one crawling inside my clothes just now," said Theodoric in a voice that hardly seemed his own. "It was most awkward."

"It must have been, if you wear your clothes at all tight," she observed. "But mice have strange ideas of comfort."

"I had to get rid of it while you were asleep," he continued. Then, with a gulp, he added, "It was getting rid of it that brought me to—to this."

"Surely leaving off a small mouse wouldn't bring on a chill," she exclaimed, with a levity that Theodoric accounted abominable.

Evidently she had detected something of his predicament, and was enjoying his confusion. All the blood in his body seemed to have mobilized into one concentrated blush, and an agony of abasement, worse than a myriad of mice, crept up and down over his soul. And then, as reflection began to assert itself, sheer terror took the place of humiliation. With every minute that passed the train was rushing nearer to the bustling terminal, where dozens of prying eyes would be exchanged for the one paralyzing pair that watched him from the farther corner of the carriage. There was one slender, despairing chance, which the next few minutes must decide. His fellow traveler might relapse into a blessed slumber. But as the minutes throbbed by that chance ebbed away. The furtive glance which Theodoric stole at her from time to time disclosed only an unwinking wakefulness.

"I think we must be getting near now," she presently observed.

Theodoric had already noted with growing terror the recurring stacks of small, ugly dwellings that heralded the journey's end. The words acted as a signal. Like a hunted beast breaking cover and dashing madly toward some other haven of momentary safety he threw aside his rug, and struggled frantically into his disheveled garments. He was conscious of dull suburban stations racing past the window, of a choking, hammering sensation in his throat and heart, and of an icy silence in that corner toward which he dared not look. Then as he sank back in his seat, clothed and almost delirious, the train slowed down to a final crawl, and the woman spoke.

"Would you be so kind," she asked, "as to get me a porter to put me into a cab? It's a shame to trouble you when you're feeling unwell, but being blind makes one so helpless at a railway station." ☾

Ben's Money 2

ADVICE FROM FRANKLIN'S LITTLE MONEY BOOK

In 1757, Benjamin Franklin compiled *The Way of Wealth* from his aphorisms about money in *Poor Richard's Almanac*. The booklet was a huge success and made Franklin wealthy. Here is some of his wisdom.

THRIFT

• *If he knows not how to save as he gets, a man may keep his nose all his life to the grindstone, and die not worth a penny.*

• *If you would be wealthy, think of saving as well as of getting: the Indies have not made Spain rich, because her outgoes are greater than her incomes. Away then with your expensive follies, and you will not have so much cause to complain of hard times and heavy taxes.*

• *What maintains one vice, would bring up two children.*

• *Beware of little expenses; a small leak will sink a great ship.*

• *Fools make feasts, and wise men eat them.*

• *Buy what thou hast no need of, and before long thou shall sell thy necessaries.*

• *You call them "goods," but if you do not take care, they will prove to be "evils" to some of you.*

• *Silks and satins, scarlet and velvets, put out the kitchen fire.* These are not the necessaries of life; they can scarcely be called the conveniencies, and yet only because they look pretty, how many want to have them. The artificial wants of mankind thus become more numerous than the natural; and, for one poor person, there are an hundred indigent.

• *A child and a fool imagine twenty shillings and twenty years can never be spent.*

DEBT

- *If you would know the value of money, go and try to borrow some.*
- *Creditors have better memories than debtors.*
- *He that goes a borrowing goes a sorrowing, and indeed so does he that lends to such people.*
- *Think what you do when you run in debt; you give to another power over your liberty. If you cannot pay at the time, you will be ashamed to see your creditor; you will be in fear when you speak to him, you will make poor pitiful sneaking excuses, and by degrees come to lose your veracity and sink into base downright lying.*
- *Poverty often deprives a man of all spirit and virtue: 'tis hard for an empty bag to stand upright.*
- *Better to go to bed supperless than rise in debt.*

OSTENTATION

- *Pride is as loud a beggar as want, and a great deal more saucy.*
- *When you have bought one fine thing you must buy ten more, that your appearance may be all of a piece. 'Tis easier to suppress the first desire than to satisfy all that follow it.*
- *'Tis as truly folly for the poor to ape the rich, as for the frog to swell in order to equal the ox.*
- *Pride breakfasts with plenty, dines with poverty, and sups with infamy.*
- *Of what use is this pride of appearance, for which so much is risked, so much is suffered? It cannot promote health; or ease pain; it makes no increase of merit in the person, it creates envy, it hastens misfortune.*

GOOD ADVICE

- *For age and want, save while you may; no morning sun lasts a whole day.*
- *'Tis easier to build two chimneys than to keep one in fuel.*
- *A ploughman on his legs is higher than a gentleman on his knees.*
- *Get what you can, and what you get, hold; 'tis the stone that will turn all your lead into gold.*
- *Be not uncharitable to those that at present seem to want it, but comfort and help them.*
- *They that won't be counseled, can't be helped.*
- *If you will not hear Reason, she'll surely rap your knuckles.* ☾

Fore Bears

HOW THE TEDDY BEAR FIRST GOT STUFFED

Some people never get over teddy bears. And why should they?
Teddy bears are about security, comfort and
non-judgmental friendship.

BELIEVE IT OR NOT, the teddy bear coincidentally sprung up on two different continents in the same year. In Germany, art student Richard Steiff had gone to work for the family business which was run by his aunt, Margaret Steiff. Confined to a wheelchair, Margaret had taught the zither to music students until she saved enough to buy a sewing machine to make dresses until 1889. Her dressmaking became popular among the stylish people, and she quickly built up the business. By 1897, she had 40 people working for her, including her brother, Richard's father. Richard went to work on the sales force, but got tired of selling dresses. In 1902, he started lollygagging around the Stuttgart Zoo, sketching monkeys and bears with the idea of designing a series of jointed stuffed animals that the company could make and sell.

Meanwhile, back in the States, President Theodore Roosevelt traveled to Mississippi to settle a border dispute. While there, he decided to engage in a peculiar but common recreation of the time—killing wild animals for fun. After several hours, however, the president was frustrated that he hadn't found anything worth wasting a bullet on. An advance team came upon a bear cub, and knowing of the president's frustration, they tied it to a tree so Roosevelt could shoot it and have a trophy to show off when he got home. When the president came upon the scene, though, he couldn't bring himself to shoot the helpless creature.

Clifford Berryman's "Drawing the Line in Mississippi"

Michtom sold so many of the toys that he closed his candy store and founded the Ideal Toy Co.

In Germany, the Steiff Company was unaware that bear mania was growing like a tree in Brooklyn. That spring, the company debuted Richard's designs at the Leipzig Toy Fair. None of the European buyers were interested, but just as they were packing up at the end of the fair, an American toy buyer, perhaps knowing of the bear mania going on at home, ran up and ordered 3,000 bears.

Today, of course, to consider shooting a bear—especially a cub and tied up, no less!—would likely get Roosevelt impeached. At that time, however, sport killing was a normal pastime, and his refusal to kill a captive cub was apparently considered an unusually kindhearted act. The moment was immortalized in a newspaper cartoon by Clifford Berryman called "Drawing the Line," and the story spread around the country. It gave Brooklyn candy store owner Morris Michtom a marketing idea.

He and his wife sketched out a pattern and made a stuffed bear that he put in his store window with a copy of the famous cartoon and a handpainted sign that said, "Teddy's Bear."

Making money in a bear market can be hard, but

In a consumer frenzy that foreshadowed fads throughout the 20th century of our own time both companies rode a bear craze in the U.S. and Europe. By 1907, Steiff had sold nearly a million bears, while Michtom had begun manufacturing a million bears a year. Steiff stuck to it and still makes very pricey stuffed toys; Ideal diversified into a variety of popular toys in the 1950s and '60s, but no longer makes stuffed bears. ❨

Stately Knowledge

12 REASONS WHY YA GOTTA LOVE MAINE

Scouring the vaults, we've come up with a dozen things to love about the state of Maine.

1 Misnomer du jour: Maine is host to the most easterly point of land in the United States. It's a small peninsula near Lubec, Maine, called, for some reason, West Quoddy Head.

2 Necessity is the mother of invention. Chester Greenwood from Farmington, Maine, invented earmuffs back in 1873 when he was only fifteen. He patented them a year later, then mass-produced them in a local factory. Chester is still honored for his important contribution to society. Every winter, folks from all over come to Farmington for a parade and festivities to celebrate—what else?—Chester Greenwood Day.

3 Ever accused of being too picky? Then Maine's the state for you—it gets the vote for being the pickiest state in the Union. More wooden toothpicks are manufactured here than in any other state.

4 Clap it out! It's easy to do because "Maine" is the only state with just one syllable.

5 Hey sports fans! Oh, sorry. Maine has no major sports teams. But it does have moose. The moose is the official state animal.

6 Do you know the muffin man? About 98% of the nation's low-bush blueberries come from Maine.

7 Isn't that spatial? Maine is pretty small, but it's the biggest state in New England.

The other five New England states, put together, would almost fit inside it.

8 Strange, but true. Even though Maine is about 89% forest, there's a desert there, too. About 200 years ago, a 40-acre area of farmland near Freeport, Maine, was ruined when its protective layer of grass was destroyed. Sand dunes swept over it and stayed there. If you choose to visit this attraction, aptly named the Desert of Maine, check out the Sand Museum where you can observe sand samples from the far reaches of the globe.

9 Our favorite Mainer is author Stephen King. King wrote his first story when he was seven, sold his first piece to a magazine at eighteen and at twenty-six, published *Carrie,* his first novel. It sold over 4 million copies and became a motion picture. More success has followed with other works including *The Shining, Christine* and *Misery.* At one time, King was on the same *New York Times* best-seller list for five books. Ever hear of author "Richard Bachman"? He's actually just King writing under a pseudonym.

10 Something's fishy about Maine. Not only do the waters around Maine's coast give the nation up to 90% of its lobsters, they also produce more tins of sardines than any other place on Earth—about 75 million little cans each year.

11 Downtown Rockport, Maine, has a bronze plaque of one Hanson Gregory, who in 1847 allegedly invented the hole in the doughnut. Townspeople still argue about whether he was a sea captain or a fifteen-year-old when it happened; other historians say that other people (including the Pennsylvania Dutch and some southwestern Indians) invented holey pastry long before Gregory was born.

12 We love Maine's sense of humor. The Roadkill Café in Greenville, Maine, claims all of its dishes are made from animals that are squashed by cars on the nearby highway, with dishes like "Bye Bye Bambi Burgers" and "The Chicken That Didn't Make It Across the Road." It's all tongue in cheek, of course. Isn't it? ☾

Elvisaurus?

GENUINE DINOSAURS WITH GREAT NAMES

Though Elvisaurus left the building millions of years ago, he lives on in paleontology. And so do the dinosaurs named after Godzilla, Bambi, a member of Monty Python and the cast of *Jurassic Park*....

ABAVORNIS was a primitive bird from about 85 million years ago. Its name means "great-great-grandfather bird."

AMBULOCETUS NATANS means "walking whale that swims," as this sea lion-sized beast had limbs that did both.

ARTHURDACTYLUS CONAN-DOYLENSIS, a pterodactyl, was named for Sir Arthur Conan Doyle, who wrote a dinosaur-heavy science fiction novel, *The Lost World*.

ATLASCOPCOSAURUS was named for the Atlas Copco, a company that provided mining tools for the expedition that discovered this Australian plant eater.

BAMBIRAPTOR was the name given a young coelurosaur found in Montana in 2000, named after the fictional young fawn of Disney fame.

Thank you... thank you very much!

BELLUSAURUS was a dinosaur with spoon-shaped teeth. Its name means "beautiful lizard," which may only be true to a lonely paleontologist far from home.

BOROGOVIA was named for the borogoves, creatures in Lewis Carroll's poem, "Jabberwocky."

CAMELOTIA, an ancient vegetarian found in England, was named for legendary Camelot.

CHUNGKINGOSAURUS was not named for prepackaged supermarket chow mein, but for the city in China.

DEINOGALERIX means "terrible hedgehog."

ELVISAURUS ("Elvis lizard") is a paleontological nickname for cryolophosaurus, which has a crest that looks like the now-extinct singer's hairdo.

EMAUSAURUS was named after good ol' E.M.A.U., Germany's Ernst-Moritz-Arndt University.

ENIGMOSAURUS was a huge meat-eating dinosaur. Little is known about it, hence its name ("mystery lizard").

ERECTOPUS was a meat-eater with big hands, which somehow translated to a name that means "upright foot."

ERIC is a specific leptocleidine pliosaur, discovered in Australia, and named after Monty Python's Eric Idle.

GALLIMIMUS was an ostrich-like dinosaur about 17 feet long. Its name means "like a rooster."

GARGOYLEOSAURUS was an armored dinosaur from the late Jurassic period. Its name means "gargoyle lizard."

GASOSAURUS ("gas lizard") got its name because it was discovered during construction by a natural gas company.

GOJIRASAURUS was a meat-eating dinosaur discovered in New Mexico in 1997. Its name means "Godzilla lizard."

HADROCODIUM was a shrew-like mammal ancestor about the size of a paperclip that ate bugs. Its name means "heavy head."

HALLUCIGENIA, a spiky worm with tentacles, was named "delusional dream" in honor of its strangeness.

HALTICOSAURUS jumped about on two legs. The name—

Artist's rendering of Ichabodcraniosaurus

probably not inspired by Little Orphan Annie — means "leaping lizard!"

ICHABODCRANIOSAURUS was the name given a specific headless velociraptorine skeleton found in Mongolia. The detached head was later discovered, leading to the "Ichabod Crane" name, inspired by *The Legend of Sleepy Hollow*.

JURASSOSAURUS NEDEGOAPEFERIMA got its name because Steven Spielberg got naming rights for donating money toward Chinese dinosaur research. He suggested *nedegoapeferima* from the names of *Jurassic Park* cast members Sam **Ne**ill, Laura **De**rn, Jeff **Go**ldblum, Richard **A**ttenborough, Bob **Pe**ck, Martin **Fe**rrero, Ariana **Ri**chards and Joseph **Ma**zzello.

MAIASAURA was a duck-billed dinosaur that cared for its young, which is how it got its name, "good mother lizard."

MASTODON, the hairy big elephant-like creature with huge tusks, has a name from Greek that means "breast tooth."

MEGARAPTOR was a large meat eater with a name that means "huge robber."

NQWEBASAURUS (pronounced N-[click with tongue]-KWE-bah-SAWR-us) means "lizard from Nqweba," the name of an African village in the Bantu language.

Eric, the half-leptocleidus

PROCOMPSOGNATHUS was a small theropod dinosaur with a long pointed snout. Its name means "before pretty jaw."

QANTASSAURUS was named for the Australian airline, Qantas, which provided transportation for the fossils.

SEISMOSAURUS is perhaps the longest dinosaur. Its name means "earthquake lizard."

STYGIMOLOCH had demonic-looking spikes and bumps on its skull. Its name means "demon from the river Styx."

TYRANNOSAURUS REX means "tyrant lizard king." Which brings to mind the lyric from Jim Morrison, still another extinct giant: "I am the lizard king / I can do anything." ☾

Zen Masters
THE ZEN OF EINSTEIN

He was quite a physicist. Philosophy, though, may best have been left to other thinkers. You be the judge with these mind-bending quotes from Albert Einstein.

• "The religion of the future will be a cosmic religion. The religion which based on experience, which refuses dogmatic. If there's any religion that would cope the scientific needs it will be Buddhism...."

• "We should take care not to make the intellect our god; it has, of course, powerful muscles, but no personality."

• "Nothing will benefit human health and increase the chances for survival of life on Earth as much as the evolution to a vegetarian diet."

• "Without deep reflection one knows from daily life that one exists for other people."

• "Things should be made as simple as possible, but not any simpler."

• "The faster you go, the shorter you are."

• "The wireless telegraph is not difficult to understand. The ordinary telegraph is like a very long cat. You pull the tail in New York, and it meows in Los Angeles. The wireless is the same, only without the cat."

• "I sometimes ask myself how it came about that I was the one to develop the theory of relativity. The reason, I think, is that a normal adult never stops to think about problems of space and time. These are things which he has thought about as a child. But my intellectual development was retarded, as a result of which I began to wonder about space and time only when I had already grown up."

Whatchamacallit?

What's that little bit between the lip and the nose called? A philtrum. There are all kinds of things we discovered that we didn't know had names. We thought you might enjoy them, too.

SNORKEL BOX: The name given to a drive-up mailbox, because of the projection of the drop slot.

BOTTS' DOTS: The raised bumps that mark off road lanes. Made of polyester, plastic or ceramic, they're named after their inventor, a California Department of Transportation chemist named Elbert Botts.

FUMET: Deer poop.

KEEPER: The loop on a belt that keeps the end in place after it has passed through the buckle.

COLUMELLA NASI: The bit on the lower edge of the nose that separates one nostril from the other.

FEAK: A dangling curl that hangs loose.

DRAGÉES: Tiny, little, silver candy balls that are used in cake and cookie decorating—particularly at holiday time.

FERRULE: The piece of metal that attaches a pencil to its eraser.

GRAWLIX, JARNS, QUIMP, NITTLES: These are all names for symbols that indicate a comics character is cursing.

ROWEL: The part of a cowboy spur that actually rotates. Usually, it's star-shaped.

FIPPLE: The lower lip.

SADDLE: The top, curved part of a "close-and-strike" matchbook.

FEAZINGS: The end of an unraveled rope.

Tom Swifties V

"I'M TEEING UP," TOM FOREWARNED

We managed to scrounge up even more weird and surreal Tom Swifty jokes. Here's the fifth and final batch. Enjoy!

"The radio jammer is working!" Tom said ecstatically.

"Let's get married," Tom said engagingly.

"I've run out of wool," said Tom, knitting his brow.

"I've gained weight," Tom said expansively.

"Elvis's daughter changed her name," Tom said expressly.

"Yes, we have no bananas today," Tom said fruitlessly.

"Love your steamroller!" Tom flattered.

"Turn 3 lefts and then go the other way," said Tom forthrightly.

"I have only diamonds, spades and clubs," said Tom heartlessly.

"Nay," said Tom hoarsely.

"The doctor removed my arm bone," Tom said humorlessly.

"Brush and floss," said Tom implacably.

"I hate that smoky sweet smell!" said Tom, incensed.

"I've borrowed my sibling's camp gear," said Tom insistently.

"I think I'm having a goat instead of a baby," Mary kidded.

"You're only average," Tom said meanly.

"I don't have a boyfriend," said Mary, guilelessly.

"I'm single, but I think I'm having a baby," said Sue, laboring under a misconception.

"This is mutiny!" said Tom bountifully.

"I should discard this low card," Tom deduced.

Ripe Ol' Corn

UNCLE JOSH IN NEW YORK CITY

"Uncle Josh Weathersby," Cal Stewart's country bumpkin, had problems figuring out modern city life (circa 1901). Here are some vignettes from a visit to hustling, bustling New York City.

UNCLE JOSH'S ARRIVAL

Well, for a long time I had my mind made up that I'd come down to New York. I was ridin' along in one of them sleepin' cars, and I felt a feller rummagin' around under my bed, and I looked out just in time to see him goin' away with my boots. Well, I knowed the way that train was a runnin' he couldn't get off with them without breakin' his durned neck. In about half an hour he brought them back—guess they didn't fit him. Well, I was sort of glad he took 'em 'cause he had shined 'em up slicker 'n a new tin whistle.

Well, when I got up in the mornin' I was so crowded up like, durned if I could get my clothes on, and when I did get 'em on durned if my pants wasn't on hind side afore, and my socks got all tangled up in that little fish net along side of the bed and I couldn't get 'em out, and I got my right boot on my left foot and the left one on the right foot, and I bumped my head on the roof of the bed over me, and then some feller stepped right square on my bunion and I let out a war whoop you coulda heard over in the next county. Well, along come that durned porter and told me I was a wakin' up everybody in the car.

Well, I got my clothes on and went into a room where they had a row of little troughs to wash in, and fast as I could pump water in the durned thing it run out of a little hole in the bottom so I just had to grab a handful and then pump some more.

When I got off the ferry boat, I commenced to think I was about the best lookin' old feller what ever come to New York, because fellers down there with buggies and carriages, the minute they seen me they all hollered, "hansom—hansom!"

Folks at home said I'd be buncoed or have my pockets picked fore I'd been here more than half an hour. Well, I fooled 'em a little bit—I was here three days before they buncoed me.

JOSH IN AN AUCTION ROOM

I was walkin' along down the street lookin' at things, when some feller throwed a banana peel on the sidewalk. Well, now I don't think much of a man what throws a banana peelin' on the sidewalk, and I don't think much of a banana what throws a man on the sidewalk, neither. My foot hit that banana peelin' and I went up in the air, and come down ker-plunk, and for about a minute I seen all the stars what astronomy tells about, and some that hadn't been discovered yet.

Well, just as I was pickin' myself up a little boy come runnin' cross the street and he said, "Oh mister, won't you please do that again, my mother didn't see you do it."

I come to a place where they was auctioneerin' off a lot of things. I stopped to see what they had to sell. Well, that place was just chuck full of old-fashioned curiosities. I saw an old book there, they said it was five hundred years old, and it belonged at one time to Louis the Seventeenth or Eighteenth, or some of them old rascals; durned if I believe anybody could read it.

Well, I commenced a biddin' on different things, but it just looked as though everybody had more money than I did, and they sort of out-bid me; but finally they put up an old-fashioned sugar bowl for sale, and I wanted to get that mighty bad, 'cause I thought as how mother would like it first rate. Well, I commenced a biddin' on it, and it was knocked down to me for $3.50. I put my hand in my pocket to get my pocket book to pay for it, and by gosh it was gone. So I went up to the feller what was a sellin' the things, and I said, "Now look here mister, will you just wait a minute. When I come in here I had a pocket book in my pocket, had fifty dollars in it, and I lost it somewheres round here; I wish you'd say to the feller what found it that I'll give five dollars for it." Another feller said, "Make it ten!" another said, "Give you twenty!" and another said, "Go you twenty-five!"

Durned if I know which one of 'em got it; when I left they was still a biddin' on it.

UNCLE JOSH IN SOCIETY

Well, I didn't suppose when I come down to New York that I was a-goin' to flop right into the middle of high toned society, but I guess that's just about what I done. You see I had an old friend a livin' down here named Henry Higgins. We was boys together down home at Punkin Centre, and I hadn't seen him in a long time.

Well, I got a feller to look up his name in the city almanac, and he showed me where Henry lived, on Avenue Five. Well, when I seen Henry's house it just about took my breath away. Henry's house is bigger'n the courthouse at Punkin Centre.

Well, I mustered up my courage, and I went up and rang some newfangled door bell. Well, Henry jist come out and grabbed me by bot hands and said, "Why Josh Weathersby, come right in!" Well, he took me into the house and introduced me to more folks than I ever seen before in all my life at one time.

After that we had somethin' to eat in the dinin' room. They had a lot of foreign dishes, somethin' what they called "beef all over mud," and another what they called "a-charlotte russia"—a little shavin' mug of cake and sweetened lather. Well, that was good eatin', though it took a lot of them, they weren't very fillin'. Then they handed me somethin' what they called ice cream, looked to me like a hunk of castile soap. Well, I stuck my fork in it, and it slipped off and got inside my vest, and in a minute I was froze from my chin to my toes. Yep, I really cut a caper at Henry's house.

JOSH IN THE DRY GOODS STORE

I'd said to mother, "I'll take a load of produce with me, and that will pay expenses of the trip." Well, I picked out a right likely lookin' store. I said to the clerk inside, "Well, be the storekeeper to home?" And presently we come to a place that had bars in front of the windows, and looked like the county jail. The clerk said, "Go in," and I said, "I hadn't done anything to be locked up for."

And that clerk commenced to laughin' though durned if I could see what he was a-laughin' about, and the store-keeper said, "Good mornin', what can I do for you?" So I said, "Do you want to buy any 'taters?" And he said, "No, sir, we don't buy pota-toes here; this a dry goods store." So I said, "Well, don't want any cabbage, do you?" And he said, "No, sir, this is a dry goods store." So I said, "Well, now, I want to know; do you need any onions?" And by chowder, he got mad-der 'n a wet hen. He said, "Now look a-here, I want you to understand once for all, this is a dry goods store, and we don't buy anything but dry goods and don't sell any-thing but dry goods; do you understand me now? DRY GOODS." And I said, "Yes, I understand; you don't need to get so riled; far as I can fig-ure, you just buy and sell dry

goods." And he said, "Yes, only dry goods." So I said, "Do you want to buy some dried apples?"

THE SIGNS SEEN IN NEW YORK

I seen a good many funny things when I was in New York, but the signs on the buildins' are 'bout as funny as anything I ever seen.

I went into the restaurant and I noticed a sign'd said "Trust in the Lord," and right under it was another what said "Try our mince pies." Well, I tried one, and I want to tell you, if you eat them pies you want to put your trust in the Lord.

Well, I come to a store, they had a sign in that window that said "Frog in your throat 10¢." It tickled me 'cause I wouldn't put one of them critters in my throat for $10!

Well, up the street I seen a sign what said "Boots blacked

on the inside." Now, any one what gets his boots blacked on the inside ain't got much respect for his socks. I get mine blacked on the outside.

A little further I seen a sign what said "Cast iron sinks." Well, now, any durned fool what don't know that cast iron sinks, ought to have some one feel his head and find out what ails him.

UNCLE JOSH AT THE OPERA

Well, I got into one of your theaters, got set down and a lot of fellers come out with horns and fiddles, and they all started in to fiddlin' and tootin'. All to once they pulled the curtain up, and there was a lot of folks having a regular family quarrel. I knowed that wasn't any of my business, and I sort of felt uneasy like; but none of the rest of the folks seemed to mind it any, so I calculated I'd see how it come out, though my hands sort of itched to get hold of one feller, 'cause I could see if he would just go 'way and tend to his own business there wouldn't be any quarrel. Well, just then a young feller handed me a piece of paper what told all about the theater doings, and it said the second act takes place five years after the first. I knowed I couldn't wait that

long to see the second part, so I got up and went out.

UNCLE JOSH ON A STREET CAR

Well, I paid 5¢ and got on one of them street cars. In one end of the car there was a little slim lady, and right along side of her was a big fleshy lady, and it didn't look as though the slim lady was gettin' more'n about 2¢ worth of room. Finally she turned to the fleshy lady and said, "They ought to charge by weight on this line," and the big lady said, "Well, if they did they wouldn't stop for you." Gosh, I had to snicker right out loud.

Three ladies got onto the car, and there weren't a place for 'em to set down, and so the big lady said to a little boy sitting nearby, "You oughta get up and let one of them ladies set down," and the little boy said, "If *you* get up, they can *all* set down."

Well, I got to talkin' to the nice feller steerin' the car. He showed me how every thing worked and when I got off I said, "Good bye, mister, hope I'll see you again some time," and he said, "Oh, I'll run across you one of these days." I told him by gosh he sure wouldn't run across me if I seen him a'comin' first. ☾

Sports Match 3
MATCH THE TEAM TO THE LOCATION

If you're not an absolute sports junkie, this one's going to be a little tough. Match the pro teams from the National Hockey League, Major League Soccer and the Women's National Basketball Association with the places they call home.

1.	Shock	New York
2.	Hurricanes	Ottawa
3.	Fire	Chicago
4.	Revolution	Carolina
5.	Crew	Washington, D.C.
6.	Sting	Atlanta
7.	Islanders	Detroit
8.	Fever	Sacramento
9.	MetroStars	New Jersey
10.	Liberty	Charlotte
11.	Senators	New York
12.	Penguins	New England
13.	Monarchs	Indiana
14.	Thrashers	Columbus
15.	United	Pittsburgh

Answers: 1. Shock: Detroit—WNBA; 2. Hurricanes: Carolina—NHL; 3. Fire: Chicago—MLS; 4. Revolution: New England—MLS; 5. Crew: Columbus—MLS; 6. Sting: Charlotte—WNBA; 7. Islanders: New York—NHL; 8. Fever: Indiana—WNBA; 9. MetroStars: New Jersey—MLS; 10. Liberty: New York—WNBA; 11. Senators: Ottawa—NHL; 12. Penguins: Pittsburgh—NHL; 13. Monarchs: Sacramento—WNBA; 14. Thrashers: Atlanta—NHL; 15. United: Washington, D.C.—MLS

Sugar Daddy
No Sucker for Commies!

What does a caramel on a stick have to do with fighting the international communist conspiracy? Plenty, mister.

ROBERT HENRY WINBORNE WELCH, JR., was born in 1899 and quickly got a reputation as a child prodigy. At age twelve, he entered the University of North Carolina and was, by his own admission years later, "the most insufferable little squirt that ever tried to associate with his elders." Raised as a fundamentalist Baptist, he tried to get his fellow students to come to Bible classes in his dorm room.

After four years, he entered the U.S. Naval Academy for two years before dropping out. He then entered Harvard Law School. Already a hard-line conservative, Welch left Harvard in the middle of his third and final year, "in disgust over what Felix Frankfurter was teaching—that labor and management were enemies." While Professor Frankfurter went on to a distinguished stint on the Supreme Court, the embittered Welch went home and began a candy company, "the one field in which it seemed least impossible to get started without either capital or experience."

His Oxford Candy Company started making fudge from a recipe Welch bought from a candy store owner. He also began making caramels. One day, inspired by lollipops, he rolled out some of his caramel and stuck a stick into it. He called his new taste treat Papa Sucker. Powered by this success, the Oxford Candy Company did well enough for him to hire an employee, his brother James.

Things went along well enough for a while, but in 1925 James left and started his own candy company. Short the help, Robert made an unusual rights deal with the Brach Candy Company to manufacture Papa Suckers from its Chicago factory. Robert spent his time flying between his Brooklyn-based company and Chicago-based Brach, overseeing the production of the caramel suckers.

WHAT'S IN A NAME?

In 1932, his candy company was hit hard by the Depression and went bankrupt. However, the James O. Welch Company, founded by his brother, was doing fine. In a reversal of fortunes, James hired Robert to take charge of his company's advertising and sales.

One of the first things Robert did in his new capacity was to start making a candy identical to the Papa Sucker. To avoid legal problems with Brach, he changed its name to Sugar Daddy, hoping the new name would insinuate easy living and wealth.

His brother's company began selling Sugar Daddies along with spin-offs like Sugar Babies, Junior Mints and Pom Poms. During the next three decades, the company's annual sales increased from $200,000 to $20 million. Robert retired in 1956, a millionaire many times over.

TOO MUCH MONEY

Despite his money, Welch was very worried about holding onto it. He sensed foreign, alien philosophies floating through the land that threatened his fortune and sense of well-being. "There is no reason on Earth why we should let ourselves be infected by such diseases as socialism and communism, and other ideological cancers," he wrote. In 1958, Welch decided to start an organization to wake America up to the grave dangers that threatened from every direction. He joined with ten other men and started the ultra-conservative John Birch Society, named after an Army intelligence agent who was killed in China ten days after World War II ended. Welch decided that Birch was the first casualty in World War III, which, as far as Welch was concerned, had already begun.

Welch believed that all Americans fell into one of four categories: "Communists, communist dupes or sympathizers, the uninformed who have yet to be awakened to the communist danger, and the ignorant." He believed it was almost too late to shake Americans out of their stupor: Wasn't America was already ruled by Dwight David Eisenhower, "a dedicated, conscious agent of the communist conspiracy"? Was not democracy itself nothing more than "a deceptive phrase, a weapon of demagoguery and a perennial fraud"? It was the Birch Society, he believed, that would bring America back to "less government, more responsibility and, with God's help, a better world."

PINKOS AND PARANOIA

But, of course, it wouldn't be easy. Welch made up a map of the world, coloring each nation various shades of pink and red to indicate how "communistic" it was. The United States was a deep pink, and even the most brutal right-wing Latin American dictatorships that machine-gunned suspected communists by the carload were painted a light pink ("somewhat communistic") instead of white ("completely free of communism").

The John Birch Society achieved a surprising level of public awareness and claimed membership in the upper five figures. In the paranoid 1950s and '60s, Welch and his cronies funded scores of books, started bookstores all over the country, published a monthly called *American Opinion* and even opened a dozen summer camps to indoctrinate kids against communism. Welch used some of his Sugar Daddy earnings to buy billboards all over the country with the message "Impeach Earl Warren," referring to the Chief Justice of the Supreme Court, whom Welch believed was leading the country down the crimson path with his pro-union and civil rights rulings.

Welch was also opposed to the fluoride in the water ("a communist plot to make Americans into mongolian idiots"), Norway ("secretly communist"), the Beatles ("Their songs are written by a communist think tank"), federal aid to education, arms negotiations, foreign aid, income taxes, collective bargaining, Social Security and much more. He wasn't even particularly happy when Ronald Reagan was elected president, considering him hopelessly liberal.

As Welch's political analysis ripened to full flagrant paranoia, he eventually decided that the "International Communist Conspiracy" was itself merely a front for something even bigger and scarier. The "inner circle that has been running the show," for two centuries, he became convinced, was an ultrasecret cabal of Masons that formed in Bavaria in May, 1776, and called itself "the Illuminati."

THE END...OR IS IT?

Welch died in 1985, and his organization fell into irrelevancy and debt. The fall of the Berlin Wall and communism in Eastern Europe made it difficult for most of the world to take its message seriously (even though, the

Society claimed, "the so-called fall of communism was just a clever hoax"). Even a move to Appleton, Wisconsin, to be close to the birthplace of their hero, senator and witch-hunter Joseph McCarthy, couldn't sufficiently bolster the troops.

James Welch disavowed his brother's views in 1961. He sold his candy company to Nabisco in 1963, but continued as a Nabisco director until 1978. James also died in 1985, just 27 days after his brother.

Coincidence? Or was it conspiracy...? ❆

Sweet Remainders

• The year was 1935. The song was *Let Me Be Your Sugar Baby.* Welch introduced Sugar Babies to the market to cash in on the popularity of the song.

• In 1963, Ann Miller and Mickey Rooney, stars of the Broadway hit *Sugar Babies,* were given the little candies by the company to toss into the audience. The promotion worked like a charm and Sugar Babies sales soared.

• Sugar Mamas were just Sugar Daddies that had been dipped in chocolate. They didn't sell well and were discontinued. No mention of them can be found in current company literature.

• Welch began including "comic cards," in Sugar Daddies in the 1940s. They were like sports trading cards, but were comic characters. In the 1970s, the company combined the two ideas and offered sports stars' heads with caricatured bodies as sort of a sports/comic trading card hybrid.

Such a Clatter

WHO WROTE "THE NIGHT BEFORE CHRISTMAS"?

Clement C. Moore has long been credited with writing the once-anonymous Christmas classic. However, some scholars now believe that the real author was probably somebody else. Here's the story.

YOU MAY NOT KNOW the title, "A Visit from St. Nicholas," but you know the poem. It's the one that begins: "'Twas the night before Christmas and all through the house...." It was an important poem in that it largely created our view of who Santa Claus is.

For centuries, Saint Nicholas had been portrayed as a stern churchman bringing whippings and punishment as often as gifts. However, in the 19th century, the image started shifting. In 1812, Washington Irving wrote about the Dutch tradition of Santa Claus "riding over the tops of the trees, in that selfsame waggon wherein he brings his yearly presents to children." In 1821, William Gilley, a New York printer, published a short poem about "Santeclaus," who drove a sleigh pulled by a reindeer. Finally, in 1823, the *Troy* (N.Y.) *Sentinel* published "An Account of a Visit from St. Nicholas," in which Santa was first depicted as a jolly fat man having eight flying reindeer and a proclivity for coming down stocking-hung chimneys with gifts.

The poem was published anonymously, and would remain so for years afterward through several reprintings. Until recently, the story that has long been accepted is that Clement Clarke Moore—a wealthy academic who dabbled in Greek and Latin, Bible studies, politics and poetry—had written it a year earlier on Christmas Eve. According to the story, a family friend had given it to the newspaper anonymously so that the ever-so-serious Moore would be spared the embarrassment of having written such a frivolous poem. Finally, 21 years later—after the

(As published in the *Troy Sentinel*, December 23, 1823)

Account of a Visit from St. Nicholas

'Twas the night before Christmas, when all thro' the house,
Not a creature was stirring, not even a mouse;
The stockings were hung by the chimney with care,
In hopes that St. Nicholas soon would be there;
The children were nestled all snug in their beds,
While visions of sugar plums danc'd in their heads,
And Mama in her 'kerchief, and I in my cap,
Had just settled our brains for a long winter's nap-
When out on the lawn there arose such a clatter,
I sprang from the bed to see what was the matter.
Away to the window I flew like a flash,
Tore open the shutters, and threw up the sash.
The moon on the breast of the new fallen snow,
Gave the lustre of mid-day to objects below;
When, what to my wondering eyes should appear,
But a miniature sleigh, and eight tiny rein-deer,
With a little old driver, so lively and quick,
I knew in a moment it must be St. Nick.
More rapid than eagles his coursers they came,
And he whistled, and shouted, and call'd them by name:
"Now! Dasher, now! Dancer, now! Prancer, and Vixen,
"On! Comet, on! Cupid, on! Dunder and Blixem;
"To the top of the porch! to the top of the wall!
"Now dash away! dash away! dash away all!"
As dry leaves before the wild hurricane fly,
When they meet with an obstacle, mount to the sky;
So up to the house-top the coursers they flew,
With the sleigh full of toys - and St. Nicholas too:
And then in a twinkling, I heard on the roof
The prancing and pawing of each little hoof.
As I drew in my head, and was turning around,
Down the chimney St. Nicholas came with a bound:
He was dress'd all in fur, from his head to his foot,
And his clothes were all tarnish'd with ashes and soot;
A bundle of toys was flung on his back,
And he look'd like a peddler just opening his pack:
His eyes - how they twinkled! his dimples how merry,
His cheeks were like roses, his nose like a cherry;
His droll little mouth was drawn up like a bow,
And the beard of his chin was as white as the snow;
The stump of a pipe he held tight in his teeth,
And the smoke it encircled his head like a wreath.
He had a broad face, and a little round belly
That shook when he laugh'd, like a bowl full of jelly:
He was chubby and plump, a right jolly old elf,
And I laugh'd when I saw him in spite of myself;
A wink of his eye and a twist of his head
Soon gave me to know I had nothing to dread.
He spoke not a word, but went straight to his work,
And fill'd all the stockings; then turn'd with a jerk,
And laying his finger aside of his nose
And giving a nod, up the chimney he rose.
He sprung to his sleigh, to his team gave a whistle,
And away they all flew, like the down of a thistle:
But I heard him exclaim, ere he drove out of sight-
Happy Christmas to all, and to all a good night.

poem had been reprinted several times — Moore stepped forward to claim credit for it.

But was he taking credit for someone else's work? According to descendents of another New York amateur poet, Moore was a fraud. They say their ancestor, Henry Livingston, a farmer and surveyor, was the true author of "A Visit from St. Nicholas." According to the recollections of Livingston's children and a neighbor, Livingston had read the poem to them in 1808, fifteen years before it was published anonymously.

The Livingstons have gotten some powerful support from Don Foster, an expert on analyzing the stylistic quirks that are every author's trademark. He is best known for identifying Shakespeare as the author of an anonymous poem and outing political writer Joe Klein as the anonymous author of *Primary Colors*. According to Foster:

• Clement Moore was a grouch whose poems were full of stern, moralistic cant. He never would've written such a playful, child-friendly poem. For example, a St. Nicholas poem he wrote for his own daughter (*see box*)

(A genuine Santa Claus poem by Clement C. Moore)

From Saint Nicholas

What! My sweet little Sis, in bed all alone;
No light in your room! And your nursy too gone!
And you, like a good child, are quietly lying,
While some naughty ones would be fretting or crying?
Well, for this you must have something pretty, my dear;
And, I hope, will deserve a reward too next year.
But, speaking of crying, I'm sorry to say
Your screeches and screams, so loud ev'ry day,
Were near driving me and my goodies away.
Good children I always give good things in plenty;
How sad to have left your stocking quite empty:
But you are beginning so nicely to spell,
And, in going to bed, behave always so well,
That, although I too oft see the tear in your eye,
I cannot resolve to pass you quite by.
I hope, when I come here again the next year,
I shall not see even the sign of a tear.
And then, if you get back your sweet pleasant looks,
And do as you're bid, I will leave you some books,
Some toys, or perhaps what you still may like better,
And then too may write you a prettier letter.
At present, my dear, I must bid you good bye;
Now, do as you're bid; and, remember, don't cry.

threatened that her "screeches and screams, so loud every day / Were near driving me and my goodies away...."

• Moore condemned "immodest verse" without a moral that had "no other recommendations that the glow of its expressions and the tinkling of its syllables, or the wanton allurement of the ideas that it conveys."

• Moore condemned tobacco as "opium's treacherous aid," yet the poem's Santa enjoyed a pipe.

• Moore's only original contribution, according to Foster, was to screw up the names of two reindeer. They had originally been named "Dunder and Blixem," a common Dutch expression meaning "thunder and lightning." Livingston spoke Dutch;

Moore did not. When Clement republished the poem under his own name, he changed the names to "Donder and Blitzen."

• In 1844, Moore contacted the *Troy Sentinel* to ask if anybody could identify the author. He was told that the staff members who had known anything about the origins of the poem had died more than a decade earlier. Shortly after, Moore published the poem as his own in a collection of his poetry.

• Livingston, on the other hand, wrote lighthearted poems with some interesting stylistic quirks. One of them was that he often wrote in the anapestic meter, emphasizing every third syllable ("da da DUM da da DUM da da DUM"), as seen in "A Visit from St. Nicholas." His annual Christmas poem was always written in the anapestic form. Moore, on the other hand, used anapestic meter in only one known poem.

• Livingston's poems often had the unusual quirk of using *all* as an adverb. So does this poem, in phrases like "all through the

(A poem example by Henry Livingston)

Epithalamium
A Marriage Poem

'Twas summer, when softly the breezes were blowing,
And Hudson majestic so sweetly was flowing,
The groves rang with music and accents of pleasure
And nature in rapture beat time to the measure,
When Helen and Jonas, so true and so loving,
Along the green lawn were seen arm in arm moving,
Sweet daffodils, violets and roses spontaneous
Wherever they wandered sprang up instantaneous.
The ascent the lovers at length were seen climbing
Whose summit is grac'd by the temple of Hymen:
The genius presiding no sooner perceived them
But, spreading his pinions, he flew to receive them;
With kindest of greetings pronounced them well come
While hollidays clangor rang loud to the welkin.

Henry Livingston, we presume

Clement Moore

"Happy Christmas" in his writings. So does Santa in this poem.

• Livingston tended to use an extravagant number of exclamation marks. Moore almost never used them. The use in the roll call of reindeer is "vintage Livingston," said Foster.

• Finally, Livingston was known for populating his poems with flying creatures, fairies, animals and people. He considered himself an expert on Lapland's reindeer. And his Dutch heritage gave him the legend of "Sint Nikolass" with his annual visits with gifts. ☾

house," "all snug in their beds," and "dressed all in fur."

• At a time when most people said "Merry Christmas," Livingston habitually used

The Roots of Christmas Traditions

JESUS WAS NOT really born on Christmas (many historians think it was more likely in autumn). In third-century Rome, though, Christianity was competing with other sects that had big winter solstice holidays. Worried that they were losing converts to the jollier sects, the early Christians began a long tradition of adopting other groups' ceremonies:

• Mithraism celebrated the birth of the sun king on that date.

• Worshipers of Saturn, god of agriculture, held feasts and parades.

• From the cult of Bacchus, the god of wine, Christians adopted lights and wreaths. Bacchus was the son of a god and mortal woman who was routinely depicted with a halo over his head. His followers ate bread and wine to symbolize his body and blood (in fact, Bacchus's blood *was* wine).

•Christmas trees? Borrowed from pagan tree worshipers in Germany.

Get a Job!

MORE SUGGESTIONS FOR A CHANGE IN CAREERS

Brachygrapher: A shorthand specialist.

Hello Girl: A telephone operator.

Eyer: One who puts eyes into sewing needles.

Bluestocking: A woman writer.

Shrimpschonger: A carver.

Tucker In: A bed-maker; a servant.

Castora: Salt and pepper shaker manufacturer.

Bang Beggar: One who tosses unwanted visitors out of town.

Shrieve: One who serves as sheriff.

Trepanger: A circular saw expert.

Gager: One who collects revenue from alcoholic beverages.

Todhunter: A city official paid to hunt foxes.

Apiarian: One who keeps bees.

Rhapsode: A professional epic poet reciter.

Nimgimmer: A physician.

Cambist: A bank employee.

Bodeys: One who makes bodices for dresses.

Stuff Gowsman: A barrister in training.

Fogger: A vendor.

Travers: Someone who works a bridge toll booth.

Cocus: A cook.

Sperviter: A sparrow specialist.

Pistor: A baker.

Woolen Billy Piecer: A mill worker responsible for salvaging broken pieces of yarn.

Banker: Ditch digger.

Times Ironer: One who irons the daily newspaper.

Ad Conveyancer: Someone who carries a sandwich board.

Claker: One who reads fortunes in the stars.

Scrutineer: A judge who investigates for misconduct in elections.

Grimbribber: An attorney.

Trencherman: A professional cook.

White Limer: A wall plasterer.

Grudge Match

WHY COKE HATES PEPSI, PART II

Continuing the story from page 231: Despite the new curvy Coke bottles and Coke attorney Harold Hirsch's constant lawsuits, one Coke-wannabe prevailed and thrived. Here's how Pepsi came alive.

PEPSI-COLA, like Coke, came from the South. It was formulated by a former Confederate Army officer, pharmacist Caleb B. Bradham. His New Bern, North Carolina, pharmacy thrived because it provided a soda fountain alternative to saloons of the town. Like other druggists at that time, Bradham began tinkering with new elixirs and patent medicines, using the knowledge he picked up in medical school.

He modeled one concoction after the wildly popular Coca-Cola. Intended to relieve stomach disorders and ulcers, "Brad's Drink," as it was called, was a pleasant mixture of vanilla, exotic oils and spices, sugar and the African kola nut. It became popular with the locals. He renamed it Pepsi-Cola in 1898, and in 1902 started peddling it to other soda fountains. Two years later, he sold shares in the business and copied Coke's franchise system to begin marketing Pepsi in bottles. By 1909, Bradham had 250 bottlers in 24 states. He was getting rich.

From 1905 to 1915, Pepsi circulated free coupons to get people to try the stuff

World War I, though, changed all that. Rapidly fluctuating sugar prices and labor costs crippled the company. By 1922, the Pepsi Company was bankrupt, and Bradham went back to filling prescriptions at his New Bern drug store.

A Wall Street money man named Roy C. Megargel bought up the company's assets and started a new Pepsi-Cola company in Richmond, Virginia. When he failed to come up with enough investment capital to keep it going, though, the company went down in flames again in 1932.

Next in line came Charles Guth, president of Loft, Inc., a candy company in Long Island, New York. Guth had a grudge against the Coca-Cola company for not giving him a volume discount on the Coke syrup he sold each year at his 115 soda fountains. He decided to make his own beverage, so he took money out of

Loft's till to buy up the Pepsi rights, including Megargel as a silent partner, and started still another new Pepsi Cola Company. He tinkered with the recipe to his own taste preferences and began serving it in his stores.

Coca-Cola, ever-vigilant in protecting its own market, sent its undercover agents into Loft stores, then filed a lawsuit, claiming they had fraudulently been served Pepsi-Cola when they had ordered Coca-Cola. Guth countersued, claiming that Coke was illegally harassing and maligning his stores and employees. The bitter court case would be played out in slow motion over the following decade.

Meanwhile, however, the Pepsi-Cola Company had other troubles. With Loft stores as its only outlet, the company was losing money fast, and Guth decided he wanted out. He even offered to sell Pepsi to Coca-Cola, for a modest price. In the blunder of its life, Coke turned him down. His partner Megargel, meanwhile, sued for funds Guth owed him, so Guth bought him out for $35,000, of which all but $500 came out of Loft's company funds.

Pepsi, now 91% owned by Guth, was about to go under

for a third time, when a used bottle dealer suggested that Guth start bottling his drink in used beer bottles. Even though the bottles held nearly twice as much as Coke's 6.5-ounce bottles, he decided to charge only a nickel since the Depression was on. Because Pepsi offered twice as much drink for the same price as a Coke, Pepsi's sales went through the roof. Guth's candy stores, however, were falling apart. Stockholders revolted, and he resigned his presidency.

The Loft Company board of directors sued Guth in 1939, after discovering he had taken most of the money for his Pepsi venture from their till. After a bruising battle, the court ruled that Loft, Inc., was the legitimate owner of Pepsi-Cola.

Regardless of the legal issues, Coke noted with alarm that Pepsi continued to do booming business. The battle soon escalated beyond sending undercover agents into Loft stores: Coke sued Pepsi over trademark violations, claiming proprietary rights to the name "Cola." On the first day of the trial, Coke lawyers made a big show of hauling out huge stacks of legal documents detailing its victories over trademark infringers.

From weighty precedence, it looked like an open and shut case. The widow of the victim of an earlier Coke lawsuit called on Walter Mack, the new president of Pepsi, to offer condolences. Her husband had been president of something called Cleo Cola. She casually mentioned that Coca-Cola had given her husband a $35,000 check to put him out of business.

A payoff? Mack couldn't believe his ears. Maybe Coke wasn't so sure of victory after all. The next day in court, Pepsi's lawyers asked about the check, and Coke's lawyers asked for a two-day recess to respond. That afternoon, Coke president, Robert Woodruff called Mack and invited him to meet the next morning. According to Mack the conversation went like this:

"Mr. Mack, I've been thinking about this lawsuit, and I think we ought to settle it. Is that agreeable to you?"

"It is, under one condition."

Mack took a piece of paper

and wrote, "I, Robert Woodruff, president and chief executive officer of the Coca-Cola Company, hereby agree that the corporation will recognize the Pepsi-Cola trademark and never attack it in the United States." He handed it to Woodruff, who drafted a similar agreement stating that Pepsi would recognize Coke. Both men signed and then shook hands on the deal.

The truce didn't last long. Coke, saying the agreement applied only to the U. S., dispatched attorneys to file trademark violation suits in countries all over the world. A lower judge in Canada ruled for Coke, but Canada's Supreme Court reversed that ruling. Because Canada was a member of the British Commonwealth, Coke appealed to the highest Commonwealth court, the Privy Council in England.

"It was a hell of a dirty trick," Mack observed later, "because it was during the war and they had lawyers over there. The Privy Council had set a date, and Coke figured we wouldn't be able to get anybody over there." Pepsi hired Wendell Willkie, who had just finished an unsuccessful presidential bid. Willkie was able to get the government to fly him over to England in an Air Force bomber, ostensibly to make speeches for the war effort. He got there in time to represent Pepsi in the courts. The Privy Council ruled in favor of Pepsi's claim that "cola" was a generic term and requested that both companies coexist in peace.

That, though, wasn't going to happen. Although the suits and countersuits stopped, the two companies continued to slash at each other in the marketplace. Coke managed to finagle a position as a quasi-government agency in World War II as a boost to the morale and energy levels of the fighting boys. Shipped

Pepsi Slogans Through the Ages

"Brad's Drink" (1898)
"Exhilarating, Invigorating, Aids Digestion" (1903)
"Pepsi-Cola—It makes you Scintillate" (1919)
"Peps You Up!" (1928)
"Join the Swing to Pepsi" (1938)
"Twice as Much for a Nickel" (1939)
"More Bounce to the Ounce" (1950)
"Be Sociable, Have a Pepsi" (1958)
"Now It's Pepsi for Those Who Think Young" (1961)
"Join the Pepsi People Feelin' Free" (1973)
"The Choice of a New Generation" (1984)
"Be Young, Have Fun, Drink Pepsi" (1993)
"The Joy of Pepsi" (2001)

with food and ammo as a "war priority item," the deal spread Coke's market worldwide at government expense. Also at U.S. expense after the war, fifty-nine new Coke plants were installed to help rebuild Europe. What

NO FINER DRINK... for Salesgirl—or Sailor

PURITY... Pepsi-Cola IN THE BIG BIG BOTTLE

isn't widely known, though, is that, despite Coke's wartime posture as an All-American icon, Coca-Cola continued bottling in Nazi Germany throughout the war, using syrup smuggled in through circuitous contacts in the international business community.

During the war, one of Coke's officers served as a consultant to the Beverage and Tobacco Board, which (according to Pepsi president Mack) he used to help Coke and hinder Pepsi. For example, one of his first directives limited sugar users to 80% of their 1941 consumption. That was acceptable for Coke's long-established bottling operation, but many of Pepsi's bottlers were not even established in 1941. After the war, Pepsi accused Coke of working to extend sugar rationing beyond necessity.

But Pepsi played dirty, too. While Coke extended its influence deeper into the Democratic executive branch, Pepsi courted Republicans, most notably Senator Joe McCarthy, who, in exchange for a $20,000 "loan," became known in the Senate as the Pepsi-Cola Kid. Two decades later, Pepsi would hire defeated presidential candidate Richard Nixon as their chief counsel. Pepsi later helped bankroll Nixon's successful presidential bid.

More legitimately, Pepsi and Coke also fought it out in the advertising world, trading slogans and marketing punches left and right. Both used elaborate advertising campaigns and giveaways. (Pepsi, for example, bought the exclusive rights to skywriting when it was new and wrote "Pepsi Cola" over nearly every city in America.) Coke's ads usually focused on cementing its image as an all-American institution; Pepsi's, on being the upstart challenger favored by youth and other non-stodgy types.

The Cola Wars continue. €

Potty Pourri
RANDOM KINDS OF FACTNESS

• Moose are lethal fighters. If one stands its ground, a wolf pack will back down and skulk away.

• Most male mammals have nipples. However, stallions and bulls don't. Zoologists speculate that's because the females have their mammary glands located between their hind legs. There simply isn't enough extra room down there on the males.

• Of course the Roosevelts were related, and the Bushes and Adamses, too, but Richard Nixon had relatives who also served in the White House. Hoover and Taft were his distant cousins.

• Although nearly all wine grapes are now machine pressed, small quantities of some of the finer ports are still pressed by foot.

• Why does "meteorology" refer to weather and not meteors? Ask Aristotle, who coined the term in 340 B.C. In Greek, *meteora* means "stuff that's up in the air," so he called snow an "aqueous meteor." Rainbows were "luminous meteors." Wind was an "aerial meteor." And he called both lightning and shooting stars "fiery meteors."

• The joystick was used in airplanes long before it was seen with computers or video games. The first reference to one goes back to 1914.

• There are lots of legends about who knocked the nose off Egypt's Sphinx. Most involve invading armies using it for target practice. Despite the legends, you can't blame Napoleon, the Germans, the British or Arab conquerors in A.D. 693. Blame the sand, wind and rain. The Sphinx is carved out of sandstone, and all of its parts have eroded over the years. The nose, being the thinnest part, has simply taken the hardest hit from it.

• Looking for sympathy? Next time you bang your elbow, tell everyone that you've developed an *ecchymosis*. That's the formal name for a bruise.

A Suppressed Gospel
MARY'S MIDWIFE GETS HER HAND BURNED

Church fathers excluded the Infancy Gospel of James (attributed to Jesus' half-brother) from the Bible during the 4th century. It tells us that Jesus was born in a cave, that Mary was given to a reluctant Joseph after being kicked out of the temple...and that the midwife who examined Mary got her hand burned off.

IN THE HISTORIES of the twelve tribes of Israel it is written that there was a man named Joachim who was exceeding rich. On the day of the Lord, Reuben told him: "It is not lawful for you to give offerings because you have not had a child for Israel." Joachim was sore grieved, and did not go home to his wife, but went into the wilderness. He pitched his tent there, and fasted forty days and forty nights, saying to himself: "I will not have either food or drink until God visits me."

His wife Anna lamented, saying: "I mourn my widowhood, and my childlessness." She prayed to the Lord, saying: "God of our fathers, bless me, and answer my prayer, as you blessed the womb of Sarah and gave her a son, Isaac." And behold an angel of the Lord appeared, saying: "Anna, the Lord has heard your prayer. You will conceive and bear, and your child will be known all over the world." Anna replied: "As God lives, I will bring my child for a gift to the Lord."

Anna's months were fulfilled, and in the ninth she gave birth. She asked the midwife: "What did I have?" The midwife said: "A girl." Anna replied: "My soul is magnified this day!" After her days were fulfilled, Anna cleansed her menstrual flow, and gave her breast to the child and named her Mary. Anna made a sanctuary in her bed chamber and allowed nothing common or unclean to pass through it. And she called for the daughters of the Hebrews that were virgins, and they were the only ones who played with Mary.

MARY BECOMES TEMPLE MASCOT...BUT THEN SHE GROWS UP

When Mary became three years old, Joachim and Anna took her to the temple of the Lord. The priest kissed her and blessed her and said: "The Lord will magnify your name through all generations; the Lord will use you to redeem the children of Israel in

Mary hangs out with the virgins

the last days." He sat Mary on the third step of the altar, and the Lord rained grace on her. She danced, and all the houses of Israel loved her. When Mary was in the temple of the Lord, she was nurtured like a dove as a dove, and she received food from the hand of an angel.

When Mary turned twelve years old, the priests met saying: "Behold Mary will reach puberty soon. What can we do with her before she pollutes the sanctuary of the Lord?" And lo, an angel of

the Lord appeared, saying: "Go forth and assemble all the widowers in the kingdom. Have every man carry a rod. The lord will give a sign, and that man shall have Mary for his wife."

RELUCTANT JOSEPH GETS A YOUNG WIFE

And the heralds went forth over all the country round, calling all the widowers. Throwing down his axe, Joseph ran to join them, and took their rods to meet the high priest. When he had finished a prayer, a dove flew out of Joseph's rod and landed on his head. The priest told Joseph: "Take the virgin of the Lord and keep her for yourself." Joseph refused, saying: "I have sons, and I am an old man, but she is just a girl. I'll become a laughingstock to the children of Israel." The priest replied: "Hear the Lord thy God, and remember what God did to Dathan, Abiram and Korah, how the earth opened up and swallowed them because of their disobedience."

So Joseph took her to his house. He said: "Mary: I have taken you from the temple of the Lord. I must leave you in my house, because I have been contracted to build a building, but I'll be back. Until then, the Lord will watch over you."

Mary was spinning cloth for the temple, and suddenly heard a voice say: "Hail! The Lord is with you: you among all women are blessed." Mary looked to her right and her left to see where the voice came from, and behold an angel of the Lord stood before her saying: "Fear not, Mary, for you have found grace before the Lord, and you shall conceive from his word."

"Will I have to conceive from the Lord as all women conceive?"

Hearing this, Mary was distraught. She asked, "Will I have to conceive from the Lord in the same way all women conceive?"

The angel replied: "Not like that, Mary. The power of the Lord will come over you, and the holy child born from you will be called the Son of the Highest. Name him Jesus, for he shall save his people from their sins."

HOW DO YOU FORGET AN ANGEL?

Mary rejoiced and went to the house of her cousin, Elizabeth. When Elizabeth opened the door, she blessed Mary and said: "Why should the mother of my Lord come to me? See how the child within me leaps and blesses you." Mary, however, had forgotten the mysteries which the angel Gabriel had told her, and she looked to the heaven and asked: "Who am I, Lord, that all the generations of the earth do bless me?"

Mary stayed three months with Elizabeth, and then went home and hid from the children of Israel. Day by day, her womb grew. She was sixteen years old when these mysteries came to pass.

Now it was the sixth month with her, and Joseph came home from his building. He entered into his house and found her swollen with child. He struck his face and cast himself down upon the ground, weeping: "How can I face my Lord? For I received a virgin out of the temple, and have not kept her safe. Who has done this evil in my house? Has not the story of Adam repeated itself, when the serpent came and found Eve alone and deceived her, so has it not happened to me, too?"

Joseph arose and said to Mary: "Why have you forgotten the Lord your God, you who was fed by the hand of an angel?"

But she wept bitterly, saying: "I am pure and I have not had sex with a man." Joseph said: "So where did this thing in your belly come from?" She replied: "As the Lord my God lives, I don't know how it got there."

Joseph became frightened and left her alone, wondering what he should do with her: "If I hide her sin, I break the law of the Lord. But what if I expose her sin? If what is inside her is the seed of an angel, I will be delivering up innocent blood to a death penalty. What then should I do? I will send her away from me secretly."

ANGELS IN THE NIGHT

That night, an angel appeared to him in a dream, saying: "Do not fear this child, for it came from the Holy Ghost. She will

bear a son you will name Jesus, for he shall save his people from their sins." When Joseph arose from sleep, he glorified God, and watched over Mary.

Annas the scribe* came later and said to Joseph: "Why didn't you come to the assembly?" Annas turned and saw that Mary was swollen with child. He went hastily to the priest and told him that Joseph had sinned grievously. "He has defiled the virgin he received out of the temple and stolen her virginity."

Mary in a cave again

[*The priest gave them "water of the Lord's wrath" and sent them out to the wilderness to meet their fate. They returned unscathed, which surprised all. The priest said, "If God didn't judge your sins, then I won't either" and released them.*]

CHRISTMAS DELIVERY

Now there went out a decree from Augustus the king that all that were in Judea should be recorded. And Joseph said: "I will record my sons, but how will I explain this child? How shall I

* A few years later, Jesus later got his revenge — in another suppressed gospel (see page 98), the Boy Savior killed Annas's son for messing up his mud.

record Mary? As my wife? No, I am ashamed. As my daughter? But all the children of Israel know that she is not my daughter...." As they drew within three miles of Bethlehem, Mary said unto him: "Take me down from the ass, for this child is pressing to come out." He replied: "Where can I shelter you in your labor? This place is a desert."

Joseph found a cave there, and left his sons to care for her, and he went out and returned with a midwife. As they reached the cave, a bright cloud overshadowed it. Immediately the cloud disappeared, and a bright light blinded them. When the light went out, the young child appeared and took the breast of its mother Mary.

The midwife cried aloud: "This is a great day for I have seen a miracle!" She left the cave and met her friend Salome. She said to her: "Salome, a virgin has given birth, even though her body shouldn't allow it."And Salome said, "As the Lord my God lives, if I don't insert my finger and feel her hymen myself, I will not believe that a virgin has given birth."

"A bright light blinded them."

The midwife went to Mary and said: "Position yourself for a test, because there is a disagreement here about you." Salome inserted her finger into Mary and screamed: "Woe is me for not believing the living God and insisting on a test. Look, my hand has fallen off and is burning up in fire!" And she bowed her knees to the Lord. And lo, an angel of the Lord appeared, saying: "Salome, the Lord has heard you. Lift the child, and you will get salvation and joy." Immediately Salome was healed.

There came wise men, saying: "Where is he that is born king of the Jews? For we have seen his star in the east and have come to worship him." When Herod heard this he was troubled. He said: "If you find him, tell me so I may also worship him." They brought gifts of gold, frankincense and myrrh. Being warned by an angel that they should not enter into Judea, they went into their own country by another way.

Salome gets her hand back after an unfortunate gynecological incident

When Herod figured out that he had been tricked by the wise men, he told his men to kill all children younger than two years old. When Mary heard that the children were being slain, she was afraid. She wrapped the baby in swaddling clothes and laid him in an ox-manger.

Now I, James, wrote in Jerusalem, at a time of tumult after Herod died. I withdrew myself into the wilderness until the unrest died down, glorifying the Lord God, who gave me the gift and the wisdom to write this history. ☾

The Secret Gospel of Mark

OF THE DOZENS of gospels written in the century after Jesus' death, one of the most intriguing is "The Secret Gospel of Mark," of which only a fragment exists that was quoted by an early church father, Clement of Alexandria, to "Theodore." Available only to advanced initiatives of the church, it was a more extensive version of the Gospel of Mark that appears in the Bible. What's in there? The surviving fragments are intriguing. The first, meant to be inserted between Mark 10.34 and 35, reads:

They came to Bethany. There was one woman there whose brother had died. She came and prostrated herself before Jesus and spoke to him. "Son of David, pity me!" But the disciples rebuked her. Jesus was angry and went with her into the garden where the tomb was. Immediately a great cry was heard from the tomb. And going up to it, Jesus rolled the stone away from the door of the tomb, and immediately went in where the young man was. Stretching out his hand, he lifted him up, taking hold his hand. And the youth, looking intently at him, loved him and started begging him to let him remain with him. And going out of the tomb, they went into the house of the youth, for he was rich. And after six days Jesus gave him an order and, at evening, the young man came to him wearing nothing but a linen cloth. And he stayed with him for the night, because Jesus taught him the mystery of the Kingdom of God. And then when he left he went back to the other side of the Jordan.

The second fragment of "Secret Mark" was meant to be inserted into Mark 10:46. It reads:

Then he came into Jericho. And the sister of the young man whom Jesus loved was there with his mother and Salome, but Jesus would not receive them.

Gee Man

The Strange Life of J. Edgar Hoover

America's premiere law enforcement agent for fifty years was also its chief blackmailer and unelected despot. Ironically, there's evidence that he ignored America's worst criminals because he, himself, was being blackmailed. Read on....

• By the time he was thirteen, J. Edgar Hoover had already discarded his first name, John, and begun his habit of keeping tabs on people. He began compulsively filing away accounts of the personalities and habits of his teachers and friends, and the clothing sizes of his loved ones.

• Edgar's father, Dickerson Hoover, Sr., suffered from clinical depression and was in and out of asylums for years until his death. His mother was overprotective and controlling.

• After college, Hoover used his government job to avoid being drafted into World War I. Fifty years later he would incessantly pursue Vietnam War draft resisters.

• J. Edgar lived with his mother until her death in 1938, when Edgar was forty-three.

• After his mother's death, Hoover started seeking out the company of women, notably Lela Rogers, Ginger Rogers's mother. Four years older than Edgar, Lela's ultra-conservative political views were a perfect complement to his. Marriage was never seriously considered, but Edgar and Lela remained friends until her death in 1955.

• Hoover made a career out of anti-communism, starting in 1919 while an ambitious desk jockey in the Bureau of Investigation (the "Federal" had not yet been tacked on). He began amassing files on suspected "Bolsheviks," cross-referencing half a million names at a time when the country had only

110 million people. The day after his twenty-fifth birthday, Hoover celebrated with the biggest "Red Raid" in America's history, in which 10,000 people were arrested in one day. Most of the suspects were found to be innocent and eventually released, and the Bureau took a great deal of heat for its police-state tactics. Still, the raids did the trick—Communist Party membership, 80,000 strong before the raids, dwindled to 6,000 after 1920 and continued to dwindle down to 2,800 by 1971.

• William Sullivan's job in the FBI was monitoring the Party. He suggested in 1970 that Hoover release membership figures to show that the FBI was winning the war against subversion. "How do you think I'm going to get my Appropriations out of Congress if you keep downplaying the Communist Party?" Hoover asked him angrily. Years later, after Hoover was safely dead, Sullivan announced that the "communist threat" had long been "a lie perpetrated on the American people."

• Hoover considered Supreme Court Justice Felix Frankfurter "the most dangerous man in America" for his support of civil rights. Hoover kept a file on Frankfurter for fifty years, and bugged his offices and those of at least eleven other Supreme Court justices.

• Hoover never voted in an American election. In fact, he never even registered to vote. He claimed to be apolitical, but in fact was a staunch supporter of the right wing of the Republican Party, feeding its candidates dirt on opponents.

• Hoover was apparently homosexual. He wrote hundreds of increasingly explicit and infatuated letters to his young protégé, Melvin Purvis. Things didn't work out, however—alas, the handsome younger man turned out to be heterosexual. The last straw was when Purvis started getting publicity for capturing some high-profile criminals, threatening to overshadow Hoover. Purvis was forced out of the FBI. During the next decade, Hoover used the FBI to harass Purvis, getting him fired from jobs, spying on him and spreading false stories about him to the press. Purvis committed suicide in 1960.

• Hoover's next big infatuation centered on a young, handsome FBI rookie named Clyde Tolson.

• The two men became inseparable, traveling together on taxpayer-financed junkets and even dressing alike. Every day the were in Washington, they ate the same lunch for free from the same restaurant.

• The romance between the two men was

Later on this New Year's Eve in 1936, model Luisa Stuart (right) claimed she saw Tolson (left) and Hoover (middle) holding hands in their limo

the source of a great deal of speculation. In the 1960s, agents joked regularly about "J. Edna" and "Mother Tolson."

• For decades, despite evidence that was obvious to everybody else, Hoover claimed there was no such thing as "organized crime." He refused to allow the FBI's resources to be used to fight the mob, instead going after "communists" and petty criminals. Why? According to author Anthony Summers in *Official and Confidential: The Secret Life of J. Edgar Hoover*, it was because the mob had explicit photos of Hoover and Tolson having sex, and information about an arrest of Hoover in New Orleans on a morals charge in the 1920s.

• Ironically, one of Hoover's favorite smears, offered without any apparent evidence, was that somebody was gay. For example, that's how he characterized Martin Luther King, Jr., Adlai Stevenson and three top aides of Richard Nixon.

• Hoover learned his lesson from being blackmailed by the mob, wrote Summers. For four decades, he had agents collect any allegation of sexual, political or financial misconduct they could find on every politician in Washington. Every president from Roosevelt on wanted to retire Hoover but backed down when they saw what he had on them. John and Robert Kennedy, whom Hoover despised, were particularly vulnerable to the volume of information Hoover had on their womanizing. In fact, some accounts have it that Hoover used his clout to demand that JFK choose Hoover's friend Lyndon Johnson as his running mate.

• His fear of germs was legendary. He installed a special ultraviolet lighting system that he believed would kill viruses, and kept a servant on staff to swat flies in his office.

• Hoover refused to hire black agents. Robert Kennedy pressured him on this in the 1960s, so Hoover merely "promoted" his black servants on staff, calling them "agents" while they performed the same menial duties as before. When he died, the FBI had only 70 black agents out of a total of 6,000.

• Hoover absolutely despised Martin Luther King, Jr., and was enraged when King won a Nobel Peace Prize in 1965, an honor that he himself coveted. Shortly before King was to pick up his prize in Sweden, Hoover had an unmarked parcel sent to King's wife. It contained a tape of King allegedly having sex with another woman, along with an anonymous note to King threatening to expose him to the world and suggesting that suicide was the only honorable way out.

• King was demoralized for several months. The FBI stepped up the pressure, harassing King with anonymous phone calls, threats and midnight false fire alarms. Hoover gleefully reviewed the wiretap transcripts for signs that the constant badgering was having an effect; one transcript quoted King as telling a friend, "They are out to break me, out to get me, harass me, break my spirit." King fell into a period of insomnia and deep depression. Finally, he rallied and decided that the cause was just, and that "we are not going to let Hoover and the FBI turn us around."

• When King was killed three years later, Atlanta FBI agents cheered; one shouted, "We finally got the son of a bitch!" Hoover "personally" took over the investigation. The first day he spent getting his photo taken for public relations purposes. The next day, as he had the day after Kennedy's assassination, he went to the racetrack for the day. In the weeks that followed, he failed to show up for meetings with the attorney general on the subject.

• The fingerprints of James Earl Ray, small-time criminal and prison escapee, had immediately been found on the scene, as well as a radio with his prison number on it. But it took two weeks for the FBI to issue an alert for him. For two months, Ray traveled freely around the country.

- When caught, Ray was carrying a large amount of cash, the source of which was not pursued with any vigor.

- For years afterward Hoover continued to smear King as a "communist and a scoundrel," leaking information and copies of the FBI tapes. He adopted a new goal: to stop Congress from making King's birthday a national holiday. His efforts were successful for several years; King's birthday wasn't honored until 1982.

Johnny and Clyde lunched every day (for free) at the Mayflower Hotel in D.C., until Hoover's death in 1972

- Hoover felt that female criminals were far more vicious and dangerous than males. He also claimed that female criminals always have red hair—if not naturally, "she either adopts a red wig or has her hair dyed red."

- During the student unrest of the 1960s, Hoover set up the COINTELPRO program to harass lawful protesters, using everything from threatening letters and phone calls to goon squads.

- On May 2, 1972, J. Edgar Hoover was found dead next to his bed. He had been in good health, and had had no previous heart problems. The cause of death was officially "hypertensive cardiovascular disease," but no autopsy was done to validate this. When undertakers arrived shortly after, they found 15–20 men in suits on the scene, ransacking books, files and papers, and emptying out drawers.

- Before his death, Hoover had somehow managed to amass millions of dollars on his civil servant's pay ($43,000 a year was his peak salary). Although he projected an air of incorruptibility, he made a lot of money from unethical and illegal dealings. Hoover received hundreds of thousands of dollars in illegal gifts, some from mob connections, and he and Tolson converted FBI Library and Recreation funds to their own uses.

- Hoover left all his earthly belongings to Clyde Tolson, bypassing relatives and other friends. Tolson died a recluse in 1975. He was buried, by mutual request, ten yards away from his former boss. ☾

Kitchen Scientist
CUTTING FRUIT INSIDE THE PEEL

Your hapless victim peels a banana for morning cereal—and finds that it comes pre-sliced! What gives? Is this the result of some fiendishly clever genetic engineering?

1 Get together a ripe banana, a thin needle and some thread.

2 Push the threaded needle into an unobtrusive spot on the ridge of the banana, angled along the inside of the peel. Bring it out at the next ridge, leaving a few inches of thread sticking out of the first hole.

3 Push the needle back through the second hole, angled toward the next ridge.

4 Keep repeating until you have gone completely around the banana and the needle has come out of your first hole again.

5 Hold both ends of the thread and pull. The thread will pull out through the banana, slicing it cleanly in two.

6 Repeat the process in other spots until you've made several slices. Make sure your victim picks the right banana from the bowl. Peeling the banana will reveal that the fruit has been presliced.

Variation: Try it with another fruit like a pear or an apple. The needle holes will be more visible, so you should take the doctored fruit this time. You'll be able to hold it in two hands and calmly twist it into neat halves. ☾

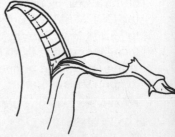

Life of the Party!

PART TWO

Not just anyone can do hand shadows. So why not bone up with these from Henry Bursill's *Hand Shadows*, and become entertainer extraordinaire at your next shindig?

Sheep

Mrs. Gump

Eagle

Bulldog

Bird on the Wing

Elephant

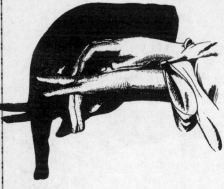

Mule

Frightened Man

Eyewitness

I Saw Vesuvius's Eruption Destroy Pompeii

Gaius Plinius Caecilius Secundus, known as Pliny the Younger, was asked to relate the story of his uncle's death. The uncle, Gaius Plinius Secundus ("Pliny the Elder"), died during the eruption of Vesuvius in A.D. 79 while trying to save others. Special thanks to Cynthia Damon of Amherst College for her translation.

My Dear Tacitus,

You ask me to write you something about the death of my uncle so that the account you transmit to posterity is as reliable as possible. I am grateful to you, for I see that his death will be remembered forever if you put it in your *Histories*.

He perished in a devastation of the loveliest of lands, in a memorable disaster shared by peoples and cities, but this will be a kind of eternal life for him.

He was at Misenum in his capacity as commander of the fleet on the 24th of August [A.D. 79]. Between 2 and 3 in the afternoon my mother drew his attention to a cloud of unusual size and appearance. He had had a sun bath, then a cold bath, and was reclining after lunch with his books.

He called for his shoes and climbed up to where he could get the best view of the phenomenon. The cloud was rising from a mountain—at such a distance we couldn't tell which, but afterwards learned that it was Vesuvius. I can best describe its shape by likening it to a pine tree. It rose into the sky on a very long "trunk" from which spread some "branches." I imagine it had been

Vesuvius erupts again in 1906

raised by a sudden blast, which then weakened, leaving the cloud unsupported so that its own weight caused it to spread sideways. Some of the cloud was white, in other parts there were dark patches of dirt and ash. The sight of it made the scientist in my uncle determined to see it from closer at hand.

Pliny the Elder's 20-mile journey from Misenum, trying to save refugees and satisfy scientific curiosity

My uncle ordered a boat made ready. He offered me the opportunity of going along, but I preferred to study—he himself happened to have set me a writing exercise. As he was leaving the house he was brought a letter from Tascius' wife Rectina,

who was terrified by the looming danger. Her villa lay at the foot of Vesuvius, and there was no way out except by boat. She begged him to get her away. He changed his plans. The expedition that started out as a quest for knowledge now called for courage. My uncle launched the quadriremes [galley boats with four banks of oarsmen] and likewise embarked, a source of aid for more people than just Rectina, for that delightful shore was a populous one. He hurried to a place from which others were fleeing, and held his course directly into danger. Was he afraid? It seems not, as he kept up a continuous observation of the various movements and shapes of that evil cloud, dictating what he saw.

Ash was falling onto the ships now, darker and denser the closer they went. Now it was bits of pumice, and rocks that were blackened and burned and shattered by the fire. Here the sea had become like a sandbar; debris from the mountain blocked the shore. He paused for a moment wondering whether to turn back as the helmsman urged him. "Fortune helps the brave," he said. "Head for the house of Pomponianus."

At Stabiae, on the far side of the bay formed by the gradually curving shore, Pomponianus had loaded up his ships even before the danger arrived, though it was visible and indeed extremely close, once it intensified. He planned to put out as soon as the contrary wind let up. That very wind carried my uncle right in, and he embraced the frightened man and gave him comfort and courage.

To lessen the other's fear by showing his own unconcern, my uncle asked to be taken to the baths. He bathed and dined, carefree or at least appearing so (which is equally impressive). Meanwhile, broad sheets of flame were lighting up many parts of Vesuvius; their light and brightness were the more vivid for the darkness of the night. To alleviate people's fears my uncle claimed that the flames came from the deserted homes of farmers who had left in a panic with the hearth fires still alight. Then he rested, and gave every indication of actually sleeping; people who passed by his door heard his snores, which were rather resonant since he was a heavy man.

As he slept, the ground outside his room rose so high

Pompeii Rises from the Ashes

On August 24, A.D. 79, the cities of Herculaneum, Pompeii and Stabiae were covered by ashes and lava several yards deep. Pompeii had not been a particularly remarkable city, but it became significant to historians because its location was lost for seventeen centuries. When Pompeii was rediscovered by a farmer digging in a vineyard in 1748, the ruins had remained largely undisturbed for all that time, providing a rich trove of historical artifacts that show what life was like at the time.

Graffiti and campaign posters still adorned the city walls (an election campaign had been in progress when the volcano erupted). Remains of about 2,000 of the 20,000 residents have been found; their bodies rotted away, but the lava and ash created perfect molds of their features, allowing archeologists to make replicas of the dead by pouring plaster into them.

About a quarter of the city is still unexcavated.

with the mixture of ash and stones that if he had spent any more time there escape would have been impossible. He got up and came out to be with Pomponianus and the others who had been unable to sleep. They discussed what to do, whether to remain under cover or to try the open air. The buildings were being rocked by a series of strong tremors, and appeared to have come loose from their foundations and to be sliding this way and that. Outside, however, there was danger from the rocks that were com-

ing down, light and fire-consumed as these bits of pumice were. Weighing the relative dangers they chose the outdoors; in my uncle's case it was a rational decision, others just chose the alternative that frightened them the least.

They tied pillows on top of their heads as protection against the shower of rock. It was daylight now elsewhere in the world, but there the darkness was darker and thicker than any night. But they had torches and other lights. They decided to go down to the shore to see if it were yet possible to escape by sea, but it remained as rough and uncooperative as before.

Resting in the shade of a sail he drank once or twice from the cold water he had asked for. Then came a smell of sulfur, announcing the flames, and the flames themselves, sending others into flight but reviving him. Supported by two small slaves he stood up, and immediately collapsed. As I understand it, his breathing was obstructed by the dust-laden air, and his innards, which were never strong and often blocked or upset, simply shut down. When daylight came again two days after he died, his body was

Despite this 18th-century engraving of Pliny the Elder's death, the guy was fifty-five and quite chunky. He likely died of a heart attack.

found untouched, unharmed, in the clothing that he had been wearing. He looked more asleep than dead.

Meanwhile at Misenum, my mother and I—but this has nothing to do with history, and you only asked for information about his death. I'll stop here then. But I will say one more thing: that I had written out everything while memories were still fresh. Use the important bits, for it is one thing to write a letter, another to write history; one thing to write to a friend, another to write for the public. Farewell, Pliny.

MEANWHILE, BACK IN MISENUM (LETTER #2)

My dear Tacitus,

You say that you want to know of my fearful ordeal at Misenum (where I broke off in my letter). "The mind shudders to remember...but here's the tale."

After my uncle's departure I finished up my studies, as I had planned. Then I had a bath, then dinner, and a short and unsatisfactory night. There had been tremors for many days previously, a common occurrence in Campania and no cause for panic. But that night the shaking grew stronger and people thought it was an upheaval, not just a tremor. My mother burst into my room and I got up. I said she should rest, and I would rouse her if need be.

We sat out on a terrace between the house and the sea. I sent for a volume of Livy; I read and even took notes from where I had left off, as if it were a moment of free time; I hardly know whether to call it bravery, or foolhardiness (I was seventeen at the time).

Up came a friend of my uncle's, recently arrived from Spain. When he saw my mother and me sitting there, and me even reading a book, he scolded her for her calm and me for my lack of concern. But I kept on with my book.

The day began with a hesitant and almost lazy dawn. All around us buildings were shaken. We were in the open, but it is only a small area and we were afraid—no, certain actually—that there would be a collapse. We finally decided to leave the town. A dazed crowd followed us, preferring our plan to their own (this is what passes for wisdom in a panic). Their numbers were so large that they slowed our departure, and then swept us along. We stopped once we had left the buildings behind us. Many strange things happened to us there, and we had much to fear: The carts that we had ordered up were rolling in opposite directions, though the ground was perfectly flat, and they wouldn't stay in place even with their wheels blocked by stones. In addition, it seemed as though the sea was being sucked backwards, as if it were being pushed back by the shaking of the land. Certainly the shoreline moved outwards, and many sea creatures were left on dry sand. Behind us were frightening dark clouds rent by lightning, opening to reveal huge figures of flame like lightning, but bigger.

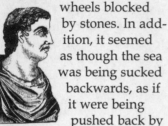

Pliny the Younger

At that point our Spanish friend urged us strongly: "If your brother and uncle is alive, he wants you to be safe. If he has perished, he wanted you to survive him. So why are you reluctant to escape?" We responded that we would not look to our own safety as long as we were uncertain about his. Waiting no longer, he himself ran from the danger at a mad pace.

It wasn't long thereafter that the cloud stretched down to the ground and covered the sea. It girdled Capri and made it vanish, it hid Misenum's headlands. My mother begged, then urged, then ordered me to flee however I might, saying that a young man could make it, but that she, weighed down in years and body, would die happy if she escaped being the cause of my death. I replied that I wouldn't save myself without her, and then I took her hand and made her walk a little faster. She obeyed with difficulty, and blamed herself for delaying me.

Now came the dust, though still thinly. I looked back: a dense cloud loomed behind us, following us like a flood pouring across the land. "Let us turn aside while we can still see, lest we be knocked over and crushed by the crowd of our companions." We had scarcely sat down when a darkness came that was not like a moonless or cloudy night, but more like the black of closed and unlighted rooms. You could hear women lamenting, children crying, men shouting. Some were calling for parents, others for children or spouses; they could only have recognized each other by voices.

Some bemoaned their own lot, others that of their loved ones. Some were so afraid of death that they prayed for death. Many raised their hands to the gods, and even more believed that there were no gods any longer and that this was one last unending night for the world. Nor were we without people who magnified real dangers with fictitious horrors. Some claimed that one or another part of Misenum had collapsed or burned; lies, but they found believers.

It grew lighter, though that seemed not a return of day, but a sign that the fire was approaching. The fire itself actually stopped some distance away, but darkness and ashes came again, a great weight of them. We stood and shook the ash off again and again, otherwise we would have been covered with it and crushed by the weight. I might boast that no groan escaped me in such perils, no cowardly word, but that I believed that I was perishing with the world, and the world with me, which was a great consolation for death.

Pliny's villa in Misenum

At last the cloud thinned out and dwindled to no more than smoke or fog. Soon there was real daylight. The sun was even shining, though with the lurid glow it has after an eclipse. The sight that met our still terrified eyes was a changed world, buried in ash like snow. We returned to Misenum and took care of our bodily needs, but spent the night dangling between hope and fear. Fear was the stronger, for the earth was still quaking and a number of people who had gone mad were mocking the evils that had happened to them and others with terrifying predictions. We still refused to go until we heard news of my uncle, although we had felt danger and expected more.

You will read what I have written, but will not take up your pen, as the material is not the stuff of history. You have only yourself to blame if it seems not even proper stuff for a letter.

Farewell, Pliny ☾

Pot Shots

Even *more* of Privy's favorite privy shots. Send us yours!
(See page 476.)

This picture (below) of the Porcupine cabin outhouse in the Crazy Mountains, Montana, is courtesy of Tom Böttger.

Each house, above, has its own sanitary privy in this 1920s neighborhood. This was a new idea to most rural folks, who were used to sharing facilities with their neighbors.

A camper (below) peeks into the facilities in the Samburu National Reserve, Kenya.

(Above) The childhood home privy of President Calvin Coolidge.

TV Dinners
HOW TV DINNERS BECAME "TRAY CHIC"

Today, frozen dinners are yupscale and pretentious, and there are those who say that TV dinners of the past were best: the trays were aluminum, the choices were scanty (turkey, beef, chicken or Salisbury steak), and they weren't too proud to call it a "TV dinner."

FROZEN FOOD in your local grocery is a relatively recent thing. True, seventeenth-century scientist Sir Francis Bacon had some ideas about freezing as a preservative and even did some experiments that looked promising. (Unfortunately, he died of hypothermia after spending a cold afternoon stuffing snow into a dead chicken.) But the modern-day frozen food industry owes its existence to Clarence Birdseye, who liked to be called Bob and pronounced his name BIRD-zee.

Birdseye, a naturalist and writer of books on wildflowers, birds and mammals, had gone to Labrador in 1917 to conduct a survey of fish and wildlife for the U.S. government. While there, he noticed that the Native Canadians' meat and poultry didn't get mushy when frozen and thawed. It felt and tasted nearly fresh, unlike food he had tried freezing back in the States.

He figured that it was because of the extreme cold that the food froze quicker. When he got back, he tested the theory. He bought $7 worth of ice, salt water and an electric fan. Sure enough, he found that slow freezing allowed large ice crystals to form, bursting the food's cell walls. Fast freezing prevented that, saving the cellular integrity, texture and flavor for months on end. As a side benefit, he also found that he could entertain dinner guests by bouncing frozen steaks off the kitchen floor before cooking them for dinner.

In 1923, Birdseye gambled everything he owned designing a practical large-scale fast freezer and setting up Birdseye Foods, Inc. He nearly went broke. When the Postum Company (which changed its name to General Foods that same year) offered to buy his patented process for $22 million, Birdseye jumped at the chance.

The corporation already had a distribution system set up, which had been Birdseye's undoing. It also could afford to buy advertis-ing to convince America that it needed frozen food. By 1934, 80 percent of the frozen food market belonged to General Food's Birds Eye Division. (They added the space in Birdseye's name and began pronouncing it like it was spelled.)

For his part, Birdseye went on tinkering, amassing over 250 patents on a range of things from recoilless harpoons to a way to turn sugar cane waste into paper. Like Bacon, he died with his inventor's boots on — in 1956, while in Peru trying to figure out how to make paper out of the agave plant, he had a fatal heart attack from the high altitude. But he lived long enough to see the preeminent use for his fast-freezing process: the TV Dinner, invented by the Swanson brothers.

Gilbert and Clarke Swanson had a problem: they were surrounded by turkeys. Real turkeys. They owned the largest turkey processing plant in the country, C. A. Swanson & Sons, and it drove them crazy that most Americans ate turkey on only one day a year: Thanksgiving. The Swansons made it their goal to insinuate more turkey meat into America's diet. First they started making frozen turkey pot pies. These became so popular that people started clamoring for more varieties. This was good news for business, but not good news for the turkey problem.

In 1951, the Swanson kitchens began experimenting with individual portion meals that could be popped into the oven and eaten without much preparation. Inspired by the segmented plates used in diners for "Blue Plate Specials," they made similar trays out of aluminum and put dinner courses in them.

Television was the hot new fad sweeping the country. The Swanson Company arranged to sponsor its own show, *Ted Mack's Family Hour.* Gilbert Swanson invited some friends over to have dinner and watch the premiere show.

While eating in front of Swanson's console TV, one of the guests remarked about how odd it was to see everybody balancing food trays on their laps in front of the TV. Swanson suddenly thought of

TV and dinner...a perfect match!

the individual portion meals his company was working on. They'd be perfect for eating while watching TV, and tying them in to the TV craze couldn't hurt. In fact, if you rounded the corners of the aluminum trays, they'd sort of look like a TV screen.... Why not call them TV Dinners?

The next morning Gilbert told his brother about the idea. Clarke liked it, and suggested putting a picture of a TV on the box with the dinner coming off the screen.

In January 1952, the first Swanson's TV Dinners rolled off the line in Omaha. They contained turkey, cornbread stuffing, gravy, buttered peas and sweet potatoes in orange and butter sauce—and cost 98¢. The dinners did well. Soon the company introduced fried chicken TV Dinners, which sold quickly until consumers started noticing that the chicken tasted like bananas.

It turned out that the yellow ink on the box used a solvent that smelled like bananas, and that the smell was seeping into the food. Swanson recalled the chicken dinners and changed the ink, but one food chain in Florida complained because it said that its customers actually preferred the banana-flavored variety. Swanson pragmatically shipped its entire recalled inventory to Florida.

In the 1960s, after TV became a guilty pleasure instead of a harmless fad, Swanson's redesigned its package to downplay the TV Dinner brand name, allowing it to more or less become a generic term. In 1984, the Swanson Company replaced the aluminum tray with a microwaveable plastic one. As a sop to the health-conscious times, the company replaced the brownie with a fruit dessert in 1986, but soon reversed the decision after a deluge of customer complaints.

We can hope that with a consumer crusade they might bring back the classic aluminum tray as well. The dinner's don't quite taste the same without that faint metallic tinge to the vegetables. And if that works, maybe next we can work toward the return of that banana-flavored chicken. ❧

True Adventure

CANOEING THE DELAWARE RIVER, PART 2

When we left the intrepid canoeists on page 66, they were preparing
to confront the monster rapids of the Big Foul. As the fourth day
breaks, the three adventurers nervously pack their canoes....

IN THE MORNING A SWIM, a solid breakfast, and an extra careful
packing of the canoes. No one spoke of it; but that morning
we each paid a particular attention to the trim of the boats
and the stowing of dunnage. At about noon we would reach
Belvidere; and the Great Foul Rift was only a mile farther.

There was a camp of bass fishers near us, and they came to
see us start. They learned our intention of going down without
portage, rift or no rift. They did not dissuade us. One of them
said he knew the Big Foul, and he gave us precise, too precise,
instructions. All I could recall half an hour later was: "Keep to
the right when you come to the big white stone—if there's
water enough to float your boats."

We came to the town of Belvidere. The mill-workers came
down to have a chat. "Keep to the right of the big white rock,
and you will strike the channel," shouted a man as we started.

A discussion in *Forest and Stream* a few years ago directed the
attention of canoemen to its alleged dangers and extreme rapidity of current. Two canoemen of East Orange, N.J., who ran the
rapids in 1878 and claimed to be the first to do so, wrote:

> "After passing through two or three small rifts, we arrived at Great Foul
> Rift, which is considered the most dangerous one in the river, on account
> of the number of rocks and the swiftness of the current. How to describe
> our passage through here, we hardly know; all we can say is, we saw it,
> we entered it, and we passed it. You can see big slate rocks on all sides,
> and are unable to tell what minute you will strike them. This rift is two
> miles long, and we passed through it in three minutes exactly, being car-
> ried that fast by the current, without using our paddles." This statement

was received with astonishment. Two miles in three minutes, or 40 miles an hour, is not the speed of a rapid, but almost that of a waterfall.

Among the critics was Mr. A. H. Siegfried of Louisville, who had also run the Great Foul Rift. He wrote: "We were warned against Foul Rift for two days above it, and came to it determined not merely to run it, but to examine it carefully, and see if it is as dangerous as the natives think. We went through it without paddle, save for steering purposes, and were just eleven minutes from the time we entered until we left the swift water. That we thought a quick run, considering the windings of the channel, following which the distance is fully three miles, though a straight line will measure nearly one-third less. The rift is very swift and crooked, whirling among many and such recklessly distributed boulders that the speed claimed by 'F. P. and E. P. D.' would have been sure death to both boats and men if it had been possible."

Half a mile or so below Belvidere, we felt the water quicken and sweep to the right. We knew we were in the first reach of the rapid that had been roaring for us since we started.

There are two distinct rapids—the Little Foul and the Great Foul—divided by swift water of half a mile. From the moment we struck the Little Foul Rift, we knew we were in the grip of a giant. We were as much astonished as if we had never run a rapid before. We shot down the river—each one finding his own channel; and, with all our careful steering, we grazed several dangerous stones.

Moseley paddles manfully into rough water

There was no stopping at the foot of the Little Foul Rift; but we ran with the stream without paddling, and examined the entrance to the Great Rapid ahead.

There was no bar or ledge formation here, as in the minor rifts behind us. The rocks stood up like the broken teeth of a sperm whale, irregularly across the river as far ahead as we could see from the canoes. Some of the stones were twelve feet out of the water, others of lesser height, and of all shapes; some were level with the surface, and some covered with a few inches of water. These last were the dangers: to strike and get "hung up" on one of these meant certain upsetting; for no boat could stand the rush, and there was no footing for the canoeman if he tried to get out to push her over. We could steer between the teeth we saw, but we suddenly became conscious of unseen teeth that lay in wait to lacerate the boats under the waterline with irregular edges as sharp as a shattered punchbowl.

We were going into the Great Foul Rift all this time, at the rate of—but who can tell the rate of rapid water? The best canoeman I know says there is no canoeing-water in America over twelve miles an hour (I think he places this on the Susquehanna, below Columbia), and that eight miles is very rapid indeed. He may be right; but, were I asked how fast we went into the Great Foul Rift, I should say, at least twelve miles an hour and, in parts of the descent, much faster.

High water marks on the Delaware bank

Guiteras went first, but was caught on a covered flat stone in the quick, smooth water; so Moseley led into the rapid, with Guiteras, who had floated off the stone, following. I came about fifty yards behind.

From the first break of the water, the sensation was somewhat similar to that of falling through the branches of a tree. The river was twisting downhill in convulsions. We rushed through narrow slopes of ten or twenty feet as if we were falling, and then shot round a rock, flinging the whole weight of our bodies on the steering-paddle. The tall stones ahead seemed to be rushing at us with the velocity of an ocean steamer.

All the time we were painfully conscious of the incisive edges under water, as one might feel the nearness of burglars' knives in the night. If we struck one of these stones on a downward shoot, it would rip the canoe from bow to stern.

Moseley steered skillfully, and we cleared two-thirds of the tortuous descent without a shock. A quarter of a mile ahead we saw the smooth water at the foot of the rift. Suddenly, the channel divided at a great white stone, the wider water going to the left, toward the center of the river, and a narrow black streak keeping straight down to the right.

A memory of the warning came to me, "Keep to the right of the big rock—if you can." But it was too late. A man could not hear his own shout in such an uproar. The white rock rushed past us. The canoes ahead had turned with the main stream, and were in the center of the river in a flash. Suddenly both canoes ahead were shot out of the channel, their bows in the air resting on a hidden rock; and the current, just then turning a sharp curve, swept by their sterns with a rush. Fortunately they were out of the stream, driven into an eddy, or that would have been the end of them.

I had time to profit by their mishap. Kneeling in the canoe, using the long-handled paddle, I rounded the curve within a foot of the grounded canoes, and fairly leaped downhill on a rounded muscle of water. In the rush, a thrill swept my

O'Boyle and Guiteras at the bottom of the Great Foul Rift

nerves—and another—as if twice I had touched cold steel. I found later that my canoe had twice been pierced by the knife-like edges under water.

Before I realized it, the end had come, and the canoe shot across the river in a sweeping eddy. The Great Foul Rift was behind me.

A fisherman on the bank had been watching our passage. "You ought to have kept to the right of that stone," he shouted. "See, there's the channel!" And, looking up, I saw it, straight as a furrow from the big white stone, keeping swift, close to the Pennsylvania shore, unbroken, and safe. Had we kept in this straight way the Great Foul Rift would to us have been no more than an exaggerated name.

The grounded canoemen pushed free, and were down in a minute; and then we went ashore, and while Moseley photographed the Great Foul Rift, the others plunged into the delicious water, that seemed too peaceful and sweet ever to have been violent and brutal.

Half a mile below the Great Foul Rift, we came to the pastoral scene of the voyage, par excellence. It was not great or grand in any way; but simply peaceful, pastoral, lovely. It was a sloping hillside of two or three farms smothered in soft foliage. A round-arched stone bridge spanned a stream. Cows and horses stood in the shadow of trees. Children's voices at play filled the air, and a dog barked joyously in some romping game.

We laid our paddles on the canoes in front of us, and floated a full mile through the lovely picture. It can never be forgotten. In its quiet way, nothing equaled it on the whole river.

"Photograph the place," I said to Moseley.

"No," he replied. "It is too good for any thing but memory." ☾

Epilogue

• The rips in author O'Reilly's canoe turned out to be a problem. Although patched that night, they reopened on the river the next day, and he had to travel the rest of the way by canal boat.

• Stretches of the Delaware are officially designated as Wild & Scenic, so much of the beauty the men saw in 1890 is still there. However, the area around the Great Foul Rift is outside that designated area and is now littered with industrial sites. Still, canoeists and kayakers make the run regularly.

• Ironically, with modern boaters using crafts of nearly indestructable acrylics instead of canvas, wood and bark, the Great Foul Rift is now considered not that big a deal. Its designation from the American Whitewater Affiliation is only Class II (out of V), which means that it is suitable for even novices.

Something in Common 3

It's easy, really—we'll give you a list of words and you tell us the one word that goes with all of them. Answers below (don't cheat!).

1. House, alley, pole, walk, fish, boat, nap, call, gut

2. House, Christmas, apple, frog, surgeon, family

3. Fall, dish, melon, works, toilet, waste, fresh, salt

4. Attack, beat, break, take, burn, ache, land, candy, felt

5. Mr., wing, human, hander, whale, turn, angle, away

6. Core, road, crab, computer, pie, sauce, jack, green, butter

7. Evil, cross, lazy, candy, glass, black, lid, public, private

8. Body, stones, plaster, iron, original, off, on, away

9. Shoe, fly, around, hobby, sea, saw, dark, latitude, race, power

10. Fruit, cricket, baseball, brick, man, vampire

11. Saw, boy, rock, big, rubber, head, stand, cigar, marching

12. Horse, brake, tree, gym, platform, polish, running, lace

13. Well, big, fifth, barrow, potter's, steering

14. Port, brush, bag, craft, line, plane, hot, conditioner, raid

15. Row, gravy, river, house, fishing

16. Beef, hog, solid, wire, coffee, floor, ball, squirrel, speed

17. Lady, state, grounds, trade, practices, way, not

18. Agent, taker, movie, traffic, laundry, office, lottery, split

19. Clear, worm, measure, ticker, video, duct

20. Pin, out, contact, view, grade, spread, breaking, game

Life of the Party!

PART THREE

We like them enough to give you more!

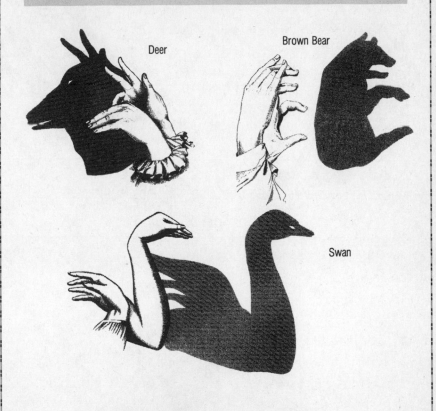

Deer

Brown Bear

Swan

Tortoise

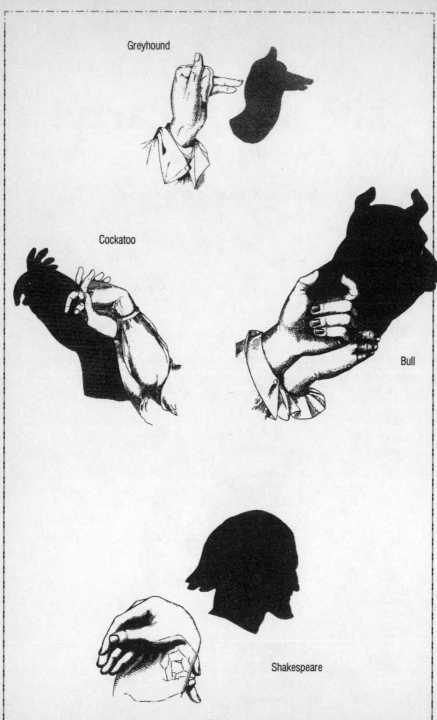

Greyhound

Cockatoo

Bull

Shakespeare

Snow Business
MAKING A SNOW PIG, OWL & FRENCH MAN

All right, so maybe the French guy isn't completely politically correct, but here is a snow sculpture guide from the 1890 *The American Boy's Handy Book* by Dan Beard, one of the founders of the American Boy Scouts.

IN THE "land of the midnight sun," the far arctic regions where Jack Frost rules supreme, where the glistening ice and thickly packed snow covers the landscape, the hardy inhabitants live in snow.

After the first good old-fashioned snow storm has covered the playground, roads, and housetops, and while the merry jingle of the sleigh bells tinkles through the wintry air, let children busy themselves rolling huge balls of snow.

THE PIGS OF SNOW

Snow statuary may be of various kinds. It is very seldom that pigs are sculptured in marble or cast in bronze, and it would be well to make some of snow, so as to have statues not likely to be found elsewhere. An oblong mass of snow forms the body (Fig. 1); the legs, nose, and ears are

FIG. I.—Making the Pig.

FIG. 2.—A Snow Pig.

made of sticks surrounded by snow, and a bit of rope nicely curled will make a very good tail. The various parts can be shaped and carved according to the skill of the young artist. A number of pigs, of different sizes, will give a lively and social air to the yard of a house. Fig. 2 shows a finished pig.

FRENCHY, THE FRENCHMAN

A statue of a Frenchman is also rather uncommon, and is not hard to make. The foundation of the body, head, and legs consists of several large snow-balls, as seen in Fig. 3, and the arms are made of smaller balls stuck on two sticks, which are inserted in the body at proper angles.

FIG. 3.—Making "Frenchy."

When the whole figure has been "blocked out," as the artists say, it must be carved, with broad wooden knives or shingles, into the proper shape, as shown in Fig. 4. The moustache should be made of icicles, which may be stuck in the face.

ARCTIC OWL

Arctic owls, which are very large and white, can also be made of snow, in the manner shown in Fig. 5 and 6. These figures can be placed on snow pedestals if they are small, but if they are monster owls, like those in the illustrations, they must be placed upon the ground. In either position, if they are fashioned properly, they will look very wise and respectable.

FIG. 4.—Frenchy.

FIG. 5.—Carving the Owl.

When the snow is too dry to make a snowball it cannot be used to make statuary, but after a slight thaw or a fresh fall of snow it readily adheres upon a slight pressure, and can be formed or fashioned in almost any shape.

Many curious objects and figures may be carved out of solidly packed balls of snow. A lawn covered with a number of large snow figures presents a most grotesque appearance, and is sure to attract the attention of all passers-by. With

FIG. 6.—An Arctic Owl.

practice not a little skill may be acquired by the young sculptor, and if the statuary be made of large proportions, they will sometimes last for weeks after the snow has disappeared from the ground and house-tops. ☾

Building a Snow House

Showing the construction of a Snow-House.

The pictures of the house show so well how it is constructed, and how it looks when it is done, that very little explanation is necessary. The walls are made of large snowballs properly placed, with snow packed between them to make the surfaces tolerably even, and then the whole shaved down with a spade, outside and inside. It will be found impossible to put one tier of balls upon the top of the others by lifting them in place, but this difficulty may be overcome by sliding the balls up an inclined plane made of a strong plank, one end of which must be placed upon the ground and the other allowed to rest upon the top of the first or foundation row of snowballs.

—**The American Boy's Handy Book**
by Dan Beard, 1890

A Snow-House Finished.

According to Mark Twain

More from *Puddin'head Wilson's Calendar*, a fictitious publication that Twain "quoted" from whenever he needed a maxim.

• "It could probably be shown by facts and figures that there is no distinctly native American criminal class except Congress."

• "We should be careful to get out of an experience only the wisdom that is in it, and stop there, lest we be like the cat that sits down on a hot stove. She will never sit down on a hot stove again. That is well, but also she will never sit on a cold one, either."

• "Everything human is pathetic. The secret source of humor itself is not joy but sorrow. There is no humor in heaven."

• "Truth is the most valuable thing we have. Let us economize it."

• "When in doubt, tell the truth."

• "It is better to have old second-hand diamonds than none at all."

• "Faith is believing what you know ain't so."

• "Names are not always what they seem. The common Welsh name Bzjxxllwcp is pronounced Jackson."

• "Few of us can stand prosperity. Another man's, I mean."

• "We can secure other people's approval, if we do right and try hard; but our own approval is worth a hundred of it, and no way has been found out of securing that."

• "It is by the goodness of God that in our country we have three unspeakably precious things: freedom of speech, freedom of conscience, and the prudence never to practice either of them."

• "Truth is stranger than fiction, but it is because fiction is obligated to stick to possibilities; truth isn't."

• "'Classic': A book which people praise and don't read."

• "Man will do many things to get himself loved, but he will do *all* things to get himself envied."

• "There are people who can do all fine and heroic things but one: keep from telling their happiness to the unhappy."

• "Man is the only animal that blushes. Or needs to."

• "There are several good protections against temptation, but the surest is cowardice."

Hopping to It

AN AMPHIBIOUS ASSAULT OF FROGS & TOADS

They're slimy and bug-eyed—not unlike your last blind date, but with a lot more appeal. Frogs and toads are the stuff that myth, legend and French dishes are made of. Sue Shipman tells us more.

• Scientists estimate that a toad can catch and devour approximately 10,000 insects during one summer.

• Some large tropical frogs eat small mammals and snakes.

• No frog lives in salt water.

• There are almost 4,000 known species of frogs and toads.

• The word for frog in Sanskrit translates to "cloud" because, in India, frogs were thought to personify thunder.

• Frogs are symbols of good luck in Japan.

• The main difference between toads and frogs is that toads don't spend as much time in the water as frogs do. As a result, their skin is thicker and retains moisture better, and they tend to be stockier in build than most frogs.

• The goliath frog from Cameroon in West Africa can be a foot long and weigh as much as a large house cat.

• The smallest known frog in the southern hemisphere is the Brazilian gold frog. Its body is less than half of an inch long.

• A group of toads is called a "knot." A group of frogs is called a "chorus."

• The desert horned lizard or "horny toad" is neither a toad nor a frog. It is a reptile. It has a spiky body that it can flatten or puff up to discourage predators.

• Some toads have glands behind their ears which they can use to squirt poison at predators. The poison of the marine toad can kill a dog within minutes if the dog ingests it. These toads were introduced to Florida and other parts of the world to try to reduce sugar cane pests.

• Some of the poison in a poisonous frog comes from its diet of toxic insects.

• Although humans use frog venom to hunt, poisonous frogs don't. They use it solely as a defense mechanism against predators.

Some South American tree frogs have webs under their legs too to help them glide from tree to ground

• Chemicals secreted by the skin of poison-arrow frogs in Central and South America are some of the deadliest biological toxins in the world— so toxic that one frog's poison could kill up to eight humans.

• South American poisonous frogs can't kill a human by touching them unless there's an abrasion on the skin, or the person otherwise ingests the poison. Scientist wear thick gloves to study them.

• Most South American hunters don't risk touching a poisonous frog at all—gloved or not—but simply skewer it on the ground with a stake and roast it to drain the poison for their darts.

• Frogs are found everywhere in the world except Antarctica. Most frogs, however, are found in the tropics.

• Presumed to be extinct, the gastric brooding frog gave birth through its mouth. It's not known whether the mother swallowed the eggs or if her tadpoles swam into her mouth and into her stomach. During gestation, she fasted and her stomach did not produce hydrochloric acid. She birthed her brood of up to 30 tadpoles by opening her mouth and letting the babies swim out.

• Frogs don't chew; they swallow their food whole.

• It is believed the phrase "frog in your throat" comes from the Old English *frogga* which meant "hoarseness."

• There are at least two theories about why the term *frog* is used as a derogatory term when speaking about the French. One is that the beef-loving English were disgusted by the French appetite for frogs' legs. Another is that the term dates from the middle ages when the British mistook the gold "fleur-de-lys" on the French flag for a frog.

• Tadpole is the name given to the aquatic larval stage of all amphibians, not just frogs and toads.

• Apart from poisonous varieties, frogs and toads won't hurt you, and they don't cause warts. Although, of course, picking up a frog or toad can be harmful to it.

• Frog legs taste like chicken. Think of it as "chicken of the swamp."

• Catherine the Great's tableware sported a frog design.

• The British dish "toad in the hole" contains no frog or toad parts. Although the origins of the name and the dish are not completely clear, it's an old recipe, dating back more than 250 years, and the name is comparable to that of our sausage and roll treat, "pigs in blankets."

• Frogs don't drink with their mouths, but absorb water through their skin.

• There are some toads that don't even need standing water to hydrate. They have a pouch on their bottoms called a "seat," that can absorb three-quarters of all the water they need from the moist soil.

• The frog's tongue attaches to the front of its mouth, not the back. It's designed for shooting out and catching bugs, not for swallowing.

• A frog's eyes are big, bulgy and are located on the top of its head. Even when its body and most of its head is submerged or buried, it can still see. The area inside the body that houses these big eyeballs is also large. When the frog swallows, it closes its eyes, pushing them down into their cavities. The eyeballs actually get shoved down into the back of the frog's mouth, helping to push the wiggling bug down its throat.

•Although the cane frog lays 30,000 to 35,000 eggs at a time, the Cuban frog lays only one. ❦

More Curses!

And more of our favorite long-forgotten, archaic insults from Jeffrey Racirk's *Long Lost Insults Knowledge Cards*.

GAMMERSTANG: "Usually applied to a female of idle, loose habits." —*Dialect of Mid-Yorkshire*, C. Clough Robinson, 1876

FUMBLER: "An unperforming husband, one that is insufficient; *fumbler's hall*, the place where such are to be put for their non-performance." —*Dictionary of the Canting Crew*, B. E., 1699

NYARGLE: "A foolish person fond of disrupting." —*Scottish Gallovidian Encyclopedia*, John Mactaggart, 1824

MOTH OF PEACE: "A mere idler; one who consumes but does not work." —*Shakespeare Cyclopædia and Glossary*, John Phin, 1902

HOGS-NORTON: "This proverbial phrase was commonly addressed to any clownish fellow, unacquainted with the rules of good society." —*Dictionary of Archaic and Provincial Words*, James Halliwell, 1855

GYLE-HATHER: "He that will stand by his master when he is at dinner, and bid him eat no raw meat, because he would eat it himself. This is a...knave that would make his master believe that the cow is wood." —*The Fraternitye of Vacabonds*, John Awdeley, 1565

QUEERE-DUKE: "A poor decayed gentleman; also a lean, half-starved fellow." —*Dictionary of the Canting Crew*, B. E., 1699

SHOOLER: "One who intrudes upon his neighbour, and forces an invitation to dinner." —*History and Antiquities of Boston*, Pishey Thompson, 1856

Retro-Futurism
MORE OF TOM SWIFT'S WORLD OF TOMORROW

Tom Swift was a boy inventor created by Victor Appleton almost a
century ago. The breathless adventure stories are great fun, but
even better are the descriptions of his inventions.

TOM SWIFT & HIS GREAT SEARCHLIGHT (1913)

"Do you notice that searchlight, and how powerful it is?"

"I do, Tom. I never knew you had one as big as that."

"Neither did I, and I haven't, really. That's one of my smallest ones,
but something seems to have happened to
it to make it throw out a beam like that.
I'm just going to look. Come on in the
shop."

The two inventors, young and old,
entered, and Tom made a quick inspec-
tion.

"Look, father!" he cried. "The alternat-
ing current from the automatic dynamo
has become crossed with direct current
from the big storage battery in a funny
way. It must have been by accident, for
never in the world would I think of connecting up in that fashion. I would have
said it would have made a short circuit
at once.

"But it hasn't. On the contrary, it has
given a current of peculiar strength and
intensity — a current that would seem to be made
especially for searchlights. Dad, I'm on the edge of a big discovery."

"I believe you, Tom," said his father. "That certainly is a queer way
for wires to be connected."

TOM SWIFT & HIS AIRSHIP (1910)

The general idea of the airship was that of the familiar aeroplane, but in addition to the sustaining surfaces of the planes, there was an aluminum, cigar-shaped tank, holding a new and very powerful gas, which would serve to keep the ship afloat even when not in motion.

Two sets of planes, one above the other, were used, bringing the airship into the biplane class. There were also two large propellers, one in

front and the other at the rear. These were carefully made, of different layers of wood "built up" as they are called, to make them stronger. They were eight feet in diameter, and driven by a twenty-cylinder, air-cooled motor, whirled around at the rate of fifteen hundred revolutions a minute. When operated at full speed the airship was capable of making eighty miles an hour against a moderate wind.

But if the use of the peculiarly-shaped planes and the gas container, with the secret but powerful vapor in it were something new in airship construction, so was the car in which the operator and travelers were to live during a voyage. It was a complete living room. There were accommodations for five persons, with sleeping berths, a small galley where food could be prepared, and several easy chairs where the travelers could rest in comfort while skimming along high in the air, as fast as the fastest railroad train.

The engine, steering apparatus, and the gas machine were within easy reach and control of the pilot, who was to be stationed in a small room in the "bow" of the ship. An electric stove served to warm the interior of the car, and also provided means for cooking the food. The airship could be launched either by starting it along the ground, on rubber-tired wheels, as is done in the case of the ordinary aeroplane, or it could be lifted by the gas, just as is done with a balloon. In short there were many novel features about the ship.

The gas test, which took place a few days later, showed that the young inventor and Mr. Sharp had made no mistake this time. No explosion followed.

TOM SWIFT & HIS GIANT TELESCOPE (1939)

"What have people on the planets got to do with the question?" asked Ned. "Huge chunks of metal break off of any heavenly body and go hurtling through space. The inhabitants don't throw them off!"

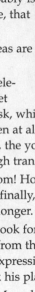

"But our meteor was no ordinary one as we have proved already," replied Tom. "I firmly believe that someone on another planet deliberately fired that missile into space, hoping it would reach this world. Since scientists agree that Mars probably is inhabited by a highly intelligent race, that planet is a reasonable guess."

"Whew!" whistled Ned. "Such ideas are beyond me."

At last Tom stepped to the giant telescope and adjusted it upon the planet Mars. He electrified the immense disk, which glowed, then could not be seen at all. Looking through the eyepiece, the young inventor stood as though transfixed.

"Tom! How does it work?" asked Ned finally, unable to restrain himself any longer.

"Look for yourself!" cried Tom, turning from the instrument. His face wore an expression of awe. Ned quickly took his place.

"Marvelous!" he exclaimed.

Before his eyes were revealed a great city, nearly seventy-five million miles distant! Peculiar people surged along the avenues, weird aircraft thronged the upper atmosphere, and gigantic buildings and palaces dotted the place. All on far-distant Mars! Ned grasped his chum's hand but could say nothing. Mr. Damon blessed the distant stars. Koku and Rad fell upon their knees. Into the eyes of Barton Swift came tears as he said: "Tom, my son, you have performed the greatest miracle of the Age!" ☾

(Interested in reading more Tom Swift theories and inventions? See pages 53 and 295.)

Speak English? 4

TRANSLATE THESE BRITISH TERMS INTO AMERICAN

Sometimes it seems like the British and Americans don't even speak the same language. How are you at translating? Translate these old and new British terms into American. (Answers below.)

1. vacuum flask
2. noughts and crosses
3. sponge bag
4. holdall
5. drummer
6. ex-directory
7. waistcoat
8. spanner
9. nought
10. courgette
11. combinations
12. plough
13. wood wool
14. torch
15. jelly
16. passage
17. portfolio
18. mate

a. cowcatcher
b. tote bag
c. zero
d. flashlight
e. tic-tac-toe
f. wrench
g. briefcase
h. traveling sales rep
i. gelatin
j. shaving kit
k. hallway
l. vest
m. union suit
n. excelsior
o. Thermos
p. buddy
q. zucchini
r. unlisted number

Fires & Plagues
MORE OF OUR FAVORITE DISASTERS

More questions and answers about famous disasters from *Just Curious About History, Jeeves*, by Erin Barrett and Jack Mingo.

CATTLE-CLYSM IN CHICAGO
Did a cow really cause the Great Chicago Fire?

No, probably not, although the fire did start in Mrs. O'Leary's barn. There's no reason to believe the fire was anything more than the result of an extraordinarily dry spell of weather mixed with the practice of keeping dry wood chips around as a cheap source of fuel. A cigarette, a match, an ember from a burning stove nearby, or even spontaneous combustion would have been more than enough to have set the blaze going.

CLAIM TO FLAME
Why did the Chicago Fire of 1871 do so much damage?

Besides the dryness in the air and the wood chips, the houses were old, wooden and packed in tightly. There may have been little anyone could do to have prevented the disaster. However, it didn't help that the firemen were misdirected when the initial call first came in. Furthermore, they had been busy with another huge blaze the day before and were exhausted. By the time they reached the site, the blaze was way beyond control.

Was the Chicago Fire the worst fire in America's history?

Heck, it wasn't even the worst fire that *day*. A much bigger, more deadly fire happened at exactly the same evening in Peshtigo, Wisconsin, begun by railroad workers clearing a way for new tracks. As a result of the same hot, dry air as Chicago's, a small brush fire turned into a blazing inferno. Before the fire

Mrs. O'Leary's; the Chicago fire started in the barn behind the house

went out, almost a week later, it had burned more than 1.2 million acres and caused more than $169 million dollars worth of damage—about the same dollar amount of the property that was lost in the Chicago Fire blaze. On top of that, more than 1,200 people were killed by the Wisconsin fire—four times as many as in the more-famous Chicago Fire.

Which was worse: the Chicago Fire or the Great London Fire?
The 1666 London Fire burned four-fifths of the city and an additional 63 acres outside the city walls. It burned longer, covered more land and wreaked more architectural devastation, notably the Custom House, the Royal Exchange and St. Paul's Cathedral. Still, the Chicago Fire was worse in some ways. First of all, the Chicago Fire

took more lives. Only 16 people died in the London fire because it burned slowly and gave enough warning for most people to escape. The fast-moving Chicago Fire claimed between 250 and 300 lives, leveling several Chicago neighborhoods—a total of 2,150 acres in less than two days. Both great fires were mass devastation with few rewards, save an architectural revitalization following the blaze and a good story about a cow.

One irrefutable bright spot came on the heels of the Great London Fire: After hundreds of years of periodic devastation, the Black Plague was finally wiped out. It had resurfaced again two years prior to the blaze, in 1664. However, after the fire, incidences suddenly declined and fizzled out, never to resurface again. It's believed, since the fire burnt everything to the ground, it took with it the old, damp breeding grounds of the plague rats, too, saving literally thousands of human lives in the long run.

PUDDING & PIE
How did the Great London Fire start?
It's reported that the 1666 fire that swept London was started by King Charles II's baker,

Thomas Farrinor, who accidentally went to bed with his oven still burning.

The phrase "from Pudding to Pie" comes directly from the great fire of London. Farrinor's house was situated on Pudding Lane. Pie Lane is located on the other side of the city where the fire finally stopped. So those clever Brits used "from Pudding to Pie" to mean the whole bloomin' city from then on.

SHOW ME YOUR BUBOES
What was the worst plague in human history?

The "Black Death" that ran through China and across to Europe in the 14th century is considered the worst plague in recorded history. Depending on the way the virus was contracted, 70–90% of those exposed to the plague died from it. During a 5-year period from 1347 to 1352, more than 25 million people in Europe alone were wiped out.

The disease was called the "Black Death" because of the color of the sores that developed on the bodies of the afflicted. However, doctors eventually figured out that there was a connection to the swollen lymph nodes called *buboes,* and "bubonic plague" seemed a better label for the affliction.

That was the world's worst plague for humanity; however, it wasn't the worst epidemic. What's the difference? A plague is a specific bacterial infection, but many of the worst diseases are caused by viruses. The worst epidemic was not a plague, but a flu in the 20th century, right after World War I in 1918-1919. The first reported case was in Kansas in 1918 and from there it spread like wildfire. After eighteen months, when the virus vanished as mysteriously as it had appeared, perhaps 37 million people worldwide had died from the disease. At no other time in recorded history have so many people died from one affliction in so little time.

How long did it take to die from the bubonic plague?
From exposure (flea bite, animal bite or exposure to mucus) to the onset of the first symptoms (headache, fever, nausea, aching and swollen buboes) took about six days. The next stage— hemorrhaging and respiratory problems stemming from severe pneumonia—came quickly, causing death within a day or two. Now, bacterial infections can usually be wiped out by antibiotics. ☾

Pot Shots

More of Privy's favorite privy shots. Send us yours! (See page 476.)

(Below, left) The privy at Alameda Beach—headquarters of the *Bathroom Companion*

A very colorful men's restroom (above), somewhere in the outback of Australia

The outhouse at Hanging Rock Raptor Observatory in Monroe County, West Virginia. At the top of Peters Mountain—elevation 3,812 feet—a cable attaches the outhouse to a tree to keep it from blowing over. Thanks fo Rodney Davis at http://www.hangingrocktower.org.

These ancient public toilets in old Ephesus could seat up to 40. An orchestra played for the crowd of users, probably to drown out sounds. Photo courtesy of Joe Garlitz.

Chicle Your Fancy

GUM THROUGH A BUBBLE OF HISTORY

A good chew has been touted as good for the mouth, nerves, digestion and sex appeal. But how did it all begin? Correspondent Elsa Bronte fills us in.

PEOPLE LIKE to chew. Through history, humanity has chewed everything from human gristle to synthetic rubber. As early as A.D. 50, the ancient Greeks chewed latex from the mastic tree, which they believed had curative powers. Upon arrival to the New World, the European settlers were introduced to spruce resin by the Native Americans. They had been chewing it for centuries. The discovery of well-chewed wads of various tree resins, unearthed along with bones and other prehistoric artifacts, leads archaeologists to believe the practice of gum chewing goes as far back as early civilization—even our primitive ancestors engaged in recreational chewing.

THE BEGINNINGS OF A BUBBLE INDUSTRY

Our more recent forebears enjoyed chewing homemade gum of spruce resin and beeswax. A man named John Curtis mixed up the first commercial batch of

Fruit and leaves of the sapodilla tree. The latex from the bark is known as "chicle."

spruce resin chewing gum in 1848. His sales were slow at first, but at two spruce chaws for a penny, the gum became an overwhelming success within a few years. By 1852, his Curtis Chewing Gum Co. employed more than 200 workers in its brand-new three-story factory in Portland, Maine.

But that was sap gum. The chicle-based chewing gum we know today came from Mexico soon after the Civil War. General Antonio Lopez de Santa Ana, infamous for leading the Mexican siege on the Alamo, was forced out of Mexico after some political upheaval. He went into exile in New York City, bringing from his native Mexico a quantity of chewing chicle, the dried sap of the sapodilla tree. The story has it that it was Santa Ana's chewing habit that gave inventor Thomas

1. Chemists test ingredients and flavors. 2. Chefs mix the gum dough. 3. Machines slice gum pieces from big sheets. 4. Gum wrapping gals wrap gum. Nowadays, they've been replaced with modern machinery.

Adams, Sr. the idea of selling a chicle gum in the United States.

In 1871, Adams received the first patent on a gum-making machine. His first gum, called "Snapping & Stretching," was pure chicle with no flavoring, but it sold enough packs to encourage Adams. He began to experiment with flavorings, beginning with sarsaparilla. In 1884, his licorice-flavored Black Jack gum premiered as the first flavored gum in America. Pepsin Tutti-Frutti chewing gum followed in 1890. Adams invented Beemans in 1898 as a cure for heartburn, and his Clove Gum got a boost during Prohibition when it was sold as a breath freshener in illegal liquor houses. (All of the gums eventually went off the market, although the current owner of Adams' gums, the

Warner-Lambert Pharmaceutical Co., irregularly reissues the century-year-old gums as a part of their "Nostalgia Gum program.")

BEEMAN'S

ORIGINAL PEPSIN CHEWING GUM

SLEEPLESSNESS, irritation, and nervous let-down are conditions that often arise from slight forms of indigestion.

The speed at which we live, and the high tension under which we work are largely responsible for the lack of care we give both to the selection of our food and its proper mastication.

I have found in my own personal practice that chewing my Original Pepsin Gum ten minutes after each meal frequently relieves these conditions.

BEEMAN'S PEPSIN CHEWING GUM

GOOD FOR DIGESTION

New York   AMERICAN CHICLE COMPANY   San Francisco
Cleveland Chicago Kansas City

RESOLVING A STICKY SITUATION

By the turn of the century, the chewing public was gobbling up new products such as Frank V. Canning's Dental Gum and Henry Fleer's candy-coated Chiclets. Henry's brother, Frank, began to work on a gum that would be elastic enough to blow into bubbles. His first prototype, Blibber-Blubber, came along in 1906, but never made it to market—it was so sticky that the only way to remove it from skin was with vigorous scrubbing and turpentine.

Walter Diemer achieved a breakthrough in August, 1928, and he wasn't even a chemist. Although Diemer was Fleer's accountant, he was messing around in the lab and discovered, through trial and error, the magic mix of ingredients that was stiff enough to get off skin, but flexible enough to blow. Bubble gum even owes it characteristic pink hue to Diemer's serendipity, because pink was the only coloring that happened to be nearby when he mixed up his first successful batch. Not long after its introduction, Fleer's Dubble Bubble became the best-selling penny candy in the United States. Fleer sold the Chiclet business in 1909 (Chiclets are now owned by Warner-Lambert), but Dubble Bubble is still made at the Fleer plant in Philadelphia.

SWEET NOTHINGS

The next major innovation in gum production came in the early 1950s, with chemically-sweetened sugarless gum. Suddenly, gum was deemed safe to chew, and its popularity surged again as dentists began recommending sugarless gum "to their patients who chew gum." (Ironically, it's been since discovered that sugared gum really isn't bad for teeth, because the sugar goes quickly as the gum stimulates saliva, and that the sugar is probably healthier than the chemical alternatives.)

A PENNY FOR YOUR CHAW

Gum machines have been dispensing gumballs and little Dentyne-sized pieces of stick gum since before the 1880s.

The stick gum machines featured mirrors in front, a smart bit of merchandising, because most people will check themselves in a mirror, and while there, maybe drop a penny into the slot.

Early gumball machines were often quite pretty — the glass globe distorting the balls to make the multicolor balls look unearthly and slightly bigger than life, the fire-engine red base creating a three-alarm wail among kids hankering for a piece. Gumball machines were simple at first — in fact, too simple, because kids learned pretty quickly how to stick their fingers up the hole and get a free ball. After that bug was worked out, however, some of them went to gimmickry — a machine made by the Pulver Company featured a little mechanical man who held the ball in his hands and dropped it down the shoot when you put in your money.

In the 20th century, much of the gumball market was taken over by the Ford Gum and Machine Co., the only U.S. company that makes both machines and the gumballs that stock them.

CHEWS FOR JESUS

The Ford Co. was founded by a roofing salesman in 1918. Named Ford S. Mason, he used his first name instead of his last name, figuring that it couldn't hurt to have people think his machines were related to the popular Model T.

At the time, the gumballs in machines were often pretty bad, and the machines unreliable. According to *The Great American Chewing Gum Book* by Robert Hendrickson

(Scarborough, 1980), Mason's father, a Baptist minister, urged him to manufacture his own machines as well as gum so that the brand would become associated with dependable quality. ("Make your own machines, my boy," he said, "and share your profits with God.") His father believed so strongly in the machines that he took time away from his sermons to design a machine for his son, one so simple yet dependable that the basic design remains unchanged to this day. Mason worked on perfecting and branding the gumball, coming up with a stamping machine to stamp FORD on each gumball at the rate of 25,000 an hour, and figuring out a waterproof glaze so that condensation inside the machine wouldn't ruin them. (Try it: Run water over a machine-bought gumball and the color probably won't come off.)

CHARITY BALLS

In 1939, an Ohio women's charity group suggested that local merchants donate their 20% cut from Ford machines to local children's charities. The idea caught on, and now 3,500 service clubs and organizations share about $2 million a year from the Fordway Program. ❦

The Dentist Hall of Fame

In honor of all those cavities that bubble gum has produced over the years (actually, science now says it's less than you'd think), we honor famous people who were also dentists.

- *Dr. Doc Holliday* helped Wyatt Earp win the OK Corral shootout.
- *Dr. G.W.A. Bonwill* invented the safety pin.
- *Dr. William Lowell* invented the wooden golf tee.
- *Dr. Pearl Zane Grey* wrote best-selling Western novels.
- *Dr. George W. Beers* created the official rules for lacrosse.
- *Dr. Edgar Buchanan* appeared in *Petticoat Junction.*
- *Dr. Allan Jones* starred in the movie *Showboat* in 1936.
- *Dr. Marlon Loomis* transmitted radio signals 27 years before Marconi.
- *Dr. Cary Middlecoff* won the U.S. Open in 1946 and 1956.
- *Dr. Charles Willson Peale* painted George Washington's portrait.
- *Dr. Paul Revere* became a silversmith and courier for the revolution.
- *Dr. Thomas Welch* bottled grape juice.
- *Dr. Painless Parker* legally changed his first name to circumvent 1880s laws against advertising, created the first national chain of dental clinics.

Word Thieves

Some Words We Borrowed from the Aztecs

You say *tomato*, we say *tomatl*. We were surprised how many English words come from Nahuatl, the language of the Aztecs and related tribes in Central and South America. Here are some of them.

avocado: Squishy, small, round—is it any surprise that the fruit's name came from *ahucatl* ("testicle")?

axolotl: Maybe you'd only know this word if you're a salamander fancier, or a *Mad* reader in the 1960s. From Aztec times to the present, these 6–8-inch amphibians have been roasted and eaten with vinegar or cayenne pepper. The name comes from *atlxotl* ("water spirit").

Axolotl, the other white meat

chili: The dish originated with the Aztecs; the Nahuati name was *chilli*.

chocolate: Called *xoclatl* from the days when cocao beans were ground up in hot water without sugar. The name meant "bitter water."

coyote: The original word was *coyotl*.

guacamole: The word comes from *ahuacatl-molli*, which means "avocado sauce."

mescal: From *mexcalli* ("agave liquor").

mesquite: From *mezquitl*.

Mexico: From *mexihco* ("place of the Mexih.")

ocelot: From *ocelotl* ("jaguar").

peyote: From *peyutl* ("caterpillar's cocoon," which is what the peyote button's silky inside looks like).

shack: From *xacalli* ("thatched hut").

tamale: From *tamal*, another Aztec dish.

tomato: From Aztec *tomatl*.

Let's Roll!

THE NITTY GRITTY ON TOILET PAPER

Toilet paper from the bottom up, by *B.C.* regular Kathie Meyer.

FIRST ATTEMPTS GO DOWN THE TOILET

Toilet paper dates back as early as the late 1300s in China. Still, the emergence of modern toilet paper in the United States is credited to New Yorker Joseph C. Gayetty who produced the first packaged bathroom tissue in 1857. Named "the Therapeutic Paper" because it contained soothing aloe, the tissue sold in flat packs of 500 sheets. In an odd sort of egotism, it had Joseph Gayetty's name printed on every sheet. Gayetty's paper didn't do well in the marketplace, in part because it was very expensive—50¢ a pack, which is comparable to almost $10 in today's money—at a time when people were willing to use old newspaper.

GREAT SCOTT

In 1879, Walter Alcock of England invented perforated toilet tissue on a roll. In the United States, Edward and Clarence Scott began manufacturing their copy of Alcock's product. Hotels and restaurants had begun installing indoor plumbing, and the traditional wiping materials— newspapers, magazines, catalogs—were not very classy. The Scott Paper Company began finding buyers in the finest places, and capitalized on this snob appeal by naming their toilet paper "Waldorf Tissue," after a famous hotel.

Consumers, initially resistant to the idea, quickly began succumbing to the snob appeal of having fancy, soft rolls of toilet paper in their bathrooms.

THE MOTHER OF INVENTION

Before the invention of modern toilet paper, people used just about anything on hand. For instance: newsprint, catalogue pages, a sponge at the end of a stick, discarded sheep's wool, straw, hay, grass, leaves, a corn cob, mussel shells, sand, the left hand, pages from a book, coconut shells, lace, hemp, a spritz of water from a bidet, snow, or tundra moss.

MYSTERY SOLVED

Have you ever wondered how manufacturers wind the toilet paper neatly onto those 3-inch cardboard tubes? Actually, they don't. The machines wind wide rolls of paper around long tubes, and then slice them into smaller rolls.

CRUEL & UNUSUAL PUNISHMENT

Prisoners in Florida jails have filed numerous complaints against the authorities because the normal allocation of toilet paper is one roll per week per person. That roll is all that's issued for all tissue needs, including nose-blowing. That's in the best case. Prisoners further said that the authorities used toilet paper as a "privilege" that was routinely revoked for up to a week as a punishment.

FOR WANT OF SOME TISSUE

Statistics say the average family has eight toilet paper rolls in reserve to avoid running out. Households run by folks younger than 30 run out more often than adults older than 50.

RUN ON THE MARKET

In 1973, *Tonight Show* host Johnny Carson joked during his monologue that there was a toilet paper shortage and people took him seriously. As a result, store shelves soon were out of t.p. as the nation began to hoard the product.

YOUR TAX DOLLARS AT WORK

The bathrooms at the Pentagon use an average of 666 rolls of toilet paper daily. The building also has twice as many bathrooms than necessary, a legacy of Virginia's laws that required separate bathrooms for white and black people.

TANKS FOR THE TP

Military toilet paper is camouflaged, since bright white could attract enemy fire at a vulnerable time. During America's war against Iraq in 1989, some tank crews reportedly t.p.'ed their tanks to hide them better.

A DIFFERENT KIND OF AIR BAG

Officials said a train crash in southern Mexico, where two trains collided head-on, killing five people and injuring 50, would have been much worse if it hadn't been for two freight cars loaded with toilet paper that helped cushion the impact.

REALITY SPONSORSHIP

In the Ivory Coast, manufacturers have named brands of toilet paper "Santa Barbara" and "Dallas Jumbo"to capitalize on the glamour of American soap operas.

NOT FOR LAZY BUMS

A pre-moistened toilet paper called Andrex is the most expensive brand on the market in Britain. It's very soft,

and, apparently, very popular.

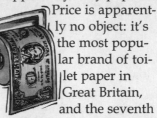

Price is apparently no object: it's the most popular brand of toilet paper in Great Britain, and the seventh best-selling product overall in that country.

TRADING THEIR PLY

• More consumers in the Western states prefer one-ply toilet paper than in the Eastern states.

• St. Andrew's Paper Mill in Walthamstow, London, gave the world the first two-ply toilet paper in 1942.

• Single-ply has one layer of 13-pound-thick paper. Double-ply has two layers of 10-pound-thick paper each. Single-ply is generally cheaper to use because folks use about the same amount of sheets regardless of the ply, and is recommended for toilet systems in recreational vehicles and boats, because it doesn't clog pipes as readily.

HOW MANY SHEETS?

• One cord of wood will yield 1,000 pounds of toilet paper.

• The standard size of a single sheet of toilet paper is 4.5 inches by 4.5 inches. Some manufacturers, however, have

come out with "cheater sheets" as small as 4 inches by 3.8 inches.

• According to the American Forest & Paper Association, the United States produces about 5.8 million tons of tissue-grade paper (consisting of toilet and facial tissue, paper napkins, towels, diapers and various other sanitary products) annually. In 1992, approximately 3.5 million tons of scrap paper were recycled into soft paper products.

GROSS NATIONAL CONSUMPTION

The number of days the average roll of bath tissue lasts in the most-used bathroom of a household is five. On average, consumers use 8.6 sheets per trip to the bathroom, or 57 sheets per day. That's a total of 20,805 sheets per year for the average person.

FRONT OR BACK?

Polls show that 60% of all respondents prefer the toilet paper to come out in the front of the roll while 29% prefer it to come out down the back of the roll. (A full 11% didn't care either way.) By more than 4 to 1, older folks prefer to have their toilet paper dispense over the front. Clearly, age brings wisdom—otherwise the paper is pressed against the wall, making it harder to get the end loose, eventually dirtying and scratching the paint below the toilet paper holder.

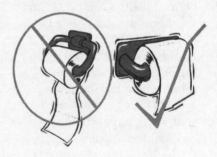

LOOSE ENDS

Why do hotels fold the loose end of the toilet paper in a **V** shape? The little nip and fold on the roll is meant to assure you that no one has used that toilet seat since it was last scoured by hotel employees. Or at the very least you know that if someone *did* use it, they didn't use toilet paper afterward. Eeew! ☾

Every Picture Tells a Story

The Spirit of '76 by Archibald M. Willard, 1875

• Most people think this painting depicts America's Revolutionary soldiers. However, most people are wrong.

• The painting was meant to be a sly commentary on drunken 4th of July celebrations that were common in the late 1800s. Note the puffy faces, the unnatural exuberance, and the guy lying on a splintered wagon wheel, who's too drunk to sit up, much less stand, as he salutes his flag.

• Anticipating a market for humorous prints with the upcoming United States 1876 centennial, commercial artist Achibald M. Willard started working on this painting of lit-up musicians clowning around in a July 4 parade. He used his father, a friend and a military cadet as models.

• Willard first called it *The 4th of July Musicians* and then *Yankee Doodle*. A print dealer renamed it *The Spirit of '76* when he sold tens of thousands of copies, making both men rich.

• Willard had no formal art training. Before discovering a lucrative market for kitsch, he mostly painted designs on wagons.

• The painting was so popular that Willard painted copies of it many times. Some subsequent editions were less comical.

Couch Potato Quiz
HOW ADDICTED ARE YOU?

Match each of the fifteen sitcom characters to their shows.

1. Sam Malone
2. Paul Buchman
3. Buffy Davis
4. Ralph Kramden
5. Rob Petrie
6. Ricky Stratton
7. Alex Keaton
8. Rhoda Morgenstern
9. Mary Ann Summers
10. Jack Tripper
11. Willie Tanner
12. Jane Hathaway
13. Alex Reiger
14. Mary Richards
15. Hawkeye Pierce

A. *Rhoda*
B. *The Honeymooners*
C. *M*A*S*H**
D. *The Beverly Hillbillies*
E. *Taxi*
F. *ALF*
G. *Family Affair*
H. *Silver Spoons*
I. *Family Ties*
J. *The Dick Van Dyke Show*
K. *Cheers*
L. *Mad About You*
M. *The Mary Tyler Moore Show*
N. *Three's Company*
O. *Gilligan's Island*

Answers: 1.K; 2.L; 3.G; 4.B; 5.J; 6.H; 7.I; 8.A; 9.O; 10.N; 11.F; 12.D; 13.E; 14.M; 15.C

Eyewitness

I LED THE CAPTURE OF JOHN WILKES BOOTH

A gun went off, the president was shot, and John Wilkes Booth gave a short, one-line speech on stage. But what then? After fleeing the Ford Theatre, Booth went south into Virginia with one of his co-conspirators, David Herold, where they were soon surrounded.

IT WAS APRIL 24, 1865, when Lieutenant Edward Doherty got orders to go to a Virginia farm owned by Richard Garrett, to hunt down fugitives David Herold and John Wilkes Booth—both wanted in relation to the death of President Abraham Lincoln. According to Doherty, this is what happened:

"I dismounted, and knocked loudly at the front door. Old Mr. Garrett came out. I seized him, and asked him where the men were who had gone to the woods when the cavalry passed the previous afternoon.

"While I was speaking with him some of the men had entered the house to search it. Soon one of the soldiers sang out, 'O Lieutenant! I have a man here I found in the corn-crib.' It was young Garrett, and I demanded the whereabouts of the fugitives. He replied, 'In the barn.'

David Herold

"Leaving a few men around the house, we proceeded in the direction of the barn, which we surrounded. I kicked on the door of the barn several times without receiving a reply. Meantime another son of the Garretts had been captured. The barn was secured with a padlock, and young Garrett carried the key. I unlocked the door, and again summoned the inmates of the building to surrender.

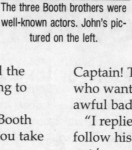

The three Booth brothers were well-known actors. John's pictured on the left.

"After some delay Booth said, 'For whom do you take me?'

"I replied, 'It doesn't make any difference. Come out.'

"He said, 'I am a cripple and alone.' I said, 'I know who is with you, and you had better surrender.'

"He replied, 'I may be taken by my friends, but not by my foes.'

"I said, 'If you don't come out, I'll burn the building.' I directed a corporal to pile up some hay in a crack in the wall of the barn and set the building on fire.

"As the corporal was picking up the hay and brush Booth said, 'If you come back here I will put a bullet through you.'

"I then motioned to the corporal to desist, and decided to wait for daylight and then to enter the barn by both doors and over power the assassins.

"Booth then said in a drawling voice, 'Oh Captain! There is a man here who wants to surrender awful bad.'

"I replied, 'You had better follow his example and come out.'

"His answer was, 'No, I have not made up my mind; but draw your men up fifty paces off and give me a chance for my life.'

"I told him I had not come to fight; that I had fifty men, and could take him.

"Then he said, 'Well, my brave boys, prepare me a stretcher, and place another stain on our glorious banner.'

"At this moment Herold reached the door. I asked him to hand out his arms; he replied that he had none. I told him I knew exactly what weapons he had. Booth replied, 'I own all the arms, and may have to use them on you, gentlemen.' I then said to Herold, 'Let me see your hands.' He put them through the partly opened door and I seized him by the wrists. I handed him over to a non-commissioned officer. Just at this moment I heard a shot, and thought Booth had shot himself. Throwing open the door, I saw that the straw and hay behind Booth were on fire. He was half-turning towards it.

"He had a crutch, and he held a carbine in his hand. I rushed into the burning barn, followed by my men, and as he was falling caught him under the arms and pulled him out of the barn. The burning building becoming too hot, I had him carried to the veranda of Garrett's house.

"Booth received his death-shot in this manner. While I was taking Herold out of the barn one of the detectives went to the rear, and pulling out some protruding straw set fire to it. I had placed Sergeant Boston Corbett at a large crack in the side of the barn, and he, seeing by the igniting hay that Booth was leveling his carbine at either Herold or myself, fired, to disable him in the arm; but Booth making a sudden move, the aim erred, and the bullet struck Booth in the back of the head, about an inch below the spot where his shot had entered the head of Mr. Lincoln. Booth asked me by signs to raise his hands. I lifted them up and he gasped, 'Useless, useless!' We gave him brandy and water, but he could not swallow it. I sent to Port Royal for a physician, who could do nothing when he came, and at seven o'clock Booth breathed his last. He had on his person a diary, a large bowie knife, two pistols, a compass and a draft on Canada for 60 pounds." ☾

Sergeant Boston Corbett—the man who shot John Wilkes Booth

Judged by Its Cover

Even More Strange Books

Can you tell a book by its title? If so, these have got to be some of the most fascinating books on the shelves, gleaned from *Bizarre Books* by Russell Ash and Brian Lake (St. Martin's, 1985).

Cooking with God—Lori David & Robert Robb (1978)

A Pickle for the Knowing Ones; or, Plain Truths in a Homespun Dress—Timothy Dexter (1802)

Daddy Was an Undertaker—McDill McCown Gassman (1952)

How I Know That the Dead Are Alive—Fanny Ruthven Paget (1917)

Gay Agony—H. A. Manhood (1930)

?—Sir Walter Newman Flower (1925)

Pernicious Pork; or, Astounding Revelations of the Evil Effects of Eating Swine Flesh—William T. Hallett (1903)

Beard Shaving, and the Common Use of the Razor, an Unnatural, Irrational, Unmanly, Ungodly and Fatal Fashion Among Christians—W. E. Painter (1847)

A Letter to the Man Who Killed My Dog—Richard Joseph (1956)

The Manliness of Christ—Thomas Hughes (1931)

Chancho: A Boy and His Pig in Peru—Sutherland Stark (1947)

I Was Hitler's Maid—Pauline Kohler (1940)

The Bright Side of Prison Life—Captain S. A. Swiggett (1897)

Why Bring That Up? A Guide To and From Seasickness—Dr. J. F. Montague (1936)

Armadillo

A LIFE ON THE HALF-SHELL

The armadillo was named by the Spanish Conquistadors; its name (pronounced arm-a-DEE-o in Spanish) means "little man in armor."

SIMPLY MARBLE-LOUS, INCREMENTALLY & EXCREMENTALLY

In Texas or Mexico, if you find what looks like clay marbles in

Nine-banded armadillo walking; rolled up (2½ ft. long, including the tail).

the middle of nowhere, it's most likely armadillo poop. Their excrement is almost perfectly round. Armadillos eat insects and small snails; in the course of picking them off the ground, they also eat a lot of soil. We're not sure if anybody has thought of picking up the poop pellets and firing them in kilns, but they could make a wonderful gift for marble-playing children.

Or maybe not. This dirt-eating habit, by the way, is the reason why armadillo teeth are dark, sometimes even black.

DON'T LOOK A GIFT ARMADILLO IN THE MOUTH

Armadillo teeth are back in their mouths and designed for grinding up insects and snails, so biting is not a part of the armadillo's self-defense repertoire. Good thing, too — armadillos are the only animals besides humans that can carry leprosy.

ROW VS. WADE

Despite common folklore and the fact that they look so heavy in their armor, an armadillo can swim. The bony plates that protect it do weigh it down, but an armadillo can still maintain

buoyancy for short swims by gulping air to inflate its intestines. However, it often prefers to cross small waterways by simply holding its breath and crawling along underwater.

ARMADILLOS ON THE ROAD

Armadillos are so commonly found as road kill because the armadillo's responses to danger are uniformly unsuitable for dealing successfully with cars. One of its strategies is to roll up into a protective ball completely surrounded by its armor, which can save it from a variety of natural things, but not a pickup truck. Another strategy is to dig straight into the

ground, which they can do in almost any soil type with re-markably speed— but not, unfortunate-ly, into blacktop. Still another strategy is to leap up into the air— which doesn't save the armadillo, but at least gives it a pyrrhic victory of making a dent in the car's front grill.

Adding to the problem is the fact that armadillos come out by night in hot weather, making them hard to see until drivers are right upon them. Unfortunately, they also live in areas of flat, straight highways that enable speeding...not to mention that those highways are oft-traveled by people who apparently have few qualms about banging into wildlife.

ARMADILLO PECCADILLOS

• Armadillo babies are identical quadruplets. The first fertilized cell splits into four identical cells, and each develops. That means that the four babies in a brood will always be the same gender.

- Armadillos sleep about 18.5 hours a day.

- Armadillos have a very low metabolic rate, so they have trouble maintaining their body temperature of about 90° F except in very warm climates. Armadillos don't have a lot of body fat, so they must forage on a daily basis. Just a few cold days in a row can be deadly to an armadillo. That's one reason why you don't see them much on the backroads of Ohio.

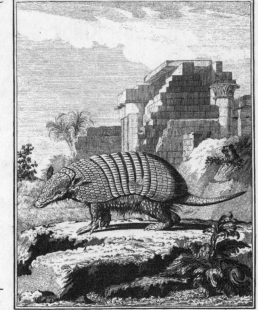

- Depending on the armadillo's species, the bands around its body will always number 3, 6 or 9.

- Armadillos can be housetrained.

- It is specifically against the law to own a pet armadillo in many states.

- Armadillos' closest relatives are sloths and anteaters.

- Armadillos don't come out of their tunnels in broad daylight. The sun hurts their eyes.

- Abandoned armadillo holes are much appreciated by other ground-dwelling animals, who sublet them.

- Armadillo meat is edible. A pound has about 780 calories.

- Fossil remains of gigantic extinct armadillos have been found in South America. This Ice Age "megadillo" was about the size of a VW bug and plated like its modern-day counterpart, but it sported a deadly cluster of spikes on the end of its tail for protection. It died out about 10,000 year ago, and we're mighty thankful for that.

- Another Ice Age armadillo is dubbed the "beautiful armadillo" (*Dasypus bellus*) for reasons unclear. It looks a lot like the not-very-pretty nine-banded armadillo of present day, although quite a bit larger. ☾

Potty Pourri
RANDOM KINDS OF FACTNESS

• England's King George V seems to have been murdered. He was administered a fatal injection minutes before midnight by his doctor on January 20, 1936. "It was evident that the last stage might endure for many hours," wrote the doctor, Lord Dawson, in his journal. "Dignity demanded a brief final scene, so I decided to determine the end."

• Sometimes a cigar is just a cigar, and sometimes a river is just aqueous liquid. The name "Nile" means "water" in ancient Egyptian.

• Sequels never get much respect. There was a second Boston Tea Party three months after the first that got lost to history. No matter. Between the two, the British tea monopoly lost $3 million in today's money.

• There's no real difference, but a burro is a smaller, more sure-footed donkey.

• In a sense, pill bugs or roly-polies are the marsupials of the crustacean world. They carry their babies in light-colored pouches on their bellies until the little roly-polies get big enough to go off on their own.

• Not just Saturn but all of the giant outer planets have rings. Saturn has six, Uranus has eleven, Jupiter has a large one and several smaller ones and Neptune has four. Saturn's are so bright that they were discovered almost 350 years ago. The other planets' rings, too dim to be seen with primitive telescopes, were discovered in the 1970s.

• Sibling rivalry can be a real motivator: Agatha Christie began writing detective stories, not for the love of the art, but to show up her older sister Madge, who insisted that Agatha didn't have the aptitude for it.

How They Work

HIDDEN STORIES BEHIND EVERYDAY THINGS

From polyester threads to scratch-and-sniff perfumes, there's an explanation behind everything, and *Bathroom Companion* science correspondent Brian Marshall is here to explain them.

HOW DO THEY MAKE PLASTIC INTO CLOTHES?

Polyester chips are hard bits of plastic, so how do manufacturers make them into cloth? The process is not unlike the way a cotton candy machine turns granulated sugar into spun candy. The plastic pellets go into a hot metal cup that has tiny holes in it. The cup rotates at a high speed, sending tiny threads of molten plastic shooting out of the little holes (called spinnerets). The molten threads instantaneously harden into a cobwebby consistency when they hit the cool air.

These are heated again, stretched, and then twisted into threads. During that process, polyester is often mixed with cotton or other fibers. The polyester lessens wrinkling; the natural fibers let your perspiration wick away from the body, alleviating the Disco Fever Sweats that plagued wearers of 100% polyester clothes in the 1970s.

HOW CAN THEY MEASURE CALORIES IN FOODS?

A little device called a "bomb calorimeter" burns foods and measures the difference between how much energy went into burning the food versus how much energy came out. A calorie is defined as the amount of energy it takes to raise 1 gram of water (about a thimbleful) 1 degree Celsius.

Here's where it gets confusing: What we call a calorie is actually a *kilocalorie*—it's equal to 1,000 scientific calories. To a scientist, a doughnut doesn't have 235 calories, but 235 *kilocalories* (235,000 calories). Better start jogging....

HOW POLAROID PHOTOS DEVELOP BEFORE YOUR EYES

When you think of the requirements of developing normal photography—most notably a light-free room—it's surprising that

Polaroid cameras could do the same thing in broad daylight. Instant photos seem like a magic trick, and in fact there is more than a little illusion in the "developing before your eyes" part. In fact, by the time you begin to see it, the photo has already fully developed.

Here's what happens after you snap your photo: First it passes through two stainless steel rollers that spread a blob of chemicals located at the edge of the plastic film sheet. These chemicals start developing the photo. But their action is hidden by a white layer of "opacifier," which is an opaque coating that keeps light from reaching photosensitive layers below.

With time, the photo underneath has already developed, yet you can't see it because the opaque layer is still in place. Finally, acid in the chemicals seeps up and reacts with the opacifier. It becomes translucent, then transparent, slowly revealing the photo that's fully developed below.

WHY DO PHONES WORK IN A POWER FAILURE?

Only corded ones do. Because the telephone system provides its own power through the phone lines, your basic corded phone will often work even when your lights won't. It's a pretty good system that gets messed up when you add those newfangled cordless phones that require household power to keep the handset charged and run the transmitter/receiver that plugs into your wall. Our advice is to make sure that at least one of your phones is of the corded variety. It could save your life in an emergency (or at least let you order pizza until you can get your microwave working again).

THE COOL PRINCIPLES BEHIND YOUR REFRIGERATOR

Bear with me now. Two ideas make refrigeration possible:

1. Gases heat up if you compress them and cool down when you let them expand. You may have seen compressed gas heat up if you've ever inflated a tire using a hand pump and found it surprisingly hot afterward. You may have noticed expanding gas cool when water evaporates off your skin on a hot day.

2. The other rule you likely learned while eating Popsicles: When two things of different temperatures come into contact, the hotter thing cools and the cooler thing heats up.

The coils and tubes of a refrigerator contain a gas. In the bad old days it was Freon, now discontinued because it was eating the Earth's ozone layer. Newer refrigerators use ammonia gas. The refrigerator motor runs a compressor that squeezes the gas, heating it up. Your refrigerator pushes the hot, compressed gas through coils on the back or bottom of your fridge. There the gas loses heat to the surrounding air and cools way down...so much so that the compressed gas turns into a liquid.

The high pressure generated from the compressor then forces that liquid through a tiny valve into the coils inside your refrigerator. This area has little pressure because its gas has been pumped into the high-compression area (*see above*). As a result, the cold, compressed liquid immediately vaporizes and expands with abandon, cooling down to arctic temperatures. The gas brings temperatures in your freezer to below freezing and then flows through the coils to cool the main part of your refrigerator. Finally, the compressor sucks the gas up and begins the process all over again.

HOW DO THEY GET SMELLS INTO SCRATCH-N-SNIFF?

Think of microscopic bubbles stuck to the paper. The oily odor extracts of the smells are placed in water and furiously mixed, breaking the oil into very tiny droplets. At that instant, a gelatinous mixture is dropped in, which settles around the oil droplets, encasing them. After they're dried, the bubbles are mixed with an inky adhesive and printed onto paper. Later, when you scratch it, some of the bubbles burst, releasing the smell. The process is called "microencapsulation," and it's also been used for carbonless copying paper. ◖

Reality Bites
DO YOU REMEMBER THESE TOOTHY SLOGANS?

Match the ad campaign to the (mostly!) toothy brand name.

don't fool
yourself

1. "Look ma, no cavities!"

2. "Kills germs by the millions."

3. "No mediciny breath."

4. "Double protection fights cavities and freshens breath."

5. "Cleans your breath while it cleans your teeth."

    A. Listerine

6. "You'll wonder where the yellow went, when you brush your teeth with..."

    B. Colgate

    C. Ultrabrite

7. "Gives your mouth (*Ting!*) sex appeal."

    D. Scope

8. "The taste you can feel."

    E. Crest

9. "Cleans teeth, freshens breath naturally."

    F. Milk Bone Dog Biscuits

    G. Aquafresh

10. "You have bad breath. BAD BREATH!"

    H. Pepsodent

Answers: 1E; 2A; 3D; 4G; 5B; 6H; 7C; 8C; 9F; 10D

Glass Eyes

HOW POLAROID CREATED AN OPTICAL EMPIRE

There are Polaroid cameras and there are Polaroid sunglasses. Wondering how in the world these two Polaroid products are connected is enough to make you a Polaroid schizophrenic.

THE NAME *POLAROID* was coined in 1934 by a Smith College professor named Clarence Kennedy to describe a plastic material created by techno-genius Edwin Herbert Land that polarized light. But Land wasn't sure he liked the name—he was leaning toward *Epibollipol* (supposedly Greek for "sheet polarizer")—but thankfully, a friend talked him out of it.

BIRTH OF A NOTION

Land had been struck by inspiration eight years earlier at age seventeen. He was strolling down Broadway in New York City, on vacation from Harvard, and was blinded by the light of an oncoming car. The boy scientist had been reading theoretical studies about polarized light. Normally, light waves travel in a forward motion, vibrating at right angles in every direction from the direction of the forward path. Polarization makes light waves go in a parallel plane instead of vibrating every which direction. Land wondered if he could develop a polarized lens that would cut the glare from headlights—without reducing their effectiveness at illuminating the road.

Other scientists had discovered the phenomenon of polarization using crystals. One, William Bird Herapath, an English physician, actually produced polarizing material in 1852 after discovering that tiny needle-shaped crystals would "comb" light. Such crystals could be formed by combining iodine with quinine salt. He dosed a student's dog with a huge dose of quinine.

To the dog's quinine-rich urine, he added iodine. Sure enough, the tiny, very fragile crystals that formed could be seen to be polarizers when you looked at them under a microscope. Herapath spent the rest of his career fruitlessly trying to create a larger and stronger polarizing crystal (maybe if he had tried dosing an elephant?) until his death 70 years later.

A LOT OF SCIENTIFIC MUMBO JUMBO ENSUES

Land, his work cut out for him, decided that the quest to make a simple and inexpensive polarizer was a matter that was worth his time and considerable intellect. He did not go back to Harvard at the end of his vacation; he stayed in New York, settling into a small apartment to figure out the problem.

By day, Land haunted the library and read everything he could find about Herapath and polarization. By night, he worked in secrecy in a science lab building at Columbia University. There was a reason for his secrecy — he didn't belong there. He climbed the fire escape each night to a window that was usually left unlocked and took advantage of the unusually well-equipped laboratory.

"It is a curious property of research activity," Land once said, "that after the problem has been solved, the solution usually seems obvious." His solution was that Herapath had gone off on a wrong path — rather than find one large crystal to work as a filter, why not align millions of microscopic crystals in rows like a comb to form an "optical grain" that would do the same thing?

Land's parents agreed to fund his quest and even provided enough money to hire an assistant, a former dental technician named Ernest Calabro, who performed tasks of plating, cutting and polishing alloy and glass plates without having any idea of what the secretive Land was up to. For his part, Land believed he would solve the problem within a relatively short time, perhaps a few months.

EUREKA!

It was more like three years, but he finally got the solution that had eluded Herapath. In the Columbia University lab, he used a powerful electromagnet to line up millions of tiny iodine-quinine crystals in a hollow glass cylinder.

Shining a light through it confirmed that Land had succeeded. He soon figured out how to do the same thing on a plastic sheet, with 1,000 billion crystals per square inch. In 1929, at the age of twenty, he had his first major invention.

About that same time, the stock market crashed, reversing his family's fortunes. Land returned to Harvard, aware that his family was sacrificing to keep him there, and began working on his degree in dead earnest. Land also continued his research, this time using a lab provided to him by a professor. It became so compelling that he dropped out of Harvard one semester shy of graduating and never returned.

FINDING THE RIGHT NICHE

He spent the next several years trying to interest the car makers in the safety features of Polaroid windshields and headlights. To remind himself of what he was trying to accomplish, Land mounted a sign in his laboratory that said, "Every night, 50 people will die on the highway from headlight glare." But the car makers believed that styling and horsepower sold cars and that safety features actually

were a mistake, because they reminded potential buyers that a car could be a dangerous thing. So even though the Polaroid materials would have added only about $4 per car and could have saved thousands of lives, Detroit turned Land down.

Other manufacturers, however, started seeing some applications for Land's new material. Out of the blue, future competitor Kodak sent a huge order for something that didn't even exist yet—a Polaroid lens to tone down glare and sky light for photos. Movie makers started looking into polarized lenses and glasses for 3-D movies. (Unfortunately, 3-D was set back for a decade when Land demonstrated it to Harry Warner of Warner Brothers. "I don't get it," said Harry after the

With a glass eye, this was the only way Harry could ever see Bugs through any lense

movie. "What's the big deal?" It wasn't until several weeks later that Land found out from a Hollywood friend that Warner had a glass eye.)

Wurlitzer began using Polaroid film for light displays on its new jukeboxes. The American Optical Company bought the rights to make Polaroid sunglasses. And with war at hand, the Polaroid Company received millions of dollars in contracts to develop optical military applications. By war's end, the Polaroid Company's sales had multiplied to $17 million.

Land, shown here with one of his early model cameras

THE NAME IS FAMILIAR....

But before that, Land began getting bored and restless. He was looking for new scientific problems to take on. In 1943, while photographing vacation scenes in Santa Fe, his three-year-old daughter asked to see the pictures he just took. When he explained that she couldn't see them until they got home, she wanted to know, "Why not?"

Why not, indeed?

Land was immediately struck by the idea of instant photography. Before the day was over, he had already worked out the basic process. The developing chemicals would have to be included in the film pack, maybe in small pods that would rupture when the film traveled through a roller system like that on an old-fashioned washing machine.

Land went back to his lab and started working with a team of technicians, including Maxfield Parrish, Jr., the son of the artist. Four years later, they had a working model to demonstrate. A year later, they introduced the camera in department stores, accompanied by near-riots. People had never seen anything like this camera in 1948. They snapped it up, even at the outrageous price of $89.75 — the equivalent of more than $500 today. ☾

Maybe he had a glass ear, too:
"Who the hell wants to hear actors talk?"
—Harry Warner of Warner Brothers Studios in 1927

Akinosuke's Dream

A SPOOKY TALE FROM ANCIENT JAPAN

Who says you need a highly paid Hollywood screenwriter to get a supernatural story with a *Twilight Zone* ending? This is an ancient legend collected by Lafcadio Hearn in 1903.

IN YAMATO PROVINCE, there lived a farmer named Miyata Akinosuke. In his garden there was an ancient cedar tree. One warm afternoon he was sitting under this tree with two of his friends, chatting and drinking wine, when he felt all of a sudden very drowsy — so drowsy that he begged his friends to excuse him for taking a nap in their presence. Then he lay down at the foot of the tree, and dreamed this dream:

As he laid there in his garden, he saw a grand procession, more imposing than anything he had ever seen before, and it was advancing toward his dwelling. Young men, richly clothed, were drawing a great lacquered palace-carriage hung with bright blue silk. When the procession arrived within a short distance of the house it halted; and a richly dressed man advanced from it, approached Akinosuke, bowed to him profoundly, and said: "Honored sir: the king, the Kokuo of Tokoyo, commands me to greet you in his august name. Please immediately enter this carriage, which he has sent for your conveyance."

Upon hearing these words Akinosuke wanted to make some fitting reply; but he was too much astonished for speech. He entered the carriage and the journey began.

In a very short time, to Akinosuke's amazement, the carriage stopped in front of a huge two-storied gateway of a Chinese style. After some little waiting, two noble-looking men came from the gateway wearing robes of purple silk and high caps of lofty rank. They bowed to him and led him to a palace whose front appeared to extend a distance of miles.

Akinosuke was shown into a reception-room of wonderful size and splendor. Serving-maids, in costume of ceremony, brought refreshments. When Akinosuke had partaken, the two purple-robed attendants bowed before him and addressed him, each speaking alternately according to the etiquette of courts: "It is now our honorable duty to inform you...as to the reason of your having been summoned hither.... Our master, the King,

augustly desires that you become his son-in-law...and it is his wish and command that you shall wed this very day...the Princess, his maiden-daughter...."

Having thus spoken, the attendants rose together, and attired Akinosuke as befit a princely bridegroom, and conducted him to the presence-room, where the Kokuo of Tokoyo was seated upon his throne, wearing a high black cap of state, and robes of yellow silk. The king greeted him with gracious words, and then said: "The wedding shall now be performed." Joyful music played and beautiful court ladies advanced from behind a curtain to conduct Akinosuke to the room in which the bride awaited him. The room was immense; but it could scarcely contain the multitude of guests. All bowed down before Akinosuke as he took his place, facing the King's daughter, on the kneeling-cushion prepared for him. The bride appeared like a maid of heaven; her robes were beautiful as a summer sky. After the wedding the couple received the congratulations of many noble persons, and wedding gifts beyond counting.

Some days later Akinosuke was again summoned to the throne-room. On this occasion he was received even more graciously than before; and the King said to him: "In the south-western part of Our dominion there is an island called Raishu. We have now appointed you Governor of that island. You will find the people loyal and docile; we entrust you with the duty of improving their social conditions and ruling them with kindness and wisdom." So Akinosuke and his bride departed from the palace of Tokoyo.

Akinosuke entered at once upon his new duties; and they did

not prove to be hard. During the first three years of his governorship he was occupied chiefly with the enactment of laws; but he had wise counselors to help him, and he never found the work unpleasant. When it was all finished, the country was so healthy and so fertile that sickness and want were unknown; and the people were so good that no laws were ever broken.

Akinosuke dwelt and ruled in Raishu for twenty years more, during which no shadow of sorrow traversed his life. But in the twenty-fourth year, a great misfortune came upon him, for his wife, who had borne him five boys and two girls, fell sick and died. She was buried, with high pomp, on the summit of a beautiful hill; and a monument, exceedingly splendid, was placed upon her grave. But Akinosuke felt such grief at her death that he no longer cared to live.

Now when the period of mourning was over, there came from the Tokoyo palace a royal messenger with condolences. "We will now send you back to your own people and country," he added. "As for the seven children, they are the grandchildren of the King, and shall be fitly cared for. Do not, therefore, allow you mind to be troubled about them."

On receiving this mandate, Akinosuke submissively prepared for his departure. When all his affairs had been settled, he was escorted with much honor to the port. There he embarked, and the ship sailed out into the blue sea, and the shape of the island of Raishu itself turned blue, then grey, and then vanished forever.... And Akinosuke suddenly awoke, under the cedar tree in his own garden!

For a moment he was stupefied and dazed. But he perceived his two friends still seated near him, drinking and chatting merrily. He stared at them in a bewildered way, and cried aloud: "How strange!"

"Akinosuke must have been dreaming," one exclaimed with a laugh. "What did you see, Akinosuke, that was strange?" Then Akinosuke told his dream of three-and-twenty years' sojourn on the island of Raishu, and they were astonished, because he had really slept for no more than a few minutes.

His friend said: "Indeed, you saw strange things. We also saw something strange while you were napping. A little yellow butterfly was fluttering over your face for a moment or two. Then it alighted on the ground beside you, close to the tree; and a big ant seized it and pulled it down into the hole. Just before you woke up, we saw that butterfly come out of the hole again, and flutter over your face as before. And then the butterfly suddenly disappeared—we do not know where."

"Perhaps it was Akinosuke's soul," the other friend said. "I thought I saw it fly into his mouth. But, even if that butterfly was Akinosuke's soul, the fact would not explain his dream."

"The ants might explain it," returned the first speaker. "Ants are queer beings—possibly goblins.... Anyhow, there is a big ant's nest under that cedar tree...." "Let us look!" cried Akinosuke. He went for a spade.

The ground beneath the cedar tree proved to have been excavated, in a most surprising way, by a prodigious colony of ants.

 The ants had furthermore built things inside their excavations; and their tiny constructions of straw, clay, and stems bore an odd resemblance to miniature towns. In the middle of a structure considerably larger than the rest there was a marvelous swarm of small ants around one very big ant, which had yellowish wings and a long black head.

"Why, there is the King of my dream!" cried Akinosuke. "And there is the palace of Tokoyo! How extraordinary! Raishu ought to lie somewhere southwest of it—to the left of that big root.... Yes! Here it is! How very strange! Now I am sure I can find the mountain, and the grave of the princess...."

In the wreck of the nest he searched, and at last discovered a tiny mound, on the top of which was fixed a water-worn pebble, in shape resembling a Buddhist monument. Underneath it he found, embedded in clay, the dead body of a female ant. ☙

Surgery Before Anesthesia

What did hospitals use for surgery before anesthesia? Until the mid-1800s in Europe and America, hospitals routinely used "holders down"—burly guys who pinned screaming patients to the operating table to keep them from writhing.

Viva la Revolución

TIDBITS FROM THE LIFE OF FIDEL CASTRO

Fidel Castro led a successful revolution in Cuba in 1958 and has ruled it for more than three and a half decades, despite repeated U.S. efforts to overthrow or kill him.

• Fidel Castro grew up in an affluent family, the oldest of seven children. His father, Angel Castro, worked for the United Fruit Company (which was eventually thrown out of Cuba). For decades, United Fruit executives who knew Angel couldn't help but shake their heads and wonder how his quiet, polite boy could have gone so bad.

• Besides the seven children, the Castro house had a flock of chickens living inside it.

• When Castro was a child, other children called him "Judio" (the Jew) because he wasn't baptized until he was six.

• At age ten, Castro got appendicitis and spent three months in the hospital. He wanted to work in medicine: "Some people thought I might make a good doctor, because I used to play with lizards and a Gillette razor blade," he told an interviewer. "I had been impressed by the operations like the one I'd been through and after that I would 'operate' on lizards—lizards that usually died, of course. Then I would enjoy watching how the ants carried them off, how hundreds of ants working together could carry the lizard and move it to their heap."

• Known as "El Loco Fidel," he was so competitive in basketball games that he would forget which side he was playing for, switching sides and making baskets for the other team.

• Castro organized a baseball team and was its pitcher, even though he had an out-of-control fastball. When his team wasn't winning, Fidel would simply halt the game and go home. He claimed later that a scout had tried to recruit him into the American major leagues.

his "letter of support and congratulations," but no ten dollar bill.

• For his honeymoon, Fidel and his new wife Mirta trav-

Castro loved baseball. He's pictured here with the Minneapolis Millers during the 1959 Junior World Series vs. Havana.

• In 1940, as a teenager, Castro wrote a letter to Franklin D. Roosevelt. "My good friend Roosevelt: I don't know very English, but I know as much as I write to you. I like to hear the radio, and I am very happy, because I heard in it that you will be president of a new era. I am a boy but I think very much but I do not think that I am writting to the President of the United States. If you like, give me a ten dollars bill green american, in the letter, because never, I have not seen a ten dollars bill green american and I would like to have one of them." He received a letter back thanking him for

eled to New York City for three months, courtesy of his new father-in-law. A friend of both families gave the couple $1,000 for spending money. His name? Fulgencio Batista, who would later become Cuban president and be overthrown by Castro's revolutionaries. In New York, Castro used part of the money to buy a huge white Lincoln Continental.

• The Castros' first son, Fidelito, was a healthy baby, but then he suddenly became gravely ill. Doctors were mystified until Mirta discovered that Fidel was force-feeding his son three times the recommended concentration of formula so that his son would grow bigger and stronger than other children. She stopped the overfeeding then—and a few months later when Fidel began doing it again.

• On Castro's first revolutionary attack on a military post, he forgot his glasses. As a result he could barely drive to the post, much less aim his gun accurately.

• He was jailed after the attack. His marriage began breaking up when he failed to follow a cardinal rule of prison: Don't write to your wife and your mistress on the same day. The prison censor switched the two letters when he put them back in their envelopes.

• While training his revolutionaries in mountain camps, he confiscated all shaving supplies, toothpaste and brushes and soap, saying true revolutionaries don't concern themselves with personal hygiene.

• Castro, knowing the power of the American press to mold opinions, once tricked Herbert Matthews, a *New York Times* reporter, into thinking he had hundreds of soldiers when he had only 20 by having them march into a clearing by ones and twos, and then march in again and again. One man had a shirt without a back, so he had to march sideways. Che Guevara then had a man come running into the clearing, feigning exhaustion, to report on a completely fictitious Army Number 2. Matthews wrote an article saying that Castro's band was so large that "General Batista cannot hope to suppress Castro's revolt."

• The Cuban Communist Party opposed Castro's rebellion, saying armed struggle was futile. On the other hand, it was supported by the Havana Lions Club and Rotarians.

• In those tense, pre-revolutionary times, Johnny Weissmuller, taking a break from playing Tarzan in the movies, was participating in a Cuban golf tournament. Suddenly, he was surrounded by group of Castro's soldiers who emerged from the rough near the 14th hole. Weissmuller pulled himself up to full height, beat his chest, and let out a Tarzan yell. After a shocked pause, the rebels shouted in delight, "Tarzan! Tarzan! Bienvenido! Welcome!"

• After Batista fled Cuba, mobs went around breaking up casinos as symbols of the American Mafia that had run

Weissmuller, second from left, once used his famous role to befriend Castro's revolutionaries

Cuba for so long. Tough-guy actor George Raft owned the Capri Hotel. When an angry mob began storming the front steps, he snarled at them in his famous gangster voice, "Yer not comin' in my casino!" The people stopped at the sound of the famous voice and retreated.

• After the revolution, Castro came again to New York, where he was wined and dined by all facets of American society — so much so that his brother Raul called from Cuba to ask if he were selling Cuba out to the Americans. His entourage went down in New York history as the ones who plucked chickens in the cities' hotels. At the time, it was assumed that the chickens were for eating — in fact, some of them were sacrificed in Santería rituals. Like many Cubans, Castro dabbles in the Santería religion. He has a mystical attachment to the number 26, picking the 26th day of a month for major speeches, decisions and actions.

• The Bay of Pigs invasion by the United States was such a talked-about "secret" in Miami's "Little Havana" that Cuban intelligence agents assumed it was some sort of disinformation campaign. On the morning before the invasion, Castro aide Carlos Franqui received a call from a *New York Times* reporter asking if he had any news about "an invasion of the island," but the security breach didn't do much harm — Castro had already stationed troops at the landing site.

• Castro always fancied himself quite a lady's man. In fact, there are dozens of children in Cuba who claim him as father. But his technique? One purported lover, a dancer at the Tropicana Hotel, said he read while he made love. A French actress complained that he smoked his damned cigar during the act. An American woman said he never took his boots off. Other women said he took them to romantic spots and then only talked for hours on end about things like agricultural reform. ☾

Life Lessons
HOW TO MAKE GIANT "OSTRICH" EGGS

These are great for displays, gifts, Easter eggs and even practical jokes. They look and feel like real eggs. Here's how to make them.

OVER THE YEARS, we've made thousands of these eggs for fun, friends, art galleries and store windows. You can make them any size, but we suggest starting small, because the bigger they are, the easier they break.

WHAT YOU'LL NEED
- Tarp and/or newspapers
- Egg-shaped balloons
- Plaster of Paris
- Water basin
- Plastic cups or Tupperware
- Stirrer
- Plastic squeeze bottle (like from shampoo or detergent)
- Small knife or scissors

HOW YOU DO IT

1 Gather your materials and fill your basin with clean water. Wear old clothes, work outdoors if you can and put down tarp and newspapers. Prepare for a mess because the balloons sometimes burst and shoot plaster in all directions.

2 Fill your cup or Tupperware container half-full with water. Begin adding plaster, stirring continuously, until it reaches the consistency of a thin milk shake. Work quickly now, because the plaster will set in 5 to 10 minutes.

3 Carefully pour the plaster into your squeeze bottle. You'll spill only a little if you approach the problem with a steady hand, an insouciant attitude and a lot of practice.

4 Put a balloon on the mouth of the squeeze bottle as if you were making a water balloon on a faucet.

5 Turn the bottle upside down. Hold the neck of

the balloon on the bottle so it doesn't slip off. Squeeze plaster into the balloon, inflating it to about the size of a tangerine.

6 Take the balloon off the bottle, squeezing its neck so the plaster doesn't escape. Blow the balloon up the rest of the way (if you don't like the idea of plaster in your mouth, use a straw), and tie it. Float it in the water tub and gently roll it around, end over end.

7 Repeat steps 4, 5 and 6 until you run out of plaster.

Quickly clean your bottle before the plaster residue inside hardens.

8 Gently turn each balloon end over end, smoothly coating its inside wall with

plaster. Do this quickly to each balloon until the plaster inside stops moving. Immediately stop turning the balloons, and let them float untouched for at least 10 minutes.

9 When the plaster has completely hardened, cut the balloon away with your blade, being careful not to gouge the surface of the plaster.

10 Trim away the excess plaster from the "navel" where the balloon neck was. And there you have it—a giant egg!

MORE IDEAS

• You can decorate the eggs after the fact, or add pigment when you mix up the plaster.

• If they break (and many of them will), use the broken shells. You can make things "hatch" out of them, or use them as small animal houses. ☾

Mascot Miracles

HOW ELSIE BECAME BORDEN'S CASH COW

Every consumer loves company mascots, but they're usually the last resort for ad agencies. Along with the Energizer Bunny (page 199) and Chiquita Banana (page 279), here's one of our favorites.

THE PUBLIC MAY LOVE Mr. Whipple (remember him?) and Betty Crocker and (especially) the cute spokesanimal cartoon characters like Tony the Tiger and Charlie Tuna. But most advertising agencies hate them because there's no challenge to them. Not only that, if they're successful, they lock the client into variations of the same kind of advertising for years into the future, making it hard to justify an ad agency's big, continuing "creative" costs.

Still, the use of "cute" has been especially successful with companies that realize that they are perceived as big, greedy, impersonal and heartless. That's how the Borden Co. got Elsie.

MASTER OF ALL TRADES

Before Gail Borden discovered how to condense milk, he was an inventor (see page 433 for more information). He had long been interested in condensing and preserving food. He poured his heart, soul and finances into a concoction he called the meat biscuit in which he boiled 120 pounds of beef down to 10 pounds of beef jelly, which he then mixed with flour and baked into long-lasting biscuits for travelers. His biscuits won awards at exhibitions, including the prestigious London International Exhibition in 1851. His meat biscuits were even taken along by a group of pioneers on their way to California.

There was only one problem: The meat biscuits tasted absolutely foul. Even though *Scientific American* called the biscuit, "one of the most valuable inventions that has ever been brought forward," the Army, with its

Gail Borden

notoriously low gastronomical standards, disagreed. After field tests, a board of Army officers reported that Borden's biscuits were "not only unpalatable, but failed to appease the craving of hunger—producing headache, nausea, and great muscular depression." His meat biscuit business failed, and Borden plummeted into bankruptcy.

The year before, however, Borden had gotten inspiration for a new invention. On the trip home from winning his London International Exhibition award, Borden had been confronted with the sight of distraught immigrant mothers holding crying, starving babies in the steerage compartment of the ship because the two cows aboard the steamer were giving infected milk. Borden is said to have been haunted by what he saw, and decided to find a way to preserve milk for long periods of time.

Borden's perverse luck from tragedy continued: If his business hadn't failed, and if he hadn't been a penniless widower, he wouldn't have sent his four children off to live with the Shaker religious colony in Lebanon, New York, where he eventually discovered the solution to preserving milk. First, though, he began living and working in a cellar in Brooklyn. He tried boiling gallons of milk down to quarts, but the dark substance that remained tasted horrible, like burnt molasses.

SHAKE, VACUUM & BOIL
He had his stroke of luck when he visited his children at the Shaker colony. The Shakers were well known for their inventive and functional designs. Borden noticed some of them making fruit preserves with a device of their own invention: a "vacuum pan" from which most of the air had been pumped out. It worked on the principle that liquids in a near-vacuum boil at a much lower temperature.

Borden made his own vacuum pan and found that milk boiled at 136° instead of 212°, leaving its color and taste essentially unchanged. He discovered he could remove 80% of the water from milk, leaving a heavy fluid that, when preserved with sugar, could last indefinitely and didn't taste too bad.

Financial success, however, eluded him. Selling the viscous liquid was not as easy as he had hoped at first. He had to sell half of his company to keep it going. Then another stroke of his perverse luck struck: A muckraking editor of *Leslie's Illustrated Weekly* launched a lurid exposé of "swill milk" with vivid word pictures of urban milk supplies from diseased cows fed on brewery refuse, milk cans and manure being hauled on the same carts, and "milk murder!" —high infant death rates from typhoid and tuberculosis. Capitalizing on the uproar, Borden bought ads extolling the purity of his condensed "country milk." Sales picked up.

MILK WARS

In fact, the Borden Company thrived so much in following decades that in the 1930s it became the subject of controversy. People began wondering why, if milk cost so much, the dairy farmers were paid so little. In the ensuing "milk wars," the big milk wholesalers, distributors and retailers were blamed for jacking up prices and pocketing obscene profits. The Borden Company, now one of the biggest "middlemen," decided it needed to quickly change its public image from rapacious and greedy to cute and cuddly.

1950s cookbook

Company executives decided to milk their obvious assets and came up with cartoon spokescows in humorous comic strips. They tried them in medical journals first, with laugh-riot hijinks like

> Calf: "Mama, I think I see a germ!"
> Cow: "Mercy, child—run quick for the Borden Inspector!"

Doctors swamped the company with requests for reprints for their waiting room walls, so Borden began running the ads in New York newspapers. There was a herd of cartoon cows with names like Bessie, Clara, Mrs. Blossom and Elsie. Then, in

1938, a radio copywriter randomly singled out Elsie's name in a commercial for Rush Hughes, a network news commentator who was sponsored by Borden. Hughes read aloud a letter, purportedly from a cow to her mother:

> Dear Mama:
> I'm so excited I can hardly chew. We girls are sending our milk to Borden now!
> Love, *Elsie*

The commercial so tickled Hughes's listeners that they started sending fan mail to Elsie. She quickly became Borden's one main sacred cow, and made her solo debut in national magazines like *Life* and *Saturday Evening Post*. For the New York World's Fair, the company bought a seven-year-old, 950-pound Jersey from Massachusetts, whose registered name was "You'll Do, Lobelia." They set up Elsie in an exhibit that was supposedly her bedroom. It was done up in "Barn Colonial" with churns used as tables, milk bottles as lamps, a wheelbarrow for a chaise longue and oil paintings of Elsie's ancestors. Elsie became such a media hit that the actress that played her, You'll Do, Lobelia, was asked to co-star in the movie *Little Men* with Jack Oakie and Kay Francis in 1940.

ELSIE'S CUTE CALVES

About the same time, the cartoon cow became married to Elmer and had two calves, Beulah and Beauregard (named after the Confederate General in the Battle of Bull Run). The family ruled the barnyard for nearly three decades. The company even named a glue after Elmer. (They didn't use Elsie's name because they feared that consumers would think the glue was made from over-the-hill dairy cows.)

In 1963, Borden introduced Elsie's Milkman Game, in which players delivered milk house to house. Despite Elsie's popularity, the game didn't go over so well.

A GOOD IDEA IN THE TOILET

In 1969, Borden's chairman, caught up in the conglomerate diversification fever of the time, decided that Elsie gave "an inaccurate message" about the company, forgetting that that had been the whole point in the first place. He decided that a company bent on diversifying into chemical manufacturing should downplay an animal that had long been meant to symbolize wholesome country goodness. Elsie was dropped as a corporate symbol, even though polls indicated she was among the best-known corporate mascots. Instead, the company settled on a logo that using an abstract red oval. Employees derided the abstract oval among themselves as "the toilet seat." Eventually, new management of Borden recognized the value of Elsie's image. On March 10, 1993, Borden readopted her to represent all of its dairy brands, building a new logo around her smiling cow face. ☾

Gail Borden Beyond "Remember the Alamo"

BEFORE GAIL BORDEN discovered how to condense whole milk in the 1850s, he was the official state surveyor for the state of Texas (among other things, he laid out the streets of Galveston) and founder of the weekly *Telegraph and Texas Register*—the newspaper that coined the phrase, "Remember the Alamo." He was also a tinkerer and inventor. We're probably fortunate that most of his inventions never amounted to anything.

• First up was a beach bathhouse that women could move around with them, and change in when out for a day in the sun.

• Borden came up with the idea for a steamboat that was self-propelled by mechanical oars.

• A special lazy susan for quick table service bombed, too.

• One of the more interesting Borden inventions had to be his "simplified method" of converting Catholics to Protestants. Something like a step-by-step guide for converters. Not surprisingly, this idea failed, too.

Battle at the Alamo

• Borden's Terraqueus Machine, although a bust, was one of his favorites. It was a contraption, made with a sail from a boat and a wagon, that could travel on both land and water. A horse would lead the wagon, equipped with the sail, to water, where the wheels and sail were supposed to take over so it could move through the sea. Unfortunately, as the story goes, Borden decided to try it out on some dinner guests with disastrous results. The contraption failed miserably once it hit the water, tipping over and dumping all his riders into the Gulf of Mexico.

Sports Match 4

MATCH THE TEAM TO THE LOCATION

Here we go again with a tough sports team match-up quiz. Match the pro teams from the NHL, MLS and the WNBA with the places they call home.

1.	Storm	San Jose
2.	Sharks	Dallas
3.	Rapids	Minnesota
4.	Sparks	Anaheim
5.	Avalanche	Nashville
6.	Rockers	Kansas City
7.	Canucks	Phoenix
8.	Burn	Colorado
9.	Wizards	Seattle
10.	Mighty Ducks	Cleveland
11.	Earthquakes	Colorado
12.	Mercury	Vancouver
13.	Predators	Los Angeles
14.	Galaxy	Los Angeles
15.	Lynx	San Jose

Answers: 1. Storm: Seattle—WNBA; 2. Sharks: San Jose—NHL; 3. Rapids: Colorado—MLS; 4. Sparks: Los Angeles—WNBA; 5. Avalanche: Colorado—NHL; 6. Rockers: Cleveland—WNBA; 7. Canucks: Vancouver—NHL; 8. Burn: Dallas—MLS; 9. Wizards: Kansas City—MLS; 10. Mighty Ducks: Anaheim—NHL; 11. Earthquakes: San Jose—MLS; 12. Mercury: Phoenix—WNBA; 13. Predators: Nashville—NHL; 14. Galaxy: Los Angeles—MLS; 15. Lynx: Minnesota—WNBA

Ripe Ol' Corn

"UNCLE JOSH AT A CIRCUS"

Uncle Josh Weathersby—a country bumpkin created by Cal Stewart—
tells about circus folks who came to town in this reprint from
W. C. Privy's original *Bathroom Companion #4*, published in 1905.

WELL, 'LONG LAST YEAR, 'bout harvest time, there was a cirkus come to Punkin Centre, and I think the whole population turned out to see it. They come paradin' into town, the bands a-playin' and banners flying, and animals pokin' their heads out of the cages, and all sorts of jim-cracks. Deacon Witherspoon said they was a sinful lot of men and wimmin, and no one oughta go and see them, but seein' as how they was there, he allowed he'd take the children and let them see the lions and tigers and things. Si Pettingill remarked, "Guess the Deacon won't put blinders on himself when he gits there." We noticed afterwards that the Deacon had a front seat where he could see and hear purty well.

Well, I said to Ezra Hoskins, "Let's you and me go down to the cirkus," and Ezra said, "All right, Joshua." So we got on our store clothes, our new boots, and put some money in our pockits, and went down to the cirkus. Well, I never seen any one in my life cut up more fool capers than Ezra did. We got in where the animals was, and Ezra he walked around the elephant three or four times, and then he said, "By gum, Josh, that's a durned handy critter—he's got two tails, and he's eatin' with one and keepin' the flies off with t'other." Durned old fool!

Well, we went on a little ways further, and all to once Ezra he said, "Gee whiz, Josh, there's Steve Jenkins over there in one of them cages." I said, "Come along you silly fool, that ain't Steve

Jenkins." Ezra said, "Well, now, I guess I'd oughter know Steve Jenkins when I see him; I jist about purty near raised Steve." Well, we went over to the cage, and it wan't no man at all, nuthin' only a durned old baboon; and Ezra wanted to shake hands with him jist 'cause he looked like Steve. Ezra said he'd bet a peck of pippins that baboon belonged to Steve's family a long ways back.

Well, then we went into where they was havin' the cirkus doin's, and I guess us two old codgers jist about busted our buttons a-laffin at that silly old clown. Well, he cut up a lot of didos, then he went out and set down right alongside of Aunt Nancy Smith; and Nancy she'd like to had histeericks. She said, "You go 'way from me you painted critter," and that clown he jist up and yelled to beat thunder—he said Nancy stuck a pin in him. Well, ev'rybody laffed, and Nancy she jist set and giggled right out.

Well, they brought a trick mule into the ring, and the ring master said he'd give any one five dollars what could ride the mule; and Ruben Hoskins allowed he could ride anything with four legs what had hair on. So he got into the ring, and that mule he took after Ruben and chased him 'round that ring so fast Ruben could see himself goin' 'round t'other side of the ring. He was mighty glad to git out of there.

Then a gal come out on horse back and commenced ridin' around. Nancy Smith said she was a brazen critter to come out there without clothes enough on her to dust a fiddle. But Deacon Witherspoon said that was the art of 'questrinism; we all allowed it, whatever he meant. And then that silly old clown he told the ring master that his uncle committed sooiside different than any man what ever committed sooiside; and the ring master said, "Well, sir, how did your uncle commit sooiside?" and that silly old clown said, "Why, he put his nose in his ear and he blowed his head off." Then he sang an old-fashioned song I

hadn't heered in a long time; it went something like this:

"From Widdletown to Waddletown is fifteen miles,
From Waddletown to Widdletown is fifteen miles,
From Widdletown to Waddletown, from Waddletown to Widdletown--
Take it all together and it's fifteen miles."

He was about the silliest cuss I ever seen.

Well, I noticed a feller a rummagin' 'round among the benches as though he might a-lost somethin'. So I said to him, "Mister, did you lose anythin' 'round here any place?" He said, "Yes, sir, I lost a ten dollar bill; if you find it I'll give you two dollars." Well, I jist made up my mind he was one of them cirkus sharpies, and when he wan't a-lookin' I pulled a ten dollar bill out of my pockit and give it to him; and the durned fool didn't know that it wasn't the same one that he lost. Gosh, I jist fooled him out of his two dollars slicker 'n a whistle.

I tell you cirkus day is a great time in Punkin Centre. ☾

• Ever wonder why the calliope always appeared at the end of a circus parade? Besides being deafening to nearby ears, there was also the safety issue—the steam-powered contraptions would occasionally blow up.

• "Leotards" were named after Jules Leotard, the man who invented the flying trapeze. He also invented the safety net...sort of. While at the Cirque Napoleon, he worked with a pile of mattresses beneath him.

Zen Masters
THE ZEN OF POP BABES

Britney Spears and Christina Aguilera—bleach-blonde pop stars—sometimes have words of wisdom for their young fans. And sometimes they don't....

Britney Says: "I always call my cousin because we're so close. We're almost like sisters, and we're also close because our moms are sisters."

"I always listen to 'NSYNC's "Tearin' Up My Heart." It reminds me to wear a bra."

"I think I'm more grounded, you know, and I know what I want out of life and I'm, you know, my morals are really, you know, strong and I have major beliefs about certain things and I think that has helped me, you know, from being, you know, coming from a really small town."

"I want to be an artist that everyone can relate to, that's young, happy and fun."

"Just because I look sexy on the cover of *Rolling Stone* doesn't mean I'm naughty."

"The cool thing about being famous is traveling. I have always wanted to travel across seas, like to Canada and stuff."

Christina Says: "I don't want to be just a straight pop singer. I'm a vocalist and that's what I want to be seen as in the long run."

"I think everybody should have a great Wonderbra. There's so many ways to enhance them, everybody does it."

"I'm not really religious but very spiritual. I give money to this company that manufactures hearing aids on a regular basis. More people should really hear me sing. I have a gift from God."

Whole Lotta Shakin'
How Jell-O Got the Wiggles & Jiggles

Although today it's a staple in kitchen pantries across the globe, Jell-O hasn't always been around. We were curious about everyone's favorite dessert, so we had intrepid reporter Don Jellyson look into Jell-O's jiggly past.

IT WIGGLES. It's colorful. It's served to patients by the finest hospitals in the world. Even the Smithsonian has done a retrospective exhibit and seminar tracing its history. Like bowling and Cheez Whiz, it's so déclassé that it's hip. We're talking about Jell-O, the salad that has no vegetables, the only pork product you can eat that's certified as kosher. Gelatin is so transformed from its original forms that rabbis have ruled it kosher and pareve—neither meat nor dairy.

Gelatin appeared in Europe centuries ago (history records that Napoleon ate it with Josephine). A specialized kind, isinglass, was milky-colored and made from the air bladders of sturgeons.

Modern-style powdered gelatin was developed by the American engineer Peter Cooper, founder of the Cooper Union for the Advancement of Science and Art, who also designed and built the Tom Thumb locomotive. In 1845, he patented the process of turning animal skin, bone and connective tissue into a highly refined flavorless wiggly clear material.

Unfortunately, Cooper never quite figured out how to make a silk purse out of his sow's ear creation. His gelatin never became a commercial success. Maybe it was because he just didn't have a promoter's sense for selling the wiggle and not the steak byproducts: His advertisements described gelatin as "a transparent substance containing all the ingredients fitting it for table use in portable form, and requiring only the addition of hot water to dissolve it."

Cooper's product sat jiggling but dormant for a half-century until 1895, when all things came to a man improbably named Pearl B. Wait. Wait was a maker of patent medicines and corn plasters in LeRoy, New York. One of his most successful products was a cough syrup, so he knew something about using flavors and colors to mask the unpleasant qualities of a product.

Wait had a neighbor with the also unlikely name of Orator Woodward, who was an inventor, too. His first invention was a pesticide-laced cement egg you could place in a chicken's nest to kill lice. Commercially, it laid an egg. However, he had more success marketing a coffee-substitute grain beverage called Grain-O.

"There's always room for J-e-l-l-O!"

The "-O" ending was a commercial fad at the time, similar to "-a-Rama" in the 1950s, or unrecognizable techno-gibberish names in the 1990s. May Wait, Pearl's wife, was inspired by Woodward's Grain-O when she named the powdered dessert mix "Jell-O."

In a Hollywood treatment of the story, Wait's fruit-flavored, brightly colored gelatin would quickly become the hit of every church potluck and picnic in LeRoy. But in real life, Wait had a devil of a time getting anybody to try it, much less buy it. Finally, in disgust, he offered to sell the whole business to Woodward for $450.

Woodward bought, figuring he could use the same manufacturing and distribution system he had already set up for Grain-O. He quickly found, though, that no matter how good your system is, it doesn't do much good if nobody wants your product. Packages of Jell-O piled up unsold in his warehouse. One day he was walking with his warehouse superintendent, A. S. Nico, and impulsively offered to sell him the entire Jell-O business for $35. Nico looked at him, looked at the pile of unsold goods—and refused the offer.

Nico soon had reason to regret the decision. Jell-O started finding its market. By 1902, Woodward was selling $250,000 worth of the stuff a year. He started advertising, using pictures of famous actresses and opera singers serving the delicate dessert from fluted glassware on silver trays. He hired famous artists like Maxfield Parrish and Norman Rockwell to illustrate his advertisements and recipe books. He began direct-mail ad campaigns, sending recipes directly to the consumer, and sent out a fleet of nattily dressed salesmen to appear at country fairs and women's clubs and demonstrate the ease and versatility of Jell-O.

Jell-O advertised heavily on radio and sponsored Jack Benny's show in the 1930s, but the true Golden Age of Jell-O came in the 1950s. Its ease of preparation and versatility of use in recipes brought forth the collective creative genius of American house-wifery. On file at Jell-O headquarters are more than 2,200 different Jell-O recipes. They range from *Joy of Jell-O Cookbook* favorites like Gelatin Poke Cake to new wave Jell-O recipes like Primordial Aspic (green Jell-O with gummy fishes and worms suspended in it). General Foods, which owns the brand, maintains an active hotline for recipes, questions and even Jell-O wisdom. (For example, did you know that there are certain fruits like pineapple, kiwi, papaya and mangoes that should only be used canned? Canning destroys an enzyme in them that keeps the Jell-O from fully hardening.)

Jell-O started falling from its slippery state of grace in the 1960s. Part of it was general anti-establishmentarianism, part was a health-conscious backlash against artificial ingredients and empty calories, and part had to do with the Baby Bust. Jell-O became a punch line signaling a lower-class mentality in jokes by people like Archie Bunker and Fred Sanford. Jell-O's sales declined precipitously from a high of 715 million packages in 1968 to 305 million by 1986.

But Jell-O started bouncing

back in 1987, thanks to the 1980s Baby Boomlet. Jigglers, a high-density finger-food Jell-O recipe, became immensely popular with the preschool set, and a vodka-laced version appealed to the young party crowd. Bill Cosby became the recognized spokesperson in TV commercials. Even President-elect Bill Clinton dined on Bing Cherry Jell-O Salad for his first post-election Thanksgiving and Christmas.

Not bad for a food product made from artificial flavor, artificial color, fresh and frozen pork skins, cattle bones and hides, and assorted connective tissue from both animals. ☾

Other Jell-O Facts

• 3 out of 4 American houses have at least one package of Jell-O in the pantry.

• America eats an average of eight boxes of Jell-O every second of the day.

• The current Jell-O Capital of America is Grand Rapids, Michigan, which consumes 82 percent more Jell-O per capita than average. Why? Maybe because of all the Protestant churches. Another strange, hopefully unrelated, fact: Grand Rapids is also the largest per capita buyer of rat poison.

• 30 percent of Jell-O is served, not straight-up, but in recipes.

• The most popular flavor? "Red" (strawberry, raspberry and cherry). Jell-O has grown from four flavors in 1897 (orange, lemon, strawberry and raspberry) to twenty today, including recent additions blueberry and watermelon.

• The key to hosting the ever-popular spectator sport called Jell-O Wrestling? Use an 8-foot padded box, pour in 55 gallons of powder, add boiling water, chill for two days and don't allow contestants to hold their opponents' heads under the Jell-O.

Eyewitness

I SAW BURR KILL HAMILTON

Many have wondered what actually went down between Alexander Hamilton and Aaron Burr on that July morning, 1804, in Weehawken, New Jersey. There were two there who wrote about what they saw of the famous duel and its aftermath.

CONSIDERING HOW it all ended, it's not surprising to find out that Alexander Hamilton and Aaron Burr began their relationship as law partners. The animosity that was built there stoked the fires of resentment that flared up later in their careers. When Burr won a Senate seat that had belonged to Hamilton's father-in-law, though, things got really tense between the two.

Burr walked away from the vice presidency in 1804, and ran a campaign for New York governor. He was unliked by many besides Hamilton, including George Washington and Thomas Jefferson. He'd developed a reputation for being untrustworthy and had a tendency to court any political party that would put him ahead. Many people were willing to try almost anything to make sure he didn't win the New York governor's race, Hamilton among them. Burr soon became the victim of a vicious smear campaign led by Hamilton. When accused by Burr of leading the slanderous attack, Hamilton refused to acknowledge it, much less apologize for the role he played. Burr, then, challenged Hamilton to a duel.

One just didn't show up for a duel unaided. Hamilton, like any other duel participant, brought a Second—a guy who prepared the guns, tended wounds and assisted the duelers with various tasks.

Hamilton's Second, Nathaniel Pendleton, and Burr's Second, W. P. Van Ness, collaborated on a summary in the aftermath of the event. Not long after, they published this account:

He then asked if they were prepared; being answered in the affirmative, he gave the

word present, as had been agreed on, and both parties presented and fired in succession. The intervening time is not expressed, as the seconds do not precisely agree on that point. The fire of Colonel Burr took effect, and General Hamilton almost instantly fell. Colonel Burr advanced toward General Hamilton with a manner and gesture that appeared to General Hamilton's friend to be expressive of regret; but, without speaking, turned about and withdrew, being urged from the field by his friend, as has been subsequently stated, with a view to prevent his being recognized by the surgeon and bargemen who were then approaching. No further communication took place between the principals, and the barge that carried Colonel Burr immediately returned to the city. We conceive it proper to add, that the conduct of the parties in this interview was perfectly proper, as suited the occasion.

Accompanying Alexander Hamilton to the duel on that day was physician David Hosack. When Hamilton fell, it was Hosack who attended to his injuries. This is what he remembered:

When called to him upon his receiving the fatal wound, I

found him half sitting on the ground, supported in the arms of Mr. Pendleton. His countenance of death I shall never forget. He had at that instant just strength to say, "This is a mortal wound, doctor"; when he sunk away, and became to all appearance lifeless. I immediately stripped up his clothes, and soon, alas I ascertained that the direction of the ball must have been through some vital part. His pulses were not to be felt, his respiration was entirely suspended, and, upon laying my hand on his heart and perceiving no motion there, I considered him as irrecoverably gone. I, however, observed to Mr. Pendleton, that the only chance for his reviving was immediately to get him upon the water. We therefore lifted him up, and carried him out of the wood to the margin of the bank, where the bargemen aided us in conveying him into the boat, which immediately put off. During all this time I could not discover the least symptom of returning life. I now rubbed his face, lips, and temples with spirits of hartshorn, applied it to his neck and breast, and to the wrists and palms of his hands, and endeavoured to pour some into his mouth.

When we had got, as I should judge, about fifty yards from the shore, some imperfect efforts to breathe were for the first time manifest; in a few minutes he sighed, and became sensible to the impression of the hartshorn or the fresh air of the water. He breathed; his eyes, hardly opened, wandered, without fixing upon any object; to our great joy, he at length spoke. "My vision is indistinct," were his first words. His pulse became more perceptible, his respiration more regular, his sight returned. I then examined the wound to know if there was any dangerous discharge of blood; upon slightly pressing his side it gave him pain, on which I desisted.

Soon after recovering his sight, he happened to cast his eye upon the case of pistols, and observing the one that he had had in his hand lying on the outside, he said, "Take care of that pistol; it is undischarged, and still cocked; it may go off and do harm. Pendleton knows" (attempting to turn his head towards him) "that I did not intend to fire at him."

"Yes," said Mr. Pendleton, understanding his wish, "I have already made Dr. Hosack acquainted with your determination as to that."

He then closed his eyes and remained calm, without any disposition to speak; nor did he say much afterward, except in reply to my questions. He asked me once or twice how I found his pulse; and he informed me that his lower extremities had lost all feeling, manifesting to me that he entertained no hopes that he should long survive.

445

The next day, Hamilton was dead. But that's not the end of the sordid tale.

Burr's "victory" meant that he was charged with murder in both New York and New Jersey. He became a social and political pariah.

He didn't let it stop him, though.... Within a few years, Burr was caught red-handed organizing a private army so that he could go and conquer portions of both Mexico and Louisiana, probably to set up his own kingdom. Although he never officially stated his purpose, Burr wrote to his co-conspirator General James Wilkinson of his intentions, "The gods invite us to glory and fortune; it remains to be seen whether we deserve the boon."

Aaron Burr's treason trial

Wilkinson, in the end, ratted him out to President Thomas Jefferson, but thanks to a legal technicality, Burr escaped being convicted of treason.

Soon after, he fled to Europe, hoping to leave his reputation behind. He did so successfully, but he sound wound up in serious debt. To avoid debtors' prison there, he had to come back home to New York.

The murder charges were eventually dropped, and Burr managed to rekindle his career as a lawyer, but the legacy he built over his lifetime never really left him. He lived a life "severed from the human race," as he put it, and died forgotten in 1833 at the age of eighty. ☾

The Long Road to American College Football

• *"I will not permit 30 men to travel 400 miles merely to agitate a bag of wind."* —Cornell president Andrew White, forbidding an intercollegiate game of football with the University of Michigan in 1873.

• *"There's murder in that game!"* —Rugged boxer John L. Sullivan, upon watching a grueling Harvard-Yale football game prior to the game's near-ban in 1909.

Rotting Grapes
A SHORT HISTORY OF WINE

"The peoples of the Mediterranean began to emerge from barbarism when they learnt to cultivate the olive and the grape vine."
—Thucydides, fifth century Greek historian

WHEN DID WINE first appear on the Earth? First, the legends. According to the Bible, Noah became the first winemaker after the flood. (Wine was important in Biblical times: In the Old Testament, all books but Jonah mention it. Isaiah even includes advice on how to plant a vineyard.)

• According to an Arabic tale recorded by Omar Khayyam in the twelfth century, a woman in a Persian king's harem discovered wine. A jar of grapes had been set aside as probably poisonous when it began foaming and smelling funny. A concubine suffering from unbearable headaches decided to kill herself with this poison. Instead, she lost her headache, she became the life of the party, and sank into a restful sleep.

• Despite the legends, though, wine dates back before history. In fact, it was probably the first alcoholic drink. Unlike beer, wine does not have to be actively fermented—it happens naturally if fruit juice is stored too long. Wine historian Hugh Johnson thinks that wine is at least 2 million years old.

• The earliest solid archaeological evidence of wine—a jar with wine residues found in Mesopotamia—dates to about 3500 B.C. The wine seems to have been made from dates.

• Egyptian wall paintings of winemaking from 3,000–5,000 years ago show that the technology of winemaking has not

Egyptians stomping grapes

changed all that much since then. One of their innovations was an overhead safety grid to keep grape stompers safe from slipping and drowning or being overcome by the car-

Bacchus, Roman God of Wine & Party Guy

bon dioxide that fermenting grapes give off. Wine was important to the Egyptians — King Tut was buried with 36 jars of it to help him make a smooth transition to the Next World.

• Romans drank their wine diluted with warm water. Many preferred the salty tang of sea water to the blandness of fresh water.

• In Rome during the second century B.C., women were forbidden to drink wine. A husband who discovered his wife soaking up the Sauvignon was allowed to divorce or even kill her with impunity.

• Many Romans worshiped Bacchus, the Roman wine god who was the miracle-working son of a god and a mortal woman. Bacchus's followers ate bread and wine to symbolically ingest the body and blood of the god.

• Some ancient wine techniques were not healthy. The Egyptians added burned sulfur to wine as a preservative. The Romans "sweetened" their wine with lead. Lead poisoning may have caused the fall of the Roman Empire, yet even after 1696, when Dr. Eberhard Gockel of Germany proved that it was a deadly poison, adding lead to wine was not banned in most countries until the mid-1800s. (Even the laws didn't stop French winemakers who continued to drop lead musketballs into their vats for several decades after.)

• Before the French got the hang of making wine, around 200 B.C., they had to buy wine from the wily Italians, exchanging a French slave for every large amphora of wine.

• Jesus' first miracle was reportedly turning water into wine. He referred to wine often, calling himself "the true vine" and used wine in the Last Supper. He even talked of humanity in grape grower terms: "Every bunch in me that beareth not fruit he taketh away; and every branch that beareth fruit, he purgeth it, that it may bring forth more fruit."

• The proper use of wine in Christian ceremony, like a lot of other apparently trivial things, has set off century-long doctrinal disputes. Greek and Armenian churches split over whether the Eucharist wine should be watered, with the Armenians refusing to water their wine and the Greeks insisting that it was a spiritual necessity. The Armenians offered a compromise in 1178—they would add water as long as it didn't have to be warm water as the Greeks demanded. The Greeks refused to budge.

Finally, a Muslim was brought in as a neutral arbiter. After listening to both sides, he issued his opinion: Since wine itself was an impure liquid forbidden by the Koran, they should skip the wine and serve the water, either hot or cold. Both sides rejected his advice.

• Wine had been banned by Muslim clerics years earlier, to the despair of Arabic doctors, then among the best in the world, who used wine as medicine and disinfectant.

• Not all Muslims followed the injunction. Even Mohammed's favorite wife (he had seven) quoted him as saying, "You may drink, but do not get drunk," while quaffing his *nabidh,* a date wine.

Wine by the Foot

Men, stripped of all their clothes, step into the vessel, and begin to tread down the floating mass, working it also with their hands. This operation is repeated several times if the wine does not ferment rapidly enough. The reason is that the bodily heat of the men aids the wine in its fermentation. The treaders form three separate rows of ten men each and, placing their arms on each other's shoulders, commence work by raising and lowering their feet, varying this, after a time, with songs and shoutings in order to keep the weaker and the lazier ones up to the work, which is quite irksome and monotonous. Taking part with them in the treading is a little band of musicians who strike up a lively tune. Walking over the pips and stalks, strewn at the bottom of the vat, becomes something like the pilgrimages of old when the devout trudged wearily along, with hard peas packed between their feet and the soles of their shoes. The treaders move slowly in a listless way. The fiddle strikes up anew, and the overseers drowsily upbraid. But all to no purpose. Music has lost its inspiration and authority its terrors, and the men, dead beat, raise one purple leg languidly after the other. —Description by an American winegrower visiting Spanish and French wine regions in 1877

- Muslims weren't alone in condemning wine, by the way. So did the Druids.

- Leif Ericson, who landed in America in the year A.D. 1000, named the new continent Vinland the Good, based on his impression the continent was completely covered in grapevines. He made two voyages and started a settlement, possibly near Cape Cod, where some historians believe that the first American wine was made.

- Not drinking wine can be a sign of fanaticism, believed King Louis XVI. In his last letter before losing his head in the French Revolution, King Louis blamed the savagery of the revolutionaries on the fact that its leader, Robespierre, drank only water.

- Louis Pasteur first developed pasteurization in the 1850s as a way to prevent

Louis Pasteur, Oenologist

wine spoilage. Afterward, he realized it could *also* be used on other substances like milk. Pasteurization came just in time: When the Prussians laid Paris under siege in the winter of 1870, there was little in the way of food in the city, but plenty of wine. One famous restaurant, Voisin, provided exactly one menu item for Christmas Day: "Chat flanqué de rats, accompagné d'un Bollinger frappé" ("Cat flanked with rats, with Bollinger wine, chilled").

- Meanwhile, in America, the wine trade had already begun thriving on both coasts half a century earlier. Franciscan monks started both the Napa and Sonoma wine regions in 1824 at the Solano Mission in Sonoma. The wine industry they began continued to the present, interrupted only by Prohibition in the 1920s.

- Surprisingly, the first large-scale American winemaking region was not on either coast, but in Ohio, of all places. So much so that it was known in the 1850s as "The Rhine of America." In 1870, America's largest winery was located on Middle Bass Island, just off the grape-growing town of Sandusky, Ohio. ☾

Modern Myths

THINGS THAT JUST AIN'T TRUE

As we hang around the ol' debunk house, we sit and swap misinformation in order to knock it down. Here are some of the most maddening bits of misinformation that we hear over and over again.

ETERNAL LIGHT

The myth: You save energy by leaving fluorescent lights on all the time instead of turning them on and off.

The truth: There was a time that fluorescents required a hefty jolt to get them started, so it was best not to flash them continuously. However, nowadays, starting a fluorescent light takes only a tiny jolt of extra electricity, so you'll save electricity by turning the lights off when they're not needed. Even if you were turning them on and off repeatedly, you'd still save electricity over the standard filament light bulb.

BEAT ME DADDY, EIGHT TO THE BAR

The myth: The phrase "rule of thumb" came from English Common Law, dictating that men could beat their wives with a stick as long as it was no wider than a thumb.

The truth: Although the myth has been cluelessly cited as fact over and over again, there was no such law in English Common Law. Likewise, there was also no such law on the books anywhere in the United States either. (In fact, wife beating was expressly against the law in the American colonies long before the revolution, and men were often punished for breaking it.) In reality, the "rule" has to do with measuring, as in "ruler." The expression comes from carpentry--essentially using the thumb to estimate an inch.

DOUBTING THOMAS

The myth: A man named Thomas Crapper invented the flush toilet.

The truth: In 1969, a writer named Wallace Reyburn wrote *Flushed with Pride*, a far-fetched "biography" of one Thomas Crapper who he said invented the flush toilet. The book was a joke, as was Reyburn's follow-up book *Bust Up: The Uplifting Tale of Otto Titzling and the Development of the Bra.* Unfortunately, not everybody got the joke, and you will still see these "inventors" erroneously credited in books and trivia games by writers who should know better.

MR. THOMAS CRAPPER.

Having said that, however, here's a twist: There is evidence that there really was a Thomas Crapper. Although he didn't invent the toilet, he manufactured toilets and accessories in the late 19th century. The evidence is actually quite convincing, consisting of old newspaper ads and so on, but one hesitates to take it unambivalently at face value considering past hoaxes and the "too-good-to-be-true" coincidence. So, to sum up: There might have been a Thomas Crapper who sold toilets; however, the flush toilet predated him by nearly 400 years. In fact, Sir John Harrington, godson of Queen Elizabeth I, created the first flush toilet in 1596. In 1775, Alexander Cumming improved Harrington's design by inventing the stink trap, which preventing odors from wafting back up from the sewers.

BEAUTIFUL HAIR WITH BODY EXTRA

The myth: Your hair and nails will continue to grow after you die.

The truth: This one is wrong, but at least it's based on what appears to be true. When a person dies, the skin loses moisture and begins to get thinner. This makes the hair and nails stick out farther, so it looks like they've grown since death.

10% OF OUR BRAINS
The myth: We use only 10% of our brains.

The truth: The myth is beloved by New Agers, human potential gurus and others with seminars and books to sell. The truth is  that you likely use all of your brain during a normal day, but not necessarily all at the same time (any more than you use all of your muscle groups at one time).

Our brains just aren't so big that we could afford to let that much of it lie fallow—it weighs only about 3 pounds. Coincidentally, 10% of that is comparable to the brain of a sheep. Don't give up on that other 90%--between eating, sleeping, work and finding your keys, every bit counts.

FIRST IN WAR, LAST IN TEETH
The myth: George Washington had wooden teeth.

The truth: Washington did have only one remaining tooth at the time of his inauguration. He didn't have wooden teeth, though. His four sets of dentures, one crafted by Paul Revere, were made of hippopotamus bone, elephant ivory and teeth from cows and dead people, held together with gold palates and springs. None of them worked well. Back then, though, nobody expected them to—the false teeth were not designed for eating, just for looking good. €

The Ups & Downs of Transportation

Elevators are about the safest form of transportation, boasting of only one fatality every 100 million miles traveled. (Stairs, in comparison, are five times more dangerous.)

Elevators owe their emergency brakes to engineer Elisha Graves Otis, founder of the elevator company that still bears his name. His invention in 1854 was a large, bow-shaped spring attached to the car and connected to the elevator cable. When taut, the cable kept the spring flexed.... However, if the cable broke, the spring would immediately flatten out, jamming its ends into notched guard rails on either side of the elevator, bringing the car to an immediate stop.

Every Picture Tells a Story

The Scream by Edvard Munch, 1893

- *The Scream,* garishly colored and crudely rendered, is the first example of Expressionism, a style of painting that's meant to express the inner experience instead of external realities.

- Edvard Munch's childhood was gloomy and tragic. Growing up in a dark Norwegian landscape was bad enough, but he lost his mother at five, and a beloved sister at fourteen.

- On the day Munch painted this, he wrote, "I was walking with two friends.... The sun was setting.... The sky turned blood-red. I stopped, and leaning against the railing, deathly tired. My friends walked on. I stood there trembling with fear, and I sensed a great, infinite scream pass through nature."

- Munch later used the same bridge setting and colors for his paintings *Anxiety* and *Despair*.

- Munch's paintings were controversial. An exhibit in Berlin was closed down after critics and the public exploded in uproar.

- Success came, but so did mental and alcohol problems. Munch committed himself to a mental institution for nine months. When he emerged, he became a brilliant printmaker, and his later work explored much less disturbing themes.

- The painting was stolen in 1994, but was recovered.

Miss Snow Death

A GHOST TALE FROM OLD JAPAN

In this story, another ancient Japanese legend collected by Lafcadio Hearn in 1903, a man is spared by a snow goddess of death...but the favor comes with a heavy obligation.

IN A VILLAGE of Musashi Province, there lived two woodcutters: Mosaku and Minokichi. At the time of which I am speaking, Mosaku was an old man; and Minokichi, his apprentice, was a lad of eighteen years. Every day they went together to a forest situated about five miles from their village. On the way to that forest there is a fast, wide river to cross; and there is a ferryboat.

Mosaku and Minokichi were on their way home one very cold evening when a great snowstorm overtook them. They reached the ferry, but they found that the boatman had gone away, leaving his boat on the other side of the river. It was no day for swimming; so the woodcutters took shelter in the ferryman's hut, thinking themselves lucky to find any shelter at all. There was no fireplace in the tiny hut, so Mosaku and Minokichi fastened the door, and lay down to rest, with their straw raincoats over them.

The old man almost immediately fell asleep; but Minokichi lay awake a long time, listening to the awful wind, and the continual slashing of the snow against the door. The river was roaring; and the hut swayed and creaked like a junk at sea. It was a terrible storm; and the air was every moment becoming colder; and Minokichi shivered under his raincoat. But at last, in spite of the cold, he too fell asleep.

He was awakened by a showering of snow in his face. The door of the hut had been forced open; and, by the snow-reflected light he saw a woman all in white. She was bending above Mosaku, and blowing her breath upon him like a bright white smoke. Almost in the same moment she turned to Minokichi, and stooped over him. He tried to cry out, but found that he could not utter any sound. The white woman bent down over him, lower and lower, until her face almost touched him; and he saw that she was very beautiful, though her eyes made him afraid. For a little time she continued to look at him. Then she smiled, and she whispered, "I intended to treat you like the other man. But I cannot help feeling some pity for you, because you are so young. You are a pretty boy, Minokichi; and I will not hurt you now. But, if you ever tell anybody—even your own mother—about what you have seen this night, then I will kill you! Remember what I say!"

With these words, she turned from him, and passed through the doorway. He suddenly found himself able to move, and he sprang up and looked out. But the woman was nowhere to be seen; and the snow was driving furiously into the hut.

Minokichi closed the door and secured it with wood. He wondered if the wind had blown it open; he thought that he might have been only dreaming, but he could not be sure. He called to Mosaku, and was frightened because the old man did not answer. He put out his hand in the dark, and touched Mosaku's face, and found that it was ice! Mosaku was dead.

By dawn the storm was over; and when the ferryman returned to his station, a little after sunrise, he found Minokichi lying senseless beside the frozen body of Mosaku. Minokichi was promptly cared for, and soon came to himself; but he remained a long time ill from the effects of the cold of that terrible night. He had been greatly frightened also by the old man's death; but he said nothing about the vision of the woman in white. As soon as he got well again, he returned to his calling, going alone every morning to the forest, and coming back at nightfall with his bundles of wood, which his mother helped him to sell.

One evening, in the winter of the following year, as he was on his way home, he overtook a girl who happened to be traveling by the same road. She was a tall, slim girl, very good-looking;

and she answered Minokichi's greeting in a voice as pleasant to the ear as the voice of a songbird. Then he walked beside her; and they began to talk. The girl said that her name was O-Yuki, a common Japanese name meaning "snow," that she had lately lost both of her parents, and that she was going to Tokyo, where she happened to have some poor relations who might help her to find a situation as a servant. Minokichi soon felt charmed by this strange girl; and the more that he looked at her, the handsomer she appeared to be. He asked her whether she was yet betrothed; and she answered, laughingly, that she was free.

By the time they reached the village, they had become very much pleased with each other. Minokichi asked O-Yuki to rest awhile at his house. After some shy hesitation, she went there with him; and his mother made her welcome, and prepared a warm meal for her. O-Yuki behaved so nicely that Minokichi's mother took an immediate fancy to her, and persuaded her to delay her journey to Yedo. And the natural end of the matter was that O-Yuki never went to Yedo at all.

O-Yuki proved a very good wife and daughter-in-law. When Minokichi's mother came to die—some five years later—her last words were of affection and praise for the wife of her son. And O-Yuki bore Minokichi ten handsome children.

The country-folk thought O-Yuki a wonderful person, by nature different from themselves. Most of the peasant-women age early; but O-Yuki, even after having become the mother of ten children, looked as young and fresh as on the day when she had first come to the village.

One night, after the children had gone to sleep, O-Yuki was sewing by the light of a paper lamp. Minokichi, watching her, said: "To see you sewing there, with the light on your face, makes me think of a strange thing that happened when I was a lad of eighteen. I then saw somebody as beautiful and white as you are now—indeed, she was very like you."

Without lifting her eyes from her work, O-Yuki responded: "Tell me about her.... Where did you see her?" Then Minokichi told her about the terrible night in the ferryman's hut, about the White Woman who had stooped above him, smiling and whispering, and about the silent death of old Mosaku. And he said: "Asleep or awake, that was the only time that I saw a being as beautiful as you. Of course, she was not a human being; and I was very much afraid of her, but she was so white! Indeed, I have never been sure whether it was a dream."

O-Yuki flung down her sewing, and bowed above Minokichi where he sat, shrieking into his face: "It was I — I — I! Yuki it was! And I told you then that I would kill you if you ever said one word about it! But for those children asleep there, I would kill you this moment! And now you had better take very, very good care of them; for if ever they have reason to complain of you, I will treat you as you deserve!"

Even as she screamed, her voice became thin, like a crying of wind; then she melted into a bright white mist that spired to the roof-beams, and shuddered away through the smoke-hole. Minokichi worked to be the best father ever, and O-Yuki was never again to be seen. ☾

Prescriptions and Second Opinions

"Nothing is more fatal to health than over-care of it." —Benjamin Franklin

"A cheerful heart is good medicine, but a crushed spirit dries up the bones." —Proverbs 17:22

"Always laugh when you can. It is cheap medicine." —Lord Byron

"Many serious illnesses are nothing but the expression of a serious dis-satis-faction with life." —Dr. Paul Tournier

"The best doctors are Doctor Diet, Doctor Quiet, and Doctor Merryman." — Jonathan Swift

"Let food be your medicine and medicine be your food." —Hippocrates

"No illness which can be treated by the diet should be treated by any other means." —Moses Maimonides of Caldova

"It requires a great faith for a man to be cured by his own placebos." —Dr. John L. McClenahan

"Early to rise and early to bed / Makes a man healthy, wealthy, and dead." — James Thurber

"Doctors are just the same as lawyers; the only difference is that lawyers merely rob you, while doctors rob you and kill you, too." —Anton Chekhov

"Don't think of organ donation as giving up part of yourself to keep total strangers alive. Think of it as total strangers giving up most of themselves to keep parts of you alive." —Anonymous

Dead Presidents

WITHOUT LOOKING, WHO'S ON A $10 BILL?

When's the last time you took a good look at the money you use every day? Match the money with the person who appears on it. Get ten or more right and you're looking like a million bucks.

1. 1¢	a. Thomas Jefferson
2. 5¢	b. Ulysses Grant
3. 10¢	c. Andrew Jackson
4. 25¢	d. John Kennedy
5. 50¢	e. Abraham Lincoln
6. $1 (coin until 1978)	f. Millard Fillmore
7. $1 (coin 1979–99)	g. Benjamin Franklin
8. $1 (coin, after 2000)	h. Dwight Eisenhower
9. $1 (bill)	i. Susan Anthony
10. $2	j. Franklin Roosevelt
11. $5	k. Ronald Reagan
12. $10	l. William McKinley
13. $20	m. George Washington
14. $50	n. Sacagawea
15. $100	o. Alexander Hamilton

ANSWERS: 1e, 2a, 3j, 4m, 5d, 6h, 7i, 8n, 9m, 10a, 11e, 12o, 13c, 14b, 15g

Words from the Wise
ADVICE TO ALWAYS, ALWAYS LIVE BY

"I always wanted to be somebody, but I should have been more specific." —Lily Tomlin

"I always keep a supply of stimulant handy in case I see a snake — which I also keep handy." —W. C. Fields

"Always acknowledge a fault. This will throw those in authority off their guard and give you an opportunity to commit more." —Mark Twain

"Always and never are two words you should always remember never to use." —Wendell Johnson

"Arguments are to be avoided; they are always vulgar and often convincing." —Oscar Wilde

"Confusion is always the most honest response." —Marty Indik

"Always get married early in the morning. That way, if it doesn't work out, you haven't wasted a whole day." —Mickey Rooney

"Always be nice to your children because they are the ones who will choose your rest home." —Phyllis Diller

"Always read stuff that will make you look good if you die in the middle of it." —P. J. O'Rourke

"Always do sober what you said you'd do drunk. That will teach you to keep your mouth shut." —Ernest Hemingway

"Always forgive your enemies; nothing annoys them so much." —Oscar Wilde

"Therefore, from a logical point of view, Always marry a woman uglier than you." —Calypso song

"Always make water when you can." —Duke of Wellington

Oh, Henry!
THE RANSOM OF RED CHIEF

One of O. Henry's best short stories is about a couple of two-bit grifters who decide to make a fortune by kidnapping the son of a prominent man. However, the plot doesn't quite work out the way they intended.

IT LOOKED LIKE A GOOD THING: but wait till I tell you. We were down South, in Alabama—Bill Driscoll and myself—when this kidnapping idea struck us. It was, as Bill afterward expressed it, "during a moment of temporary mental apparition"; but we didn't find that out till later.

There was a town down there, as flat as a flannel-cake, and called Summit, of course. It contained inhabitants of as undeleterious and self-satisfied a class of peasantry as ever clustered around a Maypole.

O Henry (William Sydney Porter)

Bill and me had a joint capital of about six hundred dollars, and we needed just two thousand dollars more to pull off a fraudulent town-lot scheme in Western Illinois with. We selected for our victim the only child of a prominent citizen named Ebenezer Dorset. The father was respectable and tight, a mortgage financier and a stern, upright collection-plate passer and forecloser. The kid was a boy of ten, with bas-relief freckles, and hair the colour of the cover of the magazine you buy at the newsstand when you want to catch a train. Bill and me figured that Ebenezer would melt down for a ransom of $2000 to a cent. But wait till I tell you.

One evening after sundown, we drove in a buggy past old Dorset's house. The kid was in the street, throwing rocks at a kitten on the opposite fence.

"Hey, little boy!" says Bill, "would you like to have a bag of candy and a nice ride?" The boy catches Bill neatly in the eye with a piece of brick.

"That will cost the old man an extra five hundred dollars," says Bill, climbing over the wheel.

That boy put up a fight like a welter-weight cinnamon bear; but, at last, we got him down in the bottom of the buggy and drove away. We took him up to the cave. After dark I drove the buggy to the little village where we had hired it, and walked back to the mountain.

Bill was pasting court-plaster over the scratches and bruises on his features. There was a fire burning, and the boy was watching a pot of boiling coffee, with two buzzard tailfeathers stuck in his red hair. He points a stick at me when I come up, and says:

"Ha! cursed paleface, do you dare to enter the camp of Red Chief, the terror of the plains?"

"He's all right now," says Bill, rolling up his trousers and examining some bruises on his shins. "We're playing Indian. I'm Old Hank, the Trapper, Red Chief's captive, and I'm to be scalped at daybreak. By Geronimo! that kid can kick hard."

Yes, sir, that boy seemed to be having the time of his life. The fun of camping out in a cave had made him forget that he was a captive himself. He immediately christened me Snake-eye, the Spy, and announced that, when his braves returned from the warpath, I was to be broiled at the stake at the rising of the sun.

Then we had supper. He made a during-dinner speech something like this: "I like this fine. I never camped out before; but I had a pet 'possum once, and I was nine last birthday. I hate school. Rats ate up sixteen of Jimmy Talbot's aunt's hen's eggs. Are there any real Indians in these woods? I want some more gravy. Amos Murray has got six toes. A parrot can talk, but a monkey or a fish can't. How many does it take to make twelve?" Every few minutes he would remember that he was a redskin. He would let out a war-whoop that made Old Hank the Trapper shiver. That boy had Bill terrorized from the start.

"Red Chief," says I to the kid, "would you like to go home?"

"Aw, what for?" says he. "I don't have any fun at home. I hate to go to school. I like to camp out. You won't take me back home again, Snake-eye, will you?"

"Not right away," says I. "We'll stay here in the cave a while."

"All right!" says he. "I never had such fun in all my life."

We went to bed about eleven o'clock. We spread down some blankets and put Red Chief between us. We weren't afraid he'd run away. He kept us awake for three hours. At last, I fell into a troubled sleep, and dreamed that I had been kidnapped and chained to a tree by a ferocious pirate with red hair.

Just at daybreak, I was awakened by a series of awful screams from Bill. They weren't yells, or howls, or whoops, or yawps, such as you'd expect from a manly set of vocal organs—they were humiliating screams, such as women emit when they see ghosts or caterpillars. It's an awful thing to hear a strong, desperate, fat man scream incontinently in a cave at daybreak.

I jumped up to see what the matter was. Red Chief was sitting on Bill's chest, with one hand twined in Bill's hair. In the other he had the knife we used for slicing bacon; and he was industriously trying to take Bill's scalp, according to the sentence that had been pronounced upon him the evening before.

I got the knife away from the kid and made him lie down again. But, from that moment, Bill's spirit was broken. He never closed an eye again in sleep as long as that boy was with us. I dozed off for a while, but along toward sun-up I remembered that Red Chief had said I was to be burned at the

"I was to be broiled at the stake at sunrise."

stake at the rising of the sun. I wasn't nervous or afraid; but I sat up and lit my pipe and leaned against a rock.

"What you getting up so soon for, Sam?" asked Bill.

"Me?" says I. "Oh, I got a kind of a pain in my shoulder. I thought sitting up would rest it."

"You're a liar!" says Bill. "You're afraid. You was to be burned at sunrise, and you was afraid he'd do it. And he would, too, if he could find a match. Ain't it awful, Sam? Do you think anybody will pay money to get a little imp like that back home?"

"Sure," said I. "A rowdy kid like that is just the kind that parents dote on. Now, you and the Chief get up and cook breakfast, while I go up on the top of this mountain and reconnoiter."

I went up on the peak of the little mountain. Over toward Summit I expected to see the sturdy yeomanry of the village armed with pitchforks beating the countryside for the dastardly kidnappers. But what I saw was a peaceful landscape dotted with one man ploughing with a dun mule. Nobody was dragging the creek; no couriers dashed hither and yon, bringing tidings of no news to the distracted parents.

"Perhaps," says I to myself, "it has not yet been discovered that the wolves have borne away the tender lambkin from the fold," says I, and I went down the mountain to breakfast.

When I got to the cave I found Bill backed up against the side of it, breathing hard, and the boy threatening to smash him with a rock half as big as a cocoanut.

"He put a red-hot boiled potato down my back," explained Bill, "and then mashed it with his foot; and I boxed his ears. Have you got a gun about you, Sam?"

I took the rock away from the boy. "I'll fix you," says the kid to Bill. "No man ever yet struck the Red Chief but what he got paid for it. You better beware!"

"We've got to fix up some plan about the ransom," says I. "There don't seem to be much excitement around Summit, but maybe his folks think he's spending the night with Aunt Jane or one of the neighbors. Anyhow, he'll be missed today. Tonight we must get a message to his father demanding $2000."

Just then we heard a kind of war-whoop, such as David might have emitted when he knocked out the champion Goliath. It was a sling that Red Chief had pulled out of his pocket, and he was whirling it around his head.

I dodged, and heard a heavy thud and a kind of a sigh from Bill, like a horse gives out when you take his saddle off. He fell in the fire. I dragged him out and poured cold water on his head for half an hour. By and by, Bill sits up and says, "You won't go away and leave me here alone, will you, Sam?"

I went out and caught that boy and shook him until his freckles rattled. "I was only funning," says he sullenly. "I didn't mean to hurt Old Hank. I'll behave, Snake-eye, if you won't send me home, and if you'll let me play the Black Scout today."

"I don't know the game," says I. "That's for you and Mr. Bill to decide. He's your playmate for the day. I'm going away for a while, on business. Now, you make friends with him and say you are sorry for hurting him, or home you go, at once."

I made him and Bill shake hands, and then I took Bill aside and told him I was going to Poplar Cove, a little village three miles from the cave, and send a peremptory letter to old man Dorset, demanding the ransom.

"You know, Sam," says Bill, "I've stood by you without batting an eye in earthquakes, fire and flood—in poker games, dynamite outrages, police raids, train robberies and cyclones. I never lost my nerve yet till we kidnapped that two-legged skyrocket of a kid. You won't leave me long with him, will you, Sam?"

"I'll be back some time this afternoon," says I. "You must keep the boy amused and quiet till I return. And now we'll write the letter to old Dorset."

Bill and I got paper and pencil and worked on the letter while Red Chief, with a blanket wrapped around him, strutted up and down, guarding the mouth of the cave. Bill begged me tearfully to make the ransom fifteen hundred dollars instead of two thousand. "I ain't attempting," says he, "to decry the celebrated moral aspect of parental affection, but it ain't human for anybody to give up $2000 for that forty-pound chunk of freckled wildcat. I'm willing to take a chance at $1500. You can charge the difference up to me."

To relieve Bill, we collaborated a letter that ran this way:

Ebenezer Dorset, Esq.:

We have your boy concealed in a place far from Summit. It is useless for you or the most skilful detectives to attempt to find him. Absolutely, the only terms on which you can have him restored to you are these: We demand fifteen hundred dollars for his return; the money to be left at midnight tonight at the same spot and as your reply—as hereinafter described. If you agree to these terms, send your answer in writing by a solitary messenger tonight at half-past eight o'clock. After crossing Owl Creek, on the road to Poplar Cove, at the bottom of the fence-post opposite the third tree, will be found a small box. The messenger will place the answer in this box and return immediately to Summit.

If you attempt any treachery or fail to comply with our demand as stated, you will never see your boy again. If you pay the money as demanded, he will be returned to you safe and well within three hours. These terms are final, and if you do not accede to them no further communication will be attempted.

—TWO DESPERATE MEN.

I addressed this letter to Dorset, and put it in my pocket. As I was about to start, the kid comes up to me and says, "Aw, Snake-eye, you said I could play the Black Scout."

"Mr. Bill will play it," says I. "What kind of a game is it?"

"I'm the Black Scout," says Red Chief, "and I have to ride to the stockade to warn the settlers that the Indians are coming."

"What am I to do?" asks Bill, looking at the kid suspiciously.

"You're the hoss," says Black Scout. "Get down on your hands and knees. How can I ride to the stockade without a hoss?"

"You'd better keep him interested," said I, "till we get the scheme going. Loosen up." Bill gets down on all fours, and a look comes in his eye like a rabbit's when you catch it in a trap.

"How far to the stockade, kid?" he asks, in a husky voice.

"Ninety miles," says the Black Scout. "And you have to hump yourself to get there on time. Whoa, now!" The Black Scout jumps on Bill's back and digs his heels in his side.

"For Heaven's sake," says Bill, "hurry back, Sam. I wish we hadn't made the ransom more than a thousand. "

I walked over to Poplar Cove and sat around the postoffice and store, talking with the chawbacons that came in to trade. One says that he hears Summit is all upset on account of Eb Dorset's boy having been lost or stolen. That was all I wanted to know. I posted my letter. The postmaster said the mail-carrier would come by in an hour to take the mail on to Summit.

When I got back to the cave Bill wabbled out of the cave.

"I tell you, Sam, a human can only stand so much," says Bill. "I was rode the ninety miles to the stockade, not barring an inch." I told him that we would get the ransom and be off with it by midnight if old Dorset fell in with our proposition. So Bill braced up enough to promise the kid to play a Russian in a Japanese war as soon as he felt a little better.

I had a scheme for collecting that ransom without danger of being caught by counterplots that ought to commend itself to professional kidnappers. The tree under which the answer was to be left—and the money later on—was close to the road fence with big, bare fields on all sides. If a gang of constables should be watching for any one to come for the note they could see him a long way off crossing the fields or in the road. But no, sirree! At half-past eight I was up in that tree as well hidden as a tree toad, waiting for the messenger to arrive.

Exactly on time, a half-grown boy rides up the road on a bicycle,

locates the box at the foot of the fencepost, slips a folded piece of paper into it and pedals away again back toward town.

I waited an hour and then slid down the tree, got the note, slipped along the fence till I struck the woods, and was back at the cave in another half an hour. I opened the note, got near the lantern and read it to Bill. The sum and substance of it was this:

Two Desperate Men.

Gentlemen: In regard to the ransom you ask for the return of my son, I think you are a little high in your demands, and I hereby make you a counter-proposition, which I am inclined to believe you will accept. You bring Johnny home and pay me $250 in cash, and I agree to take him off your hands. You had better come at night, for the neighbors believe he is lost, and I couldn't be responsible for what they would do to anybody they saw bringing him back.

Very respectfully,
EBENEZER DORSET.

"Great pirates of Penzance!" says I; "of all the impudent—"

But I glanced at Bill, and hesitated. He had the most pleading look I ever saw on the face of a dumb or a talking brute.

"Sam," says he, "what's $250, after all? We've got the money. One more night of this kid will send me to a bed in Bedlam. I think Mr. Dorset is a spendthrift for making us such a liberal offer. You ain't going to let the chance go, are you?"

"Tell you the truth, Bill," says I, "this little he ewe lamb has somewhat got on my nerves too. We'll take him home, pay the ransom and make our get-away."

We took him home that night. It was twelve o'clock when we knocked at Ebenezer's front door. At the moment when I should have been abstracting $1500 from the box under the tree, according to the original proposition, Bill was counting out $250 into Dorset's hand.

When the kid found out we were going to leave him at home he started up a howl like a calliope and fastened himself as tight as a leech to Bill's leg. His father peeled him away gradually, like a porous plaster.

"How long can you hold him?" asks Bill.

"I'm not as strong as I used to be," says old Dorset, "but I think I can promise you ten minutes."

"Enough," says Bill. "In ten minutes I shall cross the Central, Southern and Middle Western States, and be legging it trippingly for the Canadian border."

And, as dark as it was, and as fat as Bill was, and as good a runner as I am, he was a good mile and a half out of summit before I could catch up with him. ❦

SY-CLO
TRADE MARK

The Latest Word In Sanitation

The name Sy-Clo on a closet means health insurance for your home or any building in which the closet is placed; it means freedom from all those diseases which are usually traceable to noxious odors and poisonous gases arising from ordinary closets.

Sy-Clo stands for more than mere flushing; it stands for a wonderful syphonic action of great power—an action which literally pulls the contents of the bowl into the drain, cleansing the non-reachable parts, instantly sealing the outlet channel with a water trap to an unusual depth, and absolutely preventing all danger of gas.

The Sy-Clo Closet stands for an interior cleanliness and purity impossible in an iron closet, and unknown in any closet but one made of china—like the Sy-Clo. Hand-moulded of china all into one solid piece like a vase, the Sy-Clo is without crack, joint or rough surface to collect dirt or disease germs. It is as clean inside and out as a china pitcher, being made exactly the same way and of the same material.

The surface of the Sy-Clo Closet cannot chip off, is not affected by acid, water or wear, and hence cannot rust or discolor as an iron closet does. The Sy-Clo is strong, simple, durable; it cannot get out of order and, with ordinary care, will last as long as the house in which it is placed.

It costs but little more than the common closet, and when health and comfort are considered, it really costs less; in fact, *your doctor pays the bill.* Your plumber will tell you that Sy-Clo is absolutely the latest word in perfect sanitation.

Send for booklet on "Household Health"—mailed free.

POTTERIES SELLING CO.
Trenton, N. J.

Buttheads

A WHOLE HERD OF GOAT FACTS

Did you know that the term *butthead* wasn't originally an insult, but a technical term referring to goats? Most people don't know much about goats—here's your chance to be hoof and horn above the rest.

• Despite their reputation, goats don't really eat everything in sight. They do, however, explore new things with their sensitive lips, so it sometimes looks like they're chowing down on any ol' thing.

• Mohair and cashmere fabrics sound much fancier than what they really are: goat hair.

• Nanny goats have little similarity with human nannies. The name is used to denote any female goat. In England, "Nanny" was a derivative of the name *Annie*. All "billy" goats are males—it's a nickname for William. You see the same sort of naming with tom cats, and jack and jennie mules.

• Both sexes of goats have beards.

• Neutered goats are called *wethers*.

• Hey, Beavis, a "butthead" is technically any goat with horns. We kid you not.

• The most popular milk worldwide comes from goats, not cows.

• Despite a reputation for being ornery, goats are much easier to milk than cows. For one thing, they're smaller. For another, they actually like being around people. Finally, goats have only two teats instead of four like cows, cutting the work in half. (For more milking info, see next page.)

• At least four presidents had goats patrolling the White House grounds back in the days when lawnmowers were unavailable and fresh milk was hard to come by. Goat owners in the White House included Abraham Lincoln, Rutherford B.

How to Milk a Goat

• You'll need a small stool and bucket. If you milk from the side, make sure it's the same side every time. Some goat milkers prefer to milk from the rear, but that requires being fast on your feet if the goat decides to eliminate body waste.

• Tie up the goat and wash its flank and udder with warm water. Use udder cream, available at finer feed stores, on both the teats and your hands—it lubricates and acts as an antiseptic.

• Take the tops of the two teats in your two hands between your thumb and forefinger. Squeeze with those two fingers, then with the second, third and fourth fingers in fast, rolling succession.

• The milk should be creamy white. If it isn't, or if it's clotted, the goat has an easily-cured ailment called mastitis, so throw the milk away. Otherwise, keep milking. Talk to the animal gently as you milk—most goats love human attention.

Hayes, Benjamin Harrison and Harry Truman.

• Today, a *scapegoat* is usually someone who takes the rap for something gone wrong. The name, though, originally applied only to goats. It comes from "escape goat." In Leviticus 16:10, God demanded that at Yom Kippur one goat should be killed in his honor, and another released into the desert. That "escaped goat" symbolically carried away all the sins of the Israelis. Human scapegoats nowadays serve a similar function—they get burdened with the misconduct and mistakes of others.

• Don't confuse the terminology: goats don't live in flocks, they live in herds.

• Racehorses were often given goat companions to keep them calm in strange stalls. Rivals would sometimes try to upset another's horse before a race by stealing its goat friend. Etymologists tell us that that's where "getting your goat" comes from.

• Goats are consider sexually licentious. It's where the term "old goat" —implying a dirty, old man— came from.

• Goatees were likewise named in the 1840s when sporting goat-like chin-warmers became popular.

- Older siblings take note: It's said that the ancient Romans used goats to tickle prisoners to insanity and death. They'd repeatedly dip the bottom of victim's feet in salt water and let salt-loving goats lick them. After several days of this the guy would die of exhaustion and shock, laughing all the way.

- The sport that requires the fastest reflexes is jai alai. The rubber-and-goatskin ball that's used in the game can be thrown at 188 miles per hour with a curved wicker basket called a *cesta*. One hit from the ball can be deadly.

- Virginia Woolf's childhood nickname was The Goat. And, of course, there was Billy the Kid. Both were called that because a perceived resemblance to the animal. Of course, if you mentioned that to Virginia, she'd write something bad about you. Billy, though, he'd just kill you.

- Credit a lost goat for the archaeological discovery of the Dead Sea Scrolls. A herdsman wandered into a cave to see if his errant animal was there, and found the scrolls rolled up in clay jars. Whether he found his lost goat, we don't know.

- Goats were probably first tamed more than 9,000 years ago in Asia and regions of the eastern Mediterranean.

- In tropical areas, goats mate throughout the year; in cooler regions, they breed only from late summer to winter as the days become shorter.

- In the wild, does and kids travel in herds of up to fifty animals. Bucks live separately, joining the herd only during the mating season.

- Just like cows, goats chew their cud. ☾

According to Mark Twain

More from *Puddin'head Wilson's Calendar*, a
fictitious publication that Twain "quoted" from whenever
he needed a maxim to head a chapter.

• "October. This is one of the peculiarly dangerous months in which to speculate in stocks. The others are September, July, April, January, November, May, March, June, December, August, and February."

• "Nothing so needs reforming as other people's habits."

• "Behold the fool saith, 'Put not all thine eggs in the one basket,' but the wise man saith, 'Put all your eggs in the one basket and WATCH THAT BASKET."

• "If you pick up a starving dog and make him prosperous, he will not bite you. This is the principal difference between a dog and a man."

• "Even popularity can be overdone. In Rome, at first you are full of regrets that Michaelangelo died; but by and by you only regret that you didn't see him do it."

• "Few things are harder to put up with than the annoyance of a good example."

• "Some people are useless on top of the ground. They ought to be under it, inspiring the cabbages."

• "April 1. This is the day upon which we are reminded of what we are on the other 364."

• "It is often the case that the man who can't tell a lie thinks he is the best judge of one."

Be good & You will be lonesome.
Mark Twain

• "There are three infallible ways of pleasing an author: 1, to tell him you have read one of his books; 2, to tell him you have read all of his books; 3, to ask him to let you read the manuscript of his forthcoming book. No. 1 admits you to his respect; No. 2 admits you to his admiration; No. 3 carries you clear to his heart."

• "Noise proves nothing. Often a hen who has merely laid an egg cackles as if she had laid an asteroid."

• "It is easier to stay out than get out."

SPAM

TOO MANY COLD SHOULDERS

SPAM, the ultimate mystery meat. What's in it, and how did a canned meat become a beloved pop culture icon?

MARGARET THATCHER ate it for Christmas dinner in 1943. Nikita Khrushchev credited it for keeping the Soviet Army alive during World War II. Monty Python wrote a song about it. GIs in World War II joked that it was "ham that flunked its physical." Its manufacturer calls it "the Rodney Dangerfield of luncheon meat—it don't get no respect."

We're talking Spam, ladies and gentlemen, also known as "mystery meat" or (to quote those Python boys) "Spam Spam Spam Spam / Lovely Spam, oh wonderful Spam...." It's much maligned, but much eaten as well, accounting for 75 percent of all luncheon meat sales in this country. It is especially popular in Hawaii, for some reason, which has the highest per capita Spam consumption rate in the nation. (And, let the record show, the highest life expectancy in the nation as well—84 and 80 years for women and men respectively. Coincidence? We think not. Perhaps all those sodium compounds preserve more than pork products.)

In Korea, Spam is an imported luxury item, a part of the good life. A can of it is often given as a present on a date, or to coworkers and business associates, and even to newlyweds. Koreans often fry it with the peppery cabbage dish, kimchi, or roll it up into kimpap, a Spam sushi-like item made with rice and seaweed.

Why was Spam invented? Because of a surplus of pig shoulders. Every meat processor runs into the problem of what to do with the parts of the animal that are less popular than others.

Pork shoulders, for example, aren't meaty enough to sell as ham, and aren't fatty enough to make bacon. Seeing pork shoulders piling up in the coolers of the George A. Hormel Company in 1937 gave one of its executives an idea. Why not chop the meat up, add some spices and ham from other parts of the pig, and form it into small ham-like loaves? Put it in a can and fill the excess space with gelatin from the pig's leftover skin and bones—you could probably keep the meat edible for months without refrigeration.

They tried it. It worked. Hormel's Spiced Ham quickly found a niche in the market. It was inexpensive, savory, convenient and it didn't need refrigeration.

Other packers, also plagued with a surplus of pig parts, began issuing their own "Spiced Hams." Hormel offered a $100 prize for a name that would differentiate its product from the imitators. A brother of one of its workers contracted the words "Spiced Ham" and got Spam.

Spam was bolstered by a memorable ad campaign that showed how it could be served morning, noon and night and by singing commercials performed live and on the radio by the 60-strong traveling Hormel Girls ("Spam, Spam, Spam, Spam / Hormel's new miracle meat in a can / Tastes fine, saves time / If you want something grand, ask for Spam..." sung awkwardly to the tune of "My Bonnie Lies Over the Ocean").

When World War II came, Spam's price, portability and shelf life made it a staple of every GI's diet. The gospel according to Spam was also spread by American aid packages to its allies. Although many GIs swore that they'd never eat the stuff again (even Dwight Eisenhower complained about too much Spam in Army messes), they apparently got a craving once they got home and out of uniform, because Spam did booming business immediately after the war. Even now, 228 cans of Spam are eaten every minute of the day. ☾

Join Our Club!

THERE'S NO BETTER TIME than now to join W. C. Privy's special club of special friends, the Bathroom Companions of Mr. Privy. Becoming a BCOMP member has never been easier. Simply send an e-mail note to our membership committee at *membership@bathroomcompanion.com* and receive a printable membership card and a door hanger (*see below*).

Here at Bathroom Companion Central we're busy at work putting together the next installment of the BC. If you have any suggestions for stories, feel free to send them along to *ideas@bathroomcompanion.com*. If you're interested in submitting pictures for inclusion on the Pot Shots pages, please submit them to *potshots@bathroomcompanion.com*, or send anything to The Bathroom Companion, c/o St. Martin's Press, 175 Fifth Avenue, New York, N.Y. 10010.

Once again, thank you for surporting us in keeping W. C. Privy's dream flowing! ☾

Become a member today, and get your printable "Go Away!" door hanger, and your very own membership card to BCOMP—the W. C. Privy Fan Club.

Write to:
membership@bathroomcompanion.com

(For emergency use only)

(For emergency use only)